Entrepreneur®
MAGAZINE'S

ULTIMATE

GUIDE TO

FORMING

AN LLC

IN ANY STATE

MICHAEL SPADACCINI

EP
Entrepreneur®
Press

Editorial Director: Jere Calmes
Cover Design: Beth Hanson-Winter
Composition: CWL Publishing Enterprises, Inc., Madison, Wisconsin, www.cwlpub.com

This publication is designed to provide accurate and authoritative information in regard to the subject matter covered. It is sold with the understanding that the publisher is not engaged in rendering legal, accounting, or other professional services. If legal advice or other expert assistance is required, the services of a competent professional person should be sought.

—From a Declaration of Principles jointly adopted by a
Committee of the American Bar Association and
a Committee of Publishers and Associations

ISBN 1-932531-19-X

Library of Congress Cataloging-in-Publication Data

Spadaccini, Michael, 1964-
    Entrepreneur magazine's ultimate guide to forming an LLC in any state / Michael Spadaccini.
        p. cm.
    ISBN 1-932531-19-X
        1. Private companies—United States. 2. Businesspeople—United States—Handbooks,
    manuals, etc. I. Title: Entrepreneur magazine's ultimate guide to forming LLCs in any state. II. Title.
KF1380.Z9.S66 2004
346.73'0668--dc22

                                                                    2004050288

Printed in Canada

09 08 07 06 05   10 9 8 7 6 5 4 3 2 1

Contents

About the Author

Michael Spadaccini is a San Diego-based business attorney. Mr. Spadaccini has practiced business, trademark, securities, and Internet law in California from 1993 to the present. He is admitted to the California Bar, as well as the Bars of the U.S. District Court for Northern California, the U.S. Court of Appeals for the 9th Circuit, and the U.S. Court of Appeals for the U.S. Federal Circuit Appellate Court. He received his bachelor's degree from the University of Rhode Island in 1987 and his law degree from Quinnipiac University in 1992. He is the author of *Entrepreneur Magazine's Ultimate Book of Business Forms, Enterpreneur Magazine's Ultimate Guide to Incorporating in Any State*, and a periodic securities law newsletter entitled *The Securities Law Report*, available at www.learnaboutlaw.com.

Acknowledgments

I'd like to thank Jere Calmes, editorial director of Entrepreneur Press, for giving me the opportunity to write the first edition of *Entrepreneur Magazine's Ultimate Guide to Forming an LLC in Any State*.

I am also grateful to:

- Attorney, friend, and fellow golfer Dan Sweeney, who contributed to this volume by providing invaluable legal research.

- My law professors at Quinnipiac University School of Law, who taught me the foundations of corporate and business law that I now offer to you.

- My family and friends, who offered their support throughout the drafting of this volume.

- John Woods, Bob Magnan, and CWL Publishing Enterprises for turning out the book in its final form.

CHAPTER 1

Resources—What This Book Can Offer You

This book is intended for everyone: businessperson, manager, lawyer, and accountant. Its goal is to give the business professional all the tools necessary to plan, organize, form, operate, and maintain a basic LLC in any of the 50 states and the District of Columbia.

The book begins by providing a basic understanding of the law surrounding business organizations. It examines the fundamental differences and advantages of sole proprietorships, partnerships, limited liability companies, and corporations. It then compares and contrasts the various business forms.

Thereafter, this volume takes you step by step through the organization of an LLC in any of the 50 states and the District of Columbia. Among the topics covered are how to do the following:

- Select the proper state for organization of your business.
- Select a name for your business without running afoul of the law or the rights of others.
- Conduct a search for prior business names and trademarks.
- Draft the foundational documents to organize your LLC—the articles of organization. Appendix C, Appendix D, and the CD-ROM include many helpful and relevant documents that would cost thousands of dollars if drafted by an attorney.
- Choose and elect directors, officers, or managers for your company.
- Select and appoint a registered agent.
- File your organizational papers.
- Maintain proper formalities and records for your entity.
- Conduct your organization so that you can protect your personal assets and earnings from liability.

Also, this volume will assist you with the ongoing responsibilities of running an LLC. Record-keeping and internal governance are importance topics in business law. You will learn about organizing annual and special meetings of executives and owners, taking business actions by written consent in lieu of a formal vote, drafting minutes, reporting and paying annual franchise and corporate income taxes, and meeting the periodic reporting requirements that most states impose on LLCs.

Appendix A includes LLC reference information for all 50 states and the District of Columbia. The reference section includes contact information for the secretary of state's office, fee schedules and requirements for filing LLC papers, links to model organizational forms for LLCs, information on periodic reporting and tax requirements, taxation summaries, and much more.

Appendix B includes a detailed glossary of terms related to business structures and LLCs in particular.

One of this book's most valuable features is the model documents it provides. These documents, included in Appendices C and D and on the accompanying CD, can be easily modified to suit your specific needs. The CD features the documents in Microsoft Word that are easily readable on nearly any computer. There are also a few documents that are Excel templates that you can use to track various data and figures. The model documents also appear on the Web site www.learnaboutlaw.com, along with additional documents. These documents are meant to be general and can be suited to your needs with a little modification.

Understand, of course, that this volume cannot possibly serve as a substitute for the legal advice of a qual-ified attorney or accountant tailored to your specific needs. The information in this book is not intended as specific legal advice; it is intended as a broad educational overview. By using this book, you will step into the role of an attorney. But understand its limitations. If your needs are a simple, small LLC, then this book can serve your needs perfectly.

With that in mind, note that this volume occasionally warns about certain topics that present potential pitfalls and complex issues that warrant a visit to your local attorney's office. Heed these warnings because small legal errors have a way of becoming enormous legal problems over time. Business law has some simple topics and some complex ones, so if your needs are obviously complex, don't try to do everything yourself. Sometimes the best advice an attorney can give is "get a qualified attorney."

That said, let's get started.

CHAPTER 2

An Overview of Business Organizations

The most common forms of business enterprises in use in the United States are the sole proprietorship, the general partnership, the limited liability company (LLC), and the corporation. Each form has advantages and disadvantages in complexity, ease of setup, cost, liability protection, periodic reporting requirements, operating complexity, and taxation. Also, some business forms have subclasses, such as the C corporation, the S corporation, and the professional corporation. Choosing the right business form requires a delicate balancing of competing considerations. Each of these business forms is briefly discussed in this chapter. Then, in Chapter 5, we will go into detail about how to plan and organize your LLC.

THE SOLE PROPRIETORSHIP

The sole proprietorship is the simplest form for operating a business. The sole proprietorship is not a legal entity; it simply refers to a natural person who owns the business and is personally responsible for its debts. A sole proprietorship can operate under the name of its owner or it can do business under a fictitious name, such as Nancy's Nail Salon. The fictitious name is simply a trade name—it does not create a legal entity

separate from the sole proprietor owner. Fictitious names are covered at length in later chapters.

▼ **DEFINITION**

A sole proprietorship is a business owned and managed by one person. The sole proprietorship is not a legal entity; it simply refers to a natural person who owns the business and is personally responsible for its debts.

Business Names

Although a sole proprietorship is indivisible from its owner, that is not to say that the sole proprietorship cannot operate under a trade name separate from its owner. Many sole proprietorships adopt and operate under what is called a *fictitious business name*. A fictitious business name is simply a trade name (the fictitious business name) that an owner of a business (the legal name) uses in the marketplace. A business that is using a fictitious business name is said to be "doing business as" the fictitious name—the terms are interchangeable. "Doing business as" is commonly abbreviated to DBA, which some businesses often include in correspondence or in advertisements. A simple example of a DBA would be if Ritchie Rizzo, a sole proprietor, operated a business called Ritchie's Plumbing. Thus, Ritchie Rizzo is the legal name and Ritchie's Plumbing is the fictitious business name. Remember: the fictitious business name is just a name and does not create a separate entity.

> ▼ **DEFINITION**
>
> A fictitious business name is the operating name of a company that differs from its legal name.

Often, states require a person operating a sole proprietorship (or any other business form) under a fictitious business name to register that business name with either the state or the county. Requiring business owners to register fictitious names protects consumers and vendors. A consumer or creditor who has a legal dispute with a business can use the registry of fictitious names to determine what person or entity is ultimately responsible.

Sole proprietor owners can, and often do, commingle personal and business property and funds, something that partnerships, LLCs, and corporations cannot do. Sole proprietorships often have their bank accounts in the name of the owner. Sole proprietors need not observe formalities such as voting and meetings associated with the more complex business forms.

Many businesses begin as sole proprietorships and later graduate to one of the more complex business forms.

Forming a Sole Proprietorship

As noted above, you may already be operating a sole proprietorship. One of the great features of a sole proprietorship is the simplicity of formation. Little more than buying and selling goods or services is needed. In fact, no formal filing or event is required to form a sole proprietorship; it is a status that arises automatically from one's business activity.

See Chapter 3, Information for All Businesses, for information on local taxes and local licenses.

Taxes for the Sole Proprietor

Because a sole proprietorship is indistinguishable from its owner, sole proprietorship taxation is quite simple. The income earned by a sole proprietorship is income earned by its owner. A sole proprietor reports the sole proprietorship income and/or losses and expenses by filling out and filing a Schedule C along with the standard Form 1040.

> ▼ **ONLINE RESOURCE**
>
> To get IRS forms and explanatory publications, visit www.irs.gov/formspubs, and use the "Search Forms and Publications" link.

A sole proprietor need not pay unemployment tax on himself or herself, although he or she must pay unemployment tax on any employees of the business. Of course, the sole proprietor will not enjoy unemployment benefits should the business suffer.

Suing and Being Sued

Sole proprietors are personally liable for all of the debts of their businesses. Let's examine this more closely, because the potential liability can be alarming. Assume that a sole proprietor borrows money to operate, but the business loses its major customer, goes out of business, and is unable to repay the loan. The sole proprietor is liable for the amount of the loan, which can potentially consume all his or her personal assets. Imagine an even worse scenario: a sole proprietor (or even one of his or her employees!) is involved in a business-related accident in which someone is injured or killed. The resulting negligence case can be brought against the sole proprietor owner and against his or her personal assets, such as a bank account, retirement accounts, and even the proprietor's home.

Consider the preceding paragraph carefully before selecting a sole proprietorship as your business form. Accidents happen. Businesses go out of business all the time. Any sole proprietorship that suffers such an unfortunate circumstance is likely to quickly become a nightmare for its owner.

If a sole proprietor is wronged by another party, he or she can bring a lawsuit in his or her own name. Conversely, if a corporation or LLC is wronged by another party, the entity must bring its claim under the name of the company.

> The following are examples of sole proprietorships:
>
> 1. Jake is a plumber who owns his own tools and truck and has no partners.
>
> 2. Nancy has a nail salon. She rents the store-front where she operates in her own name and calls the business Nancy's Nail Salon.
>
> 3. Michael Johnson buys and sells sports memorabilia online.

The sole proprietorship is a popular business form due to its simplicity, ease of setup, and nominal cost. A sole proprietor need only register his or her name and secure local licenses and the sole proprietorship is ready for business.

The owner of a sole proprietorship typically signs contracts in his or her own name, because the sole proprietorship has no separate identity under the law. The sole proprietor owner will typically have customers write checks in the owner's name, even if the business uses a fictitious name. Sole proprietorships can bring lawsuits and can be sued using the name of the owner. Many businesses begin as sole proprietorships and graduate to more complex business forms as the business develops.

Advantages of the Sole Proprietorship

- Owners can establish a sole proprietorship instantly, easily, and inexpensively.
- Sole proprietorships carry little, if any, ongoing formalities.
- A sole proprietor need not pay unemployment tax on himself or herself (although he or she must pay unemployment tax on employees).
- Owners may freely mix business and personal assets.

Disadvantages of the Sole Proprietorship

- Owners are subject to unlimited personal liability for the debts, losses, and liabilities of the business.
- Owners cannot raise capital by selling an interest in the business.
- Sole proprietorships rarely survive the death or incapacity of their owners and so do not retain value.

THE PARTNERSHIP

A partnership is a business form created automatically when two or more persons engage in a business enterprise for profit. Consider the following language from the Uniform Partnership Act: "the association of two or more persons to carry on as co-owners of a business for profit forms a partnership, whether or not the persons intend to form a partnership." A partnership—in its various forms—offers its multiple owners flexibility and relative simplicity in organization and operation. In the case of limited partnerships and limited liability partnerships, a partnership can even offer a degree of liability protection.

DEFINITION

A partnership is a business organization formed when two or more persons or entities come together to operate a business for profit. Partnerships do not enjoy limited liability, except in the case of limited partnerships.

The following are examples of partnerships:

1. Jake and Nancy open a convenience store together and have an attorney draft a formal partnership agreement between them.

2. Jake and Nancy agree orally to join together to run a convenience store and split the profits 50/50. (However, note the warning against forming oral partnerships!)

Partnerships can be formed with a handshake—and often they are. Responsible partners, however, will seek to have their partnership arrangement memorialized in a partnership agreement, preferably with the assistance of an attorney. Because partnerships can be formed so easily, partnerships are often formed accidentally through oral agreements. A partnership is formed whenever two or more persons engage jointly in business activity to pursue profit.

▼

The following is *not* an example of a partnership:

Jake and Nancy agree that Nancy will work in Jake's existing plumbing business, he will pay her a salary, and he will pay her a bonus based on the amount of profit the business earns. Nancy is merely an employee with a profit-sharing bonus, not a partner.

Don't operate a partnership without a written partnership agreement! Because of their informality and their ease of formation, partnerships are the most likely business form to result in disputes and lawsuits between owners—and oral partnership arrangements are usually the reason.

The cost to have an attorney draft a partnership agreement can vary between $500 and $2,000, depending on the complexity of the partnership arrangement and the experience and location of the attorney.

How Partnerships Are Managed

Partnerships have very simple management structures. In the case of general partnerships, partnerships are managed by the partners themselves, with decisions ultimately resting with a majority of the percentage owners of the partnership. Partnership-style management is often called *owner management*. Corporations, on the other hand, are typically managed by appointed or elected officers, which is called *representative management*. (Representative management is discussed throughout the sections on LLCs and corporations.) Keep in mind that a majority of the percentage interest in a partnership can be very different from a majority of the partners. This is because one partner may own 60

percent of a partnership, with four other partners owning only 10 percent each. Partnerships (and corporations and LLCs) universally vest ultimate voting power with a majority of the percentage ownership interest.

Of course, partners and shareholders don't call votes every time they need to make some small business decision such as signing a contract or ordering office supplies. Small tasks are managed informally, as they should be. When voting becomes important, however, is when a dispute arises among the partners. If the dispute cannot be resolved informally, the partners call a meeting and take a vote on the matter. Those partners representing the minority in such a vote must go along with the decision of the partners representing the majority.

Partnerships do not require formal meetings of their partners like corporations do. Of course, some partnerships elect to have periodic meetings anyway. Overall, the management and administrative operation of the partnership is relatively simple, which can be an important advantage. Like sole proprietorships, partnerships often grow and graduate to LLC or corporate status.

How Partnerships Are Governed

Partnerships are governed by the law of the state in which they are organized and by the rules set out by the partners themselves. Typically, partners set forth their governing rules in a partnership agreement.

Often the governance rules determined by the partners differ from the governance rules set by state law. In most cases, the rules of the partners override state law. For example, state law typically dictates that a partnership's profits are to be divided among partners in proportion to their ownership interests. However, the partners are free to divide profits by a formula separate from their ownership interests and the decision of the partners will override state law. Thus, the governance rules in state law are default provisions that apply in the absence of any rules set by the partners in a partnership agreement.

This fact underscores the need for a partnership agreement. Otherwise, the partnership will by default be governed by state law. The laws set forth by state law may not be appropriate for every partnership. For the most part, however, the default state rules are fair and well-balanced.

An Important Concept: The Law of Agency

Agency refers to one's status as the legal representative (the *agent*) of an entity or another person. The party on whose behalf an agent acts is called a *principal*. A person is said to be the agent of a partnership or other entity if he or she has the legal authority to act on behalf of the company.

> ▼ **DEFINITION**
>
> **A**gency is status as the legal representative (the agent) of an entity or another person (a principal).

An agent can bind a partnership to contracts and other obligations through his or her actions on behalf of the partnership. Of course, when an agent acts on behalf of a partnership or another company, the company is bound by those acts and decisions. A third party dealing with an agent of a company can rely upon the agency relationship and enforce the obligations undertaken by the agent—even if the agent made a foolish or selfish decision on the company's behalf. If the agent acts within the scope of his or her authority, the partnership becomes bound by his or her actions, no matter how foolish.

The *law of agency* applies to corporations and LLCs as well as to partnerships. However, a discussion of the law of agency is particularly pertinent to a discussion of partnerships because in a general partnership, all of the partners usually have the status of agent with respect to the general partnership. The law of agency applies differently to corporations. Shareholders in a corporation are not necessarily officers and directors of that corporation and agent status will not automatically apply to them. So, partners in a partnership must be careful to delineate authority and keep abreast of decisions by their co-partners.

Partnerships can grant specific authority to specific partners, if such a grant appears in the partnership

> ▼ **DEFINITION**
>
> **T**he law of agency is the law concerned with the contractual or quasi-contractual relationship between a principal or principals and an agent who is authorized to represent the legal interests of the principal(s) and to perform legal acts that bind the principal(s).

agreement. Without an agreement to the contrary, however, any partner can bind the partnership without the consent of the other partners, as described above.

VARIETIES OF PARTNERSHIPS

There are several varieties of partnerships. They range from the simple general partnership to the limited liability partnership.

The General Partnership

By default, a standard partnership is referred to as a general partnership. General partnerships are the simplest of all partnerships. An oral partnership will almost always be a general partnership. In a general partnership, all partners share in the management of the entity and share in the entity's profits. Matters with respect to the ordinary business operations of the partnership are decided by a majority of the partners. Of course, some partners can own a greater share of the entity than

> ▼ **DEFINITION**
>
> **A** general partnership is a standard partnership, the simplest form. All partners share in the management and in the profits and decide on matters of ordinary business operations by a majority of the partners or according to the percentage ownership of each partner. All partners are responsible for the liabilities.

other partners, in which case their vote counts according to their percentage ownership—much like voting of shares in a corporation. All partners are responsible for the liabilities of the general partnership.

The Limited Partnership

The limited partnership is more complex than the general partnership. It is a partnership owned by two classes of partners: general partners manage the enterprise and are personally liable for its debts; limited partners contribute capital and share in the profits but normally do not participate in the management of the enterprise. Another notable distinction between the two classes of partners is that limited partners incur no liability for partnership debts beyond their capital contributions. Limited partners enjoy liability protection much like the shareholders of a corporation. The limited partnership is commonly used in the restaurant business, with the founders serving as general partners and the investors as limited partners.

▼ DEFINITION

A limited partnership is a business organization owned by two classes of partners: general partners, who manage the enterprise, and limited partners, who contribute capital and share in the profits but normally do not participate in the management of the enterprise. Limited partners enjoy limited personal liability while general partners have unlimited personal liability.

A limited partnership usually requires a state filing to establish the business entity. Some states, most notably California, allow the oral creation of a limited partnership. Of course, establishing a limited partnership with nothing more than an oral agreement is unwise. Oral limited partnership agreements will very likely lead to disputes and may not offer liability protection to limited partners.

Limited partnerships have fallen out of favor recently because of the rise of the limited liability company. Both forms share partnership-style taxation and partnership-style management, but the LLC offers greater liability protection because it extends liability protection to all of its managers. Thus, today the LLC is often selected instead of the limited partnership.

Because of the complexity of limited partnerships, the formation of limited partnerships is not covered in this volume. The formation of a limited partnership is best left to a qualified attorney.

The Limited Liability Partnership

Yet another form of partnership is the limited liability partnership. A limited liability partnership is one composed of licensed professionals, such as attorneys, accountants, and architects. The partners in an LLP may enjoy personal liability protection for the acts of other partners, but each partner remains liable for his or her own actions. State laws generally require an LLP to maintain generous insurance policies or cash reserves to pay claims brought against the LLP.

▼ DEFINITION

A limited liability partnership is a partnership composed of licensed professionals, each of whom may enjoy personal liability protection for the acts of other partners while remaining liable for his or her own actions.

Because of the complexity of limited liability partnerships, as well as the small audience for whom LLPs are appropriate, the formation of LLPs is not covered in this volume. That is best left to a qualified attorney.

Advantages of the Partnership

- Owners can start partnerships relatively easily and inexpensively.
- Partnerships do not require annual meetings and require few ongoing formalities.
- Partnerships offer favorable taxation for most smaller businesses.
- Partnerships often do not have to pay minimum taxes that are required of LLCs and corporations.

Disadvantages of the Partnership

- All owners are subject to unlimited personal liability for the debts, losses, and liabilities of the business (except in the cases of limited partnerships and limited liability partnerships).
- Individual partners bear responsibility for the actions of other partners.
- Poorly organized partnerships and oral partnerships can lead to disputes among owners.

THE LIMITED LIABILITY COMPANY (LLC)

The limited liability company (LLC) is America's newest form of business organization. There is little historical precedent for LLCs. They are essentially creations of the state legislatures, although some commentators trace the origin of the LLC to a 19th-century form of business organization called the *partnership association* or *limited partnership association*. The great bulk of laws authorizing LLCs in the United States were passed in the 1980s and 1990s. Wyoming passed the first law authorizing the LLC in 1977. Florida followed in 1982. The watershed event in the rise of the LLC was a 1988 Internal Revenue Service ruling that recognized partnership tax treatment for LLCs. Within six years, 46 states authorized LLCs as a business form. By 1996, Vermont, the last state to recognize LLCs, had an LLC statute in place.

▼ DEFINITION

A limited liability company is a new and flexible business organization that offers the advantages of liability protection with the simplicity of a partnership.

The LLC is often described as a hybrid business form. It combines the liability protection of a corporation with the tax treatment and ease of administration of a partnership. As the name suggests, it offers liability protection to its owners for company debts and liabilities.

Simplicity and Flexibility

While LLCs are essentially new creations of state legislatures, corporations are truly ancient—and today's corporate law still carries some unwanted baggage. The modern American corporation has antecedents that date to Roman times and that we inherited through English law. The basic principles of American corporate law have not changed significantly in centuries. Probably the single greatest disadvantage of the corporate form is the burdensome range of formalities that corporate managers must observe. A modern corporation's heavy administrative burden is a remnant of the more traditional and formal legal system under which corporate law was cultivated.

▼ INSIDER TIP

LCs are the favorite choice for entities with one to three owners working in a small local business that they do not plan to grow significantly and who do not expect to raise significant amounts of capital. As the number of owners grows, the corporation becomes a more attractive choice as a business form.

The LLC changed all that. The LLC offers the liability protection benefits of the corporation without the corporation's burdensome formalities. It is this simplicity that has made the LLC an instantly popular business form with businesspersons operating smaller companies.

Another attractive feature of LLCs that we will discuss throughout this book is their flexibility. The management of an LLC can elect to be taxed either as a partnership or as a corporation. An LLC can be managed like a partnership (a member-managed LLC) or like a corporation (manager-managed LLC). LLCs can create a board of directors and can have a president and officers just like a corporation. Management of an LLC can choose to have periodic meetings of its membership or choose to ignore such formalities altogether.

Potential Disadvantages of the Limited Liability Company

The LLC does carry some disadvantages that make it an undesirable business form for some purposes. It is a new business form and courts have not yet developed a body of legal precedent governing LLCs. Thus, LLC owners and professionals may face operating questions and issues for which they have little or no legal guidance. However, this concern lessens as the states develop a reliable body of law concerning LLCs and it is no issue at all for very small companies.

Furthermore, for companies that wish to pursue venture capital, accumulate a large number of shareholders, and/or eventually pursue an initial public offering, the LLC is not an appropriate alternative to a corporation. Venture capitalists and angel investors tend to shy away from investing in LLCs. The overwhelming number of large publicly held companies are corporations, not LLCs.

What should the owners of an LLC do if their company grows in size such that an LLC is no longer the appropriate business form? The answer is simple: it is possible to convert an LLC into a corporation. Thus, some small companies begin life as LLCs, outgrow the LLC form, and then the owners transfer the assets of the LLC to a newly formed corporation with the same owners as the LLC. Thereby, the LLC is converted to a corporation. Furthermore, as one might imagine, it is also possible to convert a corporation into an LLC—or nearly any business form into any other. It is also possible to reorganize a business in another state by transferring the assets of a business into a newly chartered entity. Converting business forms requires some sophisticated legal and tax analysis, however, and should not be attempted without the services of a qualified attorney and accountant.

The cost of setting up an LLC is roughly equivalent to the cost of setting up a corporation. The secretary of state's fees for filing articles of organization and for filing annual reports are often the same for both LLCs and corporations. Organizers that wish to seek help with organizing an LLC through an LLC formation service or through an attorney will find the fees to be roughly the same.

Advantages of the LLC

- LLCs do not require annual meetings and require few ongoing formalities.
- Owners are protected from personal liability for company debts and obligations.
- LLCs enjoy partnership-style, pass-through taxation, which is favorable to many small businesses.

Disadvantages of the LLC

- LLCs do not have a reliable body of legal precedent to guide owners and managers, although LLC law is becoming more reliable as time passes.
- An LLC is not an appropriate vehicle for businesses seeking to become public eventually or to raise money in the capital markets.
- LLCs are more expensive to set up than partnerships.
- LLCs usually require periodic filings with the state and annual fees.
- Some states do not allow the organization of LLCs for certain professional vocations.

CORPORATION

The term *corporation* comes from the Latin *corpus*, which means body. A corporation is a body—it is a legal person in the eyes of the law. It can bring lawsuits, buy and sell property, contract, be taxed, and even commit crimes.

Its most notable feature: a corporation protects its owners from personal liability for corporate debts and obligations—within limits. See the section in Chapter 7, "Protecting Yourself from Personal Liability as an Owner of an LLC," for information on the limits of corporate liability protection.

▼ **DEFINITION**

A corporation is a legal entity that has most of the rights and duties of natural persons but with perpetual life and limited liability.

A corporation has perpetual life. When shareholders pass on or leave a corporation, they can transfer their shares to others who can continue the corporation's business. A corporation is owned by its shareholders, managed by its board of directors, and in most cases operated by its officers. The shareholders elect the directors, who in turn appoint the corporate officers. In small corporations, the same person may serve multiple roles—shareholder, director, and officer.

Corporations are ideal vehicles for raising investment capital. A corporation seeking to raise capital need only sell shares of its stock. The purchasing shareholders pay cash or property for their stock and they then become part owners in the corporation. Of course, the sale of corporate stock is heavily regulated by the U.S. Securities and Exchange Commission and by state securities laws.

A corporation's shareholders, directors, officers, and managers must observe particular formalities in operating and administering the corporation. For example, decisions regarding a corporation's management must often be made by formal vote and must be recorded in the corporate minutes. Meetings of shareholders and directors must be properly noticed and must meet quorum requirements. Finally, corporations must meet annual reporting requirements in their state of incorporation and in states where they do significant business.

Advantages of the Corporation

- Owners are protected from personal liability for company debts and obligations.

- Corporations have a reliable body of legal precedent to guide owners and managers.
- A corporation is the best vehicle for eventual public companies.
- Corporations can more easily raise capital through the sale of securities.
- Corporations can easily transfer ownership through the transfer of securities.
- A corporation can have an unlimited life.
- Corporations can create tax benefits under certain circumstances, but note that C corporations may be subject to "double taxation" on profits.

Disadvantages of the Corporation

- Corporations require annual meetings and require owners and directors to observe certain formalities.
- Corporations are more expensive to set up than partnerships and sole proprietorships.
- Corporations require periodic filings with the state and annual fees.

BUSINESS FORM COMPARISON

Table 2.1 highlights the main advantages and disadvantages of each business form. Use this table to focus in on your specific needs. It outlines the various features of corporations, LLCs, partnerships, and sole proprietorships.

| TABLE 2.1 | Business Form Comparison Table

	Corporation	**Limited Liability Company**	**Partnership**	**Sole Proprietorship**
Ease of setup	More difficult	More difficult	Less difficult	Easy
Initial costs such as filing fees, state fees, and legal fees	High	High	Medium to high	Low
Owners are personally protected from liability for the organization's debts	Yes	Yes	No, except in limited partnerships	No
Entity must make annual or biennial state filings	Yes	Yes	Almost never	No
Entity must pay annual or biennial state fees	Yes	Yes	Almost never	No
Annual meetings	Required by law, except for close corporations	Not required, but recommended	Not required, but recommended	No
Formalities required in connection with voting and internal governance	Yes	Relaxed formalities	Relaxed formalities	No
Can exist indefinitely	Yes	Yes	Yes*	No
Can issue shares or interest in exchange for cash	Yes	Yes	Yes	No
Appropriate entity to raise venture capital	Yes	No	No	No
Appropriate entity to become publicly traded	Yes	No	No	No
Entity can elect to be taxed as a corporation	Yes	Yes	No	No
Entity can elect to be taxed as a partnership	Yes	Yes	Yes	No
Owner can mingle personal and business assets and funds	No	No	No	Yes
Registration required in foreign states in which company does business	Yes	Yes	No, except for limited partnerships	No
State laws governing entity are uniform throughout nation	Laws vary little	Laws vary moderately	Laws vary very little	Laws vary very little
Maximum number of members	Unlimited, except S corporation. Maximum is 75 owners	Unlimited by law**	Yes	One

*Partnerships can, conceivably, have unlimited life if new partners are admitted into the partnership as old partners exit the partnership.

**While general partnerships are not limited in size by operation of law, prudence dictates that they not have too many partners. Because each partner is liable for the acts of the other partners acting on the partnership's behalf, a large general partnership is not wise. Any general partnership of more than ten persons is likely to become difficult to manage.

CHAPTER 3

Information for All Businesses

LOCAL TAXES, LOCAL LICENSES

You can reasonably expect that your state and local jurisdiction will carry licensing and filing responsibilities for your business—regardless of the business form you choose. Local licensing rules will vary from jurisdiction to jurisdiction; expect more stringent requirements in cities. Here are some requirements to watch for:

- City and/or county business license
- City and/or county local taxation
- State sales tax registration and filings for owners who sell goods to which sales tax is applicable
- Need to pay unemployment tax on employees
- Registration for certain industries—a requirement that varies wildly from state to state
- Registration for fictitious business names

Of course, the wide variation of local regulations places this topic far beyond the scope of this book. The best ways to learn about your local regulations are to call or visit your city hall or county administration. Some municipalities even have helpful guides to get you started.

INSIDER TIP

If you get stuck in the bureaucracy trying to figure out your local regulations, call the office of an elected representative such as a county supervisor or the mayor (you probably won't reach them, you'll reach an assistant) and ask them to point you to the right person or department. Typically, elected representatives are more responsive than bureaucrats who are not elected.

PARTNERSHIP/LLC TAXATION

Partnership and LLC taxation deserve mention. A notable feature of LLCs is that they are typically taxed in the same manner as partnerships. Technically speaking, partnerships are not taxed. Their income passes freely through the partnership, but is taxed as the partnership or LLC pays the income out in the form of wages, dividends, and distributions of profits. This manner of taxation is familiarly known as *partnership taxation*. In most circumstances, smaller businesses will incur a lower overall tax liability if they follow partnership taxation. Another common term applied to partnership taxation is *pass-through taxation*—which refers to the way income passes through a partnership to its members. Although partnerships and LLCs pay no tax, they are required to disclose their earnings and distributions to the Internal Revenue Service and state tax authorities on annual information returns.

▼
DEFINITION

Pass-through taxation is when entities are not taxed on their income, but the income and profits that the entities pay out to owners and employees are taxable. Partnerships and LLCs enjoy pass-through taxation.

Partnerships report their annual income or loss on U.S. Federal Form 1065. Also, each partner submits his or her individual Schedule K-1, Partner's Share of Income, which is part of Form 1065.

How LLCs report their income depends upon if they are single-member LLCs or multimember LLCs. If a single-member LLC has an individual as its owner, the LLC income and expenses are reported just like a sole proprietorship, on Schedule C and Form 1040. Multimember LLCs (those that do not elect to be taxed as a corporation) report their annual income, loss, and expenses just as a partnership does, on Form 1065.

▼
ONLINE RESOURCE:

To get IRS forms and explanatory publications, visit www.irs.gov/formspubs and use the "Search Forms and Publications" link.

CORPORATE TAXATION

A corporation, in contrast, pays tax twice—once on its corporate profit and again when its employees or owners are taxed personally on income, distributions, and dividends. The dual effect of corporate taxation is aptly referred to as *double taxation*. Although LLCs typically follow partnership taxation, in some cases LLCs elect to be taxed as corporations. Corporations may elect partnership taxation if they elect to be taxed as subchapter S corporations. Thus, the flexibility afforded to organizers of both LLCs and corporations reveals the modern trend towards fluidity in the law of business organizations.

▼
DEFINITION

Corporate taxation is the taxation of a corporation both on its profit and when its employees or owners are taxed personally on income, distributions, and dividends.

Double taxation sounds much worse than it is. Remember that salaries are a tax-deductible expense for a corporation. Thus, only profit is subject to double taxation. Some corporations deal with the double taxation problem by simply paying out all of the corporation's profits as salaries and bonuses.

The corporate federal income tax rate (like the individual tax rate) begins at 15 percent and graduates to a maximum of 35 percent, but certain surtaxes cause tax "bubbles" at lower incomes. Table 3.1 illustrates the federal corporate income tax rates at various income levels. Note that Congress routinely adjusts income tax rates, so this table is subject to change. See the instructions to Form 1120 for current tax rates. By comparison, individual tax rates graduate to a maximum of 39.6 percent.

TABLE 3.1	U.S. Federal Corporate Income Tax Rates
Income Level	**Effective Tax Rate**
0–$50,000	15%
$50,001–$75,000	25%
$75,001–$100,000	34%
$100,001–$335,000	39%
$335,001–$10,000,000	34%
$10,000,001–$15,000,000	35%
$15,000,001–$18,333,333	38%
Above $18,333,333	35%

Corporations may choose a fiscal year that differs from the fiscal year of its shareholders. This creates opportunities to achieve tax savings through deferring income. For example, a business that receives a large increase in revenues in December can make its fiscal year end on November 30, thereby deferring the December receipts until the following fiscal year. You should seek the advice of an accountant when making decisions regarding your fiscal year.

How corporations report their annual income, loss, and expenses at the federal level depends upon whether they are C corporations or S corporations. C corporations file Form 1120, U.S. Corporation Income Tax Return. S corporations file Form 1120S, U.S. Income Tax Return for an S Corporation. Form 1120S closely mirrors a partnership return (because S corporations are taxed like partnerships) and each S corporation member must file a Schedule K-1, Shareholder's Share of Income, which is part of Form 1120S.

▼
ONLINE RESOURCE
To get IRS forms and explanatory publications, visit www.irs.gov/formspubs and use the "Search Forms and Publications" link.

Corporations are also taxed at the state level. The states have adopted a dizzying variety of approaches to corporate taxation. The most common is the corporate income tax. Corporate income tax rates are lower than federal rates and tend to range between four percent and 11 percent, depending on the state. Not all states levy an income tax. Also common are state corporate taxes based upon assets in use in the state and taxes based upon outstanding shares of stock.

A common theme in state corporate taxation is that a given state will tax only corporate activity that occurs within that state. This doctrine is called *apportionment*. For example, a state will tax corporate income only to the extent that such income flows from activities within the state.

A corporation or other business operating in more than one state must file a tax return with the IRS as well as with all states in which it operates. Of course, each state has its own legal definition of what degree of business operation will trigger taxation.

BUSINESS ENTITY TERMINOLOGY

Because LLCs, corporations, and partnerships differ fundamentally from each other, the basic language varies. For example, LLCs do not have shareholders or partners; they have "members." They do not have shares like a corporation; they have "membership interests." Understand, of course, that calling an LLC member a "shareholder" is not technically incorrect. Nevertheless, the legislators, lawyers, administrators and judges who govern the body of law surrounding LLCs will universally use the proper terminology.

Table 3.2 (next page) shows how some basic terms differ with respect to partnerships, corporations, and LLCs.

FORBIDDEN BUSINESS PURPOSES

Some licensed professions may not be conducted as LLCs and corporations. The practice of law and the practice of medicine are the most universal and most illustrative examples of this prohibition. Because lawyers and doctors face professional malpractice liability for errors that they make in the conduct of their practices, it would be unfair to the public to allow such professionals to enjoy liability protection from such errors. The types of business purposes that will be allowed in a given state will vary widely from state to state. For example, California forbids any profession that requires a "license, certification, or registration" from using the LLC or corporate form. This prohibition excludes more than 100 individual professions, including such diverse businesses as lawyers, real estate brokers, and pest control operators.

In states that allow it (not all do), licensed professionals must use a special form of LLC, the professional limited liability company (PLLC), or a special form of corporation, the professional corporation (often called a PC).

TABLE 3.2   Business Terms

	Partnership	**Corporation**	**Limited Liability Company**
Owners	Partners	Shareholders	Members
Ownership share	Partnership interest or percentage interest	Shares or stock certificate	Membership interest, percentage interest, membership unit, or unit
Charter document filed with state	Statement of partnership (for general partnerships, but it is permissive and not mandatory), certificate of limited partnership (for limited partnerships)	Articles of incorporation, or certificate of incorporation	Articles of organization or certificate of organization
Operating/governing document	Partnership agreement	Bylaws	LLC operating agreement
Company organizer	Organizer, founding partner	Incorporator	Organizer

CHAPTER 4

The Features of LLCs

LCs are formed in a manner much like corporations. Both LLCs and corporations are chartered entities. This means that, unlike some types of partnerships that can be created without state registration, LLCs can be created only by filing a charter document in the state of organization. An LLC's charter document is called its *articles of organization*—a name obviously borrowed from the corporation's equivalent, *articles of incorporation*.

Interestingly, articles of organization are very similar to articles of incorporation. For example, both state the entity's name, require the appointment of a resident agent (more on this below), and usually require a statement of purpose.

▼ DEFINITION

Articles of organization are the document by which an LLC is formed. Articles of organization cover foundational matters such as the name of the LLC, its business purpose, and its agent for service of process.

HOW LLCS ARE MANAGED

Because LLCs do not have directors like a corporation, they are managed differently than corporations. LLCs are either *member-managed* or *manager-managed*.

Member-managed LLCs are governed by the LLC's owners (members) equally, just like a standard partnership. Manager-managed LLCs are governed by one or more appointed managers, who typically need not be members of the LLC. This management by appointment is called *representative management*. Manager-managed LLCs are managed much like corporations—with an appointed body of persons other than the company's owners. The body that undertakes governing responsibilities can be in the form of a board of managers or a committee of managers.

Of course, an LLC that wishes to use a representative form of management will require operating rules. Typically, an LLC sets forth its operating rules in a document called an *operating agreement*. An operating agreement is a close equivalent of a corporation's *bylaws*. LLC operating agreements cover matters such as who governs the LLC, the appointment of managers, the manner in which members can be ousted from the LLC, and such. Operating agreements, like bylaws, are not filed with the state. In fact, typically an LLC is not required to have any operating agreement in place, although it is advised. In the absence of an operating agreement, the LLC will follow the default rules of governance set forth in the laws of the state of organization. LLCs that operate without operating agreements are extremely rare.

> ### ▼ DEFINITION
>
> An operating agreement is the document that governs the internal structure and operation of an LLC and governs the relationship between its members and its managers.

PROFESSIONAL LIMITED LIABILITY COMPANIES

Professional LLCs (sometimes called PLLCs) are simply LLCs in which the members are engaged in rendering professional services, such as the practice of medicine or law. Forming a professional LLC is slightly more difficult than forming a standard LLC. Much like professional corporation shareholders, professional LLC members may enjoy personal liability protection for the acts of other members, although each member remains liable for his or her own professional misconduct. State laws generally require professional LLCs to maintain generous insurance policies or cash reserves to pay claims brought against them.

> ### ▼ DEFINITION
>
> A professional LLC is an LLC organized to offer services that normally require a license, such as the practice of medicine or law.

Note that professional LLCs are not recognized in all states, most notably California. Professional LLCs are more sophisticated enterprises than standard LLCs, and their organization should be left to a qualified attorney.

CHAPTER 5

The Ten Steps to Organizing an LLC

Organizing an LLC yourself can seem daunting upon first glance, but it is actually a series of small, simple tasks. At the end of this chapter you will find an Organization Worksheet that will help you organize these activities. The State Reference Tables in Appendix B offer contact information and resources for all 50 states and the District of Columbia. Appendix A offers model organizational documents. Word processor versions of the documents are also included on the CD-ROM and are always available at www.learn-aboutlaw.com.

THE ROLE OF THE ORGANIZER

An LLC's organizer is the person or entity that organizes an LLC and signs and files its articles of organization or certificate of organization with the secretary of state's office or its equivalent. An organizer is necessary because a brand-new LLC does not yet have appointed managers, members, or owners. The organizer is much like the incorporator of a corporation. The organizer may be an owner or manager of the LLC, but need not be.

The organizer is the LLC's first representative and gives birth to the LLC by signing and filing the articles of organization. By signing the LLC's articles of organization, the organizer attests to

the truthfulness of the articles, but the organizer does not incur any real liability or assume any ongoing duty. When an attorney forms an LLC on behalf of a client, he or she serves as organizer. If you intend to use this book to guide you with the formation of your LLC, you will be serving as the organizer. After completing the organization of the LLC, the organizer then turns over the LLC to its owners.

THE ROLE OF MEMBERS

Members are the owners of an LLC. Once the organizer forms the LLC, persons then become owners of the LLC by purchasing membership interests in the LLC by making initial capital contributions. Typically, the founders of an LLC will join an LLC soon after the LLC is organized. When members join an LLC, they also typically execute an LLC operating agreement, discussed at length below. The LLC operating agreement is the equivalent of a corporation's bylaws—it outlines the operating rules of an LLC and governs the rights and responsibilities of its members.

THE ROLE OF MANAGERS

LLCs are managed either by the members themselves or by managers appointed or voted into office by the members. In a member-managed LLC, all members participate in management, much as the partners in a general partnership. In such cases, the managers are the members. In manager-managed LLCs, the members do not necessarily participate in the daily operations and decision making of an LLC. The managers of a manager-managed LLC are appointed by the members to operate and manage the LLC. They are the equivalent of directors and officers of a corporation.

An LLC's managers may be members of the LLC, but need not be. Again, the LLC's operating agreement will govern the relationship between members and managers, such as how managers are appointed (and, if necessary, removed). An LLC's managers enjoy broad powers. They typically have authority to take the following actions:

- Issue units of stock.
- Vote on acquisitions and mergers.
- Approve loans to the LLC.
- Approve plans for employee incentive compensation.
- Approve large purchases of real estate and capital equipment.
- Manage the LLC on a day-to-day basis.
- Hire and fire employees.
- Negotiate and sign contracts.
- Deal with customers and vendors.
- Maintain the limited liability company's records.

THE MANAGEMENT STRUCTURE OF LLCs

The management structures of LLCs are limited only by the imagination of their organizers. They can be operated like sole proprietorships or partnerships. LLCs, because of their inherent flexibility, can even be designed to imitate the management structure of a corporation. For example, an LLC can have an elected board of directors and officers such as a chief executive officer (CEO) and a president. All that is required to design an LLC management structure is an LLC operating agreement that outlines the structure. This subject is reexamined in Step 9 and Appendix C contains two examples of LLC operating agreements.

Many small LLCs will have very few members and managers, sometimes as few as one member. It is not uncommon for an LLC to have one person who is the sole owner and sole manager.

THE ROLE OF THE SECRETARY OF STATE

A secretary of state is the state official charged with the responsibility for receiving and archiving legal documents, including corporation and LLC papers. Of course, you will not deal with the secretary of state (typically an elected official) directly; you will deal with employees of the office of the secretary of state. Understand, however, that your state may have an equivalent department with a different name, such as Hawaii's Department of Commerce and Consumer Affairs or Arizona's Corporation Commission. Regardless of the name, each state's business filing office operates much the same.

Your LLC's most foundational document is its articles of organization, which you file with the secretary of state to begin the life of your LLC. But the secretary of state's role does not end there. The secretary of state's office is also the department that receives periodic information reports from LLCs and corporations and maintains records on business entities. If an LLC fails to pay its taxes or fails to file its periodic reports, the secretary of state may withdraw an LLC's good standing status. LLCs do not file their operating agreements or other records with the secretary of state.

The records of LLCs and corporations are public records and are available for inspection by anyone. In my role as an attorney, I often make requests of the secretary of state's office when trying to locate the business address of a corporation or to determine if a particular corporation still enjoys good standing status. More often than not, I seek such records when attempting to collect a debt on behalf of my clients. The secretary of state is entrusted with maintaining accurate business records and with responding to such requests for information.

If an LLC becomes seriously delinquent in its tax and reporting responsibilities, the secretary of state may eventually order an administrative dissolution of that LLC. An administrative dissolution is one way an LLC may conclude its life. Each state has different rules for what constitutes a delinquency serious enough to warrant an administrative dissolution. Both the withdrawal of good standing status and dissolution lead to a failure of a LLC's liability protection. (See Chapter 6 for further information on maintaining good standing with the secretary of state.)

STEP 1: WHERE SHOULD YOU ORGANIZE?

Your LLC's life begins when you file articles of organization with the secretary of state or an equivalent department of state government. (The federal government does not charter LLCs or corporations.) Several factors should guide your decision on which state is the best for your LLC. Those factors include the following:

- The state or states in which your business operates (the most important consideration for most companies)
- Initial LLC filing fees
- Annual filing fees and annual reporting requirements
- State-specific advantages such as privacy rights

The LLC That Does Business in Only One State

As a general rule, if your business is small and operates in and sells products or services in only one state or even just mostly in one state, you should organize your LLC in the state where you conduct business. Most readers of this book will follow this course. Corporations differ from LLCs in an important respect: because corporation law differs widely in the 50 states (especially with respect to corporate taxation, director's rights, and privacy rights), it is quite common to incorporate out-of-state.

LLC law, however, is more uniform throughout the states (especially with regard to taxation), which lessens the advantages of shopping around when picking a state in which to organize an LLC. In short, you should probably organize in your home state if your company operates solely in that state.

The LLC That Does Business in Several States

But what if your LLC operates or does business in several states? You may be required to register in all of the states where you do business—regardless of the state you choose for your organization. States generally require out-of-state LLCs (called *foreign LLCs*) to reg-

ister and pay fees in the state in which they are operating as a guest. (See Chapter 6, Operating Your LLC, for more information on foreign LLC status and reporting requirements and considerations.) For example, a Delaware LLC that transacts business in California must register in California as a foreign LLC, pay a filing fee in California, and also pay the annual minimum California franchise tax. Registration of an out-of-state LLC in a state where the LLC is conducting business operations is often called *qualification*. So the benefits of organizing out-of-state are limited by such foreign registration rules, because you will probably be required to register in your home state in any case.

> ## ▼ DEFINITION
> A foreign LLC is an LLC that operates in one state but whose articles of organization are filed in another state or another nation. In the state where its articles of organization are filed it is considered a *domestic* LLC.

This raises an important question: what constitutes "operations" or "business activity" in a particular state? Well, all states will define it somewhat differently—but universally states define business activity broadly. For example, California defines "doing business" as "actively engaging in any transaction for the purpose of financial or pecuniary gain or profit." It does not take a lawyer to get the crux of the meaning of that phrase. Quite simply, California interprets a single transaction taking place in California as doing business.

Why do states define business activity so broadly, thereby requiring local registration of out-of-state LLCs? There are two reasons. First, registered LLCs pay lucrative filing fees and franchise fees. The second reason is less sinister: each state has an interest in protecting its consumers from unscrupulous out-of-state companies, LLC or otherwise. A state can better protect its consumers from misconduct by out-of-state businesses if the state has registration and contact information on file for the company. Furthermore, a registered company automatically submits to jurisdiction (and so can be more easily sued) in jurisdictions where it is registered.

So, is every LLC in the United States properly qualified in every state in which it does business? No. Right or wrong, many thousands of LLCs regularly ignore the foreign registration requirements imposed by states. Foreign LLC registration in California, for example, runs about $1,000 per year.

STEP 2: SELECT YOUR LLC'S NAME

At this stage in the organization process, you must choose your LLC's name. Understand, of course, that you may use a trade name in the public marketplace other than your LLC's name. This is called *doing business as* (DBA) a fictitious name, as discussed earlier. For example, a company could operate a store under the trade name Evolution, but the LLC's name could be Evolution Trade Group, LLC or any other name.

The single greatest consideration when choosing a name is ensuring that no other person or entity is currently using the name. This consideration is guided by two factors. First, your use of a company name may infringe on the trademark or service mark rights of others. Infringing on the trademark rights of others may result in legal complications. Second, the secretary of state's office will not register a new LLC with the same name as an existing LLC. Keep in mind, however, that a secretary of state's office will have existing records only for company names in that state—the office will have no records for company names in the other 49 states. Thus, you may wish to search for existing trademarks and LLC names to ensure that your desired name is available.

> ### ▼ DEFINITION
>
> A trademark is any symbol, word, or combination of either, used to represent or identify a product or service. A trademark need not be registered to enjoy legal rights of protection. Trademark protection springs naturally from use of the mark in the public marketplace.

Searching for Existing Trademarks

Begin by performing a trademark search. You can hire a professional service to do a trademark search for you. The cost can range between $300 and $1,200. The value of such professional search services has been eclipsed by free services on the Internet. In my law practice, while I have used full-service search firms, I prefer to conduct trademark searches as follows.

You can search registered and pending trademarks at the U.S. Patent and Trademark Office's Web site by pointing your browser to www.uspto.gov/main/trademarks.htm and click "Search Trademarks" to use the Trademark Electronic Search System (TESS). Once there, use the New User Form Search. In the search window, enter the name that you wish to use in the box "Search Term." Make sure the "Field" term is set to "Combined Word Mark." To ensure that your search effectively locates all potential conflicts, do the following:

- Search for phonetic variants of your proposed name, because phonetically similar marks can cause a trademark conflict. For example, if your company name is Cybertech, search for Cybertek, Cybertex, Sybertex, etc.
- Search for both the plural and singular versions of your proposed name.
- If your name uses more than one word, search for each word individually.
- Follow the instructions in the use of wildcard search terms.

Searching for trademarks is an imperfect science, though, and no search can be expected to discover all users of a mark. Remember: trademark rights are created by the use of a trademark in the public marketplace and not by registration of the trademark. In fact, most trademarks are never registered, although they are used in the public marketplace. Thus, unregistered marks may be valid marks—and they are much more difficult to discover. The last step of your trademark conflict search should be an Internet search with one of the popular search engines. Such a search will probably discover any users of your proposed name.

Searching the Secretary of State's Records for Existing Company Names

Assuming that your name does not trigger a conflict with a registered or unregistered trademark, you should then search an online database of existing company names with the secretary of state in the state in which you intend to organize. Keep in mind that your LLC name must be distinguishable not only from other LLCs, but from corporations and partnerships as well. Nearly all secretary of state Web sites offer free searching of existing company names. See Appendix A, State Reference Tables, for information on locating the secretary of state's Web site in the state where you intend to organize. Alternatively, some secretary of state offices offer informal searches over the telephone. However, searching a database is always preferable.

Reserving Your LLC Name

When you have selected an appropriate name, you may wish to reserve the name of the LLC. This step is optional. In my law practice, I almost always skip reserving a company name. The form for reserving an LLC name is typically nearly as long as the form for filing the articles of organization! To me, name reservation just creates more work. If my search reveals that a name is not taken by any other company, I simply file the articles within a few days. If my filing is rejected, I work with my client to pick a new name and file again.

If name reservation is important to you, nearly all states offer a name reservation service. Typically, the service requires you to file a brief name reservation application with the secretary of state's office. See Appendix A, State Reference Tables, for information on name reservation in particular states, appropriate forms, and associated filing fees.

A Note on LLC Names

Your LLC's name should reflect LLC status. Most states require an LLC identifier. Perhaps more importantly, you should always hold yourself out to the public as an LLC to ensure maximum liability protection. Therefore, your LLC's name must include one of the following terms:

- Limited Liability Company or Limited Liability Co.
- LLC

Some states allow Limited or Ltd., but this designation may imply a limited partnership.

Your LLC's name should *not* include any of the fol-

lowing terms, which are usually restricted by state and/or federal law, unless your LLC meets the legal requirements for such terms:

- Bank
- Trust or Trustee
- Insurance
- Investment and Loan
- Thrift
- Doctor
- Mortgage
- Cooperative
- Olympic or Olympiad

STEP 3: SELECT THE REGISTERED AGENT

A registered agent is a person or entity authorized and obligated to receive legal papers on behalf of an LLC. The registered agent is identified in the articles of organization, but can typically be changed upon the filing of a notice with the secretary of state.

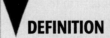

DEFINITION

A registered agent is the person or entity authorized to receive legal papers on behalf of a corporation.

The registered agent serves an important function. Because an LLC is not a physical person, service of legal papers on an LLC without such a designated representative would be impossible. The registered agent is designated by language such as the following:

The name and address in the State of California of this LLC's initial agent for service of process is John Jones, 123 Elm Street, San Francisco, California 94107.

Your state of organization may use a different term than *registered agent*. Typical equivalents include *agent for service of process*, *local agent*, and *resident agent*.

The agent can be you, a family member, a corporate officer, an attorney, or a company that specializes in corporation and business services. The registered agent's name is a public record; if you desire anonymity, hire a professional to perform this service. The agent must have a physical address in the state of organization. Thus, if your business does not operate in the state of organization, you will need to hire a registered agent in that state. You must consider this additional expense when organizing out of state. Such services typically range from $50 to $150 per year. If you wish to hire a local agent and don't know where to turn, visit www.bizfilings.com. Business Filings, Inc. offers resident agent services in all 50 states at reasonable prices.

▼ INSIDER TIP

Don't use a P.O. box as a resident agent address. First, some states don't allow it. Second, any correspondence sent to a registered agent is likely to be important; with a P.O. box you are less likely to receive that correspondence as quickly.

Having an attorney or a professional firm to serve as agent has advantages. Because the primary role of an agent is to receive service of legal papers, an attorney or a professional firm is likely to maintain a consistent address and to understand the nature of any legal papers served upon them. The agent will also receive important state and federal mail, such as tax forms, annual LLC report forms, legal notices, and the like.

▼ INSIDER TIP

If you are organizing your LLC yourself, registered agents can be valuable sources of information about the state in which you are filing. Because most registered agents work so closely with the secretary of state's office on behalf of many companies, they become experts in dealing with that office. Remember: resident agents want your yearly fees, so they won't mind answering a few questions. You might confirm with them the amount of the filing fees to include with your articles of organization or you might ask for a free sample of articles of organization that they recommend.

Note that most secretary of state's offices where you file your LLC papers will not check to see if you have properly secured the services of a registered agent. If you do not select a registered agent properly, the secretary of state will mail you documents at the registered agent's address and you will not receive them. Thus, you should hire your registered agent either before or while filing your articles of organization. Appendix C contains a sample letter suitable for hiring a registered agent.

STEP 4: SHOULD YOU ORGANIZE YOUR LLC YOURSELF OR HIRE AN ATTORNEY?

At this stage in your organization, you must decide whether you will file and organize your LLC on your own, hire a discount LLC service, or hire an attorney. Each approach has its advantages and disadvantages.

Self-Organization

Obviously, the greatest benefit of organizing your LLC yourself is initial savings. Self-organizing an LLC carries the lowest initial cost. Of course, as with any legal matter, cutting costs can often cost more later. For example, if your LLC is not properly organized, ambitious creditors may later reach your personal assets by piercing the corporate veil. (The doctrine applies equally to corporations and LLCs.) See Chapter 7 for more information on preserving your LLC's full liability protection.

Discount LLC Organization Services

A slightly more expensive alternative is to hire a discount LLC organization service. The prices range from $200 to $300 per company and the companies offer a streamlined but competent service. Such companies are essentially filing services and include only the following activities:

- They file articles of organization with the appropriate state office.
- They prepare a boilerplate operating agreement.
- They record the minutes of the initial meeting of LLC members.

Such companies generally do not include post-filing

steps, such as the following, that you must do on your own:

- Reviewing and revising the operating agreement, if necessary.
- Reviewing and revising the minutes for an organizational meeting of members, if necessary.
- Conducting the organizational meeting of members.
- Issuing units or membership interests.
- Avoiding complications with state and federal securities laws.
- Filing initial LLC reports.
- Filing periodic LLC reports.

Nevertheless, discount LLC organization services do offer value. They can often navigate the bureaucratic complexities of various states and provide prompt service and tested documents. However, the boilerplate operating agreement and proposed minutes of the organizational meeting that discount organization services provide often contain fill-in-the-blank and optional provisions that can baffle an inexperienced organizer.

Business Filings, Inc. offers competent incorporation and LLC services at reasonable prices. It also offers online filing, online customer service, and a free online name availability check. (However, name reservation services are not free.) The company can be reached at (800) 981-7183 or at www.bizfilings.com. Business Filings, Inc. can organize your business in any state; the fees range from $75 for a basic service to $295 for a comprehensive service.

Hiring an Experienced Business Attorney

Finally, you may wish to hire a business attorney to organize your LLC for you. A qualified business attorney can do the following:

- Suggest alternatives and solutions that would not occur to even the most diligent layperson.
- Assist with more complex features of LLCs, such as operating agreements and manager-managed LLCs.
- Anticipate problems before they arise.
- Prepare an operating agreement and minutes of the organizational meeting of members according to your specific needs.

- Ensure that no federal or state securities laws are violated when interests in the entity are sold to raise capital for the business.

There are several ways to find a qualified business attorney. Recommendations from friends and associates usually yield excellent matches between attorney and businessperson. Local bar associations in major metropolitan areas usually operate referral services. They prescreen attorneys, so you can be assured of the experience of any attorneys referred.

▼
INSIDER TIP

Never hire a lawyer without making inquiries. Avoid attorneys with a history of discipline problems. State bar associations—contact information, www.lawinfo.com/barassoc.html—now commonly maintain online records of attorney discipline.

What you can expect to pay varies. The hourly rate for business attorneys ranges from $100 to $350 per hour. The lower end of the scale will apply outside of major metropolitan areas and for less experienced attorneys. For services such as forming LLCs and corporations, business attorneys often charge a flat fee. You can expect to pay between $500 and $2,000 for complete organization services.

STEP 5: DETERMINE THE LLC OWNERSHIP

Your LLC will issue ownership shares, called *units*, to its members as part of the organization process. A member's units in an LLC are referred to in the aggregate as his or her percentage interest. So, if an LLC issues 100 units to its members and one member receives 60 units, that member's ownership percentage is 60 percent. You should choose your ownership structure early in the organization process, before filing your articles of organization.

The owners of an LLC will have the right to vote their units in proportion to their ownership interest. Thus, majority voting power ultimately exercises control over LLCs. Even if the LLC members choose to delegate management and operating authority to appointed managers, the members ultimately enjoy the right to elect managers and, if necessary, remove managers. In short, LLC members never delegate all of their voting power and they have ultimate authority and control over the LLC.

How Many Members?

In the early years of the development of the American LLC, many states required LLCs to have two or more members—single-member LLCs were prohibited. This led to an interesting work-around: many company organizers would simply grant a one percent ownership share to a family member or spouse and keep 99 percent ownership, thus avoiding the single-member prohibition. Today, all states allow single-member LLCs.

There are no legal prohibitions on the maximum number of LLC owners, but you should try to keep the number of members small.

Each member admitted to the LLC should execute an *investment representation letter*. We have included a sample in Appendix C. The investment representation letter offers some measure of protection to the entity because the member being admitted to the LLC makes certain representations regarding his or her qualifications and fitness to serve as a member of the LLC. Also, in the investment representation letter the member makes certain representations regarding his or her investment objectives, which are necessary representations in order to comply with state and federal securities laws.

Owners' Contributions Determine Their Percentage Ownership

Business owners contribute to a business a capital contribution of property in exchange for an interest in the business. A capital contribution is the total amount of cash, other property, services rendered, promissory notes, and/or other obligations contributed to a company for such owners' interest in a company.

As a general rule, the amounts of capital contributions made to an LLC determine the ownership percentages in that LLC. For example, let's assume three women decide to form an LLC. Anne contributes $50,000 in cash, Betty contributes $25,000 in computer equipment, and Cheryl contributes $25,000 in serv-

> ### ▼ DEFINITION
>
> A capital contribution is the total amount of cash, other property, services rendered, promissory note, and/or other obligation contributed to a company by an owner in return for that owner's interests in that company.

ices to the LLC. The proportions are easy: Anne's contribution yields her a 50 percent ownership share while Betty and Cheryl each become 25 percent owners. As a general rule, the amount of capital contributions made to an LLC determines the ownership percentages in that LLC. For example, let's assume three people come together to form an LLC.

Sometimes, however, the company organizers will want to divide the percentage ownership differently than their contributions. This is accomplished in various ways. One way is simply to alter the valuation of property contributed to the LLC. In our example above, Betty's computer equipment could be valued at $35,000, thereby entitling her to a larger percentage share in the LLC. Of course, all members must agree to the valuations. (Remember: you'll note each member's contributions in the final operating agreement.) Also, the valuations must have a reasonable basis in fact—members cannot contribute a stapler and claim a contribution of $3,000.

Members' capital contributions should be determined at the planning stage. Each member's capital contributions should be committed to writing in the LLC's operating agreement.

Multiple Classes of Ownership Units

LLCs, by default, have only one class of owners: members with voting privileges. However, they may have one or more additional classes of units. This is yet another notion borrowed from corporation law: corporations can have multiple classes of voting stock and/or additional classes of preferred stock. Secondary classes of voting and nonvoting units appear in infinite varieties. These classes of units can be broadly categorized into three groups: common, preferred, and hybrid. Common units are what are traditionally understood in corporate law as voting stock. All business entities must have one class of ownership with voting power; without a voting class of owners, the business would have no voting authority and could not function.

Small LLCs should hardly ever require multiple classes of ownership units. Multiple classes of ownership can confound even the most experienced attorneys and are used only by a miniscule fraction of business entities. The passages below should give you a basic understanding of multiple classes of ownership. But if, for some reason, you feel that you might want or need multiple classes of ownership units, you should consult an attorney.

Preferred LLC owners are typically entitled to a monetary priority or preference over another class of units. This preference is the source of the term *preferred*. What this means is that owners of preferred units are entitled to receive dividends before other owners and asset distributions upon the business' liquidation before other owners. In other words, preferred owners get paid first and common owners get what remains. Preferred units often carry no voting rights. Sometimes preferred units can be converted to common units.

Hybrid units refer to debt instruments that are convertible into units: they are not true equity ownership instruments. For example, a promissory note—a document evidencing a loan—that is convertible into units of an LLC's ownership is a hybrid unit.

The rights and privileges of all classes of owners in an LLC must be set forth in the articles of organization with a certain degree of particularity. Multiple classes of ownership shares will be appropriate for only less than only percent of all LLCs.

STEP 6: FILE THE ARTICLES OF ORGANIZATION

The life of an LLC begins with the preparation and filing of articles of organization. Typically a one-page document, the articles of organization set out the following basic information:

- The name of the LLC.
- The name and address of the agent for service of process, the person or entity authorized to receive legal papers on behalf of an LLC.
- A statement of the LLC's purpose.
- Optionally, the names of initial members or managers.
- Other optional matters, such as whether the LLC will have an infinite life or be dissolved on some date.

To begin the life of an LLC, you file articles of organization with the secretary of state (or other appropriate department) in the state of organization. See Appendix A, State Reference Tables, for contact information and fees for the appropriate department. You must file articles of organization along with a filing fee, which differs in each state.

▼ **INSIDER TIP**

Don't file articles of organization in the closing weeks of a fiscal year, such as in the last weeks of December. If you do, you may be required to file tax returns for the entire year. Wait until January 1 to file your organization papers.

Don't Disclose the Unnecessary

As a general rule, don't appoint initial members or managers in your articles of organization unless it is required. The states differ on whether appointment of initial members or managers is required in articles of organization. In California, listing the names of initial managers/members is optional. In Nevada, it's

▼ **INSIDER TIP**

Never disclose the names of the owners of an LLC if it's not required. You should always strive to operate your business entity as discreetly as possible. Although it happens only rarely, aggressive lawyers suing a company will sometimes sue the company's owners in order to harass and gain leverage—even if the owners have done nothing wrong.

required. Members and managers can easily be appointed soon after filing. Articles of organization are public documents and thus could reveal the names of an LLC's members to any member of the public.

Use the Secretary of State's Model Articles of Organization

You will find sample articles of organization for California in Appendix C, Limited Liability Company Forms. These sample articles should be used in California only and are included here as an example. Nearly every secretary of state's Web site offers sample articles of organization in either word processor or portable document format (PDF). You should always use the form recommended by the secretary of state, if one is available.

▼ ONLINE RESOURCE

You will find links to the secretary of state's office for all 50 states, the District of Columbia, Puerto Rico, Guam, and the Virgin Islands at www.learn-aboutlaw.com.

▼ INSIDER TIP

You can usually pick an exact date for the birth of your LLC. If you would like a special date of organization for your business, such as January 1 or a birthday, contact the secretary of state's office in the state in which you intend to organize. Almost all states will let you designate a special date of organization when you file.

STEP 7: ORDER YOUR LLC KIT AND SEAL (OPTIONAL)

An LLC kit (just like a corporate kit) is little more than an attractive three-ring binder where you maintain LLC records such as articles of organization, operating agreement, minutes of meetings, tax filings, business licenses, membership ledger, etc. LLC kits range in price from $50 to $100. Very fancy kits with luxury features, such as a leather-covered binder, are available for considerably more. LLC kits usually include the following:

- Model operating agreement and minutes of the organizational meeting, with optional provisions.
- Blank stock certificates.
- An LLC embossing seal.
- A blank member ledger and transfer ledger.
- LLC forms on CD or diskette.

LLC Kits Are Not Required

Neither corporate kits nor LLC kits are required by law in any state; they are completely optional. The only part of the LLC kit that I feel is totally necessary is the three-ring binder–$1.99 at an office supply store. In my law practice, I offer kits as an option. LLC kits are available from corporation supply companies and some office supply stores. You can obtain an inexpensive LLC kit by visiting www.bizfilings.com.

Whether you elect to purchase a kit or not, you should always maintain the following core LLC documents in a three-ring binder: articles of organization, operating agreement, membership ledger, and business licenses.

Sample LLC Minutes and Operating Agreement

LLC kits usually include a sample operating agreement and minutes of the LLC's organizational meeting. A sample operating agreement and minutes appear in the Appendix C. The operating agreement sets forth the internal operating rules of an LLC. See "Step 9: Prepare and Approve Your LLC's Operating Agreement" for a description of how to complete this important document.

The LLC Seal

An LLC seal is a hand-operated embossing seal that contains the name of your LLC, state of organization, and date of organization. Seals are used to impress the official company endorsement on important documents like recorded minutes of company meetings. LLC seals have a historical ancestor: the corporate seal. Corporate seals, once universally required, are no longer mandated in every state. LLC seals are standard features in almost any LLC kit, but are typically not required by law.

Stock Certificates

A stock certificate is a printed document that evidences ownership of shares in an LLC. LLC kits will include blank stock certificates. You can print the certificates by running them through a printer, typing them, or filling them out by hand.

Stock certificates are historically associated with corporations. However, LLCs operate with less formality than corporations; stock certificates are not as commonly used by LLCs. Still, the function of stock certificates is important: it gives the stockholder written evidence of his or her ownership of the company. I recommend the use of stock certificates because they minimize disputes over ownership.

Membership Ledger

A membership ledger is a written table showing the owners of an LLC. The ledger must also indicate the percentage held by each owner. As new members are added to the LLC through the sale of membership interests, their ownership is recorded on the ledger. The membership ledger should also show transfers of members' ownership interest, as when a member dies and his or her interest is transferred through his or her will.

▼
DEFINITION

A membership ledger is a ledger listing the owners of an LLC, their proportion of ownership, and the transfers or other disposition of such ownership.

The importance of the membership ledger cannot be overstated. It should be maintained diligently. The membership ledger is akin to the deed on a piece of real estate. It is the primary evidence of ownership in an LLC and carries a great degree of weight when presented in court. LLC owners should insist upon receiving updated copies of the membership ledger periodically. See Appendix C for a sample membership ledger.

STEP 8: DEFINE THE MANAGEMENT STRUCTURE AND CHOOSE MANAGERS

The next step in organizing your LLC is to decide what type of LLC your company will be: a member-managed LLC or a manager-managed LLC. Your choice is not carved in stone. A member-managed LLC can switch to a manager-managed LLC with a mere vote of its members and a new or revised operating agreement.

Who Will Manage? The Members or Appointed Managers?

Member-managed LLCs are operated by the LLC's owners, much in the manner of a general partnership. Smaller LLCs tend to be member-managed. Member management is simpler because it does not require any voting or appointment of managers—the owners themselves simply go right to work on the LLC's business. Single-member LLCs, in almost all cases, will be member-managed.

Manager-managed LLCs are operated by appointed managers, who may or may not be members. Manager-managed LLCs appear and operate much like limited partnerships or corporations. They are more complex because the appointment of managers requires voting rules to govern the process of appointment. Larger LLCs tend to be managed by appointed managers.

Two pairs of sample operating agreements are included in Appendix C. One pair creates a member-managed LLC and the other pair creates a manager-managed LLC. Each pair consists of a short-form operating agreement and a more complex long-form operating agreement.

If you select a manager-managed format for your LLC, the members will need to agree on a few points at the beginning. First, how many managers will run the LLC? One manager works fine for a small company. Larger companies might want to consider having three managers. Larger companies with more complex challenges benefit from the informed consensus that builds through a multimanager team. Put simply, three people are less likely to make a bad decision collectively than one person acting alone.

Also, multiperson boards are less likely to act in a single manager's personal interest. Managers should always avoid conflicts of interest and abstain from votes in which they have a personal interest. For example, it is improper for an LLC manager to vote on an LLC's purchase of a piece of property if the manager has an ownership interest in the property. Such a vote would obviously create a conflict of interest. A multi-person management team allows a manager with a personal interest in a particular decision to make full disclosure of his or her personal interest to the other managers, thereby ensuring an informed and fair vote.

Finally, odd-numbered manager teams are always preferable to even-numbered manager teams. Even-numbered teams can sometimes encounter deadlock on decisions, when managers split 50-50 on an issue. Extreme cases of deadlock can trigger resignation or removal fights, owner votes, and sometimes even court intervention if the deadlock cannot be resolved according to the LLC's operating rules. Deadlock can occur at the manager/director level in both LLCs and corporations and at the shareholder/member level as well.

Members' Authority over Managers

Once you determine your LLC's management structure and the number of managers, you simply select appropriate provisions for your operating agreement. If your LLC is to be manager-managed, you will select initial managers and name them in the LLC's operating agreement. LLC managers can, but need not, be LLC members.

Ultimately, LLC managers serve on behalf of an LLC's members. Keep in mind that a proper operating agreement should always give the members the right to oust a manager who is not serving to the satisfaction of members. It is also wise to require that managers be appointed every year or every few years. Managers should not be appointed for indefinite terms.

Typically, the removal of a manager will require some formality. For example, a well-drafted operating agreement will allow the removal of a manager by a vote of the majority of the LLC members—but only after notice and a properly held vote.

Managers' Liability and the Business Judgment Rule

Bear in mind that LLC managers—like directors and officers of corporations—can be held liable for mis-

managing the LLCs that they serve. Courts recognize, however, that in a competitive business environment managers must be given wide latitude in fulfilling their duties. Thus, courts are reluctant to second-guess a manager's management decision. Their rule here is called the *business judgment rule*. It states that courts will not review manager's business decisions or hold managers liable for errors or mistakes in judgment, so long as the directors meet the following criteria:

- They were independent; in other words, they did not have a personal interest in a transaction underlying the business decision.
- They acted in good faith.
- They were reasonably diligent in informing themselves of the facts.

STEP 9: PREPARE AND APPROVE YOUR LLC'S OPERATING AGREEMENT

The operating agreement governs an LLC's internal operations, much like bylaws govern a corporation's internal operations. Operating agreements govern such matters as holding meetings, voting, quorums, elections, and the powers of members and managers. Operating agreements are usually set out in a five- to 20-page document. A sample operating agreement suitable for use in any state appears in Appendix C. Your LLC kit, if you choose to purchase one, may contain a sample operating agreement that may be more appropriate for your particular state. Operating agreements are not filed with the state, like articles of organization. In fact, operating agreements should be kept confidential. Yours should remain with the LLC's core records.

The preparation of your operating agreement takes work. Don't simply sign any sample agreement. You must read through the entire document and make sure that you understand all of its provisions. You and your co-owners should execute the operating agreement only after you have all thoroughly digested its contents.

Is an Operating Agreement Necessary?

Operating agreements are vitally necessary. While many states do not legally require your LLC to have a written operating agreement, it is unwise to operate an LLC without one. The first reason is simple: oral agreements lead to misunderstandings. You are overwhelmingly less likely to have a dispute among members if all parties commit their understandings to a mutual written document.

If your LLC members do not adopt an operating agreement, your LLC will be governed by the state default rules. The default rules are set out in each state's statutes. Naturally, these rules don't cover every possible circumstance; they cover just the basics. For example, the default rules might say that an owner with a minimum of 10 percent ownership has the right to call a meeting and that members have a right to 20 days' notice before the meeting is called to order.

You should not rely on the default rules because they might not be right for your company. For example, some states have a default rule that requires LLCs to divide profits into equal shares for each member, regardless of whether each member's ownership is equal. An operating agreement can set forth the manner in which your LLC divides profits and losses among members.

Finally, adopting an operating agreement can protect the members from personal liability in connection with LLC business. Members should always endeavor to give the LLC separate existence, to hold the LLC out to the public. An LLC without a written operating agreement can appear much like a sole proprietorship or partnership. LLCs require fewer formalities than corporations, but that doesn't mean that they require no formalities at all.

Percentage of Ownership

How the ownership percentages of an LLC are divided among its members is one of the most important decisions a company's organizers will face. Choose wisely, because in most cases more than 50.01 percent of the vote of an LLC's members can dictate significant decisions regarding the LLC. This is why many company founders so often jockey for 51 percent ownership—to maintain company control. Furthermore, if an LLC is ever sold, the money received for the LLC will probably be divided among the owners in proportion to their ownership.

The owners' percentage ownership should be set forth in writing as part of the operating agreement. This written record will eliminate any later misunder-

standings or disputes with respect to share ownership. All of the sample operating agreements in this book have a table at the end where you should indicate each member's percentage interest.

Distributive Share

A *distributive share* is each owner's percentage share of the LLC profits and losses. Most often, a member's distributive share is equal to that member's percentage ownership share. This is how most people set up their LLC. For example, Nancy is a 55-percent owner and Sheila a 45-percent owner of an LLC. At the end of the year, they have profits of $10,000 to divide between them as owners. They will divide these profits according to their ownership share. Nancy would receive 55 percent of the profits as his distributive share, or $5,500. Sheila would receive 45 percent of the profits as her distributive share, or $4,500.

But what if you want to divide profits in a proportion that is not equal to ownership shares? This is called a *special allocation*. While special allocations are legal, the IRS watches them carefully. It wants to be sure that LLC owners are not using a special allocation to hide income or to allocate losses to the LLC owner in the highest tax bracket. The rules on special allocations are hopelessly complex. If you want to set up a special allocation for profits and losses, you should seek the help of an accountant or attorney.

What Your Operating Agreement Should Cover

Your operating agreement will cover the following matters:

- The powers and duties of members and managers.
- The date and time of annual meetings of members and managers.
- Procedures for electing managers.
- Procedures for removing managers, if you choose to operate a manager-managed LLC.
- Quorum requirements for member votes.
- Quorum requirements for manager votes, if you choose to operate a manager-managed LLC.
- Procedures for voting by written consent without appearing at a formal meeting.
- Procedures for giving proxy to other members.

- How profits and losses will be allocated among members.
- Buy-sell rules, which set forth procedures for transfer when a member wants to sell his interest or dies.

The owners of an LLC formally adopt the operating agreement by all signing the agreement and agreeing that it shall govern the operations of the LLC. An operating agreement is a contract among the members of an LLC; once it is executed, the LLC's members are bound by its terms.

STEP 10: OBTAIN A FEDERAL TAX IDENTIFICATION NUMBER FOR YOUR LLC

Because your LLC is a legal entity, federal law requires that you obtain a Federal Employer Identification Number (EIN or FEIN). In addition, most banks require you to give an EIN before opening a bank account. You obtain your EIN by filling out Form SS-4, Application for Employer Identification Number, or by applying online. The online application is a recent and welcome simplification of the EIN process. If you mail the form, expect to wait up to six weeks to receive your EIN. If you fax your form to a service center, you will receive your EIN in about five days. You can also obtain an EIN immediately by telephoning an IRS service center during business hours.

How to Apply for an EIN on the Internet

In order to make an online application of an SS-4, point your Web browser to https://sa2.www4.irs.gov/sa_vign/newFormSS4.do.

A form will appear in your browser. This clever form will take you step by step through the process of applying online for your SS-4. Simply follow the instructions for filling out the form and you will receive your EIN in a few minutes. Print and save a copy of the form and keep it with your entity's records. You do not need to mail a copy of the form to the IRS.

How to Apply for an EIN over the Telephone

To obtain your EIN immediately, do the following (which works in only some states):

- Either print the blank Form SS-4 in Appendix C or download and print a PDF file of the form from the IRS Web site, www.irs.gov.
- Follow the form's instructions and fill in the form's first page.
- Find your state of organization in the "Where to Apply" section of Form SS-4 on pages 2 and 3. There will be a phone number for the IRS service center that handles your region. You must have the form filled out before you call or the representative will ask you to call back.
- The IRS service centers are always busy, so be prepared to get a busy signal or wait on hold. Some service centers will give out EINs over the phone and some will not.
- When you reach a representative, she will ask you to recite the information on the form. The representative will enter the information directly into the IRS computer system. The call will take about ten minutes.
- The representative will then issue you an EIN and give a telephone number to which you must fax your completed form.

Your LLC's Fiscal Year

LLCs must have the same fiscal year-end as their members. While LLCs can have corporations as owners, it's more common for LLCs to be owned by natural persons. Natural persons, like you and me, have fiscal years that end on December 31—our fiscal year is a calendar year. LLCs that are owned by natural persons must select December 31 as their fiscal year. Thus, the LLC's tax returns will be due on April 15 in the year following each fiscal year. See Chapter 6, Operating Your LLC, for more information on filing tax returns with the IRS and with state tax authorities.

| FIGURE 5.1 | LLC Organization Worksheet |

1. Proposed name of LLC: _____

   a. Trademark search for name has been completed: _____

   b. Secretary of state's office search for name has been completed: _____

2. Address of principal office: _____

3. State of organization: _____

4. Corporate purpose: ❏ General ❏ Professional practice

5. Organizer name and address:

6. LLC will be managed by: ❏ Members ❏ Managers

7. The number of managers will be designated:
   ❏ In the Articles of Organization
   ❏ In the Operating Agreement

8. The number of directors that will be authorized:

9. Names and addresses of directors:

10. Name and address of registered agent/local agent/agent for service of process:

11. Names and addresses of initial officers:

   a. Chief Executive Officer/President: _____

   b. Treasurer/Chief Financial Officer: _____

   c. Secretary: _____

   d. Vice President(s) (optional): _____

                                  _____

                                  _____

12. Authorized number of shares of common stock: _____

13. Shareholders:

   Name/Address: _____

   Number and class of shares of stock: _____

   Type and amount of consideration to be paid: _____

14. LLC's fiscal year: _____

CHAPTER 6

Operating Your LLC

Now you have your LLC fully formed and filed. But your duties do not end there. All business entities require some ongoing formalities, responsibilities, and administration. This chapter examines how to perform the day-to-day operations and administration of your LLC.

PROTECTING YOURSELF FROM LIABILITY

The most notable feature of an LLC is that an LLC's individual owners are protected from personal liability for the LLC's debts and obligations. However, liability protection for owners of LLCs is not absolute! The doctrines of alter ego liability and piercing the corporate veil (which applies to LLCs as well) give courts the power to disregard the LLC liability shield and impose liability on owners in extraordinary cases of owner and manager misconduct. Because these important doctrines apply equally to LLCs and corporations, we will discuss them together in Chapter 7, Protecting Yourself from Personal Liability as an Owner of an LLC.

LLC FORMALITIES

LLC organizers and member should never assume that LLCs observe no formalities at all. LLCs observe fewer formalities than corporations, but still must observe certain formalities. After all, an LLC is a business entity and therefore it must observe rules and keep records. The crux of the matter is that LLCs generally do not require periodic formalities such as annual meetings, but must still observe state law and their own operating agreement and maintain adequate records.

LLCs are not required to observe certain formalities:

- LLCs are not required to have annual meetings of their members.
- LLCs are not required to elect managers periodically. Managers are free to serve year upon year until a vote of the LLC membership decides to change.
- LLCs are not required to have annual meetings of managers.
- Managers need not keep a written record of all significant formal decisions made in the course of managing the LLC—but they should do so.

On the other hand, LLCs should observe other formalities:

- LLCs should have in place a written operating agreement in which the capital contributions and percentage ownership shares of each member are clearly outlined.
- When an LLC member calls a meeting of the LLC members, the LLC must observe all formalities with respect to providing adequate notice to all LLC members.
- All votes of the LLC members, whether by written consent or by formal meeting, must be recorded in written minutes and kept with the LLC's records.
- The LLC managers, when making significant and formal decisions, should record their vote in written minutes and maintain the minutes in the LLC's records.
- LLCs must file all periodic information reports with the secretary of state in their state of organization as well as in any state in which they are qualified as a foreign corporation.
- LLCs must pay all annual state franchise taxes, if required.
- LLCs must file annual tax reports with the IRS and with each state in which they do business.
- Managers and members must respect the boundaries of conflicts of interest when entering personal transactions with the LLC.

Meetings of Members

LLCs are not required by law to hold scheduled annual meetings, so unless the LLC's operating agreement calls for such a meeting, it does not hold them. In such a case, the members must proactively call a meeting if they desire one. This proactive call to hold an annual meeting is akin to a corporation's special meeting. One reason to call a member meeting, for example, would be to make changes to the management—either by removing one, some, or all of the managers or by adding one or more managers.

In order to call a meeting of members, the members must follow several steps. The member or members calling the special meeting must collectively own a minimum percentage of an LLC's outstanding shares.

The minimum differs from state to state and from operating agreement to operating agreement; it is typically around five to 10 percent. All of the sample documents in this volume allow ten percent or more of the LLC membership to call a meeting. So, if an owner with less than ten percent ownership wishes to call a meeting, he or she will have to find one or more shareholders who agree with the need for the meeting, so these two or more persons can accumulate their ownership percentages to get over the 10 percent minimum.

If the LLC is a manager-managed LLC, the owner calling the meeting typically issues a written document, a *call*, to the LLC manager(s). Thereafter, the LLC manager or managers are charged with the responsibility of sending notice of the meeting to all of the LLC members. See Appendix C, Limited Liability Company (LLC) Forms, for a sample call letter.

DEFINITION

A call is a written document in which the owner of a manager-managed LLC typically notifies the manager(s) of a meeting. The manager or managers are charged with the responsibility of sending notice of the meeting to all the LLC members.

If the LLC is a member-managed LLC, then the owner does not issue a call to the managers. He or she simply proceeds to the next step and notices the other owners of the meeting directly.

Either the manager(s) or the owner prepares a notice of the meeting. Notice must be delivered to all members advising them of the time and place of the meeting and the proposals to be presented. See Appendix C for a sample Notice of Meeting of LLC Members.

Meetings of Managers

For the most part, appointed managers will conduct their business informally. Managers will not formally adopt resolutions for every small detail that arises in the everyday operation of an LLC. However, some significant decisions will require a meeting of the managers. For example, a decision to acquire a piece of real estate, establish a line of credit with a bank, or shut down a division will require a formal vote. The procedures for calling and noticing meetings of managers parallel the procedures for calling and noticing meetings of members.

Appearance at Member Meetings by Proxy

A *proxy* is an authorization by one member giving another person the right to vote the member's shares. Proxy also refers to the document granting such authority. Proxy rules are typically outlined in state law and an LLC's operating agreement. See Appendix C for an illustrative sample proxy form. Often proxies are granted when members do not wish to attend member meetings, but want their votes to be counted. They can therefore grant their proxy to another person to attend the meeting and vote their shares on their behalf.

Proxies can state the period of time for which they are effective. If no duration is stated, the proxy will lapse automatically by state law. Proxies tend to be used by corporations that have large numbers of shareholders. Most small corporations and LLCs will not use proxies.

Managers should not vote at meetings of managers by proxy. To do so violates a manager's duty to govern responsibly and to make informed decisions based upon adequate information.

Recording Member and Manager Meetings by Preparing Minutes

Meetings of members and of managers must be recorded. The written record of the actions taken at such meetings is called the *minutes*. Minutes are very simple to prepare and are often quite short. In Appendix C there is a simple example of LLC minutes that covers a wide range of LLC actions. Minutes of meetings should always contain the following information:

- The nature of the meeting, i.e., member's or manager's meeting.
- That either the meeting was called by notice or the persons voting waived such notice.

- Those present at the meeting.
- The date, time, and place of the meeting.
- Chairperson of the meeting.
- Actions taken at the meeting, e.g., election of directors, issuance of units, purchase of real estate, etc.

When in doubt, simply record the foregoing information in plain, conversational English. The person recording the minutes should sign the minutes, attesting to their accuracy. (There is no need to have each member sign the minutes.)

Holding Member and Manager Votes by Written Consent

Subject to certain restrictions, members and managers may take an action without a meeting if their action is memorialized in a document called a *written consent*. A written consent is simply a formal written document that sets forth a resolution or action to be taken and that is signed by the members or managers consenting to the action. Some members and managers find written consents to be invaluable—they are quicker, easier, cheaper, and more convenient. Actions taken by written consent do not require minutes, because the written consent itself serves as a memorandum of the action. See Appendix C for a sample of an action taken by written consent.

Written consents must be unanimous in some states for some LLC actions, such as the election of managers or to amend the articles of organization. A written consent should include the following information:

- The nature of the action taken, i.e., members' or managers' action
- A statement that the managers or members taking the action waive notice of a meeting
- The actions taken, i.e., election of managers, amendment of operating agreement, purchase of real estate, etc.
- A signature line for each manager or member who contributes a vote to the action

When in doubt, simply record the foregoing information in plain, conversational English.

MAINTAINING THE MEMBERSHIP LEDGER AND TRANSFERRING SHARES

One of the most important records you'll maintain for your LLC is the membership ledger. The membership ledger, as explained in Chapter 5, is simply a registry indicating the members who own the LLC, the percentage interest each owns, and the transfers or other disposition of such ownership. For all LLCs, the ledger should begin when the partnership is formed and should be updated diligently when ownership is transferred, gifted, sold, or repurchased by the partnership or when new ownership interests are issued.

Keep in mind that shares in any company are subject to comprehensive state and federal restrictions on sale and transfer unless such shares are registered with the Securities and Exchange Commission and state securities authorities. Registered shares are publicly traded shares that are sold in the public markets. So, if you sell shares in a nonpublic company, you must make sure you carefully follow the exemptions allowed by state and federal law. Unfortunately, a detailed description of such exemptions is beyond the scope of this book. However, exemptions are available for small businesses and can be easily researched by contacting the state securities department in your state.

Table 6.1, a sample ledger, shows members Patty Shay and Jane Shay receiving percentage interests upon the formation of a partnership on 1/1/2000, and also shows the transfer of Jane Shay's interest to her daughter Yoko on 12/1/2003. Note the use of plain English.

Annual Reporting Requirements

Nearly all states require LLCs to file periodic reports with the secretary of state's office or its equivalent department. An LLC files such reports in its state of organization and in states in which it is qualified as a foreign LLC. Some states, including California and Alaska, have recently relaxed their reporting requirements; these states have moved to biennial filing of LLC reports (every two years). Annual report filing fees, due dates, late penalties, and information requirements differ from state to state. See Appendix A, State Reference Tables, for information on periodic reporting requirements in your state of organization.

Some states, such as California, Georgia, and Arkansas, now offer online filing of periodic reports. We may reasonably expect that online filing will be offered by more states in the near future. Check the Web site of the appropriate office of your state of organization, listed in Appendix A, to see if your state offers an online filing program.

QUALIFYING AS A FOREIGN LLC

An LLC conducting business in a state other than its state of organization is deemed a foreign LLC in the state in which it is a guest. Conducting business in a foreign state may require you to register your LLC in the state in which you are operating. For example, an Oregon LLC that sells products in California must register as a foreign LLC with the Secretary of State in

TABLE 6.1 Sample LLC Ledger

Date of Original Issue	Member Name	Percentage Interest	Disposition of Interest
1/1/2000	Patty Shay	72.5%	
1/1/2000	Jane Shay	27.5%	On 12/1/2003, shareholder transferred shares to her daughter Yoko Shay. Share certificate surrendered and reissued as certificate number 3 to Y. Shay.
12/1/2003	Yoko Shay	27.5%	

California. Thereafter, the Oregon LLC must file biennial reports to the California Secretary of State as long as it is doing business in California.

This process of registering in a foreign state is known as *qualification*. In general, you will have to register as a foreign LLC in any state in which you are conducting business. What constitutes conducting business for the purposes of determining the qualification threshold will differ from state to state, but universally states define business activity broadly. Consider California's definition: it defines doing business as "actively engaging in any transaction for the purpose of financial or pecuniary gain or profit." Thus, California interprets a single transaction taking place in California as doing business there.

Qualifying as a foreign LLC closely mirrors the process of organizing an LLC: the LLC must typically file its articles of organization in the foreign state, along with an additional filing that includes information specific to the foreign state, such as the resident agent there. The filing fees for qualification are always at least the same as for filing articles of organization, but often are higher.

But why do states require foreign LLCs to suffer the expensive and burdensome task of filing for qualification as a foreign LLC? There are several reasons.

First, foreign LLCs must pay for the privilege of doing business in a particular state. After all, an Oregon LLC competing for sales in California competes with California LLCs and California corporations—all of which paid organizational fees in California. Thus, requiring uniform registration/qualification for all evens the playing field.

The second reason is for consumer protection. Once an LLC qualifies as a foreign LLC, it admits to jurisdiction in the foreign state and it can be sued there. Also, foreign LLCs must appoint agents for service of process in the foreign state. It is much easier to serve a company in one's home state than in another, especially at a distance. Thus, the consumers in the state where the LLC is qualified are more protected from misdeeds committed by the LLC.

The decision whether to qualify in a foreign state must be made cautiously. Once qualified, an LLC must file periodic information reports in the foreign state, will probably need to file tax returns and pay taxes in the foreign state, and must have a local agent appointed in the foreign state. Also, qualification in a foreign state makes it much easier for creditors to serve process and bring lawsuits against your corporation in the foreign state.

While the requirements of foreign qualification are clear and obvious, in practice smaller companies routinely ignore such requirements. Smaller companies simply lack the resources to register in each state in which they do business. However, this is not to say that such a practice is wise. The law is the law—and you should always endeavor to obey it.

REPORTING AND PAYING TAXES

Internal Revenue Service

The way you report your LLC's income or loss to the Internal Revenue Service depends on how many owners share in the LLC.

If you operate an LLC as a sole owner, your LLC is treated as sole proprietorship for tax purposes. You will file Form 1040, Individual Tax Return, and Schedule C, Profit or Loss from Business.

If your LLC has two or more owners, the IRS automatically treats your LLC as a partnership for tax purposes. LLCs file Form 1065, Partnership Return of Income. LLC management must also furnish copies of Schedule K-1 to each owner at the time the partnership return is due. The Schedule K-1 sets forth the LLC's distribution of profits or losses to each member.

Both single-member and multimember LLCs can elect to be treated as corporations for tax purposes. If you want to treat your LLC as a corporation for tax purposes, you can elect to do so by filing Form 8832, Entity Classification Election. See a qualified accountant before making this election, because it can have potentially undesirable tax consequences.

State Revenue Authorities

Much as you report personal income to both the federal government and your home state, LLCs must report and pay taxes at both the federal and state level. Obviously, state tax forms differ for all 50 states. Some states have separate forms for LLCs and partnerships; some states have one form for both LLCs and partnerships. Organized summaries of each state's taxation and filing requirements are in Appendix A.

But in which state or states does your LLC file a return? Most likely, you must file an LLC tax return in the state in which you are organized—although this depends on the state of organization. Your LLC must also file a tax return in any state in which the LLC is qualified as a foreign LLC. It is presumed that your LLC is doing business in a state in which it is qualified as a foreign LLC. Finally, your LLC must file a tax return in any state in which your LLC is doing business. We discussed above that all states define doing business somewhat differently—but universally states define it broadly.

AMENDING ARTICLES OF ORGANIZATION AND OPERATING AGREEMENT

Members may amend an LLC's articles of organization. They may vote on proposed amendments at a meeting called for that purpose. Alternatively, the members may approve an amendment by written consent. Any amendment to an LLC's articles of organization must be filed with the secretary of state. In fact, most states have a recommended form for recording and reporting the amendment of the articles. The amendment will not be legally effective until the secretary of state accepts the filing. Some states require either a supermajority vote or a unanimous vote to approve particular amendments. All of the model documents included with this volume require the unanimous vote of members.

Common amendments to articles of incorporation include the following:

- A provision changing the name of the LLC
- A change in the business purpose of the LLC
- A provision adopting an additional class of units

Typically, both members and managers enjoy the right to amend an LLC's operating agreement. This procedure will be outlined in your operating agreement. Because operating agreements are not filed with the state, amendments to operating agreements need not be filed with the state. They become effective immediately upon their adoption by the members or managers. All of the model documents included with this volume require the unanimous vote of members to amend the operating agreement.

ENDING THE LIFE OF YOUR LLC: DISSOLUTION

An LLC's life can be cut short by dissolution. A dissolution is the process of shutting down an LLC, settling its affairs, paying its creditors, distributing its remaining assets to its shareholders, and ending its life. A dissolution may be one of three types:

- A *voluntary* dissolution is the intentional dissolution of an LLC by its management.
- An *administrative* dissolution is a dissolution ordered either by the secretary of state or equivalent department or by another authorized state official.
- A *judicial* dissolution is a dissolution ordered by a court of law.

An LLC's members may vote for voluntary dissolution either at a meeting of members or by written consent. A notice of dissolution or application for dissolution form is then filed with the secretary of state. In some states the secretary of state will not approve the voluntary dissolution of LLC that either is not in good standing or has an outstanding tax liability. This is an interesting irony, because the eventual penalty for delinquency in periodic LLC filings is administrative dissolution.

The secretary of state enjoys the power to order an LLC's administrative dissolution. The secretary of state may exercise this power if an LLC becomes seriously delinquent in meeting its statutory requirements such as periodic filing and tax reporting. What constitutes a delinquency serious enough to warrant an administrative dissolution will differ from state to state. Some states allow LLCs to be reinstated in good standing following an administrative dissolution if they apply and pay all overdue fees. Typically, reinstatement may also require the LLC to pay penalties.

A court of law may order the judicial dissolution of an LLC upon the request of a state attorney general, an LLC owner, or a creditor. A member, for example, may bring an action to dissolve an LLC if the LLC is committing a waste of business assets, if other members are abusing the member's rights, or if there is a voting deadlock among members.

You should always endeavor to avoid dissolution. Dissolution can lead to a failure of an LLC's liability protection. See Appendix A, State Reference Tables, for information on periodic reporting requirements and tax requirements in your state of organization. You should always exercise great care when voluntarily dissolving an LLC. If you are a shareholder of an LLC with outstanding liabilities, do not allow it to become dissolved. If your LLC is dissolved while in debt, those liabilities may be attributed to you personally.

CHAPTER 7

Protecting Yourself from Personal Liability as an Owner of an LLC

The most notable feature of both LLCs and corporations is that an LLC's members and a corporation's shareholders are protected from personal liability for the company's debts and obligations. This is a valuable tool for businesspeople. In fact, the corporation developed historically as a means by which individuals could pool their investments in order to finance large business projects while protecting the individuals from liability. Without this liability shield, individuals would be less likely to invest in companies and the projects they undertake; it would be a very different world without corporations and LLCs.

Consider the following, from California's LLC statute:

no member of a limited liability company shall be personally liable ... for any debt, obligation, or liability of the limited liability company, whether that liability or obligation arises in contract, tort, or otherwise, solely by reason of being a member of the limited liability company.

As you can see, the protection afforded to LLC members in California is strong—and typical of statutes nationwide. Of course, in law there are always exceptions.

Understand that liability protection for LLC members is not absolute! In a legal sense, a corporation or an LLC is a legal entity separate from its owners. This separation, as we will learn, must be vigilantly maintained. Legal errors, personal dealings, ignoring formalities, failure to pay taxes, and other misdeeds and missteps can destroy the legal protection afforded to corporation and liability shareholders, thereby exposing them to liability.

THE IMPERFECT LIABILITY SHIELD: ALTER EGO LIABILITY

In cases of owner misconduct, courts will find and have found individual LLC and corporation owners liable to creditors. Corporation and LLC laws grant business owners strong liability protection, but are necessarily balanced by the needs of consumers and creditors. An LLC that is allowed to operate recklessly without any consequences is certainly not in the public's interest. Thus, we need to examine the rules that can lead to the erosion of the liability shield.

Our corporation law has roots in the Roman Empire. But LLCs are a more recent invention. So, where did LLC law come from? Because the LLC lawmakers had no existing law to draw upon, they did the obvious thing: they borrowed doctrines from corporate law. Because the liability shield laws of both LLCs and corporations are so closely related, they are discussed together.

The doctrines of alter ego liability and piercing the corporate veil give courts the power to disregard the LLC liability shield and impose liability on LLC owners in extraordinary cases of owner misconduct. These two doctrines (different in name, but essentially the same) will apply universally to LLCs and corporations. The states offer dozens of individual tests for alter ego liability. One common theme, however, is that a unity of interest and ownership between the entity and its owners can erode liability protection.

> ## ▼ DEFINITION
>
> Alter ego liability, as the name implies, means that a company's owner or owners have treated the company as indistinct from themselves. Without separateness between owner and company, the owner is liable for the company's obligations.

> ## ▼ DEFINITION
>
> Piercing the corporate veil, as the name implies, means that in some cases a creditor can ask a court to ignore the company liability shield and reach its owners.

Because of owner misuse of the LLC/corporate form in the following situations, courts may find that a member or members are merely the company's alter ego and that personal liability may attach to them.

- *Owners make distributions/dividends of cash and/or property to themselves when their company faces outstanding liabilities from creditors.* Say an LLC purchases $50,000 of merchandise on credit from Creditor Company. The LLC then sells the merchandise, distributes $100,000 of profit to its two owners as a year-end bonus, but does not pay Creditor Company's bill. A court would probably find that the LLC had made a wrongful distribu-

tion and Credit Company could get a judgment against LLC's owners. Bear in mind that the rule applies to distributions of profits, but not to salaries for members who also work for the company.

- *Members do not respect the separate identity of an LLC or a corporation.* An example of this would be when owners fail to identify the business entity in correspondence, advertisements, and, most importantly, contractual documents. The creditor's argument is quite simple here: "I did not know I was dealing with an entity; I thought I was dealing with an individual, so I should get a judgment against the individual." (See the sidebar for a well-known case on this point.)

- *Members commingle personal and company funds in a common bank account.* The reasoning here goes right to the heart of separateness. Without separate finances, business owners invite the argument that the separateness of the corporation or LLC be ignored. Also, commingling of funds makes the LLCs finances an impossible mess.

- *Members treat corporate assets as their own property.*

> ## ▼
>
> Here is a well-known corporate veil case.
>
> Wurzburg Brothers extended trade credit to Coleman American (a corporation). Coleman American fell behind on its payments. Wurzburg then insisted that Coleman American sign a promissory note. The note read, "Coleman American Moving Services, Inc. promises to pay $44,419.68." The note was signed "James H. Coleman" (the corporation's president at the time) and did not indicate Coleman's representative capacity as president of Coleman American. Coleman American defaulted on the payments. Wurzburg then sued James Coleman to personally repay the debt. The court pierced the corporate veil and ruled that he was personally liable for the debt because he had not followed the proper procedure for signing corporate instruments in a representative capacity as president.

How to sign documents as an LLC officer:

As the Coleman American case shows, you must represent yourself as an officer of your entity, not as an individual. When you sign contractual and other documents, use the following form:

By: Judy Doe (signature)

Name: Judy Doe

Title: President of Doe, LLC

The Imperfect Entity Can Lead to Alter Ego Liability

An LLC that is formed or maintained improperly can lead to alter ego liability for its owners. Obviously, an LLC that is not properly filed in its ostensible state of organization can offer no liability protection. Failure to follow initial and ongoing formalities can erode the liability shield as well.

A DEAD COMPANY OFFERS LITTLE LIABILITY PROTECTION

If an LLC is not in good standing or has been dissolved, the entity's ability to shield its owners from liability can be undermined. An LLC is in good standing when it is in full compliance with the law, its taxes are paid, and all periodic reports have been timely filed. An LLC can be subject to an administrative dissolution by the secretary of state if its taxes are not paid and its periodic filings are not made on time. A dissolution is the end of an LLC's life. Such an entity offers significantly reduced liability protection to its owners.

The following oversights by management can threaten an LLC's ability to shield its owners from liability:

- Managers or members fail to pay corporate and franchise taxes in the state of organization.
- Managers or members fail to file annual and periodic reports in the state of organization.
- Managers or members fail to notify the secretary of state of a change of address.
- Managers or members fail to pay the annual fees

of the resident agent or fail to advise the resident agent of a change of address.

LIABILITY PROTECTION: CORPORATION VS. LLC

Does an LLC offer greater liability protection than a corporation? In short, yes—although the LLC wins by just a hair. The reason is that LLCs do not require periodic formalities, such as annual meetings, as corporations do. Such formalities consume time and resources. Although it is not recommended, many small corporations fall behind on their formalities, especially annual meetings and elections of directors. Failing to observe these formalities weakens the corporate liability shield. Because LLCs are not subject to such formalities, LLC liability protection cannot be weakened by failure to follow formalities.

THE SEVEN MOST IMPORTANT LIABILITY PROTECTION RULES

In order to maintain liability protection for you and other owners, you should strictly abide by the following rules:

- *The most important rule of all is to pay creditors before you make distributions to owners.* Both LLCs and corporations owe an important obligation to pay creditors before distributing profits to owners. Universally, state law will force LLC owners to give back distributions of profits made to entity owners in lieu of paying creditors.
- *Always hold yourself out as an officer/manager of the entity—not as an individual.* Sign documents in your capacity as a representative of the entity, not personally, e.g., "John Jones, President, OldeCraft, LLC." You should always endeavor to prevent a creditor from arguing that you personally guaranteed an obligation. Identify your LLC in advertisements and on correspondence, invoices, statements, business cards, your Web site, etc.
- *Follow your own LLC operating agreement.* A crafty creditor's attorney can have an easy time asserting alter ego liability if you do not follow your entity's written procedures.

- *Keep proper records.* When owners and managers meet, be sure to prepare minutes of the meetings. If the owners or managers reach a decision, even informally, commit that decision to writing in the form of a written consent. Creditors wishing to pierce the liability veil will always seek to discover improper record-keeping.

- *Obtain and maintain a business checking account in the name of the entity.* Furthermore, always keep your personal assets and entity assets separate. Also, if you operate more than one entity (many people do), keep each entity's assets separate. Keep accurate business records for your entity.

- *Always keep your company in good standing with the secretary of state.* An LLC is subject to administrative dissolution if it fails to meet its ongoing responsibilities. This means that you must always file all tax returns, including franchise tax returns, and file all periodic reporting forms. Also, maintain close contact with your registered agent and always pay his or her bills on time.

- *Never dissolve a company that has debts outstanding.* If the company is dissolved, these debts can be imputed to you personally.

State Reference Tables

The following tables set forth a wealth of contact information, as well as summaries of law for each of the 50 states and the District of Columbia. Please keep in mind that the information in these tables is subject to the whims of each state's legislature, so the information is constantly changing. It is a good idea to do a reality check with the relevant secretary of state's office to confirm that the information is still current.

Alabama

Contact Information for Business Formation Assistance

Alabama Secretary of State
Corporations Division
P.O. Box 5616
Montgomery, AL 36103-5616
11 S. Union St. Suite 207
Montgomery, AL 36104
phone: (334) 242-5324
fax: (334) 240-3138
www.sos.state.al.us

LLC Organization Information and Fees

The fee for filing Articles of Organization is $40 payable to the Alabama Secretary of State but filed with the probate judge in the county of organization. Articles of Organization must be filed in the county where the LLC's registered office is located. There are additional local fees payable to the probate judge and the county. (Fees vary by county; the minimum is $35.) Foreign LLCs must pay a filing fee of $75 for qualification in Alabama.

LLC Name Reservation Information

Alabama does not reserve names for limited liability companies, only for corporations.

Where to Get LLC Formation Forms

www.sos.state.al.us/business/corpdl.cfm

Periodic LLC Reporting Requirements

There is no requirement to file an annual report with the Alabama Secretary of State's Office. There is a requirement to file a Privilege Tax Form annually with the Alabama Department of Revenue. Call (334) 353-7923 for details.

Where to Get LLC Tax Forms

www.ador.state.al.us/incometax/bpt_index.htm

LLC Tax Summary

Alabama's Corporate Franchise Tax was ruled unconstitutional in 1999. Alabama recently repealed the Corporate Entrance Fee and the Corporate Permit Fee. Alabama has unified its business entity tax under the Business Privilege Tax, to which Alabama LLCs and foreign LLCs operating in Alabama are subject. The Privilege Tax ranges from .25% up to 1.75%, with a maximum of $15,000 for LLCs. There is a helpful summary of Alabama's taxation scheme at www.ador.state.al.us/gensum.pdf

LLC Statute
Section 10-12-1 through 10-12-61 of the Code of Alabama

Alaska
Contact Information for Business Formation Assistance
Corporations Section
Alaska Department of Community and Economic Development
P.O. Box 110808
Juneau, AK 99101-0808
phone: (907) 465-2530
fax: (907) 465-2549
www.dced.state.ak.us/bsc/corps.htm

LLC Organization Information and Fees
The fee for filing Articles of Organization is $250 ($150 filing fee plus a biennial license fee of $100). Foreign LLCs wishing to conduct business in Alaska must register as a foreign limited liability company. The filing fee is $350 ($150 filing fee plus a biennial license fee of $200).

LLC Name Reservation Information
Alaska organizers may pay a $25 name reservation fee to reserve an LLC name. The name reservation remains effective for 120 days.

Where to Get LLC Formation Forms
www.dced.state.ak.us/bsc/cforms.htm

Periodic LLC Reporting Requirements
Alaska LLCs and qualified foreign LLCs must file a biennial report by January 2 of each alternate year with the Corporations Section. The biennial corporation tax is $100 for domestic corporations and $200 for foreign corporations.

Where to Get LLC Tax Forms
www.tax.state.ak.us/forms.asp

LLC Tax Summary
Alaska LLCs are treated as partnerships, enjoy pass-through taxation, and are subject to the biennial license fee described above.

LLC Statute
Title 10, Chapter 10.50 of the Alaska Statutes

Arizona
Contact Information for Business Formation Assistance
Corporations Division
Arizona Corporation Commission
1300 W. Washington Street
Phoenix, AZ 85007
phone: (602) 542-3026, 800 345-5819
www.sosaz.com

LLC Organization Information and Fees
The fee for filing Articles of Organization is $50 for Arizona domestic LLCs and $150 for foreign LLCs registering in Arizona. Within 60 days after filing their Articles of Organization, domestic LLCs must publish a Notice for Publication (sample at www.cc.state.az.us/corp/filings/forms/) advising the public of the LLC's business address and statutory agent in a newspaper of general circulation in the county where the LLC conducts business. For a list of acceptable newspapers of general circulation, see www.cc.state.az.us/corp/filings/forms/newspubs.htm. Thereafter, within 90 days of filing their Articles of Organization and publishing the notice, domestic LLCs must file with the Corporation Commission an affidavit evidencing the publication of notice. There is no form for the affidavit; the newspaper filing your notice will usually draft the affidavit and may even file it on your behalf. Be sure to ask before publishing your notice.

LLC Name Reservation Information
The Arizona Corporation Commission offers informal preliminary name availability information by Internet at www.cc.state.az.us/corp/filings/namesrch.htm and by telephone at (602) 542-3230. Arizona organizers may reserve an LLC name by filing a reservation of name form with the Arizona Corporation Commission along with a $10 fee. The reservation is effective for 120 days. Use the form provided on the Web site to reserve a name.

Where to Get LLC Formation Forms
www.cc.state.az.us/corp/filings/forms/index.htm

Periodic LLC Reporting Requirements
Arizona LLCs are not required to file periodic reports.

Where to Get LLC Tax Forms
www.revenue.state.az.us/

LLC Tax Summary
If the limited liability company is classified as a partnership for federal income tax purposes, the limited liability company must report its income to Arizona as a partnership on Arizona Form 165. If the limited liability company is classified as a corporation for federal income tax purposes, the limited liability company must report its income to Arizona as a corporation on Arizona Form 120.

LLC Statute
Title 10, Chapter 29 of the Arizona Revised Statutes

Arkansas
Contact Information for Business Formation Assistance
Corporations Division
Arkansas Secretary of State
State Capitol, Room 256
Little Rock, AR 72201-1094
phone: (501) 682-3409, 888 233-0325
sos.state.ar.us

LLC Organization Information and Fees
The fee for filing a domestic LLC's Articles of Organization is $50. Foreign LLCs must pay a $300 filing fee along with their Application for Certificate of Registration of Limited Liability Company. Online filing is available for most forms at the Secretary of State's Web site, but you'll have to register and give a credit card number. Organizers must also file a Limited Liability Company Franchise Tax Registration form at the time of filing of Articles of Organization or registration of foreign LLC. The purpose of this form is so LLCs will receive their annual Franchise Tax Report form (see below).

LLC Name Reservation Information
Arkansas organizers may reserve an LLC name by filing a name reservation application with the Arkansas Secretary of State along with a $25 name reservation fee. The name reservation remains effective for 120 days.

Where to Get LLC Formation Forms
sos.state.ar.us/corp_forms.html

Periodic LLC Reporting Requirements
Arkansas LLCs are required to file an annual LLC Franchise Tax Report. The Franchise Tax Report is mailed to LLCs in February of each year and must be filed with the Arkansas Secretary of State by June 1 of each year.

Where to Get LLC Tax Forms
sos.state.ar.us/corp_forms.html

LLC Tax Summary
Both foreign and domestic LLCs pay a $50 franchise tax at the time of filing their LLC Franchise Tax Report.

LLC Statute
Title 4, Chapter 32 of the Arkansas Code

California
Contact Information for Business Formation Assistance
California Secretary of State
(for LLCs: Note "LLC Unit")
1500 11th Street
Sacramento, CA 95814
phone: (916) 657-5448
www.ss.ca.gov

LLC Organization Information and Fees
The fee for filing Articles of Organization is $70.

LLC Name Reservation Information
California organizers may pay a $10 fee to reserve a name. The name reservation remains effective for 60 days.

Where to Get LLC Formation Forms
www.ss.ca.gov/business/corp/corp_formsfees.htm

Periodic LLC Reporting Requirements
California LLC and registered foreign LLCs must file an initial Statement of Information (Form LLC-12) within 90 days of organization accompanied by a $20 fee. Thereafter LLCs must file an annual Statement of Information Renewal Form (Form LLC-12R) accompanied by a $20 fee.

Where to Get LLC Tax Forms
www.ftb.ca.gov/businesses

LLC Tax Summary
California LLCs and foreign LLCs doing business in

California are required to pay a minimum $800 annual limited liability company tax due within three months of the close of the accounting year.

LLC Statute
Title 2.5 of the California Corporation Code

Colorado
Contact Information for Business Formation Assistance
Business Division Colorado Secretary of State
1560 Broadway, Suite 200
Denver, CO 80202
phone: (303) 894-2251
www.sos.state.co.us

LLC Organization Information and Fees
The fee for filing Articles of Organization is $50.

LLC Name Reservation Information
Colorado organizers may reserve an LLC name by filing an Application for Reservation of Name on Form 038, accompanied by a $10 fee. The name reservation remains effective for 120 days.

Where to Get LLC Formation Forms
www.sos.state.co.us/pubs/info_center/main.htm

Periodic LLC Reporting Requirements
As of January 1, 2002, LLC reports are due annually by the end of the second month in which the report is mailed to the LLC. The biennial fee is $25 for domestic LLCs and $100 for foreign LLCs. However, Colorado now offers an e-filing service that offers a substantially discounted fee ($10 for domestic LLCs and $50 for foreign LLCs). For more information on e-filing, see www.sos.state.co.us/pubs/business/almost_free.htm.

Where to Get LLC Tax Forms
www.revenue.state.co.us/TPS_Dir/wrap.asp?incl=forms_download

LLC Tax Summary
Colorado LLCs and foreign LLCs doing business in Colorado must file a Colorado Partnership or S Corporation Return of Income on Form 106. Colorado's treatment of LLCs is complex due to its nonresident member rules; nonresident members of LLCs must file a special Statement of Colorado Tax Remittance for Nonresident Partner or Shareholder

on Forms 107 and 108. See the instructions to Form 106 for detailed information.

LLC Statute
Title 7, Article 80 of the Colorado Revised Statutes

Connecticut
Contact Information for Business Formation Assistance
Connecticut Secretary of the State
30 Trinity Street
Hartford, CT 06106
phone: (860) 509-6002
www.sots.state.ct.us

LLC Organization Information and Fees
The fee for filing Articles of Organization is $60. A foreign LLC must file an Application for Registration, along with a $60 filing fee.

LLC Name Reservation Information
The Secretary of the State's office provides informal information regarding LLC name availability by calling (860) 509-6002. Connecticut organizers may reserve LLC names by filing the form Application for Reservation of Name for Domestic or Foreign Stock & Non-Stock Corp, LLC, LP, LLP & Statutory Trust. The fee is $30 and the name reservation remains effective for 120 days.

Where to Get LLC Formation Forms
www.sots.state.ct.us/commercialrecording/crdform.html

Periodic LLC Reporting Requirements
Connecticut LLCs must file annual reports by the end of the anniversary month of the LLC's initial filing with the division. The annual report fee is $10. Annual report forms are not available online.

Where to Get LLC Tax Forms
www.ct.gov/drs/taxonomy/ct_taxonomy.asp?DLN=40823&drsNav=|40823|

LLC Tax Summary
If the LLC is classified as a partnership for federal income tax purposes, it must report its income to Connecticut as a partnership using the Department of Revenue's CT-1065 form. If the LLC is classified as a corporation for federal income tax purposes, it must report its income to the state as a corporation

using the Connecticut Department of Revenue's CT-1120 form.

LLC Statute
Volume 10, Title 34 of the General Statutes of Connecticut

Delaware

Contact Information for Business Formation Assistance
Corporate Filing Section
Division of Corporations
Delaware Secretary of State
John G. Townsend Building
401 Federal Street, Suite # 4
Dover, DE 19901
phone: (302) 739-3073
www.state.de.us/corp/default.shtml

LLC Organization Information and Fees
The fee for filing a Certificate of Formation is $90. A foreign LLC must domesticate and form, which carries a combined fee of $190.

LLC Name Reservation Information
Name availability can be checked by calling (302) 739-3073. Delaware organizers may pay $75 to reserve a name. The name reservation remains effective for 120 days.

Where to Get LLC Formation Forms
www.state.de.us/corp/incbook.htm

Periodic LLC Reporting Requirements
An LLC's Annual Franchise Tax Report is due in March. Forms are mailed to resident agents in December. The filing fee is $25.

Where to Get LLC Tax Forms
www.state.de.us/revenue/taxformmain.htm

LLC Tax Summary
All Delaware LLCs are required to pay a minimum franchise tax of $200, due by June 1 of each year.

LLC Statute
Title 6, Chapter 18, Delaware Code

District of Columbia

Contact Information for Business Formation Assistance
Corporations Division
District of Columbia
Department of Consumer and Regulatory Affairs
941 North Capitol Street, N.E.
Washington, DC 20002
phone: (202) 442-4430
www.dcra.dc.gov/main.shtm

LLC Organization Information and Fees
The fee for filing Articles of Organization is $100. A completed Written Consent to Act as Registered Agent form must be attached to the Articles of Organization. A Combined Business Tax Registration Application, Form F500, must also be filed with the LLC's articles. Foreign LLC's must file an Application for Certificate of Registration for a Foreign Limited Liability Company and submit a filing fee of $150.

LLC Name Reservation Information
District of Columbia organizers may pay a $25 fee to reserve an LLC name by filing an Application for LLC Name Reservation Information form, available on the Department of Consumer and Regulatory Affairs Web site. The name reservation remains effective for 60 days.

Where to Get LLC Formation Forms
www.dcra.dc.gov/information/build_pla/business_ser vices/corporations_division.shtm

Periodic LLC Reporting Requirements
District of Columbia LLCs must file a Two-Year Report for Foreign and Domestic Limited Liability Companies. The reports are due on or before the first June 16 following the LLC's registration and on or before June 16 every two years thereafter.

Where to Get LLC Tax Forms
www.cfo.dc.gov/services/tax/forms/index.shtm

LLC Tax Summary
LLCs must file the District of Columbia's Declaration of Estimated Franchise Tax Voucher if they expect their franchise tax liability to exceed $1,000 for the taxable year. LLCs engaging in business activity in which their receipts exceed $12,000 for the taxable year must also file an Unincorporated Business Franchise Tax Return.

LLC Statute
Title 29, Chapter 13 of the Code of Laws of the District of Columbia

Florida

Contact Information for Business Formation Assistance

Division of Corporations
Florida Department of State
Corporate Filings
P.O. Box 6327
Tallahassee, FL 32314
phone: (850) 488-9000
www.sunbiz.org

LLC Organization Information and Fees

The fee for filing Articles of Organization is $100, which must be accompanied by a completed Designation of RA (Resident Agent) form. The fee for filing the Designation of RA form is $25. A foreign LLC must file an Application by Foreign Limited Liability Company for Authority to Transact Business in Florida. The filing fee is $100 and the application must be accompanied by a Designation of Registered Agent ($25 filing fee).

LLC Name Reservation Information

Florida no longer maintains a name reservation program. However, the Secretary of State's Web site allows free searches of existing corporation and LLC names.

Where to Get LLC Formation Forms

www.dos.state.fl.us/doc/form_download.html

Periodic LLC Reporting Requirements

LLCs must complete and file Florida's Limited Liability Company Uniform Business Report (UBR) annually by May 1. The fee for filing the UBR is $50.

Where to Get LLC Tax Forms

www.state.fl.us/dor/forms/download/

LLC Tax Summary

Most LLCs will be required to file the Florida Partnership Information Return (Form F-1065). This is for informational purposes only. LLCs classified as corporations for federal tax purposes must file the Florida Corporate Income/Franchise and Emergency Excise Tax Return (Form F-1120).

LLC Statute

Title XXXVI, Chapter 608 of the Florida Statutes

Georgia

Contact Information for Business Formation Assistance

Georgia Secretary of State
Corporations Division
Suite 315 West Tower
2 Martin Luther King, Jr. Drive
Atlanta, GA 30334
phone: (404) 656-2817
fax: (404) 657-2248
www.sos.state.ga.us

LLC Organization Information and Fees

The fee for filing Articles of Organization is $75. Foreign LLCs must file an Application for Certificate of Authority for Foreign Limited Liability Company, accompanied by a filing fee of $200.

LLC Name Reservation Information

Georgia charges $25 for reserving LLC names. Georgia organizers may reserve names online by visiting www.sos.state.ga.us/cgi-bin/namerequest.asp. The name reservation remains effective for 90 days. The Corporations Division maintains a searchable list of available and unavailable names.

Where to Get LLC Formation Forms

www.sos.state.ga.us/corporations/forms.htm

Periodic LLC Reporting Requirements

LLCs operating in Georgia must file an annual registration by April 1. Registration forms can be found online. Registrations can also be filed online at the Corporation Division's Web site.

Where to Get LLC Tax Forms

www2.state.ga.us/departments/dor/forms.shtml

LLC Tax Summary

LLCs engaged in business or deriving income from property located in Georgia must file the Georgia Partnership Income Tax Return (Form 700).

LLC Statute

Title 14, Chapter 11 of the Code of Georgia

Hawaii

Contact Information for Business Formation Assistance

Department of Commerce and Consumer Affairs
Business Registration Division
P.O. Box 3469
Honolulu, HI 96801
phone: (808) 586-2744

fax: (808) 586-2733

www.hawaii.gov/dcca

LLC Organization Information and Fees

The fee for filing Articles of Organization is $100. A foreign LLC must file an Application for Certificate of Authority, along with a filing fee of $100.

LLC Name Reservation Information

Hawaii organizers may reserve an LLC name online at www.ehawaiigov.org/dcca/bizsearch/exe/bizsearch.cgi. The reservation fee is $25.

Where to Get LLC Formation Forms

www.businessregistrations.com/registration/index.htm

Periodic LLC Reporting Requirements

LLCs must file an annual report each year. Annual report forms and specific filing instructions will be automatically mailed to the LLC in March.

Where to Get LLC Tax Forms

www.state.hi.us/tax/taxforms.html

LLC Tax Summary

LLCs are subject to Hawaii's general excise tax. The tax rate is .4% to .5%, depending on the source of the LLC's income. Hawaii's franchise tax is levied only on financial institutions and thus is generally not applicable to LLCs.

LLC Statute

Chapter 428 of the Hawaii Revised Statutes

Idaho

Contact Information for Business Formation Assistance

Office of the Secretary of State

700 W Jefferson, Room 203

P.O. Box 83720

Boise, ID 83720-0080

phone: (208) 334-2300

fax: (208) 334-2282

www.idsos.state.id.us

LLC Organization Information and Fees

The fee for filing Articles of Organization is $100. Foreign LLCs must file an Application for Registration of Foreign Limited Liability Company, accompanied by a filing fee of $100. For an excellent discussion on starting a business in Idaho, visit www.idoc.state.id.us/business/idahoworks/substartbusiness.htm.

LLC Name Reservation Information

Idaho organizers may reserve an LLC name by filing an Application for Reservation of Legal Entity Name and paying a $20 fee. The name reservation remains effective for four months.

Where to Get LLC Formation Forms

www.idsos.state.id.us/corp/corindex.htm

Periodic LLC Reporting Requirements

LLCs must file an annual report with the Secretary of State by the end of the month in which the LLC organized. The filing fee is $30.

Where to Get LLC Tax Forms

www2.state.id.us/tax/forms.htm

LLC Tax Summary

Most LLCs must file the Idaho Partnership Return of Income (Form 65). The tax rate is 7.6%, with a minimum payment of $20. LLCs classified as corporations for federal tax purposes must file the Idaho Corporation Income Tax Return (Form 41).

LLC Statute

Title 53, Chapter 6 of the Idaho Statutes

Illinois

Contact Information for Business Formation Assistance

Department of Business Services

Illinois Secretary of State

501 S. Second Street, Suite 328

Springfield, IL 62756

phone: (217) 782-6961

www.sos.state.il.us

LLC Organization Information and Fees

The fee for filing Articles of Organization is $400. Foreign LLCs must register by filing an Application for Admission to Transact Business, along with a filing fee of $400.

LLC Name Reservation Information

Illinois organizers may reserve a LLC name by filing for LLC-1.15 and paying a $300 fee per reserved name. The name reservation remains effective for 90 days. Available names can be searched at the Department of Business Services' Web site.

Where to Get LLC Formation Forms

www.sos.state.il.us/publications/businesspub.html

Periodic LLC Reporting Requirements

LLCs must file an Annual Report (Form LLC-50.1) each year prior to the anniversary date of their initial filing with the section. The filing fee is $200.

Where to Get LLC Tax Forms

Franchise tax is reported on the annual report form, discussed above. Income tax forms can be found at www.revenue.state.il.us/app/forms/index.jsp.

LLC Tax Summary

Most LLCs must file an Illinois Partnership Replacement Tax Return (Form IL-1065). The replacement tax rate is 1.5% of the LLCs net income. LLCs classified as corporations for federal tax purposes must file an Illinois Corporation Income and Replacement Tax Return (Form IL-1120).

LLC Statute

Chapter 805, Subheading 180 of the Illinois Compiled Statutes

Indiana

Contact Information for Business Formation Assistance

Business Services Division
Indiana Secretary of State
302 West Washington Street, Room E018
Indianapolis, IN 46204
phone: (317) 232-6576
www.state.in.us/sos

LLC Organization Information and Fees

The fee for filing Articles of Organization is $90. A foreign LLC may register by filing an Application for Certificate of Authority of a Foreign Limited Liability Company and submitting a filing fee of $90.

LLC Name Reservation Information

Indiana offers free preliminary name availability information by telephone (317) 232-6576 or online at www.ai.org/sos/business/corps/searches.html. Indiana organizers may reserve an LLC name by filing a name reservation application, along with a $20 fee. The reservation is effective for 120 days.

Where to Get LLC Formation Forms

www.state.in.us/sos/business/forms.html

Periodic LLC Reporting Requirements

Indiana LLCs must file an Indiana Business Entity Report every two years by the last day of the month in which the LLC was originally registered. The fee filing for the report is $30.

Where to Get LLC Tax Forms

www.in.gov/dor/taxforms

LLC Tax Summary

Most LLCs must file Indiana's Partnership Return (Form IT-65). The return is purely informational. LLCs classified as corporations for federal tax purposes must file a Corporation Income Tax Return (IT-20).

LLC Statute

Title 23, Article 18 of the Indiana State Code

Iowa

Contact Information for Business Formation Assistance

Business Services Division
Office of the Secretary of State
First Floor, Lucas Building
Des Moines, IA 50319
phone: (515) 281-5204
fax: (515) 242-5953, (515) 242-6556
www.sos.state.ia.us

LLC Organization Information and Fees

The fee for filing Articles of Organization is $50. Foreign LLCs must file an Application for Certificate of Registration along with the fee of $50.

LLC Name Reservation Information

Iowa incorporators may reserve a name by filing an Application to Reserve LLC name and paying a $10 fee. The name reservation remains effective for 120 days. To search available names, visit the Secretary of State's Web site.

Where to Get LLC Formation Forms

www.sos.state.ia.us/business/form.html

Periodic LLC Reporting Requirements

Iowa does not require LLCs to file periodic reports.

Where to Get LLC Tax Forms

www.state.ia.us/tax/forms/loadform.html

Additional Information

Iowa's Department of Revenue publishes an informative guide to starting a business in Iowa at www.state.ia.us/tax/business/newbus.html.

LLC Tax Summary

Most LLCs must file an Iowa Partnership Return (Form IA-1065), but are not required to pay state income tax. LLCs classified as corporations for federal tax purposes must file an Iowa Corporation Return (Form IA-1120).

LLC Statute

Title XII, Chapter 490A of the Iowa Code

Kansas

Contact Information for Business Formation Assistance

Kansas Secretary of State
Corporation Division
First Floor, Memorial Hall
120 S.W. 10th Avenue
Topeka, KS 66612-1594
phone: (785) 296-4564
fax: (785) 296-4570
www.kssos.org

LLC Organization Information and Fees

The fee for organizing an LLC is $150. Foreign LLCs may file a Foreign Limited Liability Company form and submit a filing fee of $150.

LLC Name Reservation Information

Name reservation is not available for LLCs.

Where to Get LLC Formation Forms

www.kssos.org/forms/forms.html

Periodic LLC Reporting Requirements

LLCs must file an annual report by the 15th day of the fourth month following the close of the tax year. The annual report must be accompanied by a franchise tax payment equal to $1 for every $1,000 of net capital accounts located in Kansas. The minimum franchise tax payment is $20.

Where to Get LLC Tax Forms

www.ksrevenue.org/forms-bustax.htm

Additional Information

The Secretary of State publishes a thorough and helpful Corporate Handbook, available from Web site www.kssos.org/pubs/pubs_handbooks.html.

LLC Tax Summary

Most LLCs must file a Partnership Return (Form K-65). This is an informational return only. LLCs classi-

fied as corporations for federal tax purposes must file a Corporation Income Tax Return (Form K-120). LLCs must also pay an annual franchise tax (see Periodic LLC Reporting Requirements above).

LLC Statute

Chapter 17, Article 76 of the Kansas Statutes

Kentucky

Contact Information for Business Formation Assistance

Kentucky Secretary of State
700 Capital Avenue
Suite 152, State Capitol
Frankfort, KY 40601
phone: (502) 564-3490
fax: (502) 564-5687
www.kysos.com

LLC Organization Information and Fees

The fee for filing Articles of Organization is $40. A foreign LLC must file an Application for a Certificate of Authority, accompanied by a filing fee of $90.

LLC Name Reservation Information

Kentucky organizers may reserve an LLC name for 120 days. The filing fee is $15. Informal searches are available online at www.sos.state.ky.us/obdb and by calling (502) 564-2848.

Where to Get LLC Formation Forms

www.kysos.com/busser/busfil/forms.asp

Periodic LLC Reporting Requirements

LLCs must file an annual report, due by June 30 of each year beginning with the calendar year following the date of the LLC's initial filing. The filing fee is $15. The annual report form is not available online; however, the Secretary of State's office mails the form to registered agents between January and March each year.

Where to Get LLC Tax Forms

www.revenue.ky.gov/needforms.htm

LLC Tax Summary

Most LLCs must file a Kentucky Partnership Income Return (Form 765). The return is for informational purposes only. LLCs classed as corporations for federal tax purposes must file the Kentucky Corporations Income and License Tax Return (Form 720).

LLC Statute
Chapter 275 of the Kentucky Revised Statutes

Louisiana
Contact Information for Business Formation Assistance
Commercial Division
Louisiana Secretary of State
P.O. Box 94125
Baton Rouge, LA 70804-9125
phone: (225) 925-4704
fax: (225) 925-4727
www.sec.state.la.us

LLC Organization Information and Fees
The fee for filing Articles of Organization is $60. Foreign LLCs must file an Application for Authority to Transact Business in Louisiana and submit a filing fee of $100.

LLC Name Reservation Information
Informal inquiries regarding LLC name availability may be made by phone at (225) 925-4704, by fax at (225) 925-4727, or by mail to P.O. Box 94125, Baton Rouge, LA 70804-9125. Louisiana organizers may reserve an LLC name by filing Form 398. Reservations are effective for 60 days. Two 30-day extensions are available upon request. The fee for reservations is $20.

Where to Get LLC Formation Forms
www.sec.state.la.us/comm/corp/corp-filings.htm

Periodic LLC Reporting Requirements
LLCs must file annual reports before the anniversary date of the LLCs initial filing in Louisiana. The Secretary of State mails the form to the corporation at least 30 days prior to the anniversary date. The Secretary of State does not provide blank forms. The filing fee is $10.

Where to Get LLC Tax Forms
www.rev.state.la.us/sections/taxforms

LLC Tax Summary
Most LLCs must file a Partnership Return of Income (Form IT-565). The return is required for informational purposes only. LLCs classified as corporations for federal tax purposes must file a Corporation Income and Franchise Tax Return (Form 620).

LLC Statute
Title 12 of the Louisiana Revised Statutes

Maine
Contact Information for Business Formation Assistance
Bureau of Corporations
Maine State Department
101 State House Station
Augusta, ME 04333
phone: (207) 287-3676
fax: (207) 287-5874
www.state.me.us/sos

LLC Organization Information and Fees
The fee for filing Articles of Organization (Form No. MLLC-6) is $125. A foreign LLC must file an Application for Authority to Do Business (Form MLLC-12) and submit a filing fee of $250.

LLC Name Reservation Information
Maine organizers may reserve a name by filing form MLCC-1 and submitting a filing fee of $25. The reservation is effective for 120 days.

Where to Get LLC Formation Forms
www.state.me.us/sos/cec/corp/corp.htm

Periodic LLC Reporting Requirements
Domestic and qualified foreign LLCs must file an annual report by June 1. The filing fee is $60. Annual Report forms are not available online but may be ordered by contacting the Corporate Reporting and Information Section at (207) 624-7752.

Where to Get LLC Tax Forms
www.state.me.us/revenue/forms/homepage.html

LLC Tax Summary
Most LLCs must file Maine's Partnership Return (1065ME). The return is required for informational purposes only. LLCs classified as corporations for federal tax purposes must file a Corporation Income Tax Return (1120ME).

LLC Statute
Title 31, Chapter 13 of the Maine Revised Statutes

Maryland
Contact Information for Business Formation Assistance
Maryland Secretary of State
301 West Preston Street
Baltimore, MD 21201-2395
phone: (410) 974-5521, 888 874-0013

fax: (410) 974-5190
www.sos.state.md.us

LLC Organization Information and Fees
The fee for filing Articles of Organization is $50. Foreign LLCs wishing to conduct business in Maryland must file a Limited Liability Company Registration and submit a $50 filing fee with the Division.

LLC Name Reservation Information
Organizers may reserve a name by filing a written request and a payment of $7 with the Division.

Where to Get LLC Formation Forms
www.dat.state.md.us/sdatweb/sdatforms.html

Periodic LLC Reporting Requirements
Maryland LLCs and qualified foreign LLCs must file an annual Personal Property Report (Form 1) no later than April 15. The annual report fee is $300.

Where to Get LLC Tax Forms
business.marylandtaxes.com/taxforms/default.asp

LLC Tax Summary
LLCs must file Maryland's Pass-Through Entity Income Tax Return (Form 510). Generally the return is made for informational purposes only; however, LLCs are required to pay the personal income tax on behalf of non-residents at a rate of 4.8%.

LLC Statute
Title 4A of the Corporations and Associations Section of the Maryland Code

Massachusetts

Contact Information for Business Formation Assistance
Corporations Division
Massachusetts Secretary of State
One Ashburton Place, 17th Floor
Boston, MA 02108
phone: (617) 727-9640
www.state.ma.us/sec

LLC Organization Information and Fees
The fee for filing a Certificate of Organization is $500. A foreign LLC wishing to do business in Massachusetts must file an Application for Registration as a Foreign Limited Liability Company, along with a filing fee of $500.

LLC Name Reservation Information
An organizer may reserve an LLC name for a period of 30 days. The filing fee is $15.

Where to Get LLC Formation Forms
www.state.ma.us/sec/cor/functionality/download-form.htm

Periodic LLC Reporting Requirements
An LLC must file an annual report each year with the Division on or before the anniversary date of the filing of the LLC's original Certificate of Organization or Application for Registration. The filing fee is $500.

Where to Get LLC Tax Forms
www.dor.state.ma.us/forms/formlist.htm

LLC Tax Summary
Most LLCs must file a Massachusetts Partnership Return (Form 3). The return is for informational purposes only. LLCs that are classified as corporations for federal tax purposes must file the Corporate Excise Return (Form 355).

LLC Statute
Title XXII, Chapter 156 of the General Laws of Massachusetts

Michigan

Contact Information for Business Formation Assistance
Bureau of Commercial Services
Corporation Division
P.O. Box 30702
Lansing, MI 48909-8202
phone: (517) 241-6470
fax: (517) 334-8048 (filing service)
www.michigan.gov/cis

LLC Organization Information and Fees
To organize, an LLC must file Articles of Organization and submit a $50 filing fee. Foreign LLCs must file an Application for Certificate of Authority to Transact Business in Michigan, accompanied by a filing fee of $50.

LLC Name Reservation Information
Michigan organizers may reserve an LLC name by filing an Application for Reservation of Name, accompanied by a $25 filing fee. The reservation is effective for six months.

Where to Get LLC Formation Forms
www.michigan.gov/cis

Periodic LLC Reporting Requirements
All LLCs doing business in Michigan are required to file an annual statement each year by February 15. LLCs organized after September 30 need not file an annual statement until the second February 15th after their formation.

Where to Get LLC Tax Forms
www.michigan.gov/treasury

LLC Tax Summary
Michigan does not levy a business income tax. However, it does collect a single business tax on any business with adjusted gross receipts that exceed $250,000 in a tax year. LLCs are generally exempt from this tax. However, LLCs classified as corporations for federal tax purposes may be required to pay.

LLC Statute
Michigan Statutes Section 450.4101 through 450.5200

Minnesota
Contact Information for Business Formation Assistance
Minnesota Secretary of State
Business Services
180 State Office Building
100 Rev. Dr. Martin Luther King Jr. Boulevard
St. Paul, MN 55155-1299
phone: (651) 296-2803, 877 551-6767
fax: (651) 297-7067
www.sos.state.mn.us

LLC Organization Information and Fees
An LLC may organize by filing Articles of Organization, along with a fee of $135. Foreign LLCs must file a Certificate of Authority for a Foreign Limited Liability Company and pay a filing fee of $185.

LLC Name Reservation Information
Minnesota organizers may reserve an LLC name by filing a Request for Reservation of Name with the Secretary of State and paying a $35 filing fee. The name reservation remains effective for one year.

Where to Get LLC Formation Forms
www.sos.state.mn.us/business/forms.html

Periodic LLC Reporting Requirements
Domestic and foreign LLCs must file an Annual

Registration accompanied by a filing fee of $35 each year by December 31. The Secretary of State's office now offers online filing through its Web site.

Where to Get LLC Tax Forms
www.taxes.state.mn.us/taxes/current_forms.shtml

LLC Tax Summary
Most LLCs must file a Minnesota Partnership Return (Form M3). LLCs filing the Partnership Return may be subject to a fee of $100 through $5,000. LLCs classified as corporations for federal tax purposes must file a Corporation Franchise Tax Return (Form M4).

LLC Statute
Chapter 322B of the Minnesota Statutes

Mississippi
Contact Information for Business Formation Assistance
Mississippi Secretary of State
Business Services Division
P.O. Box 136
Jackson, MS 39205-0136
phone: (601) 359-1350
fax: (601) 359-1499
www.sos.state.ms.us

LLC Organization Information and Fees
Domestic LLCs must file a Certificate of Formation with Business Services and pay a filing fee of $50. A foreign LLC must file an Application for Registration of Foreign Limited Liability Company along with a filing fee of $250 with Business Services.

LLC Name Reservation Information
Mississippi organizers may reserve an LLC name by filing a Reservation of Name (Form F0016) with the Secretary of State. The filing fee is $25 and the name reservation remains effective for 180 days.

Where to Get LLC Formation Forms
www.sos.state.ms.us/forms/forms.asp

Periodic LLC Reporting Requirements
LLCs are not required to file annual reports.

Where to Get LLC Tax Forms
www.mstc.state.ms.us/downloadforms/main.htm

LLC Tax Summary
LLCs must file a Mississippi Partnership/Limited

Liability Company/Limited Liability Partnership income tax return (Form 86-105) each year by April 15. However, Mississippi LLCs do not pay tax on their incomes unless classified as corporations for federal tax purposes.

LLC Statute
Title 79, Chapter 29 of the Mississippi Code

Missouri
Contact Information for Business Formation Assistance
Missouri Corporations Division
James C. Kirkpatrick State Information Center
P.O. Box 778
Jefferson City, MO 65102-0778
phone: (573) 751-4153
www.sos.mo.gov

LLC Organization Information and Fees
To organize, an LLC must file Articles of Organization and submit a filing fee of $105. Foreign LLCs must file an Application for Registration as a Foreign Limited Liability Company.

LLC Name Reservation Information
Missouri organizers may reserve an LLC name by filing an Application for Reservation of Name. The filing fee is $25. The name reservation remains effective for 60 days.

Where to Get LLC Formation Forms
www.sos.mo.gov/business/corporations/forms.asp

Periodic LLC Reporting Requirements
Missouri LLCs are not required to file periodic reports.

Where to Get LLC Tax Forms
www.dor.state.mo.us/tax/forms

LLC Tax Summary
Most LLCs must file a Partnership Return of Income (Form MO-1065). This return is informational only. LLCs classified as corporations for federal tax purposes must file a corporation income tax return (Form MO-1120).

LLC Statute
Title XXII, Chapter 347 of the Missouri Revised Statutes

Montana
Contact Information for Business Formation Assistance
Montana Office of the Secretary of State
Business Service Bureau
Room 260, Capitol
P.O. Box 202801
Helena, MT 59620-2801
phone: (406) 444-2034
fax: (406) 444-3976
www.sos.state.mt.us

LLC Organization Information and Fees
To organize, domestic LLCs must file Articles of Organization for Domestic Limited Liability Company. The filing fee is $70. Foreign LLCs wishing to conduct business in Montana must file an Application for Certificate of Authority of Foreign Limited Liability Company, with a filing fee of $70.

LLC Name Reservation Information
Montana organizers may reserve an LLC name by filing an Application for Reservation of Name, accompanied by a $10 filing fee. The name reservation remains effective for 120 days.

Where to Get LLC Formation Forms
www.sos.state.mt.us/css/bsb/filing_forms.asp

Periodic LLC Reporting Requirements
Montana LLCs must file an annual report, accompanied by a $10 fee, by April 15.

Where to Get LLC Tax Forms
www.state.mt.us/revenue/css/2forindividuals/06forms.asp

LLC Tax Summary
Most LLCs must file a Partnership Return of Income (Form PR-1). The Partnership Return is informational only. LLCs classified as corporations for federal tax purposes must file a Corporation License Tax Return (Form CLT-4).

LLC Statute
Title 35, Chapter 8 of the Missouri Code Annotated

Nebraska
Contact Information for Business Formation Assistance
Nebraska Corporations Division
Room 1301

State Capitol
P.O. Box 94608
Lincoln, NE 68509-4608
phone: (402) 471-4079
fax: (402) 471-3666
www.sos.state.ne.us

LLC Organization Information and Fees
Domestic LLCs may organize by filing Articles of Organization and submitting a filing fee of $100. A fee of $10 must also be submitted for the Certificate of Organization. A foreign LLC wishing to conduct business in Nebraska must file an Application for Certificate of Authority and submit a filing fee of $120.

LLC Name Reservation Information
Nebraska organizers may reserve an LLC name by filing an Application for Reservation of LLC Name, accompanied by a filing fee of $15. The name reservation remains effective for 120 days.

Where to Get LLC Formation Forms
www.sos.state.ne.us/corps/corpform.htm

Periodic LLC Reporting Requirements
LLCs are not required to file annual reports.

Where to Get LLC Tax Forms
www.revenue.state.ne.us/businc.htm

LLC Tax Summary
LLCs must file a Nebraska Partnership Return of Income each year by the 15th day of the fourth month of the fiscal year. An LLC with members that are all Nebraska individual residents and income that is solely derived from Nebraska is not required to file the Partnership Return.

LLC Statute
Section 21-2601 through 21-2653 of the Nebraska Statutes

Nevada
Contact Information for Business Formation Assistance
Nevada Secretary of State, Annex Office
Commercial Recordings Division
202 North Carson Street
Carson City, NV 89701-4201
phone: (775) 684-5708
http://sos.state.nv.us/comm_rec

LLC Organization Information and Fees
To organize, domestic LLCs must file Articles of Organization and submit a filing fee of $75. Foreign LLCs wishing to do business in Nevada must file an Application for Registration of Foreign Limited Liability Company, accompanied by the $175 filing fee. LLCs, domestic or foreign, must also file an Initial List of Managers or Members and Resident Agent by the first day of the second month after initially filing with the Division. The filing fee for the Initial List is $165.

LLC Name Reservation Information
Nevada organizers may reserve an LLC name by paying a $40 fee. Application can be made through the Secretary of State's Web site. The name reservation remains effective for 90 days.

Where to Get LLC Formation Forms
http://sos.state.nv.us/comm_rec/crforms/crforms.htm

Periodic LLC Reporting Requirements
Domestic and foreign LLCs must also file an Initial List of Managers or Members and Resident Agent, as mentioned above. Thereafter, Nevada LLCs must file an Annual List of Managers or Members and Registered Agent; the filing fee is a minimum of $125, but graduates upward for larger companies, based on capitalization.

Where to Get LLC Tax Forms
Nevada does not levy a corporate, partnership, or LLC income tax.

LLC Tax Summary
Nevada does not levy a corporate, partnership, or LLC income tax.

LLC Statute
Chapter 86 of the Nevada Revised Statutes

New Hampshire
Contact Information for Business Formation Assistance
Corporation Division
State House
107 North Main Street
Concord, NH 03301
phone: (603) 271-3244
www.sos.nh.gov

LLC Organization Information and Fees
To organize, an LLC must file a Certificate of

Formation (Form LLC 1) and submit a filing fee of $35 (www.sos.nh.gov/corporate/LLCforms.html). A foreign LLC must file an Application for Registration as a Foreign LLC (Form FLLC 1) and submit a filing fee of $200 (www.sos.nh.gov/corporate/LLCforms2.html).

LLC Name Reservation Information

LLCs may reserve a name by filing an Application for Reservation of Name and submitting a filing fee of $15. The name reservation remains effective for 120 days.

Where to Get LLC Formation Forms

www.sos.nh.gov/corporate/index.htm

Periodic LLC Reporting Requirements

Domestic and foreign LLCs doing business in New Hampshire must file an Annual Report with the Division each year by April 1. The Division issues preprinted forms by mail to all registered LLCs in January. To file online: www.sos.nh.gov/corporate/annualreport. The filing fee is $100.

Where to Get LLC Tax Forms

www.nh.gov/revenue/forms

LLC Tax Summary

LLCs with more than $50,000 in annual gross receipts from business activity within New Hampshire must file a Business Profits Tax return. The business profits tax rate is 8.5%. LLCs with more than $150,000 in annual gross receipts from business activity within New Hampshire must file a Business Enterprise Tax return. The business enterprise tax rate is .75% of the enterprise's value.

LLC Statute

Title XXVIII, Chapter 304-C of the New Hampshire Revised Statutes

New Jersey

Contact Information for Business Formation Assistance

New Jersey Division of Revenue
Business Services
P.O. Box 308
Trenton, NJ 08625
phone: (609) 292-9292
fax: (609) 984-6851
www.state.nj.us/treasury/revenue/dcr/dcrpg1.html

LLC Organization Information and Fees

To organize, an LLC must file a Certificate of Formation and submit a filing fee of $125. Foreign LLCs must file a Certificate of Registration for a Foreign LLC, along with a filing fee of $125.

LLC Name Reservation Information

New Jersey incorporators may reserve a LLC name by filing an Application for Reservation of Name. The fee is $50 and the reservation remains effective for 120 days.

Where to Get LLC Formation Forms

www.state.nj.us/treasury/revenue/dcr/geninfo/corp-man.html

Periodic LLC Reporting Requirements

An LLC must file an annual report each year. The filing fee is $50.

Where to Get LLC Tax Forms

www.state.nj.us/treasury/taxation/forms.htm

LLC Tax Summary

Most LLCs must file a Partnership Return of Income (Form NJ-1065). The return is for informational purposes only. LLCs classified as corporations for federal tax purposes must file a Corporation Business Tax Return (CBT-100).

LLC Statute

Section 42:2B-1 through 42:2B-70 of the New Jersey Permanent Statutes

New Mexico

Contact Information for Business Formation Assistance

Public Regulation Commission
Corporations Bureau
1120 Paseo de Peralta
PERA Building, Room 413
Santa Fe, NM 87501
P.O. Box 1269
Santa Fe, NM 87504-1269
phone: (505) 827-4508, (800) 947-4722 (NM)
fax: (505) 827-4387
www.nmprc.state.nm.us

LLC Organization Information and Fees

New Mexico organizers must file Articles of

Organization and submit a filing fee of $50. Foreign LLCs wishing to do business in New Mexico must file an Application for Registration, along with a filing fee of $100.

LLC Name Reservation Information

Request for name reservation may be made in writing to the Public Regulation Commission. The filing fee is $20.

Where to Get LLC Formation Forms

www.nmprc.state.nm.us/corporations/corpsforms.htm

Periodic LLC Reporting Requirements

LLCs are not required to file annual reports.

Where to Get LLC Tax Forms

www.state.nm.us/tax/trd_form.htm

LLC Tax Summary

New Mexico LLCs must file a New Mexico Income and Information Return for Pass-Through Entities (Form PTE). LLCs that file a federal corporate income tax return are required to pay the New Mexico franchise tax ($50 per year).

LLC Statute

Section 53-19-1 through 53-19-74 of the New Mexico Statutes Annotated

New York

Contact Information for Business Formation Assistance

New York Department of State
Division of Corporations, State Records, and Uniform Commercial Code
41 State Street
Albany, NY 12231-0001
phone: (518) 474-2492, (518) 474-1418
fax: (518) 474-1418
www.dos.state.ny.us

LLC Organization Information and Fees

To register, a domestic LLC must file Articles of Organization and submit a filing fee of $200. Foreign LLCs wishing to conduct business in New York must file an Application for Authority and submit a filing fee of $250. There's also a helpful guide, *Forming a Limited Liability Company in New York State*: www.dos.state.ny.us/corp/llcguide.html.

LLC Name Reservation Information

New York organizers may reserve an LLC name by filing an Application for Reservation of Name Form, accompanied by a filing fee of $20. The name reservation remains effective for 60 days.

Where to Get LLC Formation Forms

www.dos.state.ny.us/corp/llcfile.html

Periodic LLC Reporting Requirements

LLCs must file a biennial statement every two years. Shortly before the due date, the Division will mail a statement form to the LLC. The filing fee is $9.

Where to Get LLC Tax Forms

www.tax.state.ny.us/forms/corp_cur_forms.htm

LLC Tax Summary

LLCs are usually considered partnerships for New York tax purposes and must pay the Department of Revenue's annual filing fee ($325 to $10,000, depending on the number of LLC members). An LLC that is treated as a partnership for federal income tax purposes will be treated as a partnership for New York personal income and corporate franchise tax purposes.

LLC Statute

Chapter 34 of the Consolidated Laws of New York

North Carolina

Contact Information for Business Formation Assistance

Corporations Division
North Carolina Secretary of State
P.O. Box 29622
Raleigh, NC 27626-0622
phone: (919) 807-2225, (888) 246 7636 (call-back line)
www.secstate.state.nc.us

LLC Organization Information and Fees

Domestic LLCs may register with the Division by filing Articles of Organization and submitting a filing fee of $125. A foreign LLC wishing to conduct business in North Carolina must file an Application for Certificate of Authority and submit a filing fee of $125.

LLC Name Reservation Information

North Carolina organizers may reserve an LLC name by filing an Application to Reserve an LLC name, accompanied by a filing fee of $10. The name reservation remains effective for 120 days.

Where to Get LLC Formation Forms

www.secretary.state.nc.us/corporations/indxfees.asp

Periodic LLC Reporting Requirements

Domestic and foreign LLCs must file an annual report by the 15th day of the fourth month after the close of the fiscal year. The filing fee is $200.

Where to Get LLC Tax Forms

www.dor.state.nc.us/downloads/corporate.html

LLC Tax Summary

LLCs are not subject to North Carolina's corporate income or franchise taxes.

LLC Statute

Chapter 57C of the North Carolina General Statutes

North Dakota

Contact Information for Business Formation Assistance

North Dakota Secretary of State
Business Division
600 East Boulevard Avenue
Bismark, ND 58505-0500
phone: (701) 328-4284, (800) 352-0867 ext. 8-4284
fax: (701) 328-2992
www.state.nd.us/sec

LLC Organization Information and Fees

Domestic LLCs may organize by filing Articles of Organization and submitting a filing fee of $135. A foreign LLC wishing to conduct business in North Dakota must file a Certification of Authority Application and submit a filing fee of $135.

LLC Name Reservation Information

North Dakota organizers may reserve an LLC name by filing a Reserve Name Application (Form SFN 13015), accompanied by a filing fee of $10. The name reservation remains effective for 12 months.

Where to Get LLC Formation Forms

www.state.nd.us/sec/businessserv/registrations/types/companies/limitedliability/index.html

Periodic LLC Reporting Requirements

LLCs that engage in business or provide professional services must file an annual report by November 15. LLCs engaged in farming or ranching must file by April 15. The filing fee for both is $50.

Where to Get LLC Tax Forms

www.state.nd.us/taxdpt/business

LLC Tax Summary

LLCs typically must file a North Dakota Return of Income (Form 1065) and will benefit from pass-through taxation. LLCs classified as corporations for federal tax purposes will be required to file a Corporation Income Tax Return (Form 40).

LLC Statute

North Dakota Century Code, Chapter 10-32

Ohio

Contact Information for Business Formation Assistance

Ohio Secretary of State
Office of Business Services
P.O. Box 670
Columbus, OH 43216
phone: (614) 466-3910, (877) 767-3453
fax: (614) 466-3899
www.state.oh.us/sos

LLC Organization Information and Fees

Domestic and foreign LLCs may register by filing an Organization/Registration of Limited Liability Company. The filing fee is $125.

LLC Name Reservation Information

Ohio offers informal name availability information by telephone at (614) 466-3910 or (877) 767-3453 and by e-mail at busserv@sos.state.oh.us. Ohio organizers may reserve an LLC name by submitting Form 534 along with a filing fee of $50. The name reservation remains effective for 180 days.

Where to Get LLC Formation Forms

www.sos.state.oh.us/sos/busiserv/index.html

Periodic LLC Reporting Requirements

LLCs are not required to file annual reports.

Where to Get LLC Tax Forms

http://tax.ohio.gov/business.html

LLC Tax Summary

LLCs are not subject to the Ohio Corporate Franchise Tax Report.

LLC Statute

Title XVII, Chapter 1705 of the Ohio Revised Code

Oklahoma

Contact Information for Business Formation Assistance

Oklahoma Secretary of State
Business Filing Department
2300 N. Lincoln Blvd., Room 101
Oklahoma City, OK 73105-4897
phone: (405) 521-3912
fax: (405) 521-3771
www.sos.state.ok.us

LLC Organization Information and Fees

To organize, LLCs must file Articles of Organization, along with a filing fee of $100. Foreign LLCs must file an Application for Registration of Foreign Limited Liability Company and submit a filing fee of $300.

LLC Name Reservation Information

Oklahoma organizers may reserve an LLC name by either submitting an Application for Reservation of Name form to the Secretary of State or by telephone. The filing fee is $10. The name reservation remains effective for 60 days.

Where to Get LLC Formation Forms

www.sos.state.ok.us/forms/forms.htm

Periodic LLC Reporting Requirements

LLCs must file an annual report each year by July 1. The Department will automatically mail forms to registered LLCs in May. The filing fee is $25.

Where to Get LLC Tax Forms

www.oktax.state.ok.us/btforms.html

LLC Tax Summary

LLCs are not required to file a return for the Oklahoma Franchise Tax.

LLC Statute

Section 18-2001 through 18-2060 of the Oklahoma Statutes

Oregon

Contact Information for Business Formation Assistance

Oregon Office of the Secretary of State
Corporation Division
Public Service Building Suite 151
255 Capitol Street NE
Salem, OR 97310-1327
phone: (503) 986-2200
fax: (503) 378-4381
www.sos.state.or.us

LLC Organization Information and Fees

To organize, domestic LLCs must file Articles of Organization and submit a filing fee of $20. Foreign LLCs must submit an Application for Authority to transact business, along with a filing fee of $20.

LLC Name Reservation Information

Oregon organizers may pay a $10 fee to reserve a name for 120 days.

Where to Get LLC Formation Forms

www.sos.state.or.us/corporation/forms/

Periodic LLC Reporting Requirements

An annual reports and a filing fee of $20 are due by an LLC's anniversary date. The Division mails an Annual Report form to the LLC by approximately 45 days prior to the due date. The annual report is filed only the first year after organizing. In subsequent years, LLCs must only file a renewal coupon with the Division, with a filing fee is $20. The Division mails a Renewal Coupon form approximately 45 days prior to the due date.

Where to Get LLC Tax Forms

www.dor.state.or.us/forms.html

LLC Tax Summary

Most LLCs will be required to file a Partnership Return (Form 65). The return is generally for informational purposes only and no tax will be due. LLCs classified as corporations for federal tax purposes must file an Oregon Corporation Excise Tax Return (Form 20).

LLC Statute

Chapter 63 of the Oregon Revised Statutes

Pennsylvania

Contact Information for Business Formation Assistance

Department of State
Corporation Bureau
206 North Office Building
Commonwealth Avenue & North Street
Harrisburg, PA 17120
phone: (717) 787-1057
fax: (717) 783-2244
www.dos.state.pa.us

LLC Organization Information and Fees

To organize, an LLC must file a Certificate of Organization and submit a filing fee of $100. Organizers must also file a docketing statement along with the certificate; the form is available on the Secretary of State's Web site. A foreign LLC must file an Application for Registration and submit a filing fee of $180.

LLC Name Reservation Information

Pennsylvania organizers may reserve an LLC name by submitting a written or faxed request to the Corporation Bureau. The fee is $52. The name reservation remains effective for 120 days.

Where to Get LLC Formation Forms

www.dos.state.pa.us/corps/site/default.asp

Periodic LLC Reporting Requirements

Pennsylvania and foreign LLCs doing business in the state are not required to file annual reports; however, they are required to notify the Bureau upon a change in the name or address of the registered agent by filing a Statement of Change of Registered Agent.

Where to Get LLC Tax Forms

www.revenue.state.pa.us/revenue/site/default.asp

LLC Tax Summary

Most LLCs must file a PA S Corporation/Partnership Information Return (Form PA-20S/PA-65), which is for informational purposes only. LLCs may also have to file form RCT-101 for Pennsylvania's Capital Stock and Franchise Tax.

LLC Statute

Title 15, Chapter 89 of the Pennsylvania Consolidated Statutes

Rhode Island

Contact Information for Business Formation Assistance

Rhode Island Secretary of State
Corporations Division
100 North Main Street, First Floor
Providence, RI 02903-1335
phone: (401) 222-3040
fax: (401) 222-1309
www.sec.state.ri.us

LLC Organization Information and Fees

The fee for filing Articles of Organization is $150. A foreign LLC must file an Application for Registration and submit a filing fee of $150.

LLC Name Reservation Information

Rhode Island organizers may reserve an LLC name by filing an Application for Reservation of Entity Name with the Corporations Division, accompanied by a $50 filing fee. The name reservation remains effective for 120 days.

Where to Get LLC Formation Forms

www2.corps.state.ri.us/corporations/forms

Periodic LLC Reporting Requirements

Annual reports must be filed between September 1 and November 1. Annual report forms are available on the Division's Web site, www2.corps.state.ri.us/Forms/Corps/PDF/632.htm or by calling (401) 222-3040. The filing fee is $50.

Where to Get LLC Tax Forms

www.tax.state.ri.us/form/form.htm

LLC Tax Summary

Most LLCs must pay only the Rhode Island franchise tax of $250. LLCs classified as corporations for federal tax purposes must file Rhode Island's corporate income tax return.

LLC Statute

Chapter 7–16 of the General Laws of Rhode Island

South Carolina

Contact Information for Business Formation Assistance

South Carolina Secretary of State
Edgar Brown Building
1205 Pendleton Street, Suite 525
Columbia, SC 29201
P.O. Box 11350
Columbia, SC 29211
phone: (803) 734-2158
fax: (803) 734-1614
www.scsos.com

LLC Organization Information and Fees

The fee for filing Articles of Organization is $110. A foreign LLC must file an Application for a Certificate of Authority by a Foreign Limited Liability Company to Transact Business in South Carolina. The filing fee for foreign LLCs is also $110.

LLC Name Reservation Information

South Carolina organizers may reserve an LLC name by filing an Application to Reserve LLC Name with the Secretary of State accompanied by a $25 filing fee. The name reservation remains effective for 120 days.

Where to Get LLC Formation Forms

www.scsos.com/forms.htm

Periodic LLC Reporting Requirements

LLCs conducting business in South Carolina must file an annual report and a filing fee of $10. The first annual report must be filed between January 1 and April 1 the year after the LLC first organizes or registers in South Carolina. Thereafter, an LLC must file its annual report by the 15th day of the fourth month after the close of the LLCs taxable year.

Where to Get LLC Tax Forms

www.sctax.org

LLC Tax Summary

Typically, domestic and foreign LLCs conducting business in South Carolina must file a Partnership return (Form SC-1605). LLCs classified as corporations for federal tax purposes must file a Corporate Income Tax return (Form SC-1120).

LLC Statute

Section 33-44 of the South Carolina Code of Laws

South Dakota

Contact Information for Business Formation Assistance

South Dakota Secretary of State
Capitol Building
500 East Capitol Avenue, Suite 204
Pierre, SD 57501-5070
phone: (605) 773-4845
fax: (605) 773-4550
www.sdsos.gov

LLC Organization Information and Fees

To organize, an LLC must file Articles of Organization. To register, Foreign LLCs must file a Certificate of Authority Application. Articles of Organization and the Certificate of Authority Application must be accompanied by the First Annual Report. The fee schedule for the First Annual Report varies from $100 to $16,000, according to the total of member contributions (www.sdsos.gov/fees).

LLC Name Reservation Information

South Dakota organizers may reserve an LLC name by filing an Application for Reservation of Name with the Secretary of State, accompanied by a $15 filing fee. The name reservation remains effective for 120 days.

Where to Get LLC Formation Forms

www.state.sd.us/sos/corporations/forms.htm

Periodic LLC Reporting Requirements

An LLC must file an annual report before the first day of the second month following the anniversary month of the LLC's initial filing.

Where to Get LLC Tax Forms

www.state.sd.us/drr2/forms/btaxforms.htm

LLC Tax Summary

South Dakota does not have a corporate or personal income tax. LLCs conducting business in South Dakota may be subject to a sales and use tax.

LLC Statute

Title 47, Chapter 34A of the South Dakota Code

Tennessee

Contact Information for Business Formation Assistance

Tennessee Department of State
Division of Business Services
312 Eighth Avenue North
6th Floor, William R. Snodgrass Tower
Nashville, TN 37243
phone: (615) 741-2286
www.state.tn.us/sos

LLC Organization Information and Fees

Tennessee LLCs may organize by filing Articles of Organization. Foreign LLCs may register by filing an Application for Certificate of Authority to Transact Business. The fees for organizing or registering are $50 per member in existence at the date of filing, with a minimum of $300 and a maximum of $3,000. LLCs must also obtain a Certificate of Formation by paying a filing fee of $20. The Division of Business Services publishes a "Limited Liability Companies Filing Guide," which can be found at www.state.tn.us/sos/service.htm.

LLC Name Reservation Information

Tennessee offers an online search of name availability at www.tennesseeanytime.org/sosname. Tennessee organizers may reserve a LLC name by filing an Application for Reservation of Name with the Division of Business Services, accompanied by a $20 fee. The name reservation remains effective for four months.

Where to Get LLC Formation Forms

www.state.tn.us/sos/forms.htm

Periodic LLC Reporting Requirements

LLCs conducting business in Tennessee must file an annual report on the first day of the fourth month following the close of the fiscal year. The filing fees are identical to those for organizing or registering an LLC.

Where to Get LLC Tax Forms

www.state.tn.us/revenue/forms/fae/index.htm

LLC Tax Summary

Tennessee LLCs must file a Franchise and Excise Tax Return (FAE 170). The franchise tax is $.25 per $100 of the LLC's net worth at the close of the tax year (minimum tax is $100). The excise tax is 6.5% on LLC earnings from business conducted in Tennessee.

LLC Statute

Title 48, Chapters 201–248 of the Tennessee Code

Texas

Contact Information for Business Formation Assistance

Texas Secretary of State
Corporations Section
P.O. Box 13697
Austin, TX 78711-3697
phone: (512) 463-5555
fax: (512) 463-5709
www.sos.state.tx.us

LLC Organization Information and Fees

The fee for filing Articles of Organization is $200. Foreign LLCs may register by filing an Application for a Certificate of Authority by a Limited Liability Company, along with a filing fee of $500.

LLC Name Reservation Information

Texas organizers may reserve an LLC name by filing an Application for Reservation of Entity Name, accompanied by a filing fee of $25. The name reservation remains effective for 120 days.

Where to Get LLC Formation Forms

www.sos.state.tx.us/corp/business.shtml

Periodic LLC Reporting Requirements

LLCs are not required to file an annual report with the Secretary of State.

Where to Get LLC Tax Forms

www.window.state.tx.us/taxinfo/taxforms/05-forms.html

LLC Tax Summary

LLCs doing business in Texas must file and pay a franchise tax (Form 05-143). The tax rate is .25% on the LLC's net taxable capital.

LLC Statute

Title 32, Article 1528n of the Texas Civil Statutes

Utah

Contact Information for Business Formation Assistance

Division of Corporations and Commercial Code
Utah Department of Commerce
P.O. Box 146705
160 East 300 South
Salt Lake City, UT 84114-6705
phone: (801) 530-4849, (877) 526-3994 (UT)
fax: (801) 530-6438, (801) 530-6111
www.commerce.state.ut.us

LLC Organization Information and Fees

To organize, LLCs must file Articles of Organization accompanied by a $52 filing fee. Foreign LLCs may register with the Division of Corporations by filing an Application for Authority to Transact Business, along with a filing fee of $52.

LLC Name Reservation Information

Utah organizers may reserve an LLC name by filing an Application for Reservation of Business Name, accompanied by a filing fee of $22. The name reservation remains effective for 120 days.

Where to Get LLC Formation Forms

www.commerce.utah.gov/cor/corpforms.htm

Periodic LLC Reporting Requirements

LLCs conducting business in Utah must file an

Annual Report/Renewal Form, by the anniversary date of the original filing with the Division.

Where to Get LLC Tax Forms
www.tax.utah.gov/forms/current.html

LLC Tax Summary
Most LLCs must file Utah's Partnership Limited Liability Company Return of Income (Form TC-65). If an LLC is classified as a corporation for federal tax purposes, the LLC is subject to the Utah corporate income and franchise taxes.

LLC Statute
Title 48, Chapter 2C of the Utah Code

Vermont
Contact Information for Business Formation Assistance
Corporations Division
Vermont Secretary of State
Heritage I Building
81 River Street
Montpelier, VT 05609-1104
phone: (802) 828-2386
fax: (802) 828-2853
www.sec.state.vt.us

LLC Organization Information and Fees
The fee for filing Articles of Organization of $75. Foreign LLCs may also register by filing Vermont's Articles of Organization form with a filing fee of $100. Foreign LLCs must also submit a Good Standing Certificate from their state of organization.

LLC Name Reservation Information
Vermont incorporators and LLC organizers may reserve a name by filing an Application to Reserve a Name, available at www.sec.state.vt.us/tutor/dobiz/forms/reservat.htm. The filing fee is $20. The name reservation remains effective for 120 days. Vermont offers informal name searches at www.sec.state.vt.us/seek/database.htm.

Where to Get LLC Formation Forms
www.sec.state.vt.us/tutor/dobiz/dobizdoc.htm

Periodic LLC Reporting Requirements
LLCs doing business in Vermont must file an annual report within the first two and a half months following the end of a fiscal year. The filing fee is $20.

Where to Get LLC Tax Forms
www.state.vt.us/tax/forms/formsbusiness.htm

LLC Tax Summary
LLCs must file a Vermont Business Income Tax Return. Pass-through taxation is granted to LLCs, but they must pay a minimum tax of $250.

LLC Statute
Title II, Chapter 21 of the Vermont Statutes

Virginia
Contact Information for Business Formation Assistance
Office of the Clerk
Virginia State Corporation Commission
P.O. Box 1197
Richmond, VA 23218
1300 East Main Street
Richmond, VA 23219
phone: (804) 371-9967, (800) 552-7945 (VA)
www.state.va.us/scc/index.html

LLC Organization Information and Fees
To organize, an LLC must file Articles of Organization with a filing fee of $100. Foreign LLCs may register by filing an Application for Registration as a Foreign Limited Liability Company, accompanied by a filing fee of $100.

LLC Name Reservation Information
Virginia organizers may reserve an LLC name by filing an Application for Reservation or for Renewal of Reservation of LLC name on form LLC-1013, accompanied by a filing fee of $10. The name reservation remains effective for 120 days.

Where to Get LLC Formation Forms
www.state.va.us/scc/division/clk/fee_bus.htm

Periodic LLC Reporting Requirements
The Commission collects an annual registration fee of $50 from each LLC doing business in Virginia. The fee is due each year by September 1.

Where to Get LLC Tax Forms
www.tax.state.va.us/

LLC Tax Summary
LLCs are not required to file an annual return with the Virginia Department of Taxation.

LLC Statute
Title 13.1, Chapter 12 of the Code of Virginia

Washington
Contact Information for Business Formation Assistance
Corporations Division
Washington Secretary of State
801 Capitol Way S.
P.O. Box 40234
Olympia, WA 98504-0234
phone: (360) 753-7115
www.secstate.wa.gov

LLC Organization Information and Fees
To organize, an LLC must file an Application to Form a Limited Liability Company and submit a filing fee of $175. A foreign LLC may register by filing an Application for Foreign Limited Liability Company Registration, accompanied by a filing fee of $175. Newly filed LLCs must also file an Initial Report within 120 days of the LLC's initial filing.

LLC Name Reservation Information
Washington organizers may reserve an LLC name by paying a $30 name reservation fee. The form is not available online. Contact the Division for more information. Online searches at www.secstate.wa.gov/corps/search.aspx.

Where to Get LLC Formation Forms
www.secstate.wa.gov/corps/registration_forms.aspx

Periodic LLC Reporting Requirements
Washington LLCs may file their annual reports online at www.dol.wa.gov/bpd/cr.htm.

Where to Get LLC Tax Forms
www.dor.wa.gov/content/forms

LLC Tax Summary
LLCs must pay the business and occupation tax each year. The tax is levied on gross income, proceeds of sales, or value of the LLC's products. There's an online brochure, "Tax Reporting Tips," at www.dor.wa.gov/content/doingbusiness/doingBus_NwBus.aspx.

LLC Statute
Chapter 25.15 of the Revised Code of Washington

West Virginia
Contact Information for Business Formation Assistance
Business Organizations Division
West Virginia Secretary of State
Building 1, Suite 157-K
1900 Kanawha Boulevard East
Charleston, WV 25305-0770
phone: (304) 558-8000
fax: (304) 558-0900
www.wvsos.com

LLC Organization Information and Fees
To organize, an LLC must file Articles of Organization and submit a filing fee of $100. Foreign LLCs must register by filing an Application for Certificate of Authority for a Limited Liability Company, along with a filing fee of $150.

LLC Name Reservation Information
West Virginia organizers may reserve an LLC name by filing an Application for Reservation of Name on Form NR-1 accompanied by a $15 filing fee. The name reservation remains effective for 120 days.

Where to Get LLC Formation Forms
www.wvsos.com/business/services/formindex.htm

Periodic LLC Reporting Requirements
LLCs doing business in West Virginia must file an annual report by April 1 each year. The filing fee is $10.

Where to Get LLC Tax Forms
www.state.wv.us/taxrev/forms.html

LLC Tax Summary
LLCs doing business in West Virginia must file a Business Franchise Tax Return each year. The tax rate is $.75 per $100 of taxable income, with a minimum annual tax of $50.

LLC Statute
Chapter 31B of the West Virginia Code

Wisconsin
Contact Information for Business Formation Assistance
Corporation Section
Division of Corporate and Consumer Services
Department of Financial Institutions
P.O. Box 7846

Madison, WI 53707-7846
phone: (608) 261-7577
fax: (608) 267-6813
www.wdfi.org

LLC Organization Information and Fees

Wisconsin offers two means of filing Articles of Organization: traditional paper filing and QuickStart LLC. QuickStart LLC is a Web-based application that allows the organizer of a Wisconsin LLC to draft, sign, and deliver its Articles of Organization online. The fee for QuickStart is $130. The fee for traditional paper filing of Article of Organization is $170.

LLC Name Reservation Information

Wisconsin offers a name availability search online at www.wdfi.org/corporations/crispix. Wisconsin organizers may reserve an LLC name by filing a LLC Name Reservation Information and Fees Application on Form 1 accompanied by a filing fee of $15. Name reservation is also available by telephone for a fee of $30. The name reservation remains effective for 120 days.

Where to Get LLC Formation Forms

www.wdfi.org/corporations/forms

Periodic LLC Reporting Requirements

Wisconsin and foreign LLCs have to file an annual report with the Corporations Section. For Wisconsin LLCs, the report filing date is based on the quarter of the year of organization and the filing fee is $25. Annual reports will be mailed by the Department in the first month of each quarter to the registered agent at the registered office address as listed with the Department. For foreign LLCs, the report is due by the end of the first quarter of each calendar year and the filing fee is $80.

Where to Get LLC Tax Forms

www.dor.state.wi.us/html/formpub.html

LLC Tax Summary

Most LLCs must file a Partnership Return of Income (Form 3). The return is informational only. LLCs classified as corporations must file a Corporation Franchise or Income Tax Return (Form 4).

LLC Statute

Chapter 183 of the Wisconsin Statutes

Wyoming

Contact Information for Business Formation Assistance

Wyoming Office of the Secretary of State
Corporations Division
Capitol Building
Cheyenne, WY 82002
phone: (307) 777-7378
fax: (307) 777-6217
http://soswy.state.wy.us

LLC Organization Information and Fees

To organize, an LLC must file Articles of Organization and pay a filing fee of $100. Foreign LLCs must file an Application for Certificate of Authority for Foreign Limited Liability Company and pay a filing fee of $100.

LLC Name Reservation Information

Wyoming organizers may reserve an LLC name by filing an Application for Reservation of LLC name, accompanied by a $50 filing fee.

Where to Get LLC Formation Forms

soswy.state.wy.us/corporat/llc.htm

Periodic LLC Reporting Requirements

Annual reports may be filed online:
http://soswy.state.wy.us/Annual_Rpt_Main.asp.

Where to Get LLC Tax Forms

http://soswy.state.wy.us/Annual_Rpt_Main.asp

LLC Tax Summary

Wyoming has no income tax applicable to LLCs. LLCs doing business in Wyoming pay an Annual Report License Tax, which is two-tenths of one mil ($.0002) of all assets located and employed in Wyoming or $50, whichever is greater.

LLC Statute

Section 17-15-101 through 17-15-144 of the Wyoming Statutes

Glossary

Acquisition: The purchase of one corporation by another, through either the purchase of its shares or the purchase of its assets.

Administrative Dissolution: The involuntary dissolution of a corporation by the secretary of state, or other equivalent department, due to the failure of a corporation to meet statutory requirements such as periodic filing and tax reporting.

Advisory Board: A body that advises the board of directors and management of a corporation but does not have authority to vote on corporate matters.

Agency: Status as the legal representative (the agent) of an entity or another person (a principal).

Agent: The legal representative of an entity or another person (a principal).

Agent for Service of Process: The person or entity that is authorized to receive legal papers on behalf of a corporation.

Alter Ego Liability: Doctrine that attaches liability to corporate shareholders in cases of commingling of assets and failure to observe corporate formalities.

Amendment of Articles of Incorporation: The procedure by which one or more changes is made to a corporation's articles of incorporation.

Annual Meeting of Directors: A meeting held each year to elect officers of a corporation and to address other corporate matters. Usually follows immediately after an *annual meeting of shareholders*.

Annual Meeting of Shareholders: A meeting held each year to elect directors of a corporation and to address other corporate matters.

Apportionment: The allocation of income earned from activities in a particular state or assets present in a particular state to determine the tax due in that state.

Articles of Incorporation: The document that gives birth to a corporation by filing in the state of incorporation. Articles cover foundational matters such as the name of the corporation, the shares it is authorized to issue, its corporate purpose, and its agent for service of process.

Articles of Organization: The document that gives birth to an LLC by filing in the state of organization. Articles of organization cover foundational matters such as the name of the LLC, its business purpose, and its agent for service of process.

Articles of organization are to LLCs what articles of incorporation are to corporations.

Authorized Capital: The total number of a corporation's authorized shares multiplied by the share's par value. For example, 1,000,000 authorized shares of stock with a par value of one cent equals an authorized capital of $10,000.

Authorized Shares: The number of shares of a corporation's stock that the corporation has the authority to issue. The authorized number of shares of a class of stock is stated in a corporation's articles of incorporation.

Blue Sky Laws: The securities laws of individual states, collectively. These laws seek to protect people from investing in sham companies—companies that offer nothing more than "blue sky."

Board of Directors: The directors of a corporation, collectively. The directors of a corporation are its governing board. Elected by shareholders, they vote on major corporate matters such as the issuing of shares of stock, election of officers, and approval of mergers and acquisitions.

Bond: An interest-bearing instrument issued by a corporation or other entity that serves as evidence of a debt or obligation.

Business Judgment Rule: The rule that shields directors from liability for mismanagement of the corporations that they serve.

Bylaws: The internal operating rules of a corporation, usually set out in a five- to 20-page document. Bylaws govern such matters as holding meetings, voting, quorums, elections, and the powers of directors and officers.

Call: A written document in which the owner of a manager-managed LLC typically notifies the manager(s) of a meeting; the manager or managers are charged with the responsibility of sending notice of the meeting to all the LLC members.

Capital Contribution: The total amount of cash, other property, services rendered, promissory note, and/or other obligation contributed to a company for such owners' interest in a company.

C Corporation: Any corporation that has not elected S corporation status.

Certificate of Authority: A document issued by the secretary of state or equivalent department that authorizes a foreign corporation to operate in a state other than its state of incorporation.

Certificate of Good Standing: A document issued by the secretary of state or equivalent department that certifies that a corporation is validly existing and in compliance with all periodic and taxation requirements.

Close Corporation: A corporation owned by a small number of individuals. A corporation must elect to be a close corporation by inserting a statement in its articles of incorporation. State laws typically permit close corporations to be operated more informally than non-close corporations.

Common Stock: A corporation's primary class of stock. Common stock holders typically have voting rights.

Conversion Rights: Rights allowing the holder of shares of stock or other financial instrument to convert to other shares of stock.

Convertible Instrument: A financial instrument such as bonds or notes that can be converted into shares of stock. Shares of stock may also be convertible into shares of another class.

Corporate Secretary: A corporate officer, elected by the directors, usually charged with record-keeping responsibilities.

Corporate Taxation: *See* Taxation, Corporate.

Corporate Veil: *See* Pierce the Veil.

Corporation: A legal entity that has most of the rights and duties of natural persons but with perpetual life and limited liability.

Cumulative Voting: A system of voting shares of stock used in some states. Cumulative voting gives minority shareholders additional voting power by allowing them to "cumulate" their votes for a single director.

DBA. *See* Doing Business As.

Deadlock: The circumstance that arises when either the board of directors or shareholders are evenly split on a vote and cannot take action. Deadlock can lead to judicial resolution of the underlying dispute.

Debt Financing: A method of financing where the company receives a loan and gives its promise to repay the loan. *See also* Equity Financing.

Dilution: The effect of reducing an existing shareholder's or owner's interest in a corporation LLC, or partnership when new shares are issued.

Director: The directors of a corporation are its governing board. Elected by shareholders, they vote on major corporate matters such as the issuing of shares of stock, election of officers, and approval of mergers and acquisitions.

Dissolution: The process of shutting down a partnership, a corporation, or an LLC, settling its affairs, and ending its life. *See also* Administrative Dissolution, Involuntary Dissolution, Judicial Dissolution, Voluntary Dissolution.

Distribution: A transfer of profits or property by a business entity to its owners.

Distributive Share: Each owner's percentage share of the LLC profits and losses, most often equal to that member's percentage ownership share.

Dividend: A share of profits issued to the holders of shares in a corporation. Dividends can be paid in shares of stock or other property, such as shares in a subsidiary or parent company.

Dividend Priority: Special rights enjoyed by holders of a secondary class of stock that entitle holders to receive dividends before other shareholders.

Doing Business As (DBA): A company whose operating name differs from its legal name is said to be doing business as the operating name. Some states require DBA or fictitious business name filings to be made for the protection of consumers conducting business with the entity.

Domestic Corporation: In general, a corporation whose articles of incorporation are filed in the state in which it operates and maintains its principal office.

Double Taxation: The dual effect of corporate taxation, as a corporation pays taxes on its corporate profit and when its employees or owners are taxed personally on income, distributions, and dividends.

EIN: Employer Identification Number.

Equity Financing: A method of financing where a company issues shares of its stock and receives money. *See also* Debt Financing.

Equity Interest: Another term for an ownership interest in a company.

Federal Employer Identification Number: An account number required by the Internal Revenue Service for all employers—sole proprietors, partnerships, corporations, and LLCs— for collecting and reporting taxes withheld and wages paid to the employees.

FEIN: Federal Employer Identification Number.

Fictitious Business Name: The operating name of a company that differs from its legal name. Some states require companies to file DBA (doing business as) or fictitious business names for the protection of consumers conducting business with the entity.

Fiduciary: A person who holds or administers property for another and is held to a high standard of trust and responsibility with respect to that property.

Fiduciary Relationship: A special relationship in which one party, the fiduciary, owes heightened duties of good faith and responsibility to the other party with respect to the property and rights of the other party.

Foreign LLC: In general, an LLC that operates in one state but whose articles of organization are filed in another state; the state in which it operates refers to the out-of-state LLC as foreign. The term also refers to LLCs chartered in foreign nations.

Franchise Tax: A tax levied in consideration for the privilege of either incorporating or qualifying to do business in a state. A franchise tax may be based upon income, assets, outstanding shares, or a combination.

Fully Reporting Company: A public company that is subject to the Securities and Exchange Commission's periodic reporting requirements.

General Partner: In a limited partnership, someone who manages the enterprise and is personally liable for its debts.

General Partnership: A standard partnership, the simplest of all partnerships, in which all partners share in the management of the entity and in the entity's profits and decide on matters of ordinary business operations of the partnership by a majority of the partners or according to the percentage ownership of each partner.

Good Standing: A state a corporation enjoys when it is in full compliance with the law.

Go Public: The process of becoming a public, fully reporting company, either by filing a registration statement with the Securities and Exchange Commission or by merging with a public company.

Illiquidity Discount: A discount in the value of an interest in a business because of legal restrictions on the resale of such interest.

Incorporator: The person or entity that organizes a corporation and files its Articles of Incorporation. The incorporator can take corporate actions before directors and officers are appointed.

Initial Director(s): The first director(s) of a corporation, named in the original articles of incorporation filed with the secretary of state.

Investment Representation Letter: A document executed by each person admitted to membership in an LLC. The letter offers some measure of protection to the LLC because the member makes certain representations regarding his or her qualifications and fitness to serve as a member of the LLC and certain representations regarding his or her investment objectives, which are necessary representations in order to comply with state and federal securities laws.

Involuntary Dissolution: The forced dissolution of a corporation or LLC by a court or administrative action.

Judicial Dissolution: The forced dissolution of a corporation or LLC by a court at the request of a state attorney general, owner, or creditor.

Law of Agency: The law concerned with the contractual or quasi-contractual relationship between a principal or principals and an agent who is authorized to represent the legal interests of the principal(s) and to perform legal acts that bind the principal(s).

Liability Shield: The protection from liabilities, debts, and lawsuits enjoyed by the owners of a well-operated LLC or corporation that maintains its good standing.

The owners of such an LLC or corporation are said to be "shielded from liability."

Limited Liability Company (LLC): A new and flexible business organization that offers the advantages of liability protection with the simplicity of a partnership.

Limited Liability Partnership (LLP): A partnership composed of licensed professionals such as attorneys, accountants, and architects, each of whom may enjoy personal liability protection for the acts of other partners while remaining liable for his or her own actions.

Limited Partner: In a limited partnership, someone who contributes capital and shares in the profits but normally does not participate in the management of the enterprise.

Limited Partnership: A business organization owned by two classes of partners: general partners, who manage the enterprise, and limited partners, who contribute capital and share in the profits but normally do not participate in the management of the enterprise. The limited partners enjoy limited personal liability while general partners have unlimited personal liability.

Liquidation Preference: Certain classes of stock (usually preferred stock) may have a liquidation preference, which entitles the holders to be paid first in the event of the liquidation of a corporation's assets.

Manager(s): The person or persons granted the authority to manage and operate an LLC.

Manager-Managed LLC: An LLC that is managed by managers appointed by the members (owners) of the LLC.

Member(s): The owner or owners of an LLC.

Member-Managed LLC: An LLC that is managed by its members (owners), not by appointed managers.

Membership Ledger: A ledger recording the owners of an LLC, their proportion of ownership, and the transfers or other disposition of such ownership. A corporation's ledger is called a *share ledger*.

Merger: The combination of one or more corporations, LLCs, or other business entities into a single business entity.

Minutes: The written record of the actions taken at meetings.

Natural Person: A human being, as distinguished from a person created by law and recognized by law as the subject of rights and duties (such as a corporation).

Nonprofit Corporation: A business organization that serves some public purpose and therefore enjoys special treatment under the law. Nonprofit corporations, contrary to their name, can make a profit, but cannot be designed primarily for profit making. Distributions upon liquidation typically must be made to another nonprofit.

No-Par Shares: Shares for which there is no designated par value.

Officers: The managers of a corporation, such as the president, CFO, and secretary. The officers are appointed by the board of directors.

Operating Agreement: The document that governs the internal structure and operation of an LLC and governs the relationship between its members and its managers.

Organizer: The person or entity that organizes an LLC and signs and files its articles of organization or certificate of organization with the secretary of state's office or its equivalent, much like the incorporator of a corporation.

Outside Director: An independent member of the board of directors who is not a shareholder or a regular employee of a corporation.

Parent Corporation: A corporation that either owns outright or controls a subsidiary.

Partnership: A business organization formed when two or more persons or entities come together to operate a business for profit. Partnerships do not enjoy limited liability, except in the case of limited partnerships. *See also* General Partnership, Limited Partnership, Limited Liability Partnership.

Partnership Agreement: The agreement that governs the internal structure and operation of a partnership and governs the relationship among its partners.

Partnership Taxation: *See* Taxation, Pass-Through.

Par Value: The issued price of a security that bears no relation to the market price.

Pass-Through Taxation: *See* Taxation, Pass-Through.

Percentage Ownership: One's ownership in an LLC, a partnership, or a corporation, expressed as a percentage of the total ownership.

Pierce the Veil: Doctrine that attaches liability to corporate shareholders in cases of commingling of assets and failure to observe corporate formalities.

Preemptive Rights: Rights enjoyed by current shareholders to purchase additional shares of stock in proportion to their current holdings.

Preferred Stock: A separate and/or secondary class of stock issued by some corporations. Preferred stock typically has limited or no voting rights, but its holders receive dividends and, in the event the corporation is liquidated, receive repayment priority.

Principal: An entity or a person on whose behalf an agent acts.

Professional Corporation (PC): A corporation whose members are all licensed professionals, such as doctors, lawyers, accountants and architects.

Professional LLC (PLLC): An LLC organized to offer services that normally require a license, such as the practice of medicine or law.

Proxy: An authorization by an owner giving another person the right to vote the owner's shares. Proxy also refers to the document granting such authority.

Qualification: The process by which a foreign corporation registers in a state of operation other than its state of incorporation.

Quorum: The minimum percentage of owners, managers, or directors who must be present at a meeting in order for a vote to be legally effective.

Record Date: The date, set by a company, used to determine when an individual must own shares or units in a company in order to receive certain benefits from a company, such as dividend rights and voting rights. The record date is important for shareholders in publicly traded companies because shares are constantly changing hands.

Redemption: A repurchase of shares from shareholders by a corporation.

Redemption Rights: Right of repurchase enjoyed by a corporation for certain shares of stock.

Registered Agent: The person or entity authorized to receive legal papers on behalf of a corporation; also known as *agent for service of process*, and *resident agent*.

Registered Office: The official address of a corporation. Typically this address is the same as that of the registered agent.

Representative Management: The form of management used by modern business entities where the owners elect managers, directors, and officers to operate and manage the business entity.

Resident Agent: The person or entity authorized to receive legal papers on behalf of a corporation or an LLC.

S Corporation: A subchapter S corporation, a corporation that elects by filing with the IRS to be treated as a partnership for taxation purposes.

Secretary, Corporate: A corporate officer, elected by the directors, usually charged with record-keeping responsibilities.

Secretary of State: A state official charged with responsibility for the filing of legal documents, including corporation papers. In some states and the District of Columbia, this responsibility falls upon another department, such as Hawaii's Department of Commerce and Consumer Affairs or Arizona's Corporation Commission.

Securities: The broad term that refers to shares of stock, bonds, and some debt instruments.

Shareholder: An owner of a corporation and one who holds shares of stock in a corporation.

Shareholder's Agreement: An agreement between the shareholders of a corporation that can cover various matters, such as a commitment to vote for particular persons as directors and allowing other shareholders to have a right of first refusal to purchase the shares of departing shareholders.

Share Ledger: A record of each shareholder's ownership in a corporation and of all stock transactions. Any transaction regarding shares of a corporation—initial issuance of shares, sales, transfers, and other dispositions—must be entered in the stock ledger. Responsibility for maintaining the ledger usually vests with the corporation's secretary. An LLC's ledger is called a *membership ledger*.

Shelf Corporation: A fully formed corporation without operations, assets, or liabilities that remains in inventory (on a shelf) waiting for a buyer. The advantages: a shelf corporation can be operating within hours and uses its original formation date.

Simple Majority: With respect to shareholder and director voting, more than 50 percent.

Sole Proprietorship: A business owned and managed by one person. The sole proprietorship is not a legal entity. It simply refers to a natural person who owns the business and is personally responsible for its debts. A sole proprietorship can operate under the name of its owner or it can do business under a fictitious name. Sole proprietorships do not enjoy liability protection.

Special Allocation: A device whereby an LLC or a corporation's profits are divided in a proportion not equal to the ownership percentages of the entity.

Special Meeting of Directors: A meeting of directors, but not an annual meeting, called for a specific purpose.

Special Meeting of Shareholders: A meeting of shareholders, but not an annual meeting, called for a specific purpose.

Standard Partnership: *See* General Partnership.

Statute of Limitations: A law that sets the maximum period in which one must bring a lawsuit. Lawsuits cannot be brought after the expiration of the period. Periods vary by state.

Stockholder: An owner of a corporation and one who holds shares of stock in a corporation.

Stock Ledger: *See* Share Ledger.

Subscriber: A person who contracts to purchase the shares of a corporation.

Subscription Agreement: A contract to purchase the shares of a corporation.

Subsidiary: A corporation that is owned outright or controlled by a parent corporation.

Supermajority: With respect to shareholder and director voting, any required percentage higher than 50 percent.

Taxation, Corporate: The taxation of a corporation both on its profits and when its employees or owners are taxed personally on income, distributions, and dividends. The dual effect of corporate taxation is aptly referred to as *double taxation*.

Taxation, Pass-Through: When entities are not taxed on their income, but the income and profits that the entities pay out to owners and employees are taxable. The income is said to "pass through" the entity. Partnerships and LLCs enjoy pass-through taxation.

Trademark: Any symbol, word, or combination of either used to represent or identify a product or service.

Undercapitalization: The condition that exists when a company does not have enough cash to carry on its business and pay its creditors.

Unit: Ownership share in an LLC.

Voluntary Dissolution: The intentional dissolution of a business entity by its own management and owners.

Voting Right: The right enjoyed by shareholders to vote their shares.

Warrant: An instrument that grants its holder the option or right to purchase shares of stock at a future date at a specific price.

Winding Up: The process of paying creditors and distributing assets that occurs before the dissolution of a business entity.

Written Consent: A document executed by either the shareholders or the directors of a corporation in lieu of a formal meeting.

Limited Liability Company (LLC) Forms

The *LLC-1, California LLC Articles of Organization* is simply the form required in the State of California to organize and register a Limited Liability Company. Each state will require a different form. The *Sample Letter to Secretary of State Accompanying Articles of Organization* is a simple cover letter that you should include when submitting Limited Liability Company papers to the secretary of state.

A registered agent is a person or entity that is authorized and obligated to receive legal papers on behalf of an LLC. The *Sample Letter to Registered Agent Accompanying Articles of Organization* is a simple cover letter that you should deliver to your registered agent upon the organization of your LLC. Keep in mind that your state of organization may use a different term than registered agent. Typical equivalents include "agent for service of process," "local agent," and "registered agent."

The next group of forms are differing types of *LLC Operating Agreements* and deserve some comment. LLCs are managed in one of two ways, either "member-managed" or "manager-managed." Member-managed LLCs are governed by the LLC's owners (members) equally, just like a standard partnership. Manager-managed LLCs are governed by one or more appointed managers who often need not be members of the LLC. This manner of management by appointment is called "representative management." Manager-managed LLCs are managed much like corporations—with an appointed body of persons other than the company's ownership. The body of managers that undertakes governing responsibilities can come in the form of a board of managers or a committee of managers.

Thus, the *Short-Form Operating Agreement for Member-Managed LLC* and the *Long-Form Operating Agreement for Member-Managed LLC* are both short and long versions of operating agreements for member-managed LLCs. Similarly the *Short-Form Operating Agreement for Manager-Managed LLC* and the *Long-Form Operating Agreement for Manager-Managed LLC* are both short and long versions of operating agreements for manager-managed LLCs.

The *Membership Ledger* is a written table showing the owners of an LLC. The ledger must also indicate the percentage held by each owner. As new members are added to the LLC through the sale of membership interests, their ownership is recorded on the ledger. The membership ledger should also show transfers of members' ownership interests, as when a member passes away and transfers his or her interest through his or her will. The importance of the membership ledger cannot be overstated, and it should be diligently maintained. The membership ledger is akin to the deed on a piece of real estate. The ledger is the primary evidence of ownership in an LLC, and carries a great degree of weight when presented in court. LLC owners should insist upon receiving updated copies of the membership ledger periodically.

Each member admitted to the LLC should execute the *Investment Representation Letter*. The investment representation letter offers some measure of protection to the entity because the member being admitted to the LLC makes certain representations regarding his qualifications and fitness to serve as a member of the LLC. Also, in the investment representation letter the member makes certain representations regarding his or her investment objectives, which are necessary representations in order to comply with state and federal securities laws.

The *Appointment of Proxy for Member's Meeting* is an authorization by one member giving another person the right to vote the owner's shares in a company, in this case an LLC. The term Proxy also refers to the document granting such authority. Proxy rules are typically outlined in state law and an LLC's operating agreement. Often proxies are granted when members do not wish to attend member meetings, but they want their vote to be counted. They can therefore grant their proxy to another person to attend the meeting and vote their shares on their behalf.

The *Call for Meeting of Members* is an instruction by LLC members to the managers that the members want to call a meeting of members. This serves as official notice to the managers that the members wish to call a meeting. This call is only required by manager-managed LLCs; if a member in a member-managed LLC wants to call a meeting of members, he or she would skip the call, and simply send a notice of meeting of members to all other members. The next form in this volume is a notice of meeting of members.

The *Notice of Meeting of LLC Members* is simply an LLC's announcement to its members that a meeting of members has been called.

While LLC members and managers enjoy far fewer corporate formalities than corporation owners, an LLC must still maintain records of its meetings. When an LLC's members meet to formally vote on any matter, the results of that vote should be committed to written minutes called the *Minutes of Meeting of LLC Members.*

In the real world, most LLC votes are taken by written consent in a document called a *Action by Written Consent of LLC Members* rather than by notice and meeting and an in-person vote. Use the written consent form when you wish to take a company action in writing, rather than by a noticed meeting. Keep in mind, however, that your operating agreement and articles may require more than a simple majority to pass certain actions. Written consents are important company records and should be maintained in the record books.

The *Written Consent of Members Approving a Certificate of Amendment of Articles of Organization Changing an LLC's Name* is a specific example of a written consent. In this case, the written consent authorizes a change to the LLC's charter to change the LLC's legal name.

The *Internal Revenue Service Tax Form SS-4* is the request for a employer identification number. *Internal Revenue Service Form 2553* is for electing the form of a business entity.

LLC Form 1. LLC-1, California LLC Articles of Organization

ATTENTION: LIMITED LIABILITY COMPANY FILERS

Pursuant to California Revenue and Taxation Code section 17941, every Limited Liability Company (LLC) that is doing business in California or that has Articles of Organization accepted or a Certificate of Registration issued by the Secretary of State's office (pursuant to California Corporations Code section 17050 or 17451) *and* is not taxed as a corporation is subject to the annual LLC minimum tax of $800 (as well as the appropriate fee pursuant to Revenue and Taxation Code section 17942). The tax is paid to the California Franchise Tax Board, is due for the taxable year of organization/registration, and must be paid for each taxable year, or part thereof, until a Certificate of Cancellation of Registration or Certificate of Cancellation of Articles of Organization (pursuant to Corporations Code section 17356 or 17455) is filed with the Secretary of State's office. For further information regarding the payment of this tax, please contact the Franchise Tax Board at:

From within the United States (toll-free)
(800) 852-5711

From outside the United States (not toll-free)
(916) 845-6500

Automated toll-free phone service
(800) 338-0505

California Secretary of State
Business Programs Division
Business Filings Section
(916) 657-5448

State of California
Kevin Shelley
Secretary of State

File # _____

LIMITED LIABILITY COMPANY
ARTICLES OF ORGANIZATION

A $70.00 filing fee must accompany this form.

IMPORTANT – Read instructions before completing this form.

This Space For Filing Use Only

1.	NAME OF THE LIMITED LIABILITY COMPANY (END THE NAME WITH THE WORDS "LIMITED LIABILITY COMPANY," "LTD. LIABILITY CO.,"OR THE ABBREVIATIONS "LLC" OR "L.L.C.")
2.	THE PURPOSE OF THE LIMITED LIABILITY COMPANY IS TO ENGAGE IN ANY LAWFUL ACT OR ACTIVITY FOR WHICH A LIMITED **LIABILITY** COMPANY MAY BE ORGANIZED UNDER THE BEVERLY-KILLEA LIMITED LIABILITY COMPANY ACT.
3.	CHECK THE APPROPRIATE PROVISION BELOW AND NAME THE AGENT FOR SERVICE OF PROCESS. [ ] AN INDIVIDUAL RESIDING IN CALIFORNIA. PROCEED TO ITEM 4. [ ] A CORPORATION WHICH HAS FILED A CERTIFICATE PURSUANT TO SECTION 1505. PROCEED TO ITEM 5. AGENT'S NAME: _____ _____
4.	ADDRESS OF THE AGENT FOR SERVICE OF PROCESS IN CALIFORNIA, IF AN INDIVIDUAL: ADDRESS CITY STATE CA ZIP CODE
5.	THE LIMITED LIABILITY COMPANY WILL BE MANAGED BY: (CHECK ONE) [ ] ONE MANAGER [ ] MORE THAN ONE MANAGER [ ] ALL LIMITED LIABILITY COMPANY MEMBER(S)
6.	OTHER MATTERS TO BE INCLUDED IN THIS CERTIFICATE MAY BE SET FORTH ON SEPARATE ATTACHED PAGES AND ARE MADE A PART OF THIS CERTIFICATE. OTHER MATTERS MAY INCLUDE THE LATEST DATE ON WHICH THE LIMITED LIABILITY COMPANY IS TO DISSOLVE.
7.	NUMBER OF PAGES ATTACHED, IF ANY:
8.	TYPE OF BUSINESS OF THE LIMITED LIABILITY COMPANY. (FOR INFORMATIONAL PURPOSES ONLY)
9.	IT IS HEREBY DECLARED THAT I AM THE PERSON WHO EXECUTED THIS INSTRUMENT, WHICH EXECUTION IS MY ACT AND DEED. _____ _____ SIGNATURE OF ORGANIZER DATE _____ TYPE OR PRINT NAME OF ORGANIZER
10.	RETURN TO: NAME FIRM ADDRESS CITY/STATE ZIP CODE

SEC/STATE FORM LLC-1 (Rev. 12/2003) – FILING FEE $70.00   APPROVED BY SECRETARY OF STATE

INSTRUCTIONS FOR COMPLETING THE ARTICLES OF ORGANIZATION (LLC-1)

For easier completion, t his form is a vailable in a "fillable" version online at the Secretary of State's w ebsite at http:// www .ss.ca.go v/business/business.htm. The form can be filled in on y our computer , printed and mailed to the Secretary of State, Document Filin g Sup port Unit, P O Bo x 944228, Sacr amento, CA 94244-2280 or can be deliv ered in person to the Sacramento office, 150 0 11ᵗʰ Street, 3ʳᵈ Floor, Sacram ento, CA 95814. If you are not completing this fo rm o nlin e, please type or legibly print in black o r blue in k.

FILING FEE: The filing fee is $70.00. Make the check(s) payable to the Secretary of State and send the executed document and filing fee to the address stated above.

Statutory filing provisions can be found in California Corporations Code section **17051**. All statutory references are to the California Corporations Code, unless otherwise stated.

Pursuant to California Corporation Code section **17375**, nothing in this title shall be construed to permit a domestic or foreign limited liability company to render professional services, as defined in subdivision (a) of Section **13401**, in this state.

Complete th e Article s of Organi zation (Form LLC-1) as follo ws:

Item 1. Enter the name of the limited liability company. The name shall contain the words "Limited Liability Company," or the abbreviations "LLC" or "L.L.C." The words "Limited" and "Company" may be abbreviated to "Ltd." and "Co." The name of the limited liability company may not contain the words "bank," "trust," "trustee," incorporated," "inc.," "corporation," or "corp.," and shall not contain the words "insurer" or "insurance company" or any other words suggesting that it is in the business of issuing policies of insurance and assuming insurance risks. (Section **17052**.)

Item 2. Execution of this document confirms the following statement which has been preprinted on the form and may not be altered: "The purpose of the limited liability company is to engage in any lawful act or activity for which a limited liability company may be organized under the Beverly-Killea Limited Liability Company Act." Provisions limiting or restricting the business of the limited liability company may be included as an attachment.

Item 3. Enter the name of the agent for service of process. Check the appropriate provision indicating whether the agent is an individual residing in California or a corporation which has filed a certificate pursuant to Section **1505** of the California Corporations Code. If an individual is designated as agent, proceed to item 4. If a corporation is designated, proceed to item 5.

Item 4. If an individual is designated as the initial agent for service of process, enter an address in California. Do not enter "in care of" (c/o) or abbreviate the name of the city. DO NOT enter an address if a corporation is designated as the agent for service of process.

Item 5. Check the appropriate provision indicating whether the limited liability company is to be managed by one manager, more than one manager or all limited liability company member(s). (Section **17051(a)(5)**.)

Item 6. The Articles of Organization (LLC-1) may include other matters that the person filing the Articles of Organization determines to include. Other matters may include the latest date on which the limited liability company is to dissolve. If other matters are to be included, attach one or more pages setting forth the other matters.

Item 7. Enter the number of pages attached, if any. All attachments should be 8½" x 11", one-sided and legible.

Item 8. Briefly describe the type of business that constitutes the principal business activity of the limited liability company. Note restrictions in the rendering of professional services by Limited Liability Companies. Professional services are defined in California Corporations Code, Section **13401(a)** as: "Any type of professional services that may be lawfully rendered only pursuant to a license, certification, or registration authorized by the Business and Professions Code or the Chiropractic Act."

Item 9. The Articles of Organization (LLC-1) shall be executed with an original signature of the organizer.

The person executing the Articles of Organization (LLC-1) need not be a member or manager of the limited liability company.

If an entity is signing the Articles of Organization (LLC-1), the person who signs for the entity must note the exact entity name, his/her name, and his/her position/title.

If an attorney-in-fact is signing the Articles of Organization (LLC-1), the signature must be followed by the words "Attorney-in-fact for (name of person)."

If a trust is signing the Articles of Organization (LLC-1), the articles must be signed by a trustee as follows: _____, trustee for _____ trust (including the date of the trust, if applicable). Example: Mary Todd, trustee of the Lincoln Family Trust (U/T/A 5-1-94).

Item 10. Enter the name and the address of the person or firm to whom a copy of the filing should be returned.

∀   For further information contact the Business Filings Section at (916) 657-5448.

LLC Form 2. Sample Letter to Secretary of State
Accompanying Articles of Organization

Note: This letter is a version appropriate for use in Delaware, but can be modified for use in any state.

Michael Spadaccini
123 Elm Street
San Francisco, CA 94107
415-555-1212

(Date) _____

State of Delaware
Division of Corporations
401 Federal Street, Suite 4
Dover, DE 19901

To whom it may concern:

Enclosed you will find articles of organization for 17 Reasons, LLC. Please file the enclosed articles.

I have enclosed five copies of the filing and a check for $_____ to cover filing fees. Please return any necessary papers in the envelope that I have provided.

Yours truly,

Michael Spadaccini

LLC Form 3. Sample Letter to Registered Agent
Accompanying Articles of Organization

Michael Spadaccini
123 Elm Street
San Francisco, CA 94107
415-555-1212

(Date) _____

Harvard Business Services, Inc.
25 Greystone Manor
Lewes, DE 19958

To whom it may concern:

I have enclosed a copy of articles of incorporation I am filing today. As you can see, I have used you as our registered agents in the state of Delaware.

Please use the following contact information:

17 Reasons, LLC
c/o Michael Spadaccini
123 Elm Street
San Francisco, CA 94107

I have enclosed a check for $50.00 to cover the first year's services.

Yours truly,

Michael Spadaccini

LLC Form 4. Short-Form Operating Agreement for Member-Managed LLC

OPERATING AGREEMENT OF (insert full name of LLC)

THIS OPERATING AGREEMENT (the "Agreement") is hereby entered into by the undersigned, who are owners and shall be referred to as Member or Members.

RECITALS

The Members desire to form (insert full name of LLC), a limited liability company (the "Company"), for the purposes set forth herein, and, accordingly, desire to enter into this Agreement in order to set forth the terms and conditions of the business and affairs of the Company and to determine the rights and obligations of its Members.

NOW, THEREFORE, the Members, intending to be legally bound by this Agreement, hereby agree that the limited liability company operating agreement of the Company shall be as follows:

ARTICLE I. DEFINITIONS

When used in this Agreement, the following terms shall have the meanings set forth below.

1.1 "Act" means the Limited Liability Company Law of the State in which the Company is organized or chartered, including any amendments or the corresponding provision(s) of any succeeding law.

1.2 "Capital Contribution(s)" means the amount of cash and the agreed value of property, services rendered, or a promissory note or other obligation to contribute cash or property or to perform services contributed by the Members for such Members' Interest in the Company, equal to the sum of the Members' initial Capital Contributions plus the Members' additional Capital Contributions, if any, made pursuant to Sections 4.1 and 4.2, respectively, less payments or distributions made pursuant to Section 5.1.

1.3 "Code" means the Internal Revenue Code of 1986 and the regulations promulgated thereunder, as amended from time to time (or any corresponding provision or provisions of succeeding law).

1.4 "Interest" or "Interests" means the ownership Interest, expressed as a number, percentage, or fraction, set forth in Table A, of a Member in the Company.

1.5 "Person" means any natural individual, partnership, firm, corporation, limited liability company, joint-stock company, trust, or other entity.

1.6 "Secretary of State" means the Office of the Secretary of State or the office charged with accepting articles of organization in the Company's state of organization.

ARTICLE II. FORMATION

2.1 Organization. The Members hereby organize the Company as a limited liability company pursuant to the provisions of the Act.

2.2 Effective Date. The Company shall come into being on, and this Agreement shall take effect from, the date the Articles of Organization of the Company are filed with the Secretary of State in the state of organization or charter.

2.3 Agreement: Invalid Provisions and Saving Clause. The Members, by executing this Agreement, hereby agree to the terms and conditions of this Agreement. To the extent any provision of this Agreement is prohibited or ineffective under the Act, this Agreement shall be deemed to be amended to the least extent necessary in order to make this Agreement effective under the Act. In the event the Act is subsequently amended or interpreted in such a way to validate any provision of this Agreement that was formerly invalid, such provision shall be considered to be valid from the effective date of such amendment or interpretation.

ARTICLE III. PURPOSE; NATURE OF BUSINESS

3.1 Purpose; Nature of Business. The purpose of the Company shall be to engage in any lawful business that may be engaged in by a limited liability company organized under the Act, as such business activities may be determined by the Member or Members from time to time.

3.2 Powers. The Company shall have all powers of a limited liability company under the Act and the power to do all things necessary or convenient to accomplish its purpose and operate its business as described in Section 3.1 here.

ARTICLE IV. MEMBERS AND CAPITAL CONTRIBUTIONS

4.1 Members and Initial Capital Contribution. The name, address, Interest, and value of the initial Capital Contribution of the Members shall be set forth on Table A attached hereto.

4.2 Additional Capital Contributions. The Members shall have no obligation to make any additional Capital Contributions to the Company. The Members may make additional Capital Contributions to the Company as the Members unanimously determine are necessary, appropriate, or desirable.

ARTICLE V. DISTRIBUTIONS AND ALLOCATIONS

5.1 Distributions and Allocations. All distributions of cash or other assets of the Company shall be made and paid to the Members at such time and in such amounts as the majority of the Members may determine. All items of income, gain, loss, deduction, and credit shall be allocated to the Members in proportion to their Interests.

ARTICLE VI. TAXATION

6.1 Income Tax Reporting. Each Member is aware of the income tax consequences of the allocations made by Article V here and agrees to be bound by the provisions of Article V here in reporting each Member's share of Company income and loss for federal and state income tax purposes.

6.2 Tax Treatment. Notwithstanding anything contained herein to the contrary and only for purposes of federal and, if applicable, state income tax purposes, the Company shall be classified as a partnership for such federal and state income tax purposes unless and until the Members unanimously determine to cause the Company to file an election under the Code to be classified as an association taxable as a corporation.

ARTICLE VII. MANAGEMENT BY MEMBERS

7.1 Management by Members. The Company shall be managed by its Members, who shall have full and exclusive right, power, and authority to manage the affairs of the Company and to bind the Company to contracts and obligations, to make all decisions with respect thereto, and to do or cause to be done any and all acts or things deemed by the Members to be necessary, appropriate, or desirable to carry out or further the business of the Company.

7.2 Voting Power in Proportion to Interest. The Members shall enjoy voting power and authority in proportion to their Interests. Unless expressly provided otherwise in this Agreement or the Articles of Organization, Company decisions shall be made by majority vote.

7.3 Duties of Members. The Members shall manage and administer the day-to-day operations and business of the Company and shall execute any and all reports, forms, instruments, documents, papers, writings, agreements, and contracts, including but not limited to deeds, bills of sale, assignments, leases, promissory notes, mortgages, and security agreements and any other type or form of document by which property or property rights of the Company are transferred or encumbered, or by which debts and obligations of the Company are created, incurred, or evidenced.

ARTICLE VIII. BOOKS AND RECORDS

8.1 Books and Records. The Members shall keep, or cause to be kept, at the principal place of business of the Company true and correct books of account, in which shall be entered fully and accurately each and every transaction of the Company. The Company's taxable and fiscal years shall end on December 31. All Members shall have the right to inspect the Company's books and records at any time, for any reason.

ARTICLE IX. LIMITATION OF LIABILITY; INDEMNIFICATION

9.1 Limited Liability. Except as otherwise required by law, the debts, obligations, and liabilities of the Company, whether arising in contract, tort, or otherwise, shall be solely the debts, obligations, and liabilities of the Company, and the Members shall not be obligated personally for any such debt, obligation, or liability of the Company solely by reason of being Members. The failure of the Company to observe any formalities or requirements relating to the exercise of its powers or the management of its business or affairs under this Agreement or by law shall not be grounds for imposing personal liability on the Members for any debts, liabilities, or obligations of the Company. Except as otherwise expressly required by law, the Members, in such Members' capacity as such, shall have no liability in excess of (a) the amount of such Members' Capital Contributions, (b) such Members' share of any assets and undistributed profits of the Company, and (c) the amount of any distributions required to be returned according to law.

9.2 Indemnification. The Company shall, to the fullest extent provided or allowed by law, indemnify, save harmless, and pay all judgments and claims against the Members, and each of the Company's or Members' agents, affiliates, heirs, legal representatives, successors, and assigns (each, an "Indemnified Party") from, against, and in respect of any and all liability, loss, damage, and expense incurred or sustained by the Indemnified Party in connection with the business of the Company or by reason of any act performed or omitted to be performed in connection with the activities of the Company or in dealing with third parties on behalf of the Company, including costs and attorneys' fees before and at trial and at all appellate levels, whether or not suit is instituted (which attorneys' fees may be paid as incurred), and any amounts expended in the settlement of any claims of liability, loss, or damage, to the fullest extent allowed by law.

9.3. Insurance. The Company shall not pay for any insurance covering liability of the Members or the Company's or Members' agents, affiliates, heirs, legal representatives, successors, and assigns for actions or omissions for which indemnification is not permitted hereunder; provided, however, that nothing contained here shall preclude the Company from purchasing and paying for such types of insurance, including extended coverage liability and casualty and worker's compensation, as would be customary for any Person owning, managing, and/or operating comparable property and engaged in a similar business, or from naming the Members and any of the Company's or Members' agents, affiliates, heirs, legal representatives, successors, or assigns or any Indemnified Party as additional insured parties thereunder.

9.4 Non-Exclusive Right. The provisions of this Article IX shall be in addition to and not in limitation of any other rights of indemnification and reimbursement or limitations of liability to which an Indemnified Party may be entitled under the Act, common law, or otherwise.

ARTICLE X. AMENDMENT

10.1 Amendment. This Agreement may not be altered or modified except by the unanimous written consent or agreement of the Members as evidenced by an amendment hereto whereby this Agreement is amended or amended and restated.

ARTICLE XI. WITHDRAWAL

11.1 Withdrawal of a Member. No Member may withdraw from the Company except by written request of the Member given to each of the other Members and with the unanimous written consent of the other Members (the effective date of withdrawal being the date on which the unanimous written consent of all of the other Members is given) or upon the effective date of any of the following events:

(a) the Member makes an assignment of his or her property for the benefit of creditors;

(b) the Member files a voluntary petition of bankruptcy;

(c) the Member is adjudged bankrupt or insolvent or there is entered against the Member an order for relief in any bankruptcy or insolvency proceeding;

(d) the Member seeks, consents to, or acquiesces in the appointment of a trustee or receiver for, or liquidation of the Member or of all or any substantial part of the Member's property;

(e) the Member files an answer or other pleading admitting or failing to contest the material allegations of a petition filed against the Member in any proceeding described in Subsections 11.1 (a) through (d);

(f) if the Member is a corporation, the dissolution of the corporation or the revocation of its articles of incorporation or charter;

(g) if the Member is an estate, the distribution by the fiduciary of the estate's Interest in the Company;

(h) if the Member is an employee of the Company and he or she resigns, retires, or for any reason ceases to be employed by the Company in any capacity; or

(i) if the other Members owning more than fifty percent (50%) of the Interests vote or request in writing that a Member withdraw and such request is given to the Member (the effective date of withdrawal being the date on which the vote or written request of the other Members is given to the Member).

11.2 Valuation of Interest. The value of the withdrawing Member's Interest in all events shall be equal to the greater of the following: (a) the amount of the Member's Capital Contribution or (b) the amount of the Member's share of the Members' equity in the Company, plus the amount of any unpaid and outstanding loans or advances made by the Member to the Company (plus any due and unpaid interest thereon, if interest on the loan or advance has been agreed to between the Company and the Member), calculated as of the end of the fiscal quarter immediately preceding the effective date of the Member's withdrawal.

11.3 Payment of Value. The value shall be payable as follows: (a) If the value is equal to or less than $500, at closing, and (b) If the value is greater than $500, at the option of the Company, $500 at closing with the balance of the purchase price paid by delivering a promissory note of the Company dated as of the closing date and bearing interest at the prime rate published in *The Wall Street Journal* as of the effective date of withdrawal, with the principal amount being payable in five (5) equal annual installments beginning one (1) year from closing and with the interest on the accrued and unpaid balance being payable at the time of payment of each principal installment.

11.4 Closing. Payment of the value of the departing Member's Interest shall be made at a mutually agreeable time and date on or before thirty (30) days from the effective date of withdrawal. Upon payment of the value of the Interest as calculated in Section 11.3 above: (a) the Member's right to receive any and all further payments or distributions on account of the Member's ownership of the Interest in the Company shall cease; (b) the Member's loans or advances to the Company shall be paid and satisfied in full; and (c) the Member shall no longer be a Member or creditor of the Company on account of the Capital Contribution or the loans or advances.

11.5 Limitation on Payment of Value. If payment of the value of the Interest would be prohibited by any statute or law prohibiting distributions that would

(a) render the Company insolvent; or

(b) be made at a time that the total Company liabilities (other than liabilities to Members on account of their Interests) exceed the value of the Company's total assets;

then the value of the withdrawing Member's Interest in all events shall be $1.00.

ARTICLE XII. MISCELLANEOUS PROVISIONS

12.1 Assignment of Interest and New Members. No Member may assign such person's Interest in the Company in whole or in part except by the vote or written consent of the other Members owning more than fifty percent (50%) of the Interests. No additional Person may be admitted as a Member except by the vote or written consent of the Members owning more than fifty percent (50%) of the Interests.

12.2 Determinations by Members: Except as required by the express provisions of this Agreement or of the Act:

(a) Any transaction, action, or decision which requires or permits the Members to consent to, approve, elect, appoint, adopt, or authorize or to make a determination or decision with respect thereto under this Agreement, the Act, the Code, or otherwise shall be made by the Members owning more than fifty percent (50%) of the Interests.

(b) The Members shall act at a meeting of Members or by consent in writing of the Members. Members may vote or give their consent in person or by proxy.

(c) Meetings of the Members may be held at any time, upon call of any Member or Members owning, in the aggregate, at least ten percent (10%) of the Interests.

(d) Unless waived in writing by the Members owning more than fifty percent (50%) of the Interests (before or after a meeting), at least two (2) business days, prior notice of any meeting shall be given to each Member. Such notice shall state the purpose for which such meeting has been called. No business may be conducted or action taken at such meeting that is not provided for in such notice.

(e) Members may participate in a meeting of Members by means of conference telephone or similar communications equipment by means of which all Persons participating in the meeting can hear each other, and such participation shall constitute presence in person at such meeting.

(f) The Members shall cause to be kept a book of minutes of all meetings of the Members in which there shall be recorded the time and place of such meeting, by whom such meeting was called, the notice thereof given, the names of those present, and the proceedings thereof. Copies of any consents in writing shall also be filed in such minute book.

12.3 Binding Effect. This Agreement shall be binding upon and inure to the benefit of the undersigned Members, their legal representatives, heirs, successors, and assigns. This Agreement and the rights and duties of the Members hereunder shall be governed by, and interpreted and construed in accordance with, the laws of the Company's state of organization or charter, without regard to principles of choice of law.

12.5 Headings. The article and section headings in this Agreement are inserted as a matter of convenience and are for reference only and shall not be construed to define, limit, extend, or describe the scope of this Agreement or the intent of any provision.

12.6 Number and Gender. Whenever required by the context here, the singular shall include the plural, and vice versa, and the masculine gender shall include the feminine and neuter genders, and vice versa.

12.7 Entire Agreement and Binding Effect. This Agreement constitutes the sole operating agreement among the Members and supersedes and cancels any prior agreements, representations, warranties, or communications, whether oral or written, between the Members relating to the affairs of the Company and the conduct of the Company's business. No amendment or modification of this Agreement shall be effective unless approved in writing as provided in Section 10.1. The Articles of Organization and this Agreement are binding upon and shall inure to the benefit of the Members and Agent(s) and shall be binding upon their successors, assigns, affiliates, subsidiaries, heirs, beneficiaries, personal representatives, executors, administrators, and guardians, as applicable and appropriate.

IN WITNESS WHEREOF, this Agreement has been made and executed by the Members effective as of the date first written above.

_____ (Member)

_____ (Member)

_____ (Member)

Table A: Name, Address, and Initial Capital Contribution of the Members

Name and Address of Member	Value of Initial Capital Contribution	Nature of Member's Initial Capital Contribution (i.e., cash, services, property)	Percentage Interest of Member

LLC Form 5. Long-Form Operating Agreement for Member-Managed LLC

OPERATING AGREEMENT OF (INSERT NAME), LLC

THIS OPERATING AGREEMENT (the "Agreement") is made and entered into on _____, 20__, and those persons whose names, addresses, and signatures are set forth below, being the Members of (Insert Name), LLC (the "Company"), represent and agree that they have caused or will cause to be filed, on behalf of the Company, Articles of Organization, and that they desire to enter into an operating agreement.

The Members agree as follows:

ARTICLE I. DEFINITIONS

1.1. "Act" means the Limited Liability Company Law of the State in which the Company is organized or chartered, including any amendments or the corresponding provision(s) of any succeeding law.

1.2. "Affiliate" or "Affiliate of a Member" means any Person under the control of, in common control with, or in control of a Member, whether that control is direct or indirect. The term "control," as used herein, means, with respect to a corporation or limited liability company, the ability to exercise more than fifty percent (50%) of the voting rights of the controlled entity, and with respect to an individual, partnership, trust, or other entity or association, the ability, directly or indirectly, to direct the management of policies of the controlled entity or individual.

1.3. "Agreement" means this Operating Agreement, in its original form and as amended from time to time.

1.4. "Articles" means the Articles of Organization or other charter document filed with the Secretary of State in the state of organization forming this limited liability company, as initially filed and as they may be amended from time to time.

1.5. "Capital Account" means the amount of the capital interest of a Member in the Company, consisting of the amount of money and the fair market value, net of liabilities, of any property initially contributed by the Member, as (1) increased by any additional contributions and the Member's share of the Company's profits; and (2) decreased by any distribution to that Member as well as that Member's share of Company losses.

1.6. "Code" means the Internal Revenue Code of 1986, as amended from time to time, the regulations promulgated thereunder, and any corresponding provision of any succeeding revenue law.

1.7. "Company Minimum Gain" shall have the same meaning as set forth for the term "Partnership Minimum Gain" in the Regulations section 1.704-2(d) (26 CFR Section1.704-2(d)).

1.8. "Departing Member" means any Member whose conduct results in a Dissolution Event or who withdraws from or is expelled from the Company in accordance with Section 4.3, where such withdrawal does not result in dissolution of the Company.

1.9. "Dissolution Event" means, with respect to any Member, one or more of the following: the death, resignation, retirement, expulsion, bankruptcy, or dissolution of any Member.

1.10. "Distribution" means the transfer of money or property by the Company to the Members without consideration.

1.11. "Member" means each Person who has been admitted into membership in the Company, executes this Agreement and any subsequent amendments, and has not engaged in conduct resulting in a Dissolution Event or terminated membership for any other reason.

1.12. "Member Nonrecourse Debt" shall have the same meaning as set forth for the term "Partnership Nonrecourse Debt" in the Code.

1.13. "Member Nonrecourse Deductions" means items of Company loss, deduction, or Code Section 705(a)(2)(B) expenditures which are attributable to Member Nonrecourse Debt.

1.14. "Membership Interest" means a Member's rights in the Company, collectively, including the Member's economic interest, right to vote and participate in management, and right to information concerning the business and affairs of the Company provided in this Agreement or under the Act.

1.15. "Net Profits" and "Net Losses" mean the Company's income, loss, and deductions computed at the close of each fiscal year in accordance with the accounting methods used to prepare the Company's information tax return filed for federal income tax purposes.

1.16. "Nonrecourse Liability" has the meaning provided in the Code.

1.17. "Percentage Interest" means the percentage ownership of the Company of each Member as set forth in the column entitled "Member's Percentage Interest" contained in Table A as recalculated from time to time pursuant to this Agreement.

1.18. "Person" means an individual, partnership, limited partnership, corporation, limited liability company, registered limited liability partnership, trust, association, estate, or any other entity.

1.19. "Remaining Members" means, upon the occurrence of a Dissolution Event, those members of the Company whose conduct did not cause its occurrence.

ARTICLE II. FORMATION AND ORGANIZATION

2.1. Initial Date and Initial Parties. This Agreement is deemed entered into upon the date of the filing of the Company's Articles.

2.2. Subsequent Parties. No Person may become a Member of the Company without agreeing to and without becoming a signatory of this Agreement, and any offer or assignment of a Membership Interest is contingent upon the fulfillment of this condition.

2.3. Term. The Company shall commence upon the filing of its Articles and it shall continue in existence until December 31, 2050, unless terminated earlier under the provisions of this Agreement.

2.4. Principal Place of Business. The Company will have its principal place of business at (insert address of principal place of business) or at any other address upon which the Members agree. The Company shall maintain its principal executive offices at its principal place of business, as well as all required records and documents.

2.5. Authorization and Purpose. The purpose of the Company is to engage in any lawful business activity that is permitted by the Act.

ARTICLE III. CAPITAL CONTRIBUTIONS AND ACCOUNTS

3.1. Initial Capital Contributions. The initial capital contribution of each Member is listed in Table A attached hereto. Table A shall be revised to reflect and additional contributions pursuant to Section 3.2.

3.2. Additional Contributions. No Member shall be required to make any additional contributions to the Company. However, upon agreement by the Members that additional capital is desirable or necessary, any Member may, but shall not be required to, contribute additional capital to the Company on a pro rata basis consistent with the Percentage Interest of each of the Members.

3.3. Interest Payments. No Member shall be entitled to receive interest payments in connection with any contribution of capital to the Company, except as expressly provided herein.

3.4. Right to Return of Contributions. No Member shall be entitled to a return of any capital contributed to the Company, except as expressly provided in the Agreement.

3.5. Capital Accounts. A Capital Account shall be created and maintained by the Company for each Member, in conformance with the Code, which shall reflect all Capital Contributions to the Company. Should any Member transfer or assign all or any part of his or her membership interest in accordance with this Agreement, the successor shall receive that portion of the Member's Capital Account attributable to the interest assigned or transferred.

ARTICLE IV. MEMBERS

4.1. Limitation of Liability. No Member shall be personally liable for the debts, obligations, liabilities, or judgments of the Company solely by virtue of his or her Membership in the Company, except as expressly set forth in this Agreement or required by law.

4.2. Additional Members. The Members may admit additional Members to the Company only if approved by a two-thirds majority in interest of the Company Membership. Additional Members shall be permitted to participate in management at the discretion of the existing Members. Likewise, the existing Members shall agree upon an Additional Member's participation in Net Profits, Net Losses, and Distributions, as those terms are defined in this Agreement. Table A shall be amended to include the name, present mailing address, and percentage ownership of any Additional Members.

4.3. Withdrawal or Expulsion from Membership. Any Member may withdraw at any time after sixty (60) days' written notice to the company, without prejudice to the rights of the Company or any Member under any contract to which the withdrawing Member is a party. Such withdrawing Member shall have the rights of a transferee under this Agreement and the remaining Members shall be entitled to purchase the withdrawing Member's Membership Interest in accordance with this Agreement. Any Member may be expelled from the Company upon a vote of two-thirds majority in interest of the Company Membership. Such expelled Member shall have the rights of a transferee under this Agreement and the remaining Members shall be entitled to purchase the expelled Member's Membership Interest in accordance with this Agreement.

4.4. Competing Activities. The Members and their officers, directors, shareholders, partners, managers, agents, employees, and Affiliates are permitted to participate in other business activities which may be in competition, direct or indirect, with those of the Company. The Members further acknowledge that they are under no obligation to present to the Company any business or investment opportunities, even if the opportunities are of such a character as to be appropriate for the Company's undertaking. Each Member hereby waives the right to any claim against any other Member or Affiliate on account of such competing activities.

4.5. Compensation of Members. No Member or Affiliate shall be entitled to compensation for services rendered to the Company, absent agreement by the Members. However, Members and Affiliates shall be entitled to reimbursement for the actual cost of goods and services provided to the Company, including, without limitation, reimbursement for any professional services required to form the Company.

4.6. Transaction with the Company. The Members may permit a Member to lend money to and transact business with the Company, subject to any limitations contained in this Agreement or in the Act. To the extent permitted by applicable laws, such a Member shall be treated like any other Person with respect to transactions with the Company.

4.7. Meetings.

(a) There will be no regular or annual meeting of the Members. However, any Member(s) with an aggregate Percentage Interest of ten percent (10%) or more may call a meeting of the Members at any time. Such meeting shall be held at a place to be agreed upon by the Members.

(b) Minutes of the meeting shall be made and maintained along with the books and records of the Company.

(c) If any action on the part of the Members is to be proposed at the meeting, then written notice of the meeting must be provided to each Member entitled to vote not less than ten (10) days or more than sixty (60) days prior to the meeting. Notice may be given in person, by fax, by first class mail, or by any other written communication, charges prepaid, at the Members' address listed in Table A. The notice shall contain the date, time, and place of the meeting and a statement of the general nature of this business to be transacted there.

4.8. Actions at Meetings.

(a) No action may be taken at a meeting that was not proposed in the notice of the meeting, unless there is unanimous consent among all Members entitled to vote.

(b) No action may be taken at a meeting unless a quorum of Members is present, either in person or by proxy. A quorum of Members shall consist of Members holding a majority of the Percentage Interest in the Company.

(c) A Member may participate in, and is deemed present at, any meeting by clearly audible conference telephone or other similar means of communication.

(d) Any meeting may be adjourned upon the vote of the majority of the Membership Interests represented at the meeting.

(e) Actions taken at any meeting of the Members have full force and effect if each Member who was not present, in person or by proxy, signs a written waiver of notice and consent to the holding of the meeting or approval of the minutes of the meeting. All such waivers and consents shall become Company records.

(f) Presence at a meeting constitutes a waiver of the right to object to notice of a meeting, unless the Member expresses such an objection at the start of the meeting.

4.9. Actions Without Meetings. Any action that may be taken at a meeting of the Members may be taken without a meeting and without prior notice, if written consents to the action are submitted to the Company within sixty (60) days of the record date for the taking of the action, executed by Members holding a sufficient number of votes to authorize the taking of the action at a meeting at which all Members entitled to vote thereon are present and vote. All such consents shall be maintained as Company records.

4.10. Record Date. For the purposes of voting, notices of meetings, distributions, or any other rights under this Agreement, the Articles, or the Act, the Members representing in excess of ten percent (10%) of the Percentage Interests in the Company may fix, in advance, a record date that is not more than sixty (60) or less than ten (10) days prior to the date of such meeting or sixty (60) days prior to any other action. If no record date is fixed, the record date shall be determined in accordance with the Act.

4.11. Voting Rights. Except as expressly set forth in this Agreement, all actions requiring the vote, approval, or consent of the Members may be authorized upon the vote, approval, or consent of those Members holding a majority of the Percentage Interests in the Company. The following actions require the unanimous vote, approval, or consent of all Members who are neither the subjects of a dissolution event nor the transferors of a Membership Interest:

(a) Approval of the purchase by the Company or its nominee of the Membership Interest of a transferor Member;

(b) Approval of the sale, transfer, exchange, assignment, or other disposition of a Member's interest in the Company and admission of the transferee as a Member;

(c) A decision to make any amendment to the Articles or to this Agreement; and

(d) A decision to compromise the obligation of any Member to make a Capital Contribution or return money or property distributed in violation of the Act.

ARTICLE V. MANAGEMENT

5.1. Management by Members. The Company shall be managed by the Members. Each Member has the authority to manage and control the Company and to act on its behalf, except as limited by the Act, the Articles, or this Agreement.

5.2. Limitation on Exposing Members to Personal Liability. Neither the Company nor any Member may take any action that will have the effect of exposing any Member of the Company to personal liability for the obligations of the Company, without first obtaining the consent of the affected Member.

5.3. Limitation on Powers of Members. The Members shall not be authorized to permit the Company to perform the following acts or to engage in the following transactions without first obtaining the affirmative vote or written consent of the Members holding a majority Interest or such greater Percentage Interest as may be indicated below:

(a) The sale or other disposition of all or a substantial part of the Company's assets, whether occurring as a single transaction or a series of transactions over a 12-month period, except if the same is part of the orderly liquidation and winding up of the Company's affairs upon dissolution;

(b) The merger of the Company with any other business entity without the affirmative vote or written consent of all members;

(c) Any alteration of the primary purpose or business of the Company shall require the affirmative vote or written consent of Members holding at least sixty-six percent (66%) of the Percentage Interest in the Company;

(d) The establishment of different classes of Members;

(e) Transactions between the Company and one or more Members or one or more of any Member's Affiliates, or transactions in which one or more Members or Affiliates thereof have a material financial interest;

(f) Without limiting subsection (e) of this section, the lending of money to any Member or Affiliate of the Company;

(g) Any act which would prevent the Company from conducting its duly authorized business;

(h) The confession of a judgment against the Company.

Notwithstanding any other provisions of this Agreement, the written consent of all of the Members is required to permit the Company to incur an indebtedness or obligation greater than one hundred thousand dollars ($100,000.00). All checks, drafts, or other instruments requiring the Company to make payment of an amount less than fifty thousand dollars ($50,000.00) may be signed by any Member, acting alone. Any check, draft, or other instrument requiring the Company to make payment in the amount of fifty thousand dollars ($50,000.00) or more shall require the signature of two (2) Members acting together.

5.4. Fiduciary Duties. The fiduciary duties a Member owes to the Company and to the other Members of the Company are those of a partner to a partnership and to the partners of a partnership.

5.5. Liability for Acts and Omissions. As long as a Member acts in accordance with Section 5.4, no Member shall incur liability to any other Member or to the Company for any act or omission which occurs while in the performance of services for the Company.

ARTICLE VI. ALLOCATION OF PROFIT AND LOSS

6.1. Compliance with the Code. The Company intends to comply with the Code and all applicable Regulations, including without limitation the minimum gain chargeback requirements, and intends that the provisions of this Article be interpreted consistently with that intent.

6.2. Net Profits. Except as specifically provided elsewhere in this Agreement, Distributions of Net Profit shall be made to Members in proportion to their Percentage Interest in the Company.

6.3. Net Losses. Except as specifically provided elsewhere in this Agreement, Net Losses shall be allocated to the Members in proportion to their Percentage Interest in the Company. However, the foregoing will not apply to the extent that it would result in a Negative Capital Account balance for any Member equal to the Company Minimum Gain which would be realized by that Member in the event of a foreclosure of the Company's assets. Any Net Loss which is not allocated in accordance with the foregoing provision shall be allocated to other Members who are unaffected by that provision. When subsequent allocations of profit and loss are calculated, the losses reallocated pursuant to this provision shall be taken into account such that the net amount of the allocation shall be as close as possible to that which would have been allocated to each Member if the reallocation pursuant to this section had not taken place.

6.4. Regulatory Allocations. Notwithstanding the provisions of Section 6.3, the following applies:

(a) Should there be a net decrease in Company Minimum Gain in any taxable year, the Members shall specially allocate to each Member items of income and gain for that year (and, if necessary, for subsequent years) as required by the Code governing minimum gain chargeback requirements.

(b) Should there be a net decrease in Company Minimum Gain based on a Member Nonrecourse Debt in any taxable year, the Members shall first determine the extent of each Member's share of the Company Minimum Gain attributable to Member Nonrecourse Debt in accordance with the Code. The Members shall then specially allocate items of income and gain for that year (and, if necessary, for subsequent years) in accordance with the Code to each Member who has a share of the Company Nonrecourse Debt Minimum Gain.

(c) The Members shall allocate Nonrecourse Deductions for any taxable year to each Member in proportion to his or her Percentage Interest.

(d) The Members shall allocate Member Nonrecourse Deductions for any taxable year to the Member who bears the risk of loss with respect to the Nonrecourse Debt to which the Member Nonrecourse Deduction is attributable, as provided in the Code.

(e) If a Member unexpectedly receives any allocation of loss or deduction, or item thereof, or distributions which result in the Member's having a Negative Capital Account balance at the end of the taxable year greater than the Member's share of Company Minimum Gain, the Company shall specially allocate items of income and gain to that Member in a manner designed to eliminate the excess Negative Capital Account balance as rapidly as possible. Any allocations made in accordance with this provision shall taken into consideration in determining subsequent allocations under Article VI, so that, to the extent possible, the total amount allocated in this and subsequent allocations equals that which would have been allocated had there been no unexpected adjustments, allocations, and distributions and no allocation pursuant to Section 6.4(e).

(f) In accordance with Code Section 704(c) and the Regulations promulgated pursuant thereto, and notwithstanding any other provision in this Article, income, gain, loss, and deductions with respect to any property contributed to the Company shall, solely for tax purposes, be allocated among Members, taking into account any variation between the adjusted basis of the property to the Company for federal income tax purposes and its fair market value on the date of contribution. Allocations pursuant to this subsection are made solely for federal, state, and local taxes and shall not be taken into consideration in determining a Member's Capital Account or share of Net Profits or Net Losses or any other items subject to Distribution under this agreement.

6.5. Distributions. The Members may elect, by unanimous vote, to make a Distribution of assets at any time that would not be prohibited under the Act or under this Agreement. Such a Distribution shall be made in proportion to the unreturned capital contributions of each Member until all contributions have been paid, and thereafter in proportion to each Member's Percentage Interest in the Company. All such Distributions shall be made to those Persons who, according to the books and records of the Company, were the holders of record of Membership Interests on the date of the Distribution. Subject to Section 6.6, neither the Company nor any Members shall be liable for the making of any Distributions in accordance with the provisions of this section.

6.6. Limitations on Distributions.

(a) The Members shall not make any Distribution if, after giving effect to the Distribution, (1) the Company would not be able to pay its debts as they become due in the usual course of business, or (2) the Company's total assets would be less than the sum of its total liabilities plus, unless this Agreement provides otherwise, the amount that would be needed, if the Company were to be dissolved at the time of Distribution, to satisfy the preferential rights of other Members upon dissolution that are superior to the rights of the Member receiving the Distribution.

(b) The Members may base a determination that a Distribution is not prohibited under this section on any of the following: (1) financial statements prepared on the basis of accounting practices and principles that are reasonable under the circumstances, (2) a fair valuation, or (3) any other method that is reasonable under the circumstances.

6.7. Return of Distributions. Members shall return to the Company any Distributions received which are in violation of this Agreement or the Act. Such Distributions shall be returned to the account or accounts of the Company from which they were taken in order to make the Distribution. If a Distribution is made in compliance with the Act and this Agreement, a Member is under no obligation to return it to the Company or to pay the amount of the Distribution for the account of the Company or to any creditor of the Company.

6.8. Members Bound by These Provisions. The Members understand and acknowledge the tax implications of the provisions of this Article of the Agreement and agree to be bound by these provisions in reporting items of income and loss relating to the Company on their federal and state income tax returns.

ARTICLE VII. TRANSFERS AND TERMINATIONS OF MEMBERSHIP INTERESTS

7.1. Restriction on Transferability of Membership Interests. A Member may not transfer, assign, encumber, or convey all or any part of his or her Membership Interest in the Company, except as provided herein. In entering into this Agreement, each of the Members acknowledges the reasonableness of this restriction, which is intended to further the purposes of the Company and the relationships among the Members.

7.2. Permitted Transfers. In order to be permitted, a transfer or assignment of all or any part of a Membership Interest must have the approval of a two-thirds majority of the Members of the Company. Each Member, in his or her sole discretion, may proffer or withhold approval. In addition, the following conditions must be met:

(a) The transferee must provide a written agreement, satisfactory to the Members, to be bound by all of the provisions of this Agreement;

(b) The transferee must provide the Company with his or her taxpayer identification number and initial tax basis in the transferred interest;

(c) The transferee must pay the reasonable expenses incurred in connection with his or her admission to Membership;

(d) The transfer must be in compliance with all federal and state securities laws;

(e) The transfer must not result in the termination of the Company pursuant to Code Section 708.

(f) The transfer must not render the Company subject to the Investment Company Act of 1940, as amended; and

(g) The transferor must comply with the provisions of this Agreement.

7.3. Company's Right to Purchase Transferor's Interest and Valuation of Transferor's Interest. Any Member who wishes to transfer all or any part of his or her interest in the Company shall immediately provide the Company with written notice of his or her intention. The notice shall fully describe the nature of the interest to be transferred. Thereafter, the Company, or its nominee, shall have the option to purchase the transferor's interest at the Repurchase Price (as defined below).

(a) The "Repurchase Price" shall be determined as of the date of the event causing the transfer or dissolution event (the "Effective Date"). The date that the Company receives notice of a Member's intention to transfer his or her interest pursuant to this paragraph shall be deemed to be the Effective Date. The Repurchase Price shall be determined as follows:

i. The Repurchase Price of a Member's Percentage Interest shall be computed by the independent certified public accountant (CPA) regularly used by the Company or, if the Company has no CPA or if the CPA is unavailable, then by a qualified appraiser selected by the Company for this purpose. The Repurchase Price of a Member's Percentage Interest shall be the sum of the Company's total Repurchase Price multiplied by the Transferor's Percentage Interest as of the Effective Date.

ii. The Repurchase Price shall be determined by the book value method, as more further described herein. The book value of the interests shall be determined in accordance with the regular financial statements prepared by the Company and in accordance with generally accepted accounting principles, applied consistently with the accounting principles previously applied by the Company, adjusted to reflect the following:

(1) All inventory, valued at cost.

(2) All real property, leasehold improvements, equipment, and furnishings and fixtures valued at their fair market value.

(3) The face amount of any accounts payable.

(4) Any accrued taxes or assessments, deducted as liabilities.

(5) All usual fiscal year-end accruals and deferrals (including depreciation), prorated over the fiscal year.

(6) The reasonable fair market value of any good will or other intangible assets.

(b) The cost of the assessment shall be borne by the Company.

(c) The option provided to the Company shall be irrevocable and shall remain open for thirty (30) days from the Effective Date, except that if notice is given by regular mail, the option shall remain open for thirty-five (35) days from the Effective Date.

(d) At any time while the option remains open, the Company (or its nominee) may elect to exercise the option and purchase the transferor's interest in the Company. The transferor Member shall not vote on the question of whether the Company should exercise its option.

(e) If the Company chooses to exercise its option to purchase the transferor Member's interest, it shall provide written notice to the transferor within the option period. The notice shall specify a "Closing Date" for the purchase, which shall occur within thirty (30) days of the expiration of the option period.

(f) If the Company declines to exercise its option to purchase the transferor Member's interest, the transferor Member may then transfer his or her interest in accordance with Section 7.2. Any transfer not in compliance with the provisions of Section 7.2 shall be null and void and have no force or effect.

(g) In the event that the Company chooses to exercise its option to purchase the transferor Member's interest, the Company may elect to purchase the Member's interest on the following terms:

i. The Company may elect to pay the Repurchase Price in cash, by making such cash payment to the transferor Member upon the Closing Date.

ii. The Company may elect to pay any portion of the Repurchase Price by delivering to the transferor Member, upon the Closing Date, all of the following:

(1) An amount equal to at least 10% of the Repurchase Price in cash or in an immediately negotiable draft, and

(2) A Promissory Note for the remaining amount of the Repurchase Price, to be paid in 12 successive monthly installments, with such installments beginning 30 days following the Closing Date, and ending one year from the Closing Date, and

(3) A security agreement guaranteeing the payment of the Promissory Note by offering the Transferor's former membership interest as security for the payment of the Promissory Note.

7.4. Occurrence of Dissolution Event. Upon the death, withdrawal, resignation, retirement, expulsion, insanity, bankruptcy, or dissolution of any Member (a Dissolution Event), the Company shall be dissolved, unless all of the Remaining Members elect by a majority in interest within 90 days thereafter to continue the operation of the business. In the event that the Remaining Members to agree, the Company and the Remaining Members shall have the right to purchase the interest of the Member whose actions caused the occurrence of the Dissolution Event. The interest shall be sold in the manner described in Section 7.6.

7.5. Withdrawal from Membership. Notwithstanding Section 7.4, in the event that a Member withdraws in accordance with Section 4.3 and such withdrawal does not result in the dissolution of the Company, the Company and the Remaining Members shall have the right to purchase the interest of the withdrawing Member in the manner described in Section 7.6.

7.6. Purchase of Interest of Departing Member. The purchase price of a Departing Member's interest shall be determined in accordance with the procedure provided in Section 7.3.

(a) Once a value has been determined, each Remaining Member shall be entitled to purchase that portion of the Departing Member's interest that corresponds to his or her percentage ownership of the Percentage Interests of those Members electing to purchase a portion of the Departing Member's interest in the Company.

(b) Each Remaining Member desiring to purchase a share of the Departing Member's interest shall have thirty (30) days to provide written notice to the Company of his or her intention to do so. The failure to provide notice shall be deemed a rejection of the opportunity to purchase the Departing Member's interest.

(c) If any Member elects not to purchase all of the Departing Member's interest to which he or she is entitled, the other Members may purchase that portion of the Departing Member's interest. Any interest which is not purchased by the Remaining Members may be purchased by the Company.

(d) The Members shall assign a closing date within 60 days after the Members' election to purchase is completed. At that time, the Departing Member shall deliver to the Remaining Members an instrument of title, free of any encumbrances and containing warranties of title, duly conveying his or her interest in the Company and, in return, he or she shall be paid the purchase price for his or her interest in cash. The Departing Member and the Remaining Members shall perform all acts reasonably necessary to consummate the transaction in accordance with this agreement.

7.7. No Release of Liability. Any Member or Departing Member whose interest in the Company is sold pursuant to Article VII is not relieved thereby of any liability he or she may owe the Company.

ARTICLE VIII. BOOKS, RECORDS, AND REPORTING

8.1. Books and Records. The Members shall maintain at the Company's principal place of business the following books and records: a current list of the full name and last known business or residence address of each Member together with the Capital Contribution, Capital Account, and Membership Interest of each Member; a copy of the Articles and all amendments thereto; copies of the Company's federal, state; and local income tax or information returns and reports, if any; for the six (6) most recent taxable years; a copy of this Agreement and any amendments to it; copies of the Company's financial statements, if any; the books and records of the Company as they relate to its internal affairs for at least the current and past four (4) fiscal years; and true and correct copies of all relevant documents and records indicating the amount, cost, and value of all the property and assets of the Company.

8.2. Accounting Methods. The books and records of the Company shall be maintained in accordance with the accounting methods utilized for federal income tax purposes.

8.3. Reports. The Members shall cause to be prepared and filed in a timely manner all reports and documents required by any governmental agency. The Members shall cause to be prepared at least annually all information concerning the Company's operations that is required by the Members for the preparation of their federal and state tax returns.

8.4. Inspection Rights. For purposes reasonably related to their interests in the Company, all Members shall have the right to inspect and copy the books and records of the Company during normal business hours, upon reasonable request.

8.5. Bank Accounts. The Members shall maintain all of the funds of the Company in a bank account or accounts in the name of the Company, at a depository institution or institutions to be determined by a majority of the Members. The Members shall not permit the funds of the Company to be commingled in any manner with the funds or accounts of any other Person. The Members shall have the powers enumerated in Section 5.3 with respect to endorsing, signing, and negotiating checks, drafts, or other evidence of indebtedness to the Company or obligating the Company money to a third party.

ARTICLE IX. DISSOLUTION, LIQUIDATION, AND WINDING UP

9.1. Conditions Under Which Dissolution Shall Occur. The Company shall dissolve and its affairs shall be wound up upon the happening of the first of the following: at the time specified in the Articles; upon the happening of a Dissolution Event and the failure of the Remaining Members to elect to continue, in accordance with Section 7.4; upon the vote of all of the Members to dissolve; upon the entry of a decree of judicial dissolution pursuant to the Act; upon the happening of any event specified in the Articles as causing or requiring dissolution; or upon the sale of all or substantially all of the Company's assets.

9.2. Winding Up and Dissolution. If the Company is dissolved, the Members shall wind up its affairs, including the selling of all of the Company's assets and the provision of written notification to all of the Company's creditors of the commencement of dissolution proceedings.

9.3. Order of Payment. After determining that all known debts and liabilities of the Company in the process of winding up have been paid or provided for, including, without limitation, debts and liabilities to Members who are creditors of the Company, the Members shall distribute the remaining assets among the Members in accordance with their Positive Capital Account balances, after taking into consideration the profit and loss allocations made pursuant to Section 6.4. Members shall not be required to restore Negative Capital Account Balances.

ARTICLE X. INDEMNIFICATION

10.1. Indemnification. The Company shall indemnify any Member and may indemnify any Person to the fullest extent permitted by law on the date such indemnification is requested for any judgments, settlements, penalties, fines, or expenses of any kind incurred as a result of the Person's performance in the capacity of Member, officer, employee, or agent of the Company, as long as the Member or Person did not behave in violation of the Act or this Agreement.

ARTICLE XI. MISCELLANEOUS PROVISIONS

11.1. Assurances. Each Member shall execute all documents and certificates and perform all acts deemed appropriate by the Members and the Company or required by this Agreement or the Act in connection with the formation and operation of the Company and the acquisition, holding, or operation of any property by the Company.

11.2. Complete Agreement. This Agreement and the Articles constitute the complete and exclusive statement of the agreement among the Members with respect to the matters discussed herein and therein and they supersede all prior written or oral statements among the Members, including any prior statement, warranty, or representation.

11.3. Section Headings. The section headings which appear throughout this Agreement are provided for convenience only and are not intended to define or limit the scope of this Agreement or the intent of subject matter of its provisions.

11.4. Binding Effect. Subject to the provisions of this Agreement relating to the transferability of Membership Interests, this Agreement is binding upon and shall inure to the benefit of the parties hereto and their respective heirs, administrators, executors, successors, and assigns.

11.5. Interpretation. All pronouns and common nouns shall be deemed to refer to the masculine, feminine, neuter, singular, and plural, as the context may require. In the event that any claim is made by any Member relating to the drafting and interpretation of this Agreement, no presumption, inference, or burden of proof or persuasion shall be created or implied solely by virtue of the fact that this Agreement was drafted by or at the behest of a particular Member or his or her counsel.

11.6. Applicable Law. Each Member agrees that all disputes arising under or in connection with this Agreement and any transactions contemplated by this Agreement shall be governed by the internal law, and not the law of conflicts, of the state of organization.

11.7. Specific Performance. The Members acknowledge and agree that irreparable injury shall result from a breach of this Agreement and that money damages will not adequately compensate the injured party. Accordingly, in the event of a breach or a threatened breach of this Agreement, any party who may be injured shall be entitled, in addition to any other remedy which may be available, to injunctive relief to prevent or to correct the breach.

11.8. Remedies Cumulative. The remedies described in this Agreement are cumulative and shall not eliminate any other remedy to which a Person may be lawfully entitled.

11.9. Notice. Any notice or other writing to be served upon the Company or any Member thereof in connection with this Agreement shall be in writing and shall be deemed completed when delivered to the address specified in Table A, if to a Member, and to the resident agent, if to the Company. Any Member shall have the right to change the address at which notices shall be served upon ten (10) days' written notice to the Company and the other Members.

11.10. Amendments. Any amendments, modifications, or alterations to this Agreement or the Articles must be in writing and signed by all of the Members.

11.11. Severability. Each provision of this Agreement is severable from the other provisions. If, for any reason, any provision of this Agreement is declared invalid or contrary to existing law, the inoperability of that provision shall have no effect on the remaining provisions of the Agreement, which shall continue in full force and effect.

11.12. Counterparts. This Agreement may be executed in counterparts, each of which shall be deemed an original and all of which shall, when taken together, constitute a single document.

IN WITNESS WHEREOF, this Agreement has been made and executed by the Members effective as of the date first written above.

_____ (Member)

_____ (Member)

_____ (Member)

Table A: Name, Address, and Initial Capital Contribution of the Members

Name and Address of Member	Value of Initial Capital Contribution	Nature of Member's Initial Capital Contribution (i.e., cash, services, property)	Member's Percentage Interest

LLC Form 6. Short-Form Operating Agreement for Manager-Managed LLC

OPERATING AGREEMENT OF (insert full name of LLC)

THIS OPERATING AGREEMENT (the "Agreement") is hereby entered into by the undersigned, who are owners and shall be referred to as Member or Members.

RECITALS

The Members desire to form (insert full name of LLC), a limited liability company (the "Company"), for the purposes set forth herein, and, accordingly, desire to enter into this Agreement in order to set forth the terms and conditions of the business and affairs of the Company and to determine the rights and obligations of its Members.

NOW, THEREFORE, the Members, intending to be legally bound by this Agreement, hereby agree that the limited liability company operating agreement of the Company shall be as follows:

ARTICLE I. DEFINITIONS

When used in this Agreement, the following terms shall have the meanings set forth below.

1.1 "Act" means the Limited Liability Company Law of the State in which the Company is organized or chartered, including any amendments or the corresponding provision(s) of any succeeding law.

1.2 "Capital Contribution(s)" means the amount of cash and the agreed value of property, services rendered, or a promissory note or other obligation to contribute cash or property or to perform services contributed by the Members for such Members' Interest in the Company, equal to the sum of the Members' initial Capital Contributions plus the Members' additional Capital Contributions, if any, made pursuant to Sections 4.1 and 4.2, respectively, less payments or distributions made pursuant to Section 5.1.

1.3 "Code" means the Internal Revenue Code of 1986 and the regulations promulgated thereunder, as amended from time to time (or any corresponding provision or provisions of succeeding law).

1.4 "Interest" or "Interests" means the ownership Interest, expressed as a number, percentage, or fraction, set forth in Table A, of a Member in the Company.

1.5 "Manager" or "Managers" means the natural person or persons who have authority to govern the Company according to the terms of this Agreement.

1.6 "Person" means any natural individual, partnership, firm, corporation, limited liability company, joint-stock company, trust, or other entity.

1.7 "Secretary of State" means the Office of the Secretary of State or the office charged with accepting articles of organization in the Company's state of organization.

ARTICLE II. FORMATION

2.1 Organization. The Members hereby organize the Company as a limited liability company pursuant to the provisions of the Act.

2.2 Effective Date. The Company shall come into being on, and this Agreement shall take effect from, the date the Articles of Organization of the Company are filed with the Secretary of State in the state of organization or charter.

2.3 Agreement: Invalid Provisions and Saving Clause. The Members, by executing this Agreement, hereby agree to the terms and conditions of this Agreement. To the extent any provision of this Agreement is prohibited or ineffective under the Act, this Agreement shall be deemed to be amended to the least extent necessary in order to make this Agreement effective under the Act. In the event the Act is subsequently amended or interpreted in such a way to validate any provision of this Agreement that was formerly invalid, such provision shall be considered to be valid from the effective date of such amendment or interpretation.

ARTICLE III. PURPOSE; NATURE OF BUSINESS

3.1 Purpose; Nature of Business. The purpose of the Company shall be to engage in any lawful business that may be engaged in by a limited liability company organized under the Act, as such business activities may be determined by the Manager or Managers from time to time.

3.2 Powers. The Company shall have all powers of a limited liability company under the Act and the power to do all things necessary or convenient to accomplish its purpose and operate its business as described in Section 3.1 here.

ARTICLE IV. MEMBERS AND CAPITAL CONTRIBUTIONS

4.1 Members and Initial Capital Contribution. The name, address, Interest, type of property, and value of the initial Capital Contribution of the Members shall be set forth on Table A attached hereto.

4.2 Additional Capital Contributions. The Members shall have no obligation to make any additional Capital Contributions to the Company. The Members may make additional Capital Contributions to the Company as the Members unanimously determine are necessary, appropriate, or desirable.

ARTICLE V. DISTRIBUTIONS AND ALLOCATIONS

5.1 Distributions and Allocations. All distributions of cash or other assets of the Company shall be made and paid to the Members at such time and in such amounts as a majority of the Managers may determine. All items of income, gain, loss, deduction, and credit shall be allocated to the Members in proportion to their Interests.

ARTICLE VI. TAXATION

6.1 Income Tax Reporting. Each Member is aware of the income tax consequences of the allocations made by Article V here and agrees to be bound by the provisions of Article V here in reporting each Member's share of Company income and loss for federal and state income tax purposes.

6.2 Tax Treatment. Notwithstanding anything contained herein to the contrary and only for purposes of federal and, if applicable, state income tax purposes, the Company shall be classified as a partnership for such federal and state income tax purposes unless and until the Members determine to cause the Company to file an election under the Code to be classified as an association taxable as a corporation.

ARTICLE VII. MANAGERS AND AGENTS

7.1 Management by Manager(s). The Members shall elect and appoint the Manager(s), who shall have the full and exclusive right, power, and authority to manage the affairs of the Company and to bind the Company to contracts and obligations, to make all decisions with respect thereto, and to do or cause to be done any and all acts or things deemed by the Members to be necessary, appropriate, or desirable to carry out or further the business of the Company. All decisions and actions of the Manager(s) shall be made by majority vote of the Manager(s) as provided in Section 12.3. No annual meeting shall be required to reappoint Manager(s). Such Person(s) shall serve in such office(s) at the pleasure of the Members and until his, her, or their successors are duly elected and appointed by the Members. Until further action of the Members as provided herein, the Manager(s) whose names appear on Table B below are the Manager(s) of the Company.

7.2 Agents. Without limiting the rights of the Members, the Manager(s), or the Company, the Manager(s) shall appoint the Person(s) who is (are) to act as the agent(s) of the Company to carry out and further the decisions and actions of the Members or the Manager(s), to manage and the administer the day-to-day operations and business of the Company, and to execute any and all reports, forms, instruments, documents, papers, writings, agreements, and contracts, including but not limited to deeds, bills of sale, assignments, leases, promissory notes, mortgages, and security agreements and any other type or form of document by which property or property rights of the Company are transferred or encumbered, or by which debts and obligations of the Company are created, incurred, or evidenced, which are necessary, appropriate, or beneficial to carry out or further such decisions or actions and to manage and administer the day-to-day operations and business.

ARTICLE VIII. BOOKS AND RECORDS

8.1 Books and Records. The Managers shall keep, or cause to be kept, at the principal place of business of the Company true and correct books of account, in which shall be entered fully and accurately each and every transaction of the Company. The Company's taxable and fiscal years shall end on December 31. All Members shall have the right to inspect the Company's books and records at any time, for any reason.

ARTICLE IX. LIMITATION OF LIABILITY; INDEMNIFICATION

9.1 Limited Liability. Except as otherwise required by law, the debts, obligations, and liabilities of the Company, whether arising in contract, tort, or otherwise, shall be solely the debts, obligations, and liabilities of the Company, and the Members shall not be obligated personally for any such debt, obligation, or liability of the Company solely by reason of being Members. The failure of the Company to observe any formalities or requirements relating to the exercise of its powers or the management of its business or affairs under this Agreement or by law shall not be grounds for imposing personal liability on the Members for any debts, liabilities, or obligations of the Company. Except as otherwise expressly required by law, the Members, in such Members' capacity as such, shall have no liability in excess of (a) the amount of such Members' Capital Contributions, (b) such Members' share of any assets and undistributed profits of the Company, and (c) the amount of any distributions required to be returned according to law.

9.2 Indemnification. The Company shall, to the fullest extent provided or allowed by law, indemnify, save harmless, and pay all judgments and claims against the Members or Manager(s), and each of the Company's, Members', or Manager(s)' agents, affiliates, heirs, legal representatives, successors, and assigns (each, an "Indemnified Party") from, against, and in respect of any and all liability, loss, damage, and expense incurred or sustained by the Indemnified Party in connection with the business of the Company or by reason of any act performed or omitted to be performed in connection with the activities of the Company or in dealing with third parties on behalf of the Company, including costs and attorneys' fees before and at trial and at all appellate levels, whether or not suit is instituted (which attorneys' fees may be paid as incurred), and any amounts expended in the settlement of any claims of liability, loss, or damage, to the fullest extent allowed by law.

9.3. Insurance. The Company shall not pay for any insurance covering liability of the Members or the Manager(s) or the Company's, Members', or Manager(s)' agents, affiliates, heirs, legal representatives, successors, and assigns for actions or omissions for which indemnification is not permitted hereunder; provided, however, that nothing contained here shall preclude the Company from purchasing and paying for such types of insurance, including extended coverage liability and casualty and worker's compensation, as would be customary for any Person owning, managing, and/or operating comparable property and engaged in a similar business, or from naming the Members or the Manager(s) and any of the Company's, Members', or Manager(s)' agents, affiliates, heirs, legal representatives, successors, or assigns or any Indemnified Party as additional insured parties thereunder.

9.4 Non-Exclusive Right. The provisions of this Article IX shall be in addition to and not in limitation of any other rights of indemnification and reimbursement or limitations of liability to which an Indemnified Party may be entitled under the Act, common law, or otherwise.

ARTICLE X. AMENDMENT

10.1 Amendment. This Agreement may not be altered or modified except by the unanimous written consent or agreement of the Members as evidenced by an amendment hereto whereby this Agreement is amended or amended and restated.

ARTICLE XI. WITHDRAWAL

11.1 Withdrawal of a Member. No Member may withdraw from the Company except by written request of the Member given to each of the other Members and with the unanimous written consent of the other Members (the effective date of withdrawal being the date on which the unanimous written consent of all of the other Members is given) or upon the effective date of any of the following events:

(a) the Member makes an assignment of his or her property for the benefit of creditors;

(b) the Member files a voluntary petition of bankruptcy;

(c) the Member is adjudged bankrupt or insolvent or there is entered against the Member an order for relief in any bankruptcy or insolvency proceeding;

(d) the Member seeks, consents to, or acquiesces in the appointment of a trustee or receiver for, or liquidation of the Member or of all or any substantial part of the Member's property;

(e) the Member files an answer or other pleading admitting or failing to contest the material allegations of a petition filed against the Member in any proceeding described in Subsections 11.1 (a) through (d);

(f) if the Member is a corporation, the dissolution of the corporation or the revocation of its articles of incorporation or charter;

(g) if the Member is an estate, the distribution by the fiduciary of the estate's Interest in the Company;

(h) if the Member is an employee of the Company and he or she resigns, retires, or for any reason ceases to be employed by the Company in any capacity; or

(i) if the other Members owning more than fifty percent (50%) of the Interests vote or request in writing that a Member withdraw and such request is given to the Member (the effective date of withdrawal being the date on which the vote or written request of the other Members is given to the Member).

11.2 Valuation of Interest. The value of the withdrawing Member's Interest in all events shall be equal to the greater of the following: (a) the amount of the Member's Capital Contribution or (b) the amount of the Member's share of the Members' equity in the Company, plus the amount of any unpaid and outstanding loans or advances made by the Member to the Company (plus any due and unpaid interest thereon, if interest on the loan or advance has been agreed to between the Company and the Member), calculated as of the end of the fiscal quarter immediately preceding the effective date of the Member's withdrawal.

11.3 Payment of Value. The value shall be payable as follows: (a) If the value is equal to or less than $500, at closing, and (b) If the value is greater than $500, at the option of the Company, $500 at closing with the balance of the purchase price paid by delivering a promissory note of the Company dated as of the closing date and bearing interest at the prime rate published in *The Wall Street Journal* as of the effective date of withdrawal, with the principal amount being payable in five (5) equal annual installments beginning one (1) year from closing and with the interest on the accrued and unpaid balance being payable at the time of payment of each principal installment.

11.4 Closing. Payment of the value of the departing Member's Interest shall be made at a mutually agreeable time and date on or before thirty (30) days from the effective date of withdrawal. Upon payment of the value of the Interest as calculated in Section 11.3 above: (a) the Member's right to receive any and all further payments or distributions on account of the Member's ownership of the Interest in the Company shall cease; (b) the Member's loans or advances to the Company shall be paid and satisfied in full; and (c) the Member shall no longer be a Member or creditor of the Company on account of the Capital Contribution or the loans or advances.

11.5 Limitation on Payment of Value. If payment of the value of the Interest would be prohibited by any statute or law prohibiting distributions that would

(a) render the Company insolvent; or

(b) be made at a time that the total Company liabilities (other than liabilities to Members on account of their Interests) exceed the value of the Company's total assets;

then the value of the withdrawing Member's Interest in all events shall be $1.00.

ARTICLE XII. MISCELLANEOUS PROVISIONS

12.1 Assignment of Interest and New Members. No Member may assign such person's Interest in the Company in whole or in part except by the vote or written consent of the other Members owning more than fifty percent (50%) of the Interests. No additional Person may be admitted as a Member except by the vote or written consent of the Members owning more than fifty percent (50%) of the Interests.

12.2 Determinations by Members: Except as required by the express provisions of this Agreement or of the Act:

(a) Any transaction, action, or decision which requires or permits the Members to consent to, approve, elect, appoint, adopt, or authorize or to make a determination or decision with respect thereto under this Agreement, the Act, the Code, or otherwise shall be made by the Members owning more than fifty percent (50%) of the Interests.

(b) The Members shall act at a meeting of Members or by consent in writing of the Members. Members may vote or give their consent in person or by proxy.

(c) Meetings of the Members may be held at any time, upon call of any Manager or a Member or Members owning, in the aggregate, at least ten percent (10%) of the Interests.

(d) Unless waived in writing by the Members owning more than fifty percent (50%) of the Interests (before or after a meeting), at least two (2) business days' prior notice of any meeting shall be given to each Member. Such notice shall state the purpose for which such meeting has been called. No business may be conducted or action taken at such meeting that is not provided for in such notice.

(e) Members may participate in a meeting of Members by means of conference telephone or similar communications equipment by means of which all Persons participating in the meeting can hear each other, and such participation shall constitute presence in person at such meeting.

(f) The Managers shall cause to be kept a book of minutes of all meetings of the Members in which there shall be recorded the time and place of such meeting, by whom such meeting was called, the notice thereof given, the names of those present, and the proceedings thereof. Copies of any consents in writing shall also be filed in such minutes book.

12.3 Determinations by Managers. Except as required by the express provisions of this Agreement or of the Act and if there shall be more than one Manager:

(a) Any transaction, action, or decision which requires or permits the Managers to consent to, approve, elect, appoint, adopt, or authorize or to make a determination or decision with respect thereto under this Agreement, the Act, the Code, or otherwise shall be made by a majority of the Managers.

(b) The Managers shall act only at a meeting of the Managers or by consent in writing of the Managers. Managers may vote or give their consent in person only and not by proxy.

(c) Meetings of the Managers may be held at any time, upon call of any agent of the Company appointed pursuant to Section 7.2 of this Agreement or any Manager.

(d) Notice of any meeting shall be given to a majority of the Managers at any time prior to the meeting, in writing or by verbal communication. Such notice need not state the purpose for which such meeting has been called.

(e) The Managers may participate in a meeting of the Managers by means of conference telephone or similar communications equipment by means of which all Persons participating in the meeting can hear each other, and such participation shall constitute presence in person at such meeting.

(f) The Managers may cause to be kept a book of minutes of all meetings of the Managers in which there shall be recorded the time and place of such meeting, by whom such meeting was called, the notice thereof given, the names of those present, and the proceedings thereof. Copies of any consents in writing shall also be filed in such minute book.

12.4 Binding Effect. This Agreement shall be binding upon and inure to the benefit of the undersigned, their legal representatives, heirs, successors, and assigns. This Agreement and the rights and duties of the Members hereunder shall be governed by, and interpreted and construed in accordance with, the laws of the State of Florida, without regard to principles of choice of law.

12.5 Headings. The article and section headings in this Agreement are inserted as a matter of convenience and are for reference only and shall not be construed to define, limit, extend, or describe the scope of this Agreement or the intent of any provision.

12.6 Number and Gender. Whenever required by the context here, the singular shall include the plural, and vice versa, and the masculine gender shall include the feminine and neuter genders, and vice versa.

12.7 Entire Agreement and Binding Effect. This Agreement constitutes the sole operating agreement among the Members and supersedes and cancels any prior agreements, representations, warranties, or communications, whether oral or written, between the Members relating to the affairs of the Company and the conduct of the Company's business. No amendment or modification of this Agreement shall be effective unless approved in writing as provided in Section 10.1. The Articles of Organization and this Agreement are binding upon and shall inure to the benefit of the Members and Agent(s) and shall be binding upon their successors, assigns, affiliates, subsidiaries, heirs, beneficiaries, personal representatives, executors, administrators, and guardians, as applicable and appropriate.

IN WITNESS WHEREOF, this Agreement has been made and executed by the Members effective as of the date first written above.

_____ (Member)

_____ (Member)

_____ (Member)

Table A: Name, Address, and Initial Capital Contribution of the Members

Name and Address of Member	Value of Initial Capital Contribution	Nature of Member's Initial Capital Contribution (i.e., cash, services, property)	Percentage Interest of Member

Table B: Managers

Name of Manager	Address of Manager

LLC Form 7. Long-Form Operating Agreement for Manager-Managed LLC

OPERATING AGREEMENT OF (insert full name), LLC

THIS OPERATING AGREEMENT (the "Agreement") is made and entered into on _____, 20__, and those persons whose names, addresses and signatures are set forth below, being the Members of (insert name), LLC (the "Company"), represent and agree that they have caused or will cause to be filed, on behalf of the Company, Articles of Organization, and that they desire to enter into an operating agreement.

The Members agree as follows:

ARTICLE I. DEFINITIONS

1.1. "Act" means the Limited Liability Company Law of the State in which the Company is organized or chartered, including any amendments or the corresponding provision(s) of any succeeding law.

1.2. "Affiliate" or "Affiliate of a Member" means any Person under the control of, in common control with, or in control of a Member, whether that control is direct or indirect. The term "control," as used herein, means, with respect to a corporation or limited liability company, the ability to exercise more than fifty percent (50%) of the voting rights of the controlled entity, and with respect to an individual, partnership, trust, or other entity or association, the ability, directly or indirectly, to direct the management of policies of the controlled entity or individual.

1.3. "Agreement" means this Operating Agreement, in its original form and as amended from time to time.

1.4. "Articles" means the Articles of Organization or other charter document filed with the Secretary of State in the state of organization forming this limited liability company, as initially filed and as they may be amended from time to time.

1.5. "Capital Account" means the amount of the capital interest of a Member in the Company, consisting of the amount of money and the fair market value, net of liabilities, of any property initially contributed by the Member, as (1) increased by any additional contributions and the Member's share of the Company's profits; and (2) decreased by any distribution to that Member as well as that Member's share of Company losses.

1.6. "Code" means the Internal Revenue Code of 1986, as amended from time to time, the regulations promulgated thereunder, and any corresponding provision of any succeeding revenue law.

1.7. "Company Minimum Gain" shall have the same meaning as set forth for the term "Partnership Minimum Gain" in the Regulations section 1.704-2(d) (26 CFR Section1.704-2(d)).

1.8. "Departing Member" means any Member whose conduct results in a Dissolution Event or who withdraws from or is expelled from the Company in accordance with Section 4.3, where such withdrawal does not result in dissolution of the Company.

1.9. "Dissolution Event" means, with respect to any Member, one or more of the following: the death, resignation, retirement, expulsion, bankruptcy, or dissolution of any Member.

1.10. "Distribution" means the transfer of money or property by the Company to the Members without consideration.

1.11 "Manager" means each Person who has been appointed to serve as a Manager of the Company in accordance with the Act, the Articles, and this Agreement.

1.12. "Member" means each Person who has been admitted into membership in the Company, executes this Agreement and any subsequent amendments, and has not engaged in conduct resulting in a Dissolution Event or terminated membership for any other reason.

1.13. "Member Nonrecourse Debt" shall have the same meaning as set forth for the term "Partnership Nonrecourse Debt" in the Code.

1.14. "Member Nonrecourse Deductions" means items of Company loss, deduction, or Code Section 705(a)(2)(B) expenditures which are attributable to Member Nonrecourse Debt.

1.15. "Membership Interest" means a Member's rights in the Company, collectively, including the Member's economic interest, right to vote and participate in management, and right to information concerning the business and affairs of the Company provided in this Agreement or under the Act.

1.16. "Net Profits" and "Net Losses" mean the Company's income, loss, and deductions computed at the close of each fiscal year in accordance with the accounting methods used to prepare the Company's information tax return filed for federal income tax purposes.

1.17. "Nonrecourse Liability" has the meaning provided in the Code.

1.18. "Percentage Interest" means the percentage ownership of the Company of each Member as set forth in the column entitled "Member's Percentage Interest" contained in Table A as recalculated from time to time pursuant to this Agreement.

1.19. "Person" means an individual, partnership, limited partnership, corporation, limited liability company, registered limited liability partnership, trust, association, estate, or any other entity.

1.20. "Remaining Members" means, upon the occurrence of a Dissolution Event, those members of the Company whose conduct did not cause its occurrence.

ARTICLE II. FORMATION AND ORGANIZATION

2.1. Initial Date and Initial Parties. This Agreement is deemed entered into upon the date of the filing of the Company's Articles.

2.2. Subsequent Parties. No Person may become a Member of the Company without agreeing to and without becoming a signatory of this Agreement, and any offer or assignment of a Membership Interest is contingent upon the fulfillment of this condition.

2.3. Term. The Company shall commence upon the filing of its Articles and it shall continue in existence until December 31, 2050, unless terminated earlier under the provisions of this Agreement.

2.4. Principal Place of Business. The Company will have its principal place of business at (insert address of principal place of business) or at any other address upon which the Members agree. The Company shall maintain its principal executive offices at its principal place of business, as well as all required records and documents.

2.5. Authorization and Purpose. The purpose of the Company is to engage in any lawful business activity that is permitted by the Act.

ARTICLE III. CAPITAL CONTRIBUTIONS AND ACCOUNTS

3.1. Initial Capital Contributions. The initial capital contribution of each Member is listed in Table A attached hereto. Table A shall be revised to reflect and additional contributions pursuant to Section 3.2.

3.2. Additional Contributions. No Member shall be required to make any additional contributions to the Company. However, upon agreement by the Members that additional capital is desirable or necessary, any Member may, but shall not be required to, contribute additional capital to the Company on a pro rata basis consistent with the Percentage Interest of each of the Members.

3.3. Interest Payments. No Member shall be entitled to receive interest payments in connection with any contribution of capital to the Company, except as expressly provided herein.

3.4. Right to Return of Contributions. No Member shall be entitled to a return of any capital contributed to the Company, except as expressly provided in the Agreement.

3.5. Capital Accounts. A Capital Account shall be created and maintained by the Company for each Member, in conformance with the Code, which shall reflect all Capital Contributions to the Company. Should any Member transfer or assign all or any part of his or her membership interest in accordance with this Agreement, the successor shall receive that portion of the Member's Capital Account attributable to the interest assigned or transferred.

ARTICLE IV. MEMBERS

4.1. Limitation of Liability. No Member shall be personally liable for the debts, obligations, liabilities, or judgments of the Company solely by virtue of his or her Membership in the Company, except as expressly set forth in this Agreement or required by law.

4.2. Additional Members. The Members may admit additional Members to the Company only if approved by a two-thirds majority in interest of the Company Membership. Additional Members shall be permitted to participate in management at the discretion of the existing Members. Likewise, the existing Members shall agree upon an Additional Member's participation in Net Profits, Net Losses, and Distributions, as those terms are defined in this Agreement. Table A shall be amended to include the name, present mailing address, and percentage ownership of any Additional Members.

4.3. Withdrawal or Expulsion from Membership. Any Member may withdraw at any time after sixty (60) days' written notice to the company, without prejudice to the rights of the Company or any Member under any contract to which the withdrawing Member is a party. Such withdrawing Member shall have the rights of a transferee under this Agreement and the remaining Members shall be entitled to purchase the withdrawing Member's Membership Interest in accordance with this Agreement. Any Member may be expelled from the Company upon a vote of two-thirds majority in interest of the Company Membership. Such expelled Member shall have the rights of a transferee under this Agreement and the remaining Members shall be entitled to purchase the expelled Member's Membership Interest in accordance with this Agreement.

4.4. Competing Activities. The Members and their officers, directors, shareholders, partners, managers, agents, employees, and Affiliates are permitted to participate in other business activities which may be in competition, direct or indirect, with those of the Company. The Members further acknowledge that they are under no obligation to present to the Company any business or investment opportunities, even if the opportunities are of such a character as to be appropriate for the Company's undertaking. Each Member hereby waives the right to any claim against any other Member or Affiliate on account of such competing activities.

4.5. Compensation of Members. No Member or Affiliate shall be entitled to compensation for services rendered to the Company, absent agreement by the Members. However, Members and Affiliates shall be entitled to reimbursement for the actual cost of goods and services provided to the Company, including, without limitation, reimbursement for any professional services required to form the Company.

4.6. Transaction with the Company. The Members may permit a Member to lend money to and transact business with the Company, subject to any limitations contained in this Agreement or in the Act. To the extent permitted by applicable laws, such a Member shall be treated like any other Person with respect to transactions with the Company.

4.7. Meetings.

(a) There will be no regular or annual meeting of the Members. However, any Member(s) with an aggregate Percentage Interest of ten percent (10%) or more may call a meeting of the Members at any time. Such meeting shall be held at a place to be agreed upon by the Members.

(b) Minutes of the meeting shall be made and maintained along with the books and records of the Company.

(c) If any action on the part of the Members is to be proposed at the meeting, then written notice of the meeting must be provided to each Member entitled to vote not less than ten (10) days or more than sixty (60) days prior to the meeting. Notice may be given in person, by fax, by first class mail, or by any other written communication, charges prepaid, at the Members' address listed in Table A. The notice shall contain the date, time, and place of the meeting and a statement of the general nature of this business to be transacted there.

4.8. Actions at Meetings.

(a) No action may be taken at a meeting that was not proposed in the notice of the meeting, unless there is unanimous consent among all Members entitled to vote.

(b) No action may be taken at a meeting unless a quorum of Members is present, either in person or by proxy. A quorum of Members shall consist of Members holding a majority of the Percentage Interest in the Company.

(c) A Member may participate in, and is deemed present at, any meeting by clearly audible conference telephone or other similar means of communication.

(d) Any meeting may be adjourned upon the vote of the majority of the Membership Interests represented at the meeting.

(e) Actions taken at any meeting of the Members have full force and effect if each Member who was not present in person or by proxy, signs a written waiver of notice and consent to the holding of the meeting or approval of the minutes of the meeting. All such waivers and consents shall become Company records.

(f) Presence at a meeting constitutes a waiver of the right to object to notice of a meeting, unless the Member expresses such an objection at the start of the meeting.

4.9. Actions Without Meetings. Any action that may be taken at a meeting of the Members may be taken without a meeting and without prior notice, if written consents to the action are submitted to the Company within sixty (60) days of the record date for the taking of the action, executed by Members holding a sufficient number of votes to authorize the taking of the action at a meeting at which all Members entitled to vote thereon are present and vote. All such consents shall be maintained as Company records.

4.10. Record Date. For the purposes of voting, notices of meetings, distributions, or any other rights under this Agreement, the Articles, or the Act, the Members representing in excess of ten percent (10%) of the Percentage Interests in the Company may fix, in advance, a record date that is not more than sixty (60) or less than ten (10) days prior to the date of such meeting or sixty (60) days prior to any other action. If no record date is fixed, the record date shall be determined in accordance with the Act.

4.11. Voting Rights. Except as expressly set forth in this Agreement, all actions requiring the vote, approval, or consent of the Members may be authorized upon the vote, approval, or consent of those Members holding a majority of the Percentage Interests in the Company. The following actions require the unanimous vote, approval, or consent of all Members who are neither the subjects of a dissolution event nor the transferors of a Membership Interest:

(a) Approval of the purchase by the Company or its nominee of the Membership Interest of a transferor Member;

(b) Approval of the sale, transfer, exchange, assignment, or other disposition of a Member's interest in the Company, and admission of the transferee as a Member;

(c) A decision to make any amendment to the Articles or to this Agreement; and

(d) A decision to compromise the obligation to any Member to make a Capital Contribution or return money or property distributed in violation of the Act.

ARTICLE V. MANAGEMENT

5.1. Management by Appointed Managers. The Company shall be managed by one or more appointed Managers. The number of Managers and the identity of each Manager are set forth in Table B, below. The Members shall elect and appoint the Managers (and also determine the number of managers), who shall have the full and exclusive right, power, and authority to manage the affairs of the Company and to bind the Company to contracts and obligations, to make all decisions with respect thereto, and to do or cause to be done any and all acts or things deemed by the Members to be necessary, appropriate, or desirable to carry out or further the business of the Company. All decisions and actions of the Managers shall be made by majority vote of the Managers as provided in this Agreement. There shall be no annual meetings of the Members or Managers; Managers shall serve at the pleasure of the Members and until their successors and are duly elected and appointed by the Members.

5.2. Limitation on Powers of Managers; Member Vote Required for Some Actions. The Mangers shall not be authorized to permit the Company to perform the following acts or to engage in the following transactions without first obtaining the affirmative vote or written consent of the Members holding a majority Interest or such greater Percentage Interest as may be indicated below:

(a) The sale or other disposition of all or a substantial part of the Company's assets, whether occurring as a single transaction or a series of transactions over a 12-month period, except if the same is part of the orderly liquidation and winding up of the Company's affairs upon dissolution;

(b) The merger of the Company with any other business entity without the affirmative vote or written consent of all members;

(c) Any alteration of the primary purpose or business of the Company shall require the affirmative vote or written consent of Members holding at least sixty-six percent (66%) of the Percentage Interest in the Company;

(d) The establishment of different classes of Members;

(e) Transactions between the Company and one or more Members or one or more of any Member's Affiliates, or transactions in which one or more Members or Affiliates thereof have a material financial interest;

(f) Without limiting subsection (e) of this section, the lending of money to any Member or Affiliate of the Company;

(g) Any act which would prevent the Company from conducting its duly authorized business;

(h) The confession of a judgment against the Company.

Notwithstanding any other provisions of this Agreement, the written consent of all of the Members is required to permit the Company to incur an indebtedness or obligation greater than one hundred thousand dollars ($100,000.00). All checks, drafts, or other instruments requiring the Company to make payment of an amount less than fifty thousand dollars ($50,000.00) may be signed by any Member, acting alone. Any check, draft, or other instrument requiring the Company to make payment in the amount of fifty thousand dollars ($50,000.00) or more shall require the signature of two (2) Members acting together.

5.3. Fiduciary Duties. The fiduciary duties a Member owes to the Company and to the other Members of the Company are those of a partner to a partnership and to the partners of a partnership.

5.4. Liability for Acts and Omissions. As long as a Member acts in accordance with Section 5.3, no Member shall incur liability to any other Member or to the Company for any act or omission which occurs while in the performance of services for the Company.

ARTICLE VI. ALLOCATION OF PROFIT AND LOSS

6.1. Compliance with the Code. The Company intends to comply with the Code and all applicable Regulations, including without limitation the minimum gain chargeback requirements, and intends that the provisions of this Article be interpreted consistently with that intent.

6.2. Net Profits. Except as specifically provided elsewhere in this Agreement, Distributions of Net Profit shall be made to Members in proportion to their Percentage Interest in the Company.

6.3. Net Losses. Except as specifically provided elsewhere in this Agreement, Net Losses shall be allocated to the Members in proportion to their Percentage Interest in the Company. However, the foregoing will not apply to the extent that it would result in a Negative Capital Account balance for any Member equal to the Company Minimum Gain which would be realized by that Member in the event of a foreclosure of the Company's assets. Any Net Loss which is not allocated in accordance with the foregoing provision shall be allocated to other Members who are unaffected by that provision. When subsequent allocations of profit and loss are calculated, the losses reallocated pursuant to this provision shall be taken into account such that the net amount of the allocation shall be as close as possible to that which would have been allocated to each Member if the reallocation pursuant to this section had not taken place.

6.4. Regulatory Allocations. Notwithstanding the provisions of Section 6.3, the following applies:

(a) Should there be a net decrease in Company Minimum Gain in any taxable year, the Members shall specially allocate to each Member items of income and gain for that year (and, if necessary, for subsequent years) as required by the Code governing minimum gain chargeback requirements.

(b) Should there be a net decrease in Company Minimum Gain based on a Member Nonrecourse Debt in any taxable year, the Members shall first determine the extent of each Member's share of the Company Minimum Gain attributable to Member Nonrecourse Debt in accordance with the Code. The Members shall then specially allocate items of income and gain for that year (and, if necessary, for subsequent years) in accordance with the Code to each Member who has a share of the Company Nonrecourse Debt Minimum Gain.

(c) The Members shall allocate Nonrecourse Deductions for any taxable year to each Member in proportion to his or her Percentage Interest.

(d) The Members shall allocate Member Nonrecourse Deductions for any taxable year to the Member who bears the risk of loss with respect to the Nonrecourse Debt to which the Member Nonrecourse Deduction is attributable, as provided in the Code.

(e) If a Member unexpectedly receives any allocation of loss or deduction, or item thereof, or distributions which result in the Member's having a Negative Capital Account balance at the end of the taxable year greater than the Member's share of Company Minimum Gain, the Company shall specially allocate items of income and gain to that Member in a manner designed to eliminate the excess Negative Capital Account balance as rapidly as possible. Any allocations made in accordance with this provision shall taken into consideration in determining subsequent allocations under Article VI, so that, to the extent possible, the total amount allocated in this and subsequent allocations equals that which would have been allocated had there been no unexpected adjustments, allocations, and distributions and no allocation pursuant to Section 6.4(e).

(f) In accordance with Code Section 704(c) and the Regulations promulgated pursuant thereto, and notwithstanding any other provision in this Article, income, gain, loss, and deductions with respect to any property contributed to the Company shall, solely for tax purposes, be allocated among Members, taking into account any variation between the adjusted basis of the property to the Company for federal income tax purposes and its fair market value on the date of contribution. Allocations pursuant to this subsection are made solely for federal, state, and local taxes and shall not be taken into consideration in determining a Member's Capital Account or share of Net Profits or Net Losses or any other items subject to Distribution under this agreement.

6.5. Distributions. The Members may elect, by unanimous vote, to make a Distribution of assets at any time that would not be prohibited under the Act or under this Agreement. Such a Distribution shall be made in proportion to the unreturned capital contributions of each Member until all contributions have been paid, and thereafter in proportion to each Member's Percentage Interest in the Company. All such Distributions shall be made to those Persons who, according to the books and records of the Company, were the holders of record of Membership Interests on the date of the Distribution. Subject to Section 6.6, neither the Company nor any Members shall be liable for the making of any Distributions in accordance with the provisions of this section.

6.6. Limitations on Distributions.

(a) The Members shall not make any Distribution if, after giving effect to the distribution, (1) the Company would not be able to pay its debts as they become due in the usual course of business, or (2) the Company's total assets would be less than the sum of its total liabilities plus, unless this Agreement provides otherwise, the amount that would be needed, if the Company were to be dissolved at the time of Distribution, to satisfy the preferential rights of other Members upon dissolution that are superior to the rights of the Member receiving the Distribution.

(b) The Members may base a determination that a Distribution is not prohibited under this section on any of the following: (1) financial statements prepared on the basis of accounting practices and principles that are reasonable under the circumstances, (2) a fair valuation, or (3) any other method that is reasonable under the circumstances.

6.7. Return of Distributions. Members shall return to the Company any Distributions received which are in violation of this Agreement or the Act. Such Distributions shall be returned to the account or accounts of the Company from which they were taken in order to make the Distribution. If a Distribution is made in compliance with the Act and this Agreement, a Member is under no obligation to return it to the Company or to pay the amount of the Distribution for the account of the Company or to any creditor of the Company.

6.8. Members Bound by These Provisions. The Members understand and acknowledge the tax implications of the provisions of this Article of the Agreement and agree to be bound by these provisions in reporting items of income and loss relating to the Company on their federal and state income tax returns.

ARTICLE VII. TRANSFERS AND TERMINATIONS OF MEMBERSHIP INTERESTS

7.1. Restriction on Transferability of Membership Interests. A Member may not transfer, assign, encumber, or convey all or any part of his or her Membership Interest in the Company, except as provided herein. In entering into this Agreement, each of the Members acknowledges the reasonableness of this restriction, which is intended to further the purposes of the Company and the relationships among the Members.

7.2. Permitted Transfers. In order to be permitted, a transfer or assignment of all or any part of a Membership interest must have the approval of a two-thirds majority of the Members of the Company. Each Member, in his or her sole discretion, may proffer or withhold approval. In addition, the following conditions must be met:

(a) The transferee must provide a written agreement, satisfactory to the Members, to be bound by all of the provisions of this Agreement;

(b) The transferee must provide the Company with his or her taxpayer identification number and initial tax basis in the transferred interest;

(c) The transferee must pay the reasonable expenses incurred in connection with his or her admission to Membership;

(d) The transfer must be in compliance with all federal and state securities laws;

(e) The transfer must not result in the termination of the Company pursuant to Code Section 708.

(f) The transfer must not render the Company subject to the Investment Company Act of 1940, as amended; and

(g) The transferor must comply with the provisions of this Agreement.

7.3. Company's Right to Purchase Transferor's Interest and Valuation of Transferor's Interest. Any Member who wishes to transfer all or any part of his or her interest in the Company shall immediately provide the Company with written notice of his or her intention. The notice shall fully describe the nature of the interest to be transferred. Thereafter, the Company, or its nominee, shall have the option to purchase the transferor's interest at the Repurchase Price (as defined below).

(a) The "Repurchase Price" shall be determined as of the date of the event causing the transfer or dissolution event (the "Effective Date"). The date that the Company receives notice of a Member's intention to transfer his or her interest pursuant to this paragraph shall be deemed to be the Effective Date. The Repurchase Price shall be determined as follows:

i. The Repurchase Price of a Member's Percentage Interest shall be computed by the independent certified public accountant (CPA) regularly used by the Company or, if the Company has no CPA or if the CPA is unavailable, then by a qualified appraiser selected by the Company for this purpose. The Repurchase Price of a Member's Percentage Interest shall be the sum of the Company's total Repurchase Price multiplied by the Transferor's Percentage Interest as of the Effective Date.

ii. The Repurchase Price shall be determined by the book value method, as more further described herein. The book value of the interests shall be determined in accordance with the regular financial statements prepared by the Company and in accordance with generally accepted accounting principles, applied consistently with the accounting principles previously applied by the Company, adjusted to reflect the following:

(1) All inventory, valued at cost.

(2) All real property, leasehold improvements, equipment, and furnishings and fixtures valued at their fair market value.

(3) The face amount of any accounts payable.

(4) Any accrued taxes or assessments, deducted as liabilities.

(5) All usual fiscal year-end accruals and deferrals (including depreciation), prorated over the fiscal year.

(6) The reasonable fair market value of any good will or other intangible assets.

The cost of the assessment shall be borne by the Company.

(b) The option provided to the Company shall be irrevocable and shall remain open for thirty (30) days from the Effective Date, except that if notice is given by regular mail, the option shall remain open for thirty-five (35) days from the Effective Date.

(c) At any time while the option remains open, the Company (or its nominee) may elect to exercise the option and purchase the transferor's interest in the Company. The transferor Member shall not vote on the question of whether the Company should exercise its option.

(d) If the Company chooses to exercise its option to purchase the transferor Member's interest, it shall provide written notice to the transferor within the option period. The notice shall specify a "Closing Date" for the purchase, which shall occur within thirty (30) days of the expiration of the option period.

(e) If the Company declines to exercise its option to purchase the transferor Member's interest, the transferor Member may then transfer his or her interest in accordance with Section 7.2. Any transfer not in compliance with the provisions of Section 7.2 shall be null and void and have no force or effect.

(f) In the event that the Company chooses to exercise its option to purchase the transferor Member's interest, the Company may elect to purchase the Member's interest on the following terms:

i. The Company may elect to pay the Repurchase Price in cash, by making such cash payment to the transferor Member upon the Closing Date.

ii. The Company may elect to pay any portion of the Repurchase Price by delivering to the transferor Member, upon the Closing Date, all of the following:

(1) An amount equal to at least 10% of the Repurchase Price in cash or in an immediately negotiable draft, and

(2) A Promissory Note for the remaining amount of the Repurchase Price, to be paid in 12 successive month-

ly installments, with such installments beginning 30 days following the Closing Date, and ending one year from the Closing Date, and

(3) A security agreement guaranteeing the payment of the Promissory Note by offering the Transferor's former membership interest as security for the payment of the Promissory Note.

7.4. Occurrence of Dissolution Event. Upon the death, withdrawal, resignation, retirement, expulsion, insanity, bankruptcy, or dissolution of any Member (a Dissolution Event), the Company shall be dissolved, unless all of the Remaining Members elect by a majority in interest within 90 days thereafter to continue the operation of the business. In the event that the Remaining Members to agree, the Company and the Remaining Members shall have the right to purchase the interest of the Member whose actions caused the occurrence of the Dissolution Event. The interest shall be sold in the manner described in Section 7.6.

7.5. Withdrawal from Membership. Notwithstanding Section 7.4, in the event that a Member withdraws in accordance with Section 4.3 and such withdrawal does not result in the dissolution of the Company, the Company and the Remaining Members shall have the right to purchase the interest of the withdrawing Member in the manner described in Section 7.6.

7.6. Purchase of Interest of Departing Member. The purchase price of a Departing Member's interest shall be determined in accordance with the procedure provided in Section 7.3.

(a) Once a value has been determined, each Remaining Member shall be entitled to purchase that portion of the Departing Member's interest that corresponds to his or her percentage ownership of the Percentage Interests of those Members electing to purchase a portion of the Departing Member's interest in the Company.

(b) Each Remaining Member desiring to purchase a share of the Departing Member's interest shall have thirty (30) days to provide written notice to the Company of his or her intention to do so. The failure to provide notice shall be deemed a rejection of the opportunity to purchase the Departing Member's interest.

(c) If any Member elects not to purchase all of the Departing Member's interest to which he or she is entitled, the other Members may purchase that portion of the Departing Member's interest. Any interest which is not purchased by the Remaining Members may be purchased by the Company.

(d) The Members shall assign a closing date within 60 days after the Members' election to purchase is completed. At that time, the Departing Member shall deliver to the Remaining Members an instrument of title, free of any encumbrances and containing warranties of title, duly conveying his or her interest in the Company and, in return, he or she shall be paid the purchase price for his or her interest in cash. The Departing Member and the Remaining Members shall perform all acts reasonably necessary to consummate the transaction in accordance with this agreement.

7.7. No Release of Liability. Any Member or Departing Member whose interest in the Company is sold pursuant to Article VII is not relieved thereby of any liability he or she may owe the Company.

ARTICLE VIII. BOOKS, RECORDS, AND REPORTING

8.1. Books and Records. The Members shall maintain at the Company's principal place of business the following books and records: a current list of the full name and last known business or residence address of each Member, together with the Capital Contribution, Capital Account, and Membership Interest of each Member; a copy of the Articles and all amendments thereto; copies of the Company's federal, state, and local income tax or information returns and reports, if any, for the six (6) most recent taxable years; a copy of this Agreement and any amendments to it; copies of the Company's financial statements, if any; the books and records of the Company as they relate to its internal affairs for at least the current and past four (4) fiscal years; and true and correct copies of all relevant documents and records indicating the amount, cost, and value of all the property and assets of the Company.

8.2. Accounting Methods. The books and records of the Company shall be maintained in accordance with the accounting methods utilized for federal income tax purposes.

8.3. Reports. The Members shall cause to be prepared and filed in a timely manner all reports and documents required by any governmental agency. The Members shall cause to be prepared at least annually all information concerning the Company's operations that is required by the Members for the preparation of their federal and state tax returns.

8.4. Inspection Rights. For purposes reasonably related to their interests in the Company, all Members shall have the right to inspect and copy the books and records of the Company during normal business hours, upon reasonable request.

8.5. Bank Accounts. The Managers shall maintain all of the funds of the Company in a bank account or accounts in the name of the Company, at a depository institution or institutions to be determined by a majority of the Members. The Managers shall not permit the funds of the Company to be commingled in any manner with the funds or accounts of any other Person. The Managers shall have the powers enumerated in Section 5.2 with respect to endorsing, signing, and negotiating checks, drafts, or other evidence of indebtedness to the Company or obligating the Company money to a third party.

ARTICLE IX. DISSOLUTION, LIQUIDATION, AND WINDING UP

9.1. Conditions Under Which Dissolution Shall Occur. The Company shall dissolve and its affairs shall be wound up upon the happening the first of the following: at the time specified in the Articles; upon the happening of a Dissolution Event; and the failure of the Remaining Members to elect to continue, in accordance with Section 7.4; upon the vote of all of the Members to dissolve; upon the entry of a decree of judicial dissolution pursuant to the Act; upon the happening of any event specified in the Articles as causing or requiring dissolution; or upon the sale of all or substantially all of the Company's assets.

9.2. Winding Up and Dissolution. If the Company is dissolved, the Members shall wind up its affairs, including the selling of all of the Company's assets and the provision of written notification to all of the Company's creditors of the commencement of dissolution proceedings.

9.3. Order of Payment. After determining that all known debts and liabilities of the Company in the process of winding up have been paid or provided for, including, without limitation, debts and liabilities to Members who are creditors of the Company, the Members shall distribute the remaining assets among the Members in accordance with their Positive Capital Account balances, after taking into consideration the profit and loss allocations made pursuant to Section 6.4. Members shall not be required to restore Negative Capital Account Balances.

ARTICLE X. INDEMNIFICATION

10.1. Indemnification. The Company shall indemnify any Member and may indemnify any Person to the fullest extent permitted by law on the date such indemnification is requested for any judgments, settlements, penalties, fines, or expenses of any kind incurred as a result of the Person's performance in the capacity of Member, officer, employee, or agent of the Company, as long as the Member, or Person did not behave in violation of the Act or this Agreement.

ARTICLE XI. MISCELLANEOUS PROVISIONS

11.1. Assurances. Each Member shall execute all documents and certificates and perform all acts deemed appropriate by the Members and the Company or required by this Agreement or the Act in connection with the formation and operation of the Company and the acquisition, holding, or operation of any property by the Company.

11.2. Complete Agreement. This Agreement and the Articles constitute the complete and exclusive statement of the agreement among the Members with respect to the matters discussed herein and therein and they supersede all prior written or oral statements among the Members, including any prior statement, warranty, or representation.

11.3. Section Headings. The section headings which appear throughout this Agreement are provided for convenience only and are not intended to define or limit the scope of this Agreement or the intent of subject matter of its provisions.

11.4. Binding Effect. Subject to the provisions of this Agreement relating to the transferability of Membership Interests, this Agreement is binding upon and shall inure to the benefit of the parties hereto and their respective heirs, administrators, executors, successors, and assigns.

11.5. Interpretation. All pronouns and common nouns shall be deemed to refer to the masculine, feminine, neuter, singular, and plural, as the context may require. In the event that any claim is made by any Member relating to the drafting and interpretation of this Agreement, no presumption, inference, or burden of proof or persuasion shall be created or implied solely by virtue of the fact that this Agreement was drafted by or at the behest of a particular Member or his or her counsel.

11.6. Applicable Law. Each Member agrees that all disputes arising under or in connection with this Agreement and any transactions contemplated by this Agreement shall be governed by the internal law, and not the law of conflicts, of the state of organization.

11.7. Specific Performance. The Members acknowledge and agree that irreparable injury shall result from a breach of this Agreement and that money damages will not adequately compensate the injured party. Accordingly, in the event of a breach or a threatened breach of this Agreement, any party who may be injured shall be entitled, in addition to any other remedy which may be available, to injunctive relief to prevent or to correct the breach.

11.8. Remedies Cumulative. The remedies described in this Agreement are cumulative and shall not eliminate any other remedy to which a Person may be lawfully entitled.

11.9. Notice. Any notice or other writing to be served upon the Company or any Member thereof in connection with this Agreement shall be in writing and shall be deemed completed when delivered to the address specified in Table A, if to a Member, and to the resident agent, if to the Company. Any Member shall have the right to change the address at which notices shall be served upon ten (10) days' written notice to the Company and the other Members.

11.10. Amendments. Any amendments, modifications, or alterations to this Agreement or the Articles must be in writing and signed by all of the Members.

11.11. Severability. Each provision of this Agreement is severable from the other provisions. If, for any reason, any provision of this Agreement is declared invalid or contrary to existing law, the inoperability of that provision shall have no effect on the remaining provisions of the Agreement, which shall continue in full force and effect.

11.12. Counterparts. This Agreement may be executed in counterparts, each of which shall be deemed an original and all of which shall, when taken together, constitute a single document.

IN WITNESS WHEREOF, this Agreement has been made and executed by the Members effective as of the date first written above.

_____ (Member)

_____ (Member)

_____ (Member)

Table A: Name, Address, and Initial Capital Contribution of the Members

Name and Address of Member	Value of Initial Capital Contribution	Nature of Member's Initial Capital Contribution (i.e., cash, services, property)	Member's Percentage Interest

Table B: Managers

Name of Manager	Address of Manager

LLC Form 8. Membership Ledger

Date of Original Issue	Member Name	Percentage Interest	Disposition of Shares (transferred or surrendered stock certificate)

LLC Form 9. Investment Representation Letter

Note: The following Investment Representation Letter should be executed by each LLC member and delivered to the company. The Representation Letter seeks to ensure company compliance with securities laws, by asking owners to certify that they are joining the LLC as an investment, and not to trade shares in the LLC.

(insert date)

To whom it may concern,

I am delivering this letter to Olde Craft, LLC in connection with my purchase of a 25% interest in Olde Craft, Inc. for a total sum of $75,000.00. I represent the following:

I am purchasing the shares in my own name and for my own account, for investment and not with an intent to sell or for sale in connection with any distribution of such stock; and no other person has any interest in or right with respect to the shares; nor have I agreed to give any person any such interest or right in the future.

I recognize that the shares have not been registered under the Federal Securities Act of 1933, as amended, or qualified under any state securities law, and that any sale or transfer of the shares is subject to restrictions imposed by federal and state law.

I also recognize that I cannot dispose of the shares absent registration and qualification or an available exemption from registration and qualification. I understand that no federal or state securities commission or other government body has approved of the fairness of the shares offered by the corporation and that the Commissioner has not and will not recommend or endorse the shares.

I have not seen or received any advertisement or general solicitation with respect to the sale of the shares.

I have a preexisting personal or business relationship with the Company or one or more of its officers, directors, or controlling persons and I am aware of its character and general financial and business circumstances.

I acknowledge that during the course of this transaction and before purchasing the shares I have been provided with financial and other written information about the Company. I have been given the opportunity by the Company to obtain any information and ask questions concerning the Company, the shares, and my investment that I felt necessary; and to the extent I availed myself of that opportunity, I have received satisfactory information and answers.

In reaching the decision to invest in the shares, I have carefully evaluated my financial resources and investment position and the risks associated with this investment, and I acknowledge that I am able to bear the economic risks of this investment.

_____

John Miller

LLC. Form 10. Appointment of Proxy for Member's Meeting

Note: Use the following form when a Member wants to give his or her vote to another person at a meeting of an LLC's membership.

APPOINTMENT OF PROXY FOR (Annual/Special) MEETING

MadHatter, LLC

SHAREHOLDER: John Miller

PERCENTAGE INTEREST HELD BY SHAREHOLDER: 32%

I, the undersigned, as record holder of a 32% interest in MadHatter, LLC, revoke any previous proxies and appoint the person whose name appears just below this paragraph as my proxy to attend the member's meeting on _____ and any adjournment of that meeting.

The person I want to appoint as my proxy is _____

The proxy holder is entitled to cast a total number of votes equal to, but not exceeding the number of shares which I would be entitled to cast if I were personally present.

I authorize my proxy holder to vote and otherwise represent me with regard to any business that may come before this meeting in the same manner and with the same effect as if I were personally present.

I may revoke this proxy at any time. This proxy will lapse three months after the date of its execution.

If you are signing for a business entity, state your title:

Date (*important*):_____

_____
Name

_____
Title

Note: All proxies must be signed. Sign exactly as your name appears on your stock certificate. Joint shareholders must each sign this proxy. If signed by an attorney in fact, the Power of Attorney must be attached.

LLC Form 11. Call for Meeting of Members

Note: This "call" is an instruction by LLC members to the managers that the members want to call a meeting of members. This serves as official notice. This call is required only in manager-managed LLCs; if a member in a member-managed LLC wants to call a meeting of members, he or she would skip the call and simply send a notice of meeting of members to all other members. The next form is a notice of meeting of members.

CALL FOR MEETING OF LLC MEMBERS

TO: The Managers of MadHatter, LLC

(insert date)

The party or parties whose name appears below are members of MadHatter, LLC, and own percentage interests entitled to cast not less than 10 percent of MadHatter's votes. We hereby call a meeting of the members of MadHatter to be held _____ (date), at _____ (time), for the purpose of considering and acting upon the following matters:

(Insert matters to be considered, such as "A proposal that John Jones be removed as a manager of MadHatter.")

You are directed to give notice of this meeting of the members, in the manner prescribed by MadHatter's operating agreement and by law, to all members entitled to receive notice of the meeting.

Date _____

_____

_____

_____

LLC Form 12. Notice of Meeting of LLC Members

Note: This form is an LLC's announcement to its members that a meeting of members has been called.

NOTICE OF MEETING OF MEMBERS OF OLDECRAFT, LLC

Certain members of OldeCraft, LLC, have called a meeting of the members of OldeCraft pursuant to OldeCraft's operating agreement.

Therefore, this is your official notice as an OldeCraft member that a meeting of members of OldeCraft, LLC, will be held on _____ (date), at _____ (time), at _____ (address), to consider and act on the following matters:

(insert matters to be considered, such as "A proposal that John Jones be removed from the board of directors.")

If you do not expect to be present at the meeting and wish your shares to be voted, you may complete the attached form of proxy and mail it in the enclosed addressed envelope.

Date _____

_____
John Wilson, Manager

LLC Form 13. Minutes of Meeting of LLC Members

Note: While LLC members and managers enjoy far fewer corporate formalities than corporation owners, an LLC must still maintain records of its meetings. When an LLC's members meet to formally vote on any matter, the results of that vote should be committed to written minutes.

MINUTES OF MEETING OF MEMBERS OF OLDECRAFT, LLC

The members of OLDECRAFT, LLC, held a meeting on _____ (date), at _____(time), at _____(place). The meeting was called by John Miller and the company managers mailed notice to all members that the meeting would take place.

The following members were present at the meeting, in person or by proxy, representing membership interests as indicated:

> John Jones, 50%
> John Smith, 30%
> John Miller, 20%

Also present were Michael Spadaccini, attorney to the company, and Lisa Jones, wife of John Jones, and the company's president and sole manager.

The company's president called the meeting to order and announced that she would chair the meeting, that a quorum was present, and that the meeting was held pursuant to a written notice of meeting given to all members of the company. A copy of the notice was ordered inserted in the minute book immediately preceding the minutes of this meeting.

The minutes of the previous meeting of shareholders were then read and approved.

The chairperson then announced that the election of a manager was in order. Lisa Jones stated that she could no longer serve as manager of the company. John Smith was then elected to serve until the next meeting of members, and until the manager's successor was duly elected and qualified, as follows:

(Include agreement for selecting new manager here.)

There being no further business to come before the meeting, on motion duly made, seconded, and adopted, the meeting was adjourned.

_____
John Smith, Manager

LLC Form 14. Action by Written Consent of LLC Members

Note: Most company votes are taken by written consent rather than by notice and meeting and an in-person vote. Use the following form when you wish to take a company action in writing, rather than by a noticed meeting. Keep in mind, however, that your operating agreement and articles may require more than a simple majority to pass certain actions. Written consents are important company records and should be maintained in the record books.

ACTION BY WRITTEN CONSENT OF SHAREHOLDERS OF OLDECRAFT, LLC

The undersigned members of OldeCraft, LLC, owning of record the number of shares entitled to vote as set forth, hereby consent to the following company actions. The vote was unanimous. (For actions where a unanimous vote is not required: "A vote of 66% was required to take the actions listed below, and 80% of the membership interest in the company have given their consent."):

1. Pete Wilson is hereby removed as manager of the company.

2. The number of managers of the company is increased from one to two.

John Smith and John Miller, both also members, are hereby elected to serve as company managers until the next meeting of members.

DATED: _____

_____
John Smith

Percentage Owned: _____

DATED: _____

_____
John Miller

Percentage Owned:_____

LLC Form 15. Written Consent of Members Approving a Certificate of Amendment of Articles of Organization Changing an LLC's Name

ACTION OF MEMBERS BY WRITTEN CONSENT TO APPROVE AN AMENDMENT TO ARTICLES OF ORGANIZATION CHANGING LLC NAME

The undersigned, who comprise all the members of PLASTICWORLD, LLC, agree unanimously to the following:

RESOLVED, that the Certificate of Amendment of Articles of Organization presented to the undersigned members, specifically changing the name of the company to PLASTICUNIVERSE, LLC is approved.

Date _____

_____

Scott Bess

_____

Brian Bess

LLC Form 16. Internal Revenue Service Tax Form SS-4

Form **SS-4**
(Rev. December 2001)
Department of the Treasury
Internal Revenue Service

Application for Employer Identification Number

(For use by employers, corporations, partnerships, trusts, estates, churches, government agencies, Indian tribal entities, certain individuals, and others.)

See separate instructions for each line.   Keep a copy for your records.

EIN

OMB No. 1545-0003

Type or print clearly.

1 Legal name of entity (or individual) for whom the EIN is being requested

2 Trade name of business (if different from name on line 1)

3 Executor, trustee,

4a Mailing address (room, apt., suite no. and street, or P.O. box)

5a Street address (if different) (Do not enter a P.O. box.)

4b City, state, and ZIP code

5b City, state, and ZIP code

6 County and state where principal business is located

7a Name of principal officer, general partner, grantor, owner, or trustor

7b SSN, ITIN, or EIN

8a **Type of entity** (check only one box)
- ☐ Sole proprietor (SSN) _____
- ☐ Partnership
- ☐ Corporation (enter form number to be filed) _____
- ☐ Personal service corp.
- ☐ Church or church-controlled organization
- ☐ Other nonprofit organization (specify) _____
- ☐ Other (specify)

- ☐ Estate (SSN of decedent) _____
- ☐ Plan administrator (SSN) _____
- ☐ Trust (SSN of grantor) _____
- ☐ National Guard   ☐ State/local government
- ☐ Farmers' cooperative   ☐ Federal government/military
- ☐ REMIC   ☐ Indian tribal governments/enterprises

Group Exemption Number (GEN) _____

8b If a corporation, name the state or foreign country (if applicable) where incorporated

State

Foreign country

9 **Reason for applying** (check only one box)
- ☐ Started new business (specify type) _____
- ☐ Hired employees (Check the box and see line 12.)
- ☐ Compliance with IRS withholding regulations
- ☐ Other (specify)

- ☐ Banking purpose (specify purpose) _____
- ☐ Changed type of organization (specify new type) _____
- ☐ Purchased going business
- ☐ _____
- ☐ Created a pension plan (specify type) _____

10 Date business started or acquired (month, day, year)

11 Closing month of accounting year

12 First date wages or annuities were paid or will be paid (month, day, year). **Note:** *If applicant is a withholding agent, enter date income will first be paid to nonresident alien. (month, day, year)*

13 Highest number of employees expected in the next 12 months. **Note:** *If the applicant does not expect to have any employees during the period, enter "-0-."*

Agricultural	Household	Other

14 Check **one** box that best describes the principal activity of your business.
- ☐ Construction   ☐ Rental & leasing   ☐ Transportation & warehousing
- ☐ Real estate   ☐ Manufacturing   ☐ Finance & insurance
- ☐ Health care & social assistance   ☐ Wholesale-agent/broker
- ☐ Accommodation & food service   ☐ Wholesale-other   ☐ Retail
- ☐ Other (specify)

15 Indicate principal line of merchandise sold; specific construction work done; products produced; or services provided.

16a Has the applicant ever applied for an employer identification number for this or any other business?   ☐ Yes   ☐ No
Note: *If "Yes," please complete lines 16b and 16c.*

16b If line 16a, give applicant's legal name and trade name shown on prior application if different from line 1 or 2 above.
Legal name   Trade name

16c Approximate date when, and city and state where, the application was filed. Enter previous employer identification number if known.
Approximate date when filed (month, day, year)   City and state where filed   Previous EIN

Third Party Designee	Complete this section **only** if you want to authorize the named individual to receive the entity's EIN and answer questions about the completion of this form.	
	Designee's name	Designee's telephone number (include area code) ( )
	Address and ZIP code	Designee's fax number (include area code) ( )

Under penalties of perjury, I declare that I have examined this application, and to the best of my knowledge and belief, it is true, correct, and complete.

Applicant's telephone number (include area code) ( )

Name and title (type or print clearly)

Signature   Date

Applicant's fax number (include area code) ( )

For Privacy Act and Paperwork Reduction Act Notice, see separate instructions.   Cat. No. 16055N   Form **SS-4** (Rev. 12-2001)

LLC Form 17. Internal Revenue Service Form 2553

Form **2553**
(Rev. December 2002)
Department of the Treasury
Internal Revenue Service

Election by a Small Business Corporation
(Under section 1362 of the Internal Revenue Code)
See Parts II and III on back and the separate instructions.
The corporation may either send or fax this form to the IRS. See page 2 of the instructions.

OMB No. 1545-0146

Notes:
1. ***Do not** file **Form 1120S**, U.S. Income Tax Return for an S Corporation, for any tax year before the year the election takes effect.*
2. *This election to be an S corporation can be accepted only if all the tests are met under **Who May Elect** on page 1 of the instructions; all shareholders have signed the consent statement; and the exact name and address of the corporation and other required form information are provided.*
3. *If the corporation was in existence before the effective date of this election, see **Taxes an S Corporation May Owe** on page 1 of the instructions.*

Part I   Election Information

Please Type or Print

Name of corporation (see instructions)	**A** Employer identification number
Number, street, and room or suite no. (If a P.O. box, see instructions.)	**B** Date incorporated
City or town, state, and ZIP code	**C** State of incorporation

D Check the applicable box(es) if the corporation, after applying for the EIN shown in **A** above, changed its name ☐ or address ☐

E Election is to be effective for tax year beginning (month, day, year) . . . .   /   /

F Name and title of officer or legal representative who the IRS may call for more information

G Telephone number of officer or legal representative
(   )

H If this election takes effect for the first tax year the corporation exists, enter month, day, and year of the **earliest** of the following: (1) date the corporation first had shareholders, (2) date the corporation first had assets, or (3) date the corporation began doing business . . . .   /   /

I Selected tax year: Annual return will be filed for tax year ending (month and day) - - - - - - - - - - - - - - - - - -
If the tax year ends on any date other than December 31, except for a 52-53-week tax year ending with reference to the month of December, you **must** complete Part II on the back. If the date you enter is the ending date of a 52-53-week tax year, write "52-53-week year" to the right of the date.

J Name and address of each shareholder; shareholder's spouse having a community property interest in the corporation's stock; and each tenant in common, joint tenant, and tenant by the entirety. (A husband and wife (and their estates) are counted as one shareholder in determining the number of shareholders without regard to the manner in which the stock is owned.)	**K** Shareholders' Consent Statement. Under penalties of perjury, we declare that we consent to the election of the above-named corporation to be an S corporation under section 1362(a) and that we have examined this consent statement, including accompanying schedules and statements, and to the best of our knowledge and belief, it is true, correct, and complete. We understand our consent is binding and may not be withdrawn after the corporation has made a valid election. (Shareholders sign and date below.)		**L** Stock owned		**M** Social security number or employer identification number (see instructions)	**N** Shareholder's tax year ends (month and day)
	Signature	Date	Number of shares	Dates acquired		

Under penalties of perjury, I declare that I have examined this election, including accompanying schedules and statements, and to the best of my knowledge and belief, it is true, correct, and complete.

Signature of officer	Title	Date

For Paperwork Reduction Act Notice, see page 4 of the instructions.   Cat. No. 18629R   Form **2553** (Rev. 12-2002)

Form 2553 (Rev. 12-2002)   Page **2**

Part II   Selection of Fiscal Tax Year (All corporations using this part must complete item O and item P, Q, or R.)

O   Check the applicable box to indicate whether the corporation is:

    1. ☐ A new corporation adopting the tax year entered in item I, Part I.

    2. ☐ An existing corporation retaining the tax year entered in item I, Part I.

    3. ☐ An existing corporation changing to the tax year entered in item I, Part I.

P   Complete item P if the corporation is using the automatic approval provisions of Rev. Proc. 2002-38, 2002-22 I.R.B. 1037, to request **(1)** a natural business year (as defined in section 5.05 of Rev. Proc. 2002-38) or **(2)** a year that satisfies the ownership tax year test (as defined in section 5.06 of Rev. Proc. 2002-38). Check the applicable box below to indicate the representation statement the corporation is making.

    1. Natural Business Year   ☐   I represent that the corporation is adopting, retaining, or changing to a tax year that qualifies as its natural business year as defined in section 5.05 of Rev. Proc. 2002-38 and has attached a statement verifying that it satisfies the 25% gross receipts test (see instructions for content of statement). I also represent that the corporation is not precluded by section 4.02 of Rev. Proc. 2002-38 from obtaining automatic approval of such adoption, retention, or change in tax year.

    2. Ownership Tax Year   ☐   I represent that shareholders (as described in section 5.06 of Rev. Proc. 2002-38) holding more than half of the shares of the stock (as of the first day of the tax year to which the request relates) of the corporation have the same tax year or are concurrently changing to the tax year that the corporation adopts, retains, or changes to per item I, Part I, and that such tax year satisfies the requirement of section 4.01(3) of Rev. Proc. 2002-38. I also represent that the corporation is not precluded by section 4.02 of Rev. Proc. 2002-38 from obtaining automatic approval of such adoption, retention, or change in tax year.

Note: *If you do not use item P and the corporation wants a fiscal tax year, complete either item Q or R below. Item Q is used to request a fiscal tax year based on a business purpose and to make a back-up section 444 election. Item R is used to make a regular section 444 election.*

Q   **Business Purpose**—To request a fiscal tax year based on a business purpose, you must check box Q1. See instructions for details including payment of a user fee. You may also check box Q2 and/or box Q3.

    1. Check here   ☐   if the fiscal year entered in item I, Part I, is requested under the prior approval provisions of Rev. Proc. 2002-39, 2002-22 I.R.B. 1046. Attach to Form 2553 a statement describing the relevant facts and circumstances and, if applicable, the gross receipts from sales and services necessary to establish a business purpose. See the instructions for details regarding the gross receipts from sales and services. If the IRS proposes to disapprove the requested fiscal year, do you want a conference with the IRS National Office?

    ☐ Yes   ☐ No

    2. Check here   ☐   to show that the corporation intends to make a back-up section 444 election in the event the corporation's business purpose request is not approved by the IRS. (See instructions for more information.)

    3. Check here   ☐   to show that the corporation agrees to adopt or change to a tax year ending December 31 if necessary for the IRS to accept this election for S corporation status in the event (1) the corporation's business purpose request is not approved and the corporation makes a back-up section 444 election, but is ultimately not qualified to make a section 444 election, or (2) the corporation's business purpose request is not approved and the corporation did not make a back-up section 444 election.

R   **Section 444 Election**—To make a section 444 election, you must check box R1 and you may also check box R2.

    1. Check here   ☐   to show the corporation will make, if qualified, a section 444 election to have the fiscal tax year shown in item I, Part I. To make the election, you must complete **Form 8716,** Election To Have a Tax Year Other Than a Required Tax Year, and either attach it to Form 2553 or file it separately.

    2. Check here   ☐   to show that the corporation agrees to adopt or change to a tax year ending December 31 if necessary for the IRS to accept this election for S corporation status in the event the corporation is ultimately not qualified to make a section 444 election.

Part III   Qualified Subchapter S Trust (QSST) Election Under Section 1361(d)(2)*

Income beneficiary's name and address	Social security number
Trust's name and address	Employer identification number

Date on which stock of the corporation was transferred to the trust (month, day, year) . . . .   /   /

In order for the trust named above to be a QSST and thus a qualifying shareholder of the S corporation for which this Form 2553 is filed, I hereby make the election under section 1361(d)(2). Under penalties of perjury, I certify that the trust meets the definitional requirements of section 1361(d)(3) and that all other information provided in Part III is true, correct, and complete.

Signature of income beneficiary or signature and title of legal representative or other qualified person making the election   Date

*Use Part III to make the QSST election only if stock of the corporation has been transferred to the trust on or before the date on which the corporation makes its election to be an S corporation. The QSST election must be made and filed separately if stock of the corporation is transferred to the trust after the date on which the corporation makes the S election.

✳   Form **2553** (Rev. 12-2002)

Additional Forms for Managing an LLC

As a service to entrepreneurs who choose the LLC form of structure for their business, the rest of this book includes 144 forms and documents to help you manage that business. Each section that follows will include a brief description of the forms in that section followed by the forms. There is also an accompanying CD on which you also find these items formatted in Word and Excel so you can adapt them for your own use. The forms are numbered consecutively throughout this appendix for easier identification on the CD.

You'll find forms covering the following areas:

- Appendix D1. Human Resource Recruitment Tools
- Appendix D2. Employee Records and Human Resource Management
- Appendix D3. Employee and Workplace Safety
- Appendix D4. Employee Termination
- Appendix D5. Miscellaneous Personnel Forms
- Appendix D6. Sales and Revenue Analysis Tools
- Appendix D7. Credit, Billing, and Collection Tools
- Appendix D8. Contracts and Agreements
- Appendix D9. Business Operation Tools
- Appendix D10. Cash Disbursements and Purchasing
- Appendix D11. Inventory Movement and Valuation Tools
- Appendix D12. Financial Reports
- Appendix D13. Miscellaneous Forms

Human Resource Recruitment Tools

Attracting and hiring the right employee for your firm is essential to your business success. In this section, you will find forms and worksheets that will help you attract and evaluate suitable candidates. These forms are applicable to nearly any industry. You will find two employment applications, the *Application for Employment—Short Form* and the *Application for Employment—Long Form*. The short form will likely be sufficient for most hires, while the long form is more appropriate for longer-term and executive positions.

As part of the employment application process, insist that your applicants execute the *Authorization to Release Employment Applicant Information*. This important form authorizes the applicant's former employer to release information about the applicant's work history and personal characteristics. Most former employers will insist on receiving such an authorization before divulging any information.

You will also find two versions of a *Pre-Employment Reference Check via Phone*. These two forms are scripts that you should use when making telephone contact with an applicant's former employer. If you wish to contact your applicant's former employer by letter, use the *Pre-Employment Reference Check via Letter* form.

Once you have narrowed your employee search to a handful of candidates, summarize their critical strengths and weaknesses with the *Applicant Comparison Summary Form*; rate each candidate's qualifications for critical job requirements, such as computer skills, foreign languages, and the like. You can rate each applicant's individual skills with *Applicant Rating Form, Part One* and *Applicant Rating Form, Part Two*.

Once you have found your ideal candidate, you can use the *Offer of Employment and Employment Contract*. This form formally announces the offer of employment and documents the terms of the employment agreement. Save a copy in the employee's file. Finally, once you have secured your new employee, use the *New Employee Announcement* to announce your new employee to your other employees.

1. Application for Employment–Short Form

Our policy is to provide equal employment opportunity to all qualified persons without regard to race, creed, color, religious belief, sex, age, national origin, ancestry, physical or mental disability, or veteran status.

Name
Last _____ First _____ Middle _____
Date _____
Street Address _____
City _____ State _____ ZIP _____
Telephone _____
Social Security # _____

Position applied for _____
How did you hear of this opening? _____
When can you start? _____ Desired Wage $_____

Are you a U.S. citizen or otherwise authorized to work in the U.S. on an unrestricted basis? (You may be required to provide documentation.) ❑ Yes ❑ No
Are you looking for full-time employment? ❑ Yes ❑ No
If no, what hours are you available? _____
Are you willing to work swing shift? ❑ Yes ❑ No
Are you willing to work graveyard? ❑ Yes ❑ No

Have you ever been convicted of a felony? (This will not necessarily affect your application.) ❑ Yes ❑ No
If yes, please describe conditions. _____
_____
_____
_____
_____

Education	School Name and Location	Year	Major	Degree
High School	_____	_____	_____	_____
College	_____	_____	_____	_____
College	_____	_____	_____	_____
Post-College	_____	_____	_____	_____
Other Training	_____	_____	_____	_____

In addition to your work history, are there other skills, qualifications, or experience that we should consider?
_____
_____
_____
_____
_____

Employment History (Start with most recent employer)
Company Name _____
Address _____ Telephone _____
Date Started _____ Starting Wage _____ Starting Position _____
Date Ended _____ Ending Wage _____ Ending Position _____
Name of Supervisor _____
May we contact? ❑ Yes ❑ No

Responsibilities _____
_____

Reason for leaving _____

Company Name _____
Address _____ Telephone _____
Date Started _____ Starting Wage _____ Starting Position _____
Date Ended _____ Ending Wage _____ Ending Position _____
Name of Supervisor _____
May we contact? ❑ Yes ❑ No
Responsibilities _____
_____

Reason for leaving _____

Company Name _____
Address _____ Telephone _____
Date Started _____ Starting Wage _____ Starting Position _____
Date Ended _____ Ending Wage _____ Ending Position _____
Name of Supervisor _____
May we contact? ❑ Yes ❑ No
Responsibilities _____
_____

Reason for leaving _____

Company Name _____
Address _____ Telephone _____
Date Started _____ Starting Wage _____ Starting Position _____
Date Ended _____ Ending Wage _____ Ending Position _____
Name of Supervisor _____
May we contact? ❑ Yes ❑ No
Responsibilities _____
_____

Reason for leaving _____

Attach additional information if necessary.

I certify that the facts set forth in this application for employment are true and complete to the best of my knowledge. I understand that if I am employed, false statements on this application shall be considered sufficient cause for dismissal. This company is hereby authorized to make any investigations of my prior educational and employment history.

I understand that employment at this company is "at will," which means that either I or this company can terminate the employment relationship at any time, with or without prior notice, and for any reason not prohibited by statute. All employment is continued on that basis. I understand that no supervisor, manager, or executive of this company, other than the president, has any authority to alter the foregoing.

Signature_____ Date _____

2. Application for Employment–Long Form

Our policy is to provide equal employment opportunity to all qualified persons without regard to race, creed, color, religious belief, sex, age, national origin, ancestry, physical or mental disability, or veteran status.

Name
Last _____ First _____ Middle_____
Date _____
Street Address _____
City _____ State _____ ZIP _____
Telephone _____
Social Security # _____

Position applied for _____
How did you hear of this opening? _____
When can you start? _____ Desired Wage $_____

Are you a U.S. citizen or otherwise authorized to work in the U.S. on an unrestricted basis? (You may be required to provide documentation.) ❑ Yes ❑ No
Are you looking for full-time employment? ❑ Yes ❑ No
If no, what hours are you available? _____
Are you willing to work swing shift? ❑ Yes ❑ No
Are you willing to work graveyard? ❑ Yes ❑ No

Have you ever been convicted of a felony? (This will not necessarily affect your application.) ❑ Yes ❑ No
If yes, please describe conditions. _____
_____
_____
_____
_____
_____

Employment Desired
Have you ever applied for employment here? ❑ Yes ❑ No
When? _____ Where?_____
Have you ever been employed by this company? ❑ Yes ❑ No
When? _____ Where?_____
Are you presently employed? ❑ Yes ❑ No
May we contact your present employer? ❑ Yes ❑ No
Are you available for full-time work? ❑ Yes ❑ No
Are you available for part-time work? ❑ Yes ❑ No
Will you relocate? ❑ Yes ❑ No
Are you willing to travel? ❑ Yes ❑ No   If yes, what percent? _____
Date you can start _____
Desired position _____
Desired starting salary _____
Please list applicable skills _____
_____
_____

Education: School Name and Location   Year   Major Degree

High School _____ _____ _____ _____

College _____ _____ _____ _____

College _____ _____ _____ _____

Post-College _____ _____ _____ _____

Other Training _____ _____ _____ _____

In addition to your work history, are there other skills, qualifications, or experience that we should consider?

_____

_____

_____

_____

_____

Please list any scholastic honors received and offices held in school.

_____

_____

Are you planning to continue your studies? ❏ Yes ❏ No

If yes, where and what courses of study?

_____

_____

Company Name _____

Address _____ Telephone _____

Date Started _____ Starting Wage _____ Starting Position _____

Date Ended _____ Ending Wage _____ Ending Position _____

Name of Supervisor _____

May we contact? ❏ Yes ❏ No

Responsibilities _____

_____

Reason for leaving _____

Company Name _____

Address _____ Telephone _____

Date Started _____ Starting Wage _____ Starting Position _____

Date Ended _____ Ending Wage _____ Ending Position _____

Name of Supervisor _____

May we contact? ❏ Yes ❏ No

Responsibilities _____

_____

Reason for leaving _____

Company Name _____

Address _____ Telephone _____

Date Started _____ Starting Wage _____ Starting Position _____

Date Ended _____ Ending Wage _____ Ending Position _____

Name of Supervisor _____

May we contact? ❏ Yes ❏ No

Responsibilities _____

_____

Reason for leaving _____

Company Name _____

Address _____ Telephone _____

Date Started _____ Starting Wage _____ Starting Position _____

Date Ended _____ Ending Wage _____ Ending Position _____

Name of Supervisor _____

May we contact? ❏ Yes ❏ No

Responsibilities _____

_____

Reason for leaving _____

Company Name _____

Address _____ Telephone _____

Date Started _____ Starting Wage _____ Starting Position _____

Date Ended _____ Ending Wage _____ Ending Position _____

Name of Supervisor _____

May we contact? ❏ Yes ❏ No

Responsibilities _____

_____

Reason for leaving _____

Company Name _____

Address _____ Telephone _____

Date Started _____ Starting Wage _____ Starting Position _____

Date Ended _____ Ending Wage _____ Ending Position _____

Name of Supervisor _____

May we contact? ❏ Yes ❏ No

Responsibilities _____

_____

Reason for leaving _____

References

List three personal references, not related to you, who have known you for more than one year.

Name _____ Phone _____Years Known_____

Address _____

Name _____ Phone _____Years Known_____

Address _____

Name _____ Phone _____Years Known_____

Address _____

Emergency Contact

In case of emergency, please notify:_____

Name _____ Phone _____

Address _____

Name _____ Phone _____

Address _____

Please Read Before Signing:

I certify that all information provided by me on this application is true and complete to the best of my knowledge and that I have withheld nothing that, if disclosed, would alter the integrity of this application.

I authorize my previous employers, schools, or persons listed as references to give any information regarding employment or educational record. I agree that this company and my previous employers will not be held liable in any respect if a job offer is not extended, or is withdrawn, or employment is terminated because of false statements, omissions, or answers made by myself on this application. In the event of any employment with this company, I will comply with all rules and regulations as set by the company in any communication distributed to the employees.

In compliance with the Immigration Reform and Control Act of 1986, I understand that I am required to provide approved documentation to the company that verifies my right to work in the United States on the first day of employment. I have received from the company a list of the approved documents that are required.

I understand that employment at this company is "at will," which means that either I or this company can terminate the employment relationship at any time, with or without prior notice, and for any reason not prohibited by statute. All employment is continued on that basis. I hereby acknowledge that I have read and understand the above statements.

Signature _____ Date _____

Immigration Reform and Control Act Requirement

In compliance with the Immigration Reform and Control Act of 1986, you are required to provide approved documentation that verifies your right to work in the United States prior to your employment with this company. Please be prepared to provide us with the following documentation in the event you are offered and accept employment with our company:

Any one of the following: (These establish both identity and employment authorization.)
1. U.S. Passport.
2. Certificate of U.S. Citizenship (issued by USCIS).
3. Certificate of Naturalization (issued by USCIS).
4. Resident alien card or other alien unexpired endorsement card, with photo or other approved identifying information which evidences employment authorization.
5. Unexpired foreign passport with unexpired endorsement authorizing employment.

Or one from List A and List B:

List A (These establish employment authorization.)
1. Social Security card.
2. Birth Certificate or other documentation that establishes U.S. nationality or birth.
3. Other approved documentation.

List B
1. Driver's license or similar government identification card with photo or other approved identifying information.
2. Other approved documentation of identity for applicants under age 16 or in a state that does not issue an I.D. card (other than a driver's license).

3. Authorization to Release Employment Applicant Information

Employment Applicant:

_____

_____

_____

_____

To:

_____

_____

_____

_____

I have applied for a position with _____.

I have been requested to provide information for their use in reviewing my background and qualifications. Therefore, I authorize the investigation of my past and present work, character, education, military, and employment qualifications.

The release in any manner of all information by you is authorized, whether such information is of record or not, and I do hereby release all persons, agencies, firms, companies, etc., from any damages resulting from providing such information.

This authorization is valid for 90 days from the date of my signature below. Please keep this copy of my release request for your files. Thank you for your cooperation.

Signature_____ Date_____

Note: Medical information is often protected by state laws and civil codes. Consult your attorney if you wish to seek this information.

Note: Many employers are reluctant to provide information on previous employees. If you ask each applicant to distribute this form to his or her references before you contact them, the prior employers may be more willing to release information.

4. Pre-Employment Reference Check via Phone

Applicant's Name_____ Applying for_____

"My name is _____ from _____Company.

_____ has applied for a position with our company.

I would like to verify the information provided us by _____ and

_____ has given us permission to contact you."

Person Contacted_____ Company_____

Phone_____ ❑ Personnel Department ❑ Ex-Supervisor ❑ Other _____

Comments: _____

_____

Job Title _____

Employment Date _____

Job Responsibilities _____

_____

Attendance _____

Rehire _____

Person Contacted_____ Company_____

Phone_____ ❑ Personnel Department ❑ Ex-Supervisor ❑ Other _____

Comments: _____

_____

Job Title _____

Employment Date _____

Job Responsibilities _____

_____

Attendance _____

Rehire _____

Person Contacted_____ Company_____

Phone_____ ❑ Personnel Department ❑ Ex-Supervisor ❑ Other _____

Comments: _____

_____

Job Title _____

Employment Date _____

Job Responsibilities _____

_____

Attendance _____

Rehire _____

References Checked by _____ Date _____

Checker's Comments _____

_____

_____

5. Pre-Employment Reference Check via Phone (Version Two)

Applicant_____ Position_____

Company Contacted_____ Phone_____

Name of Company Representative _____

Title of Company Representative _____

Dates of Employment: From_____ To_____

Salary Information:

Regular Pay_____ Overtime Pay_____

Bonus _____ Shift _____

Differential_____

Date of last wage increase _____

What was your relationship with the applicant? _____
_____
_____

What were the applicant's job title and duties? _____
_____
_____

How long did you supervise this employee? _____

How would you compare this employee to others doing similar work and responsibilities? _____
_____
_____

Strong Points
_____
_____
_____
_____

Areas for Improvement
_____
_____
_____
_____

How would you rate this applicant's ability on a scale of 1 to 5 (1 being the lowest) regarding the following?

Attention to Detail _____ Comment _____

Learn _____ Comment _____

Follow Directions _____ Comment _____

Accept Responsibility _____ Comment _____

Follow Through _____ Comment _____

Initiate _____ Comment _____

Supervisory Duties _____
_____

Supervisory Ability _____
_____

Leadership Potential _____
_____

Attendance/Punctuality _____
_____

Ability to Work with Others _____
_____

Reason for Leaving _____
_____

Would You Rehire? _____
_____

Other Comments _____
_____

References Checked by _____ **Date** _____

6. Pre-Employment Reference Check via Letter

From:

_____

_____

_____

_____

To:

_____

_____

_____

_____

We would appreciate your assistance in verifying the information listed below regarding an employment application. It is to be understood that all information is confidential and will be treated as such in our company personnel files. Attached, please find an authorization to release information signed by the applicant. A self-addressed, stamped envelope is enclosed for your convenience in replying. We appreciate your assistance in this matter. Thank you.

Yours truly,

Personnel Manager

The following information was provided to us by the applicant. Please make any appropriate corrections:
Name _____ SS # _____
Job Title _____ Final Salary $_____
Date of Employment _____
Reason for Termination _____

Please complete the following requested information:
Would you rehire this applicant? ❏ Yes   ❏ No
If no, why not? _____
_____

Please review and rate the applicant in these areas:

	Unsatisfactory		Average		Outstanding
Attendance	1	2	3	4	5
Quality of work	1	2	3	4	5
Quantity of work	1	2	3	4	5
Cooperation	1	2	3	4	5
Responsibility	1	2	3	4	5

Signed _____ Title _____

Date _____

7. Applicant Comparison Summary Form

Position_____ Date Interviewed _____

Interviewed by_____

Candidate 1_____

Candidate 2_____

Candidate 3_____

Candidate 4_____

Critical Job Requirements	Candidate #1	#2	#3	#4	Comments
_____	_____	_____	_____	_____	_____
_____	_____	_____	_____	_____	_____
_____	_____	_____	_____	_____	_____
_____	_____	_____	_____	_____	_____
_____	_____	_____	_____	_____	_____
_____	_____	_____	_____	_____	_____
_____	_____	_____	_____	_____	_____
_____	_____	_____	_____	_____	_____
_____	_____	_____	_____	_____	_____
_____	_____	_____	_____	_____	_____
_____	_____	_____	_____	_____	_____
_____	_____	_____	_____	_____	_____
_____	_____	_____	_____	_____	_____
_____	_____	_____	_____	_____	_____
_____	_____	_____	_____	_____	_____
_____	_____	_____	_____	_____	_____

Legend:
✓ Meets critical job requirements
+ Exceeds critical job requirements
– Does not meet critical job requirements

8. Applicant Rating Form, Part One

Applicant's Name _____

Position and Department _____

Interviewed by _____ Date _____

Critical Job Requirements	Below Average			Average		Above Average			Excellent	
_____	1	2	3	4	5	6	7	8	9	10
_____	1	2	3	4	5	6	7	8	9	10
_____	1	2	3	4	5	6	7	8	9	10
_____	1	2	3	4	5	6	7	8	9	10
_____	1	2	3	4	5	6	7	8	9	10
_____	1	2	3	4	5	6	7	8	9	10
_____	1	2	3	4	5	6	7	8	9	10
_____	1	2	3	4	5	6	7	8	9	10
_____	1	2	3	4	5	6	7	8	9	10
_____	1	2	3	4	5	6	7	8	9	10
_____	1	2	3	4	5	6	7	8	9	10
_____	1	2	3	4	5	6	7	8	9	10
_____	1	2	3	4	5	6	7	8	9	10
_____	1	2	3	4	5	6	7	8	9	10
_____	1	2	3	4	5	6	7	8	9	10
_____	1	2	3	4	5	6	7	8	9	10
_____	1	2	3	4	5	6	7	8	9	10

Comments:

Strong Points _____

_____

_____

Weak Areas _____

_____

_____

Other _____

_____

_____

9. Applicant Rating Form, Part Two

Applicant's Name _____

Position and Department _____

Interviewed by _____ Date _____

Job Experience:	Poor				Outstanding
Relevance to Position	1	2	3	4	5
Accomplishments	1	2	3	4	5
Analytical/Problem Solving	1	2	3	4	5
Leadership	1	2	3	4	5
Career Goals	1	2	3	4	5
Academics:					
Relevance of Studies to Job	1	2	3	4	5
Extent, Variety in Activities	1	2	3	4	5
Abilities as a Student	1	2	3	4	5
Characteristics:					
Grooming	1	2	3	4	5
Bearing	1	2	3	4	5
Initiative	1	2	3	4	5
Grasp of Ideas	1	2	3	4	5
Stability	1	2	3	4	5
Personality	1	2	3	4	5
Preparation for Interview:					
Knowledge of Company	1	2	3	4	5
Relevance of Questions	1	2	3	4	5

Summary of Strength and Shortcomings:
Talent, Skills, Knowledge, Energy

_____

_____

Motivation, Interests

_____

_____

Personal Qualities, Effectiveness

_____

_____

Other Comments

_____

_____

10. Offer of Employment and Employment Contract

Date

Employee Name _____

Address _____

_____

Dear _____:

We are pleased to offer you a position with _____ ("Company"). Your start date, manager, compensation, benefits, and other terms of employment will be as set forth below and on EXHIBIT A.

TERMS OF EMPLOYMENT

1. **Position and Duties.** Company shall employ you, and you agree to competently and professionally perform such duties as are customarily the responsibility of the position as set forth in the job description attached as EXHIBIT A and as reasonably assigned to you from time to time by your Manager as set forth in EXHIBIT A.

2. **Outside Business Activities.** During your employment with Company, you shall devote competent energies, interests, and abilities to the performance of your duties under this Agreement. During the term of this Agreement, you shall not, without Company's prior written consent, render any services to others for compensation or engage or participate, actively or passively, in any other business activities that would interfere with the performance of your duties hereunder or compete with Company's business.

3. **Employment Classification.** You shall be a Full-Time Employee and shall not be entitled to benefits except as specifically outlined herein.

4. **Compensation/Benefits.**
   4.1 Wage. Company shall pay you the wage as set forth in the job description attached as EXHIBIT A.
   4.2 Reimbursement of Expenses. You shall be reimbursed for all reasonable and necessary expenses paid or incurred by you in the performance of your duties. You shall provide Company with original receipts for such expenses.
   4.3 Withholdings. All compensation paid to you under this Agreement, including payment of salary and taxable benefits, shall be subject to such withholdings as may be required by law or Company's general practices.
   4.4 Benefits. You will also receive Company's standard employee benefits package (including health insurance), and will be subject to Company's vacation policy as such package and policy are in effect from time to time.

5. **At-Will Employment.** Either party may terminate this Agreement by written notice at any time for any reason or for no reason. This Agreement is intended to be and shall be deemed to be an at-will employment Agreement and does not constitute a guarantee of continuing employment for any term.

6. **Nondisclosure Agreement.** You agree to sign Company's standard Employee Nondisclosure Agreement and Proprietary Rights Assignment as a condition of your employment. We wish to impress upon you that we do not wish you to bring with you any confidential or proprietary material of any former employer or to violate any other obligation to your former employers.

7. **Authorization to Work.** Because of federal regulations adopted in the Immigration Reform and Control Act of 1986, you will need to present documentation demonstrating that you have authorization to work in the United States.

8. **Further Assurances.** Each party shall perform any and all further acts and execute and deliver any documents that are reasonably necessary to carry out the intent of this Agreement.

9. **Notices.** All notices or other communications required or permitted by this Agreement or by law shall be in writing and shall be deemed duly served and given when delivered personally or by facsimile, air courier, certified

mail (return receipt requested), postage and fees prepaid, to the party at the address indicated in the signature block or at such other address as a party may request in writing.

10. **Governing Law.** This Agreement shall be governed and interpreted in accordance with the laws of the State of California, as such laws are applied to agreements between residents of California to be performed entirely within the State of California.

11. **Entire Agreement.** This Agreement sets forth the entire Agreement between the parties pertaining to the subject matter hereof and supersedes all prior written agreements and all prior or contemporaneous oral Agreements and understandings, expressed or implied.

12. **Written Modification and Waiver.** No modification to this Agreement, nor any waiver of any rights, shall be effective unless assented to in writing by the party to be charged, and the waiver of any breach or default shall not constitute a waiver of any other right or any subsequent breach or default.

13. **Assignment.** This Agreement is personal in nature, and neither of the parties shall, without the consent of the other, assign or transfer this Agreement or any rights or obligations under this Agreement, except that Company may assign or transfer this Agreement to a successor of Company's business, in the event of the transfer or sale of all or substantially all of the assets of Company's business, or to a subsidiary, provided that in the case of any assignment or transfer under the terms of this Section, this Agreement shall be binding on and inure to the benefit of the successor of Company's business, and the successor of Company's business shall discharge and perform all of the obligations of Company under this Agreement.

14. **Severability.** If any of the provisions of this Agreement are determined to be invalid, illegal, or unenforceable, such provisions shall be modified to the minimum extent necessary to make such provisions enforceable, and the remaining provisions shall continue in full force and effect to the extent the economic benefits conferred upon the parties by this Agreement remain substantially unimpaired.

15. **Arbitration of Disputes.** Any controversy or claim arising out of or relating to this contract, or the breach thereof, shall be settled by arbitration administered by the American Arbitration Association under its National Rules for the Resolution of Employment Disputes, and judgment upon the award rendered by the arbitrator(s) may be entered by any court having jurisdiction thereof.

We look forward to your arrival and what we hope will be the start of a mutually satisfying work relationship.

Sincerely,
Company

By: _____

Acknowledged, Accepted, and Agreed

Date: _____

_____
Employee Signature

11. New Employee Announcement

Date _____

To: All Employees

From: _____

Subject: New Employee

I am pleased to announce that _____ (new employee name) has joined our staff as a _____ (job title).

In his/her new position, _____ will report to_____.

Our new employee comes to us from _____ (last employer), where he/she was _____ (job title and major responsibilities) and prior to that was _____ (job title and major responsibilities).

Please join me in welcoming our new employee to our staff and in wishing him/her much success!

Employee Records and Human Resource Management

Now that you've got the best candidate in the door, it's very important to keep him or her there and to maintain adequate records. You should always maintain a master database of your employees with the *Employee Master Database*. With this form you can maintain an accurate and convenient master list of the name, Social Security number, date of birth, address, and hire date of each current or former employee. (Always maintain records for five years after an employee leaves his or her position.) You can also maintain records of whether the employee is current or former and full or part time. The *Employee Master Database* also contains columns for whether your employees have executed an employment agreement, stock option agreement, employee handbook acknowledgment, non-disclosure agreement, and W-4 form. Once you have these documents on file, indicate so by writing "OF" in each appropriate cell.

The *Company Employee Handbook* is a full-featured handbook that outlines a company's employment-related policies. You should carefully customize this document to suit your individual needs. When you present the *Company Employee Handbook* to your employees, also present them with an *Acknowledgment of Receipt of Employee Handbook* and ensure that they return the *Acknowledgment* to you; this *Acknowledgment* is your proof that the employee has read the *Handbook* and agreed to its terms.

In each employee's file, you should insert a completed *Employee Personal Information* form. You should have the employee fill out the form immediately after he or she is hired.

The *Employee Vacation Request* is filled out by an employee desiring vacation time and presented to the human resources department.

If your human resources department deducts money from an employee's pay for any reason other than ordinary tax withholding, such as 401(k) plans, savings plans, union dues, etc., be sure to have the employee consent to such deduction by executing the *Payroll Deduction Authorization*. If your human resources department makes a direct deposit of an employee's pay, have the employee authorize direct deposit by executing the *Direct Deposit Authorization*. As with any employment record, maintain a copy of either *Authorization* in the employee's file.

If your employee's position prevents him or her from being fully relieved from all responsibilities during a meal period, you should pay the employee for the meal period and have him or her agree to the arrangement by submitting to you a *Pay for Meal Period* form.

If a department head wants to hire, he or she would submit either the *Personnel Requisition*

(Non-Management) or the *Personnel Requisition (Management)* to the human resources department. The *Salary Recommendation Form* is a valuable internal document that enables staff to determine the appropriate salary in the case of a new hire or a promotion.

The *Job Announcement: Open Position* form announces to existing staff the availability of a new position. Remember: your current employees are a great resource both for filling new positions and for getting recommendations for new employees. The *Job Posting: Open Position* announces a new position to the general public. The *Job Position Description* presents a detailed description of a new position. Use the *Description* to alert staff of the details of the position.

Employees whose contact information changes should submit a *Personnel Data Change Form* to the human resources department. When employees are promoted, are terminated, resign, go on sick leave, etc, fill out an *Employee Status Change* form to keep track. Both the *Career Development Worksheet for Management Employee Career Interests* and the *Career Development Worksheet for Non-Management Employee Career Interests* enable your employees to clarify and communicate their career development goals. You should always aspire to have your employees grow as your company grows. The *Employee Career Development Worksheet Objectives and Results* form tracks the employee's goals and progress.

Unfortunately, you may find it necessary to discipline your employees. Be careful to document each incident and the recommended discipline and to treat employees evenhandedly. The employer-employee relationship is a contractual relationship and an employer owes tremendous duties of fairness to its employees. Many employer-employee disputes ripen into expensive litigation. You can minimize this undesirable result by maintaining meticulous employee discipline records. When one or more of your employees commits misconduct worthy of disciplinary action, fill out an *Employee Incident and Discipline Documentation Form*. Once an appropriate course of employee discipline has been decided, commit the recommended course in a *Disciplinary Notice*. The *Notice* serves as a formal written warning to errant employees. The *Notice* can also serve to refute any arguments offered by the employee suggesting that he or she did not receive warnings or discipline.

To evaluate and record an employee's performance, you can use the *Employee Performance Review*.

The *Time Sheet—Hourly Employees* records the hours worked by each employee and can help calculate overtime. Note that state law differs widely on the amount and rate of overtime that must be paid. The *Annual Attendance Record* allows you to compile and analyze an employee's attendance, sick days, tardiness, vacation days, and much more for a full year. An employee who seeks a leave of absence should complete a *Request for Leave of Absence Without Pay* and deliver it to the person with human resource responsibilities.

An employee who wishes to see his or her personnel file should complete a *Request to Inspect Personnel File* and deliver it to the person with human resource responsibilities. If an employee has a serious grievance, insist that he or she complete an *Employee Grievance Form*, to accurately and fully document the grievance.

12. Employee Master Database

Employee File Information

OF = On File

Current Employee	Name	SS Number	DOB	Home Address	Date Hired	Full/Part Time	Employm't Contract	Stock Opt. Agreement	Emp Hdbk Ack	Signed NDA	W-4 on File	US Dept Just EEV

Note: This form is available as an Excel template on the CD that accompanies this book.

13. Company Employee Handbook

_____ Company Employee Handbook

Issue Date: _____

Version Number: _____

To _____ Company Employees:

This is our new Employee Handbook. Please review it and sign the attached acknowledgment and drop the acknowledgment in _____'s in box.

You may keep a copy of the Handbook if you wish, but a copy will always be available to you through the HR department. If you do not wish to keep a copy, please return it to HR.

This Employee Handbook was developed to describe some of the expectations of our employees and to outline the policies, programs, and benefits available to eligible employees. Employees should familiarize themselves with the contents of the Handbook as soon as possible, for it will answer many questions about employment with _____ Company.

Introductory Statement

This Handbook is designed to acquaint you with _____ Company and provide you with information about working conditions, employee benefits, and some of the policies affecting your employment. This Handbook is not a contract and is not intended to create any contractual or legal obligations. You should read, understand, and comply with all provisions of the Handbook. It describes many of your responsibilities as an employee and outlines the programs developed by _____ Company to benefit employees. One of our objectives is to provide a work environment that is conducive to both personal and professional growth.

No Handbook can anticipate every circumstance or question about policy. As _____ Company continues to grow, the need may arise and _____ Company reserves the right to revise, supplement, or rescind any policies or portion of the Handbook from time to time as it deems appropriate, in its sole and absolute discretion. The only exception is our employment-at-will policy permitting you or _____ Company to end our relationship for any reason at any time. The employment-at-will policy cannot be changed except in a written agreement signed by both you and the President of the Company. Employees will, of course, be notified of such changes to the Handbook as they occur.

Customers are among our organization's most valuable assets. Every employee represents _____ Company to our customers and the public. The way we do our jobs presents an image of our entire organization. Customers judge all of us by how they are treated with each employee contact. Therefore, one of our first business priorities is to assist any customer or potential customer. Nothing is more important than being courteous, friendly, helpful, and prompt in the attention you give to customers.

_____ Company will provide customer relations and services training to all employees with extensive customer contact. Our personal contact with the public, our manners on the telephone, and the communications we send to customers are a reflection not only of ourselves, but also of the professionalism of _____ Company. Positive customer relations not only enhance the public's perception or image of _____ Company, but also pay off in greater customer loyalty and increased sales and profit.

1-01 Nature of Employment

Employment with _____ Company is voluntarily entered into and is "at-will," which means that the employee is free to resign at will at any time, with or without notice or cause. Similarly, _____ Company may terminate the employment relationship at any time, with or without notice or cause, so long as there is no violation of applicable federal or state law. No one has the authority to make verbal statements that change the at-will nature of employment, and the at-will relationship cannot be changed or modified for any employee except in a written agreement signed by that employee and the President of _____ Company.

Policies set forth in this Handbook are not intended to create a contract, nor are they to be construed to constitute contractual obligations of any kind or a contract of employment between _____ Company and any of its employees. The provisions of the Handbook have been developed at the discretion of management and, except for its policy of employment-at-will, may be amended or cancelled at any time, at _____ Company's sole discretion.

These provisions supersede all existing policies and practices and may not be amended or added to without the express written approval of the CEO or person designated by the CEO of _____ Company.

1-02 Employee Relations

_____ Company believes that the work conditions, wages, and benefits it offers to its employees are competitive with those offered by other employers in this area and in this industry. If employees have concerns about work conditions or compensation, they are strongly encouraged to voice these concerns openly and directly to their supervisors.

Our experience has shown that when employees deal openly and directly with supervisors, the work environment can be excellent, communications can be clear, and attitudes can be positive. We believe that _____ Company amply demonstrates its commitment to employees by responding effectively to employee concerns.

1-03 Equal Employment Opportunity

In order to provide equal employment and advancement opportunities to all individuals, employment decisions at _____ Company will be based on merit, qualifications, and the needs of the company. _____ Company does not unlawfully discriminate in employment opportunities or practices on the basis of race, color, religion, sex, national origin, age, disability, ancestry, medical conditions, family care status, sexual orientation, or any other basis prohibited by law.

_____ Company will make reasonable accommodations for qualified individuals with known disabilities unless doing so would result in an undue hardship to the extent required by law. This policy governs all aspects of employment, including selection, job assignment, compensation, discipline, termination, and access to benefits and training.

Any employees with questions or concerns about any type of discrimination in the workplace are encouraged to bring these issues to the attention of their immediate supervisor or the Human Resources Department. Employees can raise concerns and make reports without fear of reprisal. Anyone found to be engaging in any type of unlawful discrimination will be subject to disciplinary action, up to and including termination of employment.

1-04 Business Ethics and Conduct

The successful business operation and reputation of _____ Company are built upon the principles of fair dealing and ethical conduct of our employees. Our reputation for integrity and excellence requires careful observance of the spirit and the letter of all applicable laws and regulations, as well as a scrupulous regard for the highest standards of conduct and personal integrity.

The continued success of _____ Company is dependent upon our customers' trust and we are dedicated to preserving that trust. Employees owe a duty to _____ Company, its customers, and its shareholders to act in a way that will merit the continued trust and confidence of the public.

_____ Company will comply with all applicable laws and regulations and expects its directors, officers, and employees to conduct business in accordance with the letter, spirit, and intent of all relevant laws and to refrain from any illegal, dishonest, or unethical conduct.

In general, the use of good judgment, based on high ethical principles, will guide you with respect to lines of acceptable conduct. If a situation arises where it is difficult to determine the proper course of action, the matter should be discussed openly with your immediate supervisor and, if necessary, with the Human Resources Department for advice and consultation.

Compliance with this policy of business ethics and conduct is the responsibility of every _____ Company employee. Disregarding or failing to comply with this standard of business ethics and conduct could lead to disciplinary action, up to and including possible termination of employment.

1-05 Personal Relationships in the Workplace

The employment of relatives or individuals involved in a dating relationship in the same area of an organization may cause serious conflicts and problems with favoritism and employee morale. In addition to claims of partiality in treatment at work, personal conflicts from outside the work environment can be carried over into day-to-day working relationships.

For purposes of this policy, relatives are any persons who are related to each other by blood or marriage or whose relationship is similar to that of persons who are related by blood or marriage. A dating relationship is defined as a relationship that may be reasonably expected to lead to the formation of a consensual "romantic" or sexual relationship. This policy applies to all employees without regard to the gender or sexual orientation of the individuals involved.

Relatives of current employees may not occupy a position that will be working directly for or supervising their relative except as required by law. Individuals involved in a dating relationship with a current employee may also not occupy a position that will be working directly for or supervising the employee with whom they are involved in a dating relationship. _____ Company also reserves the right to take prompt action if an actual or potential conflict of interest arises involving relatives or individuals involved in a dating relationship who occupy positions at any level (higher or lower) in the same line of authority that may affect the review of employment decisions.

If a relative relationship or dating relationship is established after employment between employees who are in a reporting situation described above, it is the responsibility and obligation of the supervisor involved in the relationship to disclose the existence of the relationship to management.

In other cases where a conflict or the potential for conflict arises because of the relationship between employees, even if there is no line of authority or reporting involved, the employees may be separated by reassignment or terminated from employment. Employees in a close personal relationship should refrain from public workplace displays of affection or excessive personal conversation.

1-07 Immigration Law Compliance

_____ Company is committed to employing only United States citizens and aliens who are authorized to work in the United States and does not unlawfully discriminate on the basis of citizenship or national origin.

In compliance with the Immigration Reform and Control Act of 1986, each new employee, as a condition of employment, must complete the Employment Eligibility Verification Form I-9 and present documentation establishing identity and employment eligibility. Former employees who are rehired must also complete the form if they have not completed an I-9 with _____ Company within the past three years or if their previous I-9 is no longer retained or valid.

Employees with questions or seeking more information on immigration law issues are encouraged to contact the Human Resources Department. Employees may raise questions or complaints about immigration law compliance without fear of reprisal.

1-08 Conflicts of Interest

Employees have an obligation to conduct business within guidelines that prohibit actual or potential conflicts of interest. This policy establishes only the framework within which _____ Company wishes the business to operate. The purpose of these guidelines is to provide general direction so that employees can seek further clarification on issues related to the subject of acceptable standards of operation. Contact the Human Resources Department for more information or questions about conflicts of interest.

An actual or potential conflict of interest occurs when an employee is in a position to influence a decision that may result in a personal gain for that employee or for a relative as a result of _____ Company's business dealings. For the purposes of this policy, a relative is any person who is related by blood or marriage or whose relationship with the employee is similar to that of persons who are related by blood or marriage.

No "presumption of guilt" is created by the mere existence of a relationship with outside firms. However, if employees have any influence on transactions involving purchases, contracts, or leases, it is imperative that they disclose to an officer of _____ Company as soon as possible the existence of any actual or potential conflict of interest so that safeguards can be established to protect all parties.

Personal gain may result not only in cases where an employee or relative has a significant ownership in a firm with which _____ Company does business, but also when an employee or relative receives any kickback, bribe, substantial gift, or special consideration as a result of any transaction or business dealings involving _____ Company.

1-12 Non-Disclosure

The protection of confidential business information and trade secrets is vital to the interests and the success of _____ Company. Such confidential information includes, but is not limited to, the following examples:

- acquisitions
- compensation data
- computer processes
- computer programs and codes
- customer lists
- customer preferences
- financial information
- investments
- labor relations strategies
- marketing strategies
- new materials research
- partnerships
- pending projects and proposals
- proprietary production processes
- research and development strategies
- scientific data
- scientific formulae
- scientific prototypes
- technological data
- technological prototypes

All employees may be required to sign a non-disclosure agreement as a condition of employment. Employees who improperly use or disclose trade secrets or confidential business information will be subject to disciplinary action, up to and including termination of employment and legal action, even if they do not actually benefit from the disclosed information.

1-14 Disability Accommodation

_____ Company is committed to complying fully with applicable disability laws and ensuring equal opportunity in employment for qualified persons with disabilities.

Hiring procedures have been reviewed and provide persons with disabilities meaningful employment opportunities. Pre-employment inquiries are made regarding only an applicant's ability to perform the duties of the position.

Reasonable accommodation is available to all disabled employees, where their disability affects the performance of job functions to the extent required by law. All employment decisions are based on the merits of the situation and the needs of the company, not the disability of the individual.

_____ Company is also committed to not unlawfully discriminating against any qualified employees or applicants because they are related to or associated with a person with a disability.

This policy is neither exhaustive nor exclusive. _____ Company is committed to taking all other actions necessary to ensure equal employment opportunity for persons with disabilities in accordance with the ADA and all other applicable federal, state, and local laws.

2-01 Employment Categories

It is the intent of _____ Company to clarify the definitions of employment classifications so that employees understand their employment status and benefit eligibility. These classifications do not guarantee employment for any specified period of time. Accordingly, the right to terminate the employment relationship at will at any time is retained by both the employee and _____ Company.

Each employee is designated as either NONEXEMPT or EXEMPT from federal and state wage and hour laws. NONEXEMPT employees are entitled to overtime pay under the specific provisions of federal and state laws. EXEMPT employees are excluded from specific provisions of federal and state wage and hour laws. An employee's EXEMPT or NONEXEMPT classification may be changed only upon written notification by _____ Company management.

In addition to the above categories, each employee will belong to one other employment category:

REGULAR FULL-TIME employees are those who are not in a temporary or introductory status and who are regularly scheduled to work _____ Company's full-time schedule. Generally, they are eligible for _____ Company's benefit package, subject to the terms, conditions, and limitations of each benefit program.

INTRODUCTORY employees are those whose performance is being evaluated to determine whether further employment in a specific position or with _____ Company is appropriate. Employees who satisfactorily complete the introductory period will be notified of their new employment classification.

TEMPORARY employees are those who are hired as interim replacements, to temporarily supplement the work force, or to assist in the completion of a specific project. Employment assignments in this category are of a limited duration. Employment beyond any initially stated period does not in any way imply a change in employment status. Temporary employees retain that status unless and until notified of a change. While temporary employees receive all legally mandated benefits (such as workers' compensation insurance and Social Security), they are ineligible for all of _____ Company's other benefit programs.

2-02 Access to Personnel Files

_____ Company maintains a personnel file on each employee. The personnel file includes such information as the employee's job application, résumé, records of training, documentation of performance appraisals and salary increases, and other employment records.

Personnel files are the property of _____ Company and access to the information they contain is restricted. Generally, only supervisors and management personnel of _____ Company who have a legitimate reason to review information in a file are allowed to do so.

Employees who wish to review their own file should contact the Human Resources Department. With reasonable advance notice, employees may review their own personnel files in _____ Company's offices and in the presence of an individual appointed by _____ Company to maintain the files.

2-04 Personal Data Changes

It is the responsibility of each employee to promptly notify _____ Company of any changes in personal data. Personal mailing addresses, telephone numbers, number and names of dependents, individuals to be contacted in the event of an emergency, educational accomplishments, and other such status reports should be accurate and current at all times. If any personal data has changed, notify the Human Resources Department.

2-05 Introductory Period

The introductory period is intended to give new employees the opportunity to demonstrate their ability to achieve a satisfactory level of performance and to determine whether the new position meets their expectations. _____ Company uses this period to evaluate employee capabilities, work habits, and overall performance. Either the employee or _____ Company may end the employment relationship at will at any time during or after the introductory period, with or without cause or advance notice.

All new and rehired employees work on an introductory basis for the first 90 calendar days after their date of hire. Any significant absence will automatically extend an introductory period by the length of the absence. If _____ Company determines that the designated introductory period does not allow sufficient time to thoroughly evaluate the employee's performance, the introductory period may be extended for a specified period.

2-08 Employment Applications

_____ Company relies upon the accuracy of information contained in the employment application, as well as the accuracy of other data presented throughout the hiring process and employment. Any misrepresentations, falsifications, or material omissions in any of this information or data may result in the exclusion of the individual from further consideration for employment or, if the person has been hired, termination of employment.

In processing employment applications, _____ Company may obtain a consumer credit report or background check for employment. If _____ Company takes an adverse employment action based in whole or in part on any report caused by the Fair Credit Reporting Act, a copy of the report and a summary of your rights under the Fair Credit Reporting Act will be provided as well as any other documents required by law.

2-09 Performance Evaluation

Supervisors and employees are strongly encouraged to discuss job performance and goals on an informal, day-to-day basis. A formal written performance evaluation will be conducted following an employee's introductory period. Additional formal performance evaluations are conducted to provide both supervisors and employees the opportunity to discuss job tasks, identify and correct weaknesses, encourage and recognize strengths, and discuss positive, purposeful approaches for meeting goals.

2-10 Job Descriptions

_____ Company maintains job descriptions to aid in orienting new employees to their jobs, identifying the requirements of each position, establishing hiring criteria, setting standards for employee performance evaluations, and establishing a basis for making reasonable accommodations for individuals with disabilities.

The Human Resources Department and the hiring manager prepare job descriptions when new positions are created. Existing job descriptions are also reviewed and revised in order to ensure that they are up to date. Job descriptions may also be rewritten periodically to reflect any changes in position duties and responsibilities. All employees will be expected to help ensure that their job descriptions are accurate and current, reflecting the work being done.

Employees should remember that job descriptions do not necessarily cover every task or duty that might be assigned, and that additional responsibilities may be assigned as necessary. Contact the Human Resources Department if you have any questions or concerns about your job description.

3-01 Employee Benefits

Eligible employees at _____ Company are provided a wide range of benefits. A number of the programs (such as Social Security, workers' compensation, state disability, and unemployment insurance) cover all employees in the manner prescribed by law.

Benefits eligibility is dependent upon a variety of factors, including employee classification. Your supervisor can identify the programs for which you are eligible. Details of many of these programs can be found elsewhere in the Handbook.

The following benefit programs are available to eligible employees:

- auto mileage
- bereavement leave
- dental insurance
- holidays
- medical insurance
- stock options
- vacation benefits

Some benefit programs require contributions from the employee, but most are fully paid by _____ Company. Many benefits are described in separate Summary Plan Descriptions, or Plans, which may change from time to time. The Summary Plan Description will have control over any policy in this Handbook. You will receive a copy of each Summary Plan Description applicable to you. Contact the Human Resources Department if you need a Summary Plan Description or have any questions.

3-03 Vacation Benefits

Vacation time off with pay is available to eligible employees to provide opportunities for rest, relaxation, and personal pursuits. Employees in the following employment classification(s) are eligible to earn and use vacation time as described in this policy:

Regular full-time employees

The amount of paid vacation time employees receive each year increases with the length of their employment, as shown in the following schedule:

- Upon initial eligibility, the employee is entitled to 10 vacation days each year, accrued monthly at the rate of 0.833 days.

- After four years of eligible service, the employee is entitled to 15 vacation days each year, accrued monthly at the rate of 1.250 days.

The length of eligible service is calculated on the basis of a "benefit year." This is the 12-month period that begins when the employee starts to earn vacation time. An employee's benefit year may be extended for any significant leave of absence except military leave of absence. Military leave has no effect on this calculation. (See individual leave of absence policies for more information.)

Once employees enter an eligible employment classification, they begin to earn paid vacation time according to the schedule. They can request use of vacation time after it is earned.

Paid vacation time can be used in minimum increments of one day. To take vacation, employees should request advance approval from their supervisors. Requests will be reviewed based on a number of factors, including business needs and staffing requirements.

Vacation time off is paid at the employee's base pay rate at the time of vacation. It does not include overtime or any special forms of compensation such as incentives, commissions, bonuses, or shift differentials.

As stated above, employees are encouraged to use available paid vacation time for rest, relaxation, and personal pursuits. In the event that available vacation is not used by the end of the benefit year, employees may carry unused time forward to the next benefit year. If the total amount of unused vacation time reaches a "cap" equal to two times the annual vacation amount, further vacation accrual will stop. When the employee uses paid vacation time and brings the available amount below the cap, vacation accrual will begin again.

Upon termination of employment, employees will be paid for unused vacation time that has been earned through the last day of work.

3-05 Holidays

_____ Company will grant holiday time off to all employees on the holidays listed below:

- New Year's Day (January 1)
- Martin Luther King, Jr. Day (third Monday in January)
- Presidents' Day (third Monday in February)
- Memorial Day (last Monday in May)
- Independence Day (July 4)
- Labor Day (first Monday in September)
- Thanksgiving (fourth Thursday in November)
- Christmas (December 25)
- New Year's Eve (December 31)

_____ Company will grant paid holiday time off to all eligible employees immediately upon assignment to an eligible employment classification. Holiday pay will be calculated based on the employee's straight-time pay rate (as of the date of the holiday) times the number of hours the employee would otherwise have worked on that day. Eligible employee classification(s):

Regular full-time employees

If a recognized holiday falls during an eligible employee's paid absence (e.g., vacation, sick leave), the employee will be ineligible for holiday pay. If eligible nonexempt employees work on a recognized holiday, they will receive holiday pay plus wages at their straight-time rate for the hours worked on the holiday. In addition to the recognized holidays previously listed, eligible employees will receive two floating holidays in each anniversary year. To be eligible, employees must complete three calendar days of service in an eligible employment classification. These holidays must be scheduled with the prior approval of the employee's supervisor.

Paid time off for holidays will be counted as hours worked for the purposes of determining whether overtime pay is owed.

3-06 Workers' Compensation Insurance

_____ Company provides a comprehensive workers' compensation insurance program at no cost to employees, pursuant to law. This program covers any injury or illness sustained in the course of employment that requires medical, surgical, or hospital treatment. Subject to applicable legal requirements, workers' compensation insurance provides benefits after a short waiting period or, if the employee is hospitalized, immediately.

Employees who sustain work-related injuries or illnesses should inform their supervisor immediately. No matter how minor an on-the-job injury may appear, it is important that it be reported immediately. This will enable an eligible employee to qualify for coverage as quickly as possible.

3-07 Sick Leave Benefits

_____ Company provides paid sick leave benefits to all eligible employees for periods of temporary absence due to illnesses or injuries. Eligible employee classification(s):

Regular full-time employees

Eligible employees will accrue sick leave benefits at the rate of 10 days per year (.83 of a day for every full month of service). Sick leave benefits are calculated on the basis of a "benefit year," the 12-month period that begins when the employee starts to earn sick leave benefits.

Paid sick leave can be used in minimum increments of one day. An eligible employee may use sick leave benefits for an absence due to his or her own illness or injury, or that of a child, parent, or spouse of the employee.

Employees who are unable to report to work due to illness or injury should notify their direct supervisor before the scheduled start of their workday if possible. The direct supervisor must also be contacted on each additional day of absence. If an employee is absent for three or more consecutive days due to illness or injury, the company may require a physician's statement verifying the illness or injury and its beginning and expected ending dates. Such verification may be requested for other sick leave absences as well and may be required as a condition to receiving sick leave benefits.

Sick leave benefits will be calculated based on the employee's base pay rate at the time of absence and will not include any special forms of compensation, such as incentives, commissions, bonuses, or shift differentials.

Sick leave benefits are intended solely to provide income protection in the event of illness or injury, and may not be used for any other absence. Unused sick leave benefits will not be paid to employees while they are employed or upon termination of employment.

3-08 Time Off to Vote

_____ Company encourages employees to fulfill their civic responsibilities by participating in elections. Generally, employees are able to find time to vote either before or after their regular work schedule. If employees are unable to vote in an election during their nonworking hours, _____ Company will grant up to two hours of paid time off to vote.

Employees should request time off to vote from their supervisor at least two working days prior to the Election Day. Advance notice is required so that the necessary time off can be scheduled at the beginning or end of the work shift, whichever causes less disruption to the normal work schedule.

Employees must submit a voter's receipt on the first working day following the election to qualify for paid time off.

3-09 Bereavement Leave

Employees who wish to take time off due to the death of an immediate family member should notify their supervisor immediately.

Up to three days of paid bereavement leave will be provided to eligible employees in the following classification(s):

Regular full-time employees

Bereavement pay is calculated based on the base pay rate at the time of absence and will not include any special forms of compensation, such as incentives, commissions, bonuses, or shift differentials.

Bereavement leave will normally be granted unless there are unusual business needs or staffing requirements. Employees may, with their supervisors' approval, use any available paid leave for additional time off as necessary.

_____ Company defines "immediate family" as the employee's spouse, parent, child, or sibling.

3-11 Jury Duty

_____ Company encourages employees to fulfill their civic responsibilities by serving jury duty when required. Employees may request unpaid jury duty leave for the length of absence. If desired, employees may use any available paid time off (for example, vacation benefits).

Employees must show the jury duty summons to their supervisor as soon as possible so that the supervisor may make arrangements to accommodate their absence. Of course, employees are expected to report for work whenever the court schedule permits.

Either _____ Company or the employee may request an excuse from jury duty if, in _____ Company's judgment, the employee's absence would create serious operational difficulties.

_____ Company will continue to provide health insurance benefits for the full term of the jury duty absence.

Vacation, sick leave, and holiday benefits will continue to accrue during unpaid jury duty leave.

3-13 Benefits Continuation (COBRA)

The federal Consolidated Omnibus Budget Reconciliation Act (COBRA) gives employees and their qualified beneficiaries the opportunity to continue health insurance coverage under _____ Company's health plan when a "qualifying event" would normally result in the loss of eligibility. Some common qualifying events are resignation, termination of employment, or death of an employee; a reduction in an employee's hours or a leave of absence; an employee's divorce or legal separation; and a dependent child no longer meeting eligibility requirements.

Under COBRA, the employee or beneficiary pays the full cost of coverage at _____ Company's group rates plus an administration fee. _____ Company provides each eligible employee with a written notice describing rights granted under COBRA when the employee becomes eligible for coverage under _____ Company's health insurance plan. The notice contains important information about the employee's rights and obligations. Contact the Human Resources Department for more information about COBRA.

3-16 Health Insurance

_____ Company's health insurance plan provides employees access to medical and dental insurance benefits. Employees in the following employment classification(s) are eligible to participate in the health insurance plan:

Regular full-time employees

Eligible employees may participate in the health insurance plan subject to all terms and conditions of the agreement between _____ Company and the insurance carrier.

A change in employment classification that would result in loss of eligibility to participate in the health insurance plan may qualify an employee for benefits continuation under the Consolidated Omnibus Budget Reconciliation Act (COBRA). Refer to the "Benefits Continuation (COBRA)" policy section 3-13 for more information.

Details of the health insurance plan are described in the Summary Plan Description (SPD). An SPD and information on cost of coverage will be provided in advance of enrollment to eligible employees. Contact the Human Resources Department for more information about health insurance benefits.

4-03 Paydays

All employees are paid monthly on the first day of the month. Each paycheck will include earnings for all work performed through the end of the previous payroll period.

In the event that a regularly scheduled payday falls on a day off, such as a weekend or holiday, employees will receive pay on the last day of work before the regularly scheduled payday.

If a regular payday falls during an employee's vacation, the employee may receive his or her earned wages before departing for vacation if a written request is submitted at least one week prior to departing for vacation.

4-05 Employment Termination

Termination of employment is an inevitable part of personnel activity within any organization and many of the reasons for termination are routine. Below are examples of some of the most common circumstances under which employment is terminated:

- Resignation—voluntary employment termination initiated by an employee.
- Discharge—involuntary employment termination initiated by the organization.
- Layoff—involuntary employment termination initiated by the organization because of an organizational change.
- Retirement—voluntary employment termination initiated by the employee meeting age, length of service, and any other criteria for retirement from the organization.

_____ Company will generally schedule exit interviews at the time of employment termination. The exit interview will afford an opportunity to discuss such issues as employee benefits, conversion privileges, repayment of outstanding debts to _____ Company, or return of _____ Company-owned property. Suggestions, complaints, and questions can also be voiced.

Nothing in this policy is intended to change the company's at-will employment policy. Since employment with _____ Company is based on mutual consent, both the employee and _____ Company have the right to terminate employment at will, with or without cause, at any time. Employees will receive their final pay in accordance with applicable state law.

Employee benefits will be affected by employment termination in the following manner. All accrued, vested benefits that are due and payable at termination will be paid. Some benefits may be continued at the employee's expense if the employee so chooses. The employee will be notified in writing of the benefits that may be continued and of the terms, conditions, and limitations of such continuance. See the "Benefits Continuation (COBRA)" policy section 3-13.

4-09 Administrative Pay Corrections

_____ Company takes all reasonable steps to ensure that employees receive the correct amount of pay in each paycheck and that employees are paid promptly on the scheduled payday.

In the unlikely event that there is an error in the amount of pay, the employee should promptly bring the discrepancy to the attention of the Human Resources Department so that corrections can be made as quickly as possible.

4-10 Pay Deductions and Setoffs

The law requires that _____ Company make certain deductions from every employee's compensation. Among these are applicable federal, state, and local income taxes. _____ Company also must deduct Social Security taxes on each employee's earnings up to a specified limit that is called the Social Security "wage base." _____ Company matches the amount of Social Security taxes paid by each employee.

_____ Company offers programs and benefits beyond those required by law. Eligible employees may voluntarily authorize deductions from their paychecks to cover the costs of participation in these programs. Pay setoffs are pay deductions taken by _____ Company, usually to help pay off a debt or obligation to _____ Company or others. If you have questions concerning why deductions were made from your paycheck or how they were calculated, the Human Resources Department can assist in having your questions answered.

5-01 Safety

To assist in providing a safe and healthful work environment for employees, customers, and visitors, _____ Company has established a workplace safety program. This program is a top priority for _____ Company. The Human Resources Department has responsibility for implementing, administering, monitoring, and evaluating the safety program. Its success depends on the alertness and personal commitment of all.

_____ Company provides information to employees about workplace safety and health issues through regular internal communication channels such as supervisor-employee meetings, bulletin board postings, e-mail, memos, or other written communications.

Some of the best safety improvement ideas come from employees. Those with ideas, concerns, or suggestions for improved safety in the workplace are encouraged to raise them with their supervisor, or with another supervisor or manager, or bring them to the attention of the Human Resources Department. Reports and concerns about workplace safety issues may be made anonymously if the employee wishes. All reports can be made without fear of reprisal.

Each employee is expected to obey safety rules and to exercise caution in all work activities. Employees must immediately report any unsafe condition to the appropriate supervisor. Employees who violate safety standards, who cause hazardous or dangerous situations, or who fail to report or, where appropriate, remedy such situations may be subject to disciplinary action, up to and including termination of employment.

In the case of accidents that result in injury, regardless of how insignificant the injury may appear, employees should immediately notify the Human Resources Department or the appropriate supervisor. Such reports are necessary to comply with laws and initiate insurance and workers' compensation benefits procedures.

5-02 Work Schedules

Work schedules for employees vary throughout our organization. 9:00 a.m.-6:00 p.m. is a standard workday. Supervisors will advise employees of their individual work schedules. Staffing needs and operational demands may necessitate variations in starting and ending times, as well as variations in the total hours that may be scheduled each day and week.

5-04 Use of Phone and Mail Systems

Personal use of the telephone for long-distance and toll calls is not permitted. Employees should practice discretion when making local personal calls and may be required to reimburse _____ Company for any charges resulting from their personal use of the telephone. To ensure effective telephone communications, employees should always use the approved greeting ("Good Morning, _____ Company" or "Good Afternoon, _____ Company," as applicable) and speak in a courteous and professional manner. Please confirm information received from the caller and hang up only after the caller has done so.

The mail system is reserved for business purposes only. Employees should refrain from sending or receiving personal mail at the workplace. The e-mail system is the property of _____ Company. Occasional use of the e-mail system for personal messages is permitted, within reasonable limits. _____ Company will not guarantee the privacy of the e-mail system except to the extent required by law.

5-05 Smoking

Smoking is prohibited throughout the workplace, as required by law. This policy applies equally to all employees, customers, and visitors.

5-06 Rest and Meal Periods

All employees are provided with one one-hour meal period each workday. Supervisors will schedule meal periods to accommodate operating requirements. Employees will be relieved of all active responsibilities and restrictions during meal periods and will not be compensated for that time. Brief rest periods will be allowed, as required by California law.

5-10 Emergency Closings

At times, emergencies such as severe weather, fires, power failures, or earthquakes can disrupt company operations. In extreme cases, these circumstances may require the closing of a work facility.

In cases where an emergency closing is not authorized, employees who fail to report for work will not be paid for the time off. Employees may request available paid leave time such as unused vacation benefits.

5-12 Business Travel Expenses

_____ Company will reimburse employees for reasonable business travel expenses incurred while on assignments away from the normal work location. All business travel must be approved in advance by the President. Employees whose travel plans have been approved should make all travel arrangements through _____ Company's designated travel agency.

When approved, the actual costs of travel, meals, lodging, and other expenses directly related to accomplishing business travel objectives will be reimbursed by _____ Company. Employees are expected to limit expenses to reasonable amounts.

Expenses that generally will be reimbursed include the following:

- airfare or train fare for travel in coach or economy class or the lowest available fare
- car rental fees, only for compact or mid-sized cars
- fares for shuttle or airport bus service, where available; costs of public transportation for other ground travel
- taxi fares, only when there is no less expensive alternative
- mileage costs for use of personal cars, only when less expensive transportation is not available
- cost of standard accommodations in low- to mid-priced hotels, motels, or similar lodgings
- cost of meals, no more than $30.00 a day
- tips not exceeding 15% of the total cost of a meal or 10% of a taxi fare
- charges for telephone calls, fax, and similar services required for business purposes

Employees who are involved in an accident while traveling on business must promptly report the incident to their immediate supervisor. Vehicles owned, leased, or rented by _____ Company may not be used for personal use without prior approval. When travel is completed, employees should submit completed travel expense reports within 30 days. Reports should be accompanied by receipts for all individual expenses. Employees should contact their supervisor for guidance and assistance on procedures related to travel arrangements, expense reports, reimbursement for specific expenses, or any other business travel issues. Abuse of this business travel expenses policy, including falsifying expense reports to reflect costs not incurred by the employee, can be grounds for disciplinary action, up to and including termination of employment.

5-14 Visitors in the Workplace

To provide for the safety and security of employees and the facilities at _____ Company, only authorized visitors are allowed in the workplace. Restricting unauthorized visitors helps maintain safety standards, protects against theft, ensures security of equipment, protects confidential information, safeguards employee welfare, and avoids potential distractions and disturbances. All visitors should enter _____ Company at the main entrance. Authorized visitors will receive directions or be escorted to their destination. Employees are responsible for the conduct and safety of their visitors. If an unauthorized individual is observed on _____ Company's premises, employees should immediately notify their supervisor or, if necessary, direct the individual to the main entrance.

5-16 Computer and E-mail Usage

Computers, computer files, the e-mail system, and software furnished to employees are _____ Company property intended for business use. Employees should not use a password, access a file, or retrieve any stored communication without authorization.

_____ Company strives to maintain a workplace free of harassment and is sensitive to the diversity of its employees. Therefore, _____ Company prohibits the use of computers and the e-mail system in ways that are disruptive, offensive to others, or harmful to morale.

For example, the display or transmission of sexually explicit images, messages, and cartoons is not allowed. Other such misuse includes, but is not limited to, ethnic slurs, racial comments, off-color jokes, or anything that may be construed as harassment or showing disrespect for others. Employees should notify their immediate supervisor, the Human Resources Department, or any member of management upon learning of violations of this policy. Employees who violate this policy will be subject to disciplinary action, up to and including termination of employment.

5-17 Internet Usage

Internet access to global electronic information resources on the World Wide Web is provided by _____ Company to assist employees in obtaining work-related data and technology. The following guidelines have been established to help ensure responsible and productive Internet usage. While Internet usage is intended for job-related activities, incidental and occasional brief personal use of e-mail and the Internet is permitted within reasonable limits.

All Internet data that is composed, transmitted, or received via our computer communications systems is considered to be part of the official records of _____ Company and, as such, is subject to disclosure to law enforcement or other third parties. Employees should expect only the level of privacy that is warranted by existing law and no more. Consequently, employees should always ensure that the business information contained in Internet e-mail messages and other transmissions is accurate, appropriate, ethical, and lawful. Any questions regarding the legal effect of a message or transmission should be brought to our General Counsel.

Data that is composed, transmitted, accessed, or received via the Internet must not contain content that could be considered discriminatory, offensive, obscene, threatening, harassing, intimidating, or disruptive to any employee or other person. Examples of unacceptable content may include, but are not limited to, sexual comments or images, racial slurs, gender-specific comments, or any other comments or images that could reasonably offend someone on the basis of race, age, sex, religious or political beliefs, national origin, disability, sexual orientation, or any other characteristic protected by law.

The unauthorized use, installation, copying, or distribution of copyrighted, trademarked, or patented material on the Internet is expressly prohibited. As a general rule, if an employee did not create material, does not own the rights to it, or has not gotten authorization for its use, it should not be put on the Internet. Employees are also responsible for ensuring that the person sending any material over the Internet has the appropriate distribution rights. Any questions regarding the use of such information should be brought to our General Counsel.

Internet users should take the necessary anti-virus precautions before downloading or copying any file from the Internet. All downloaded files are to be checked for viruses; all compressed files are to be checked before and after decompression.

Abuse of the Internet access provided by _____ Company in violation of the law or _____ Company policies will result in disciplinary action, up to and including termination of employment. Employees may also be held personally liable for any violations of this policy. The following behaviors are examples of previously stated or additional actions and activities that are prohibited and can result in disciplinary action:

- Sending or posting discriminatory, harassing, or threatening messages or images
- Using the organization's time and resources for personal gain
- Stealing, using, or disclosing someone else's code or password without authorization
- Copying, pirating, or downloading software and electronic files without permission
- Sending or posting confidential material, trade secrets, or proprietary information outside of the organization
- Violating copyright law
- Failing to observe licensing agreements
- Engaging in unauthorized transactions that may incur a cost to the organization or initiate unwanted Internet services and transmissions
- Sending or posting messages or material that could damage the organization's image or reputation
- Participating in the viewing or exchange of pornography or obscene materials
- Sending or posting messages that defame or slander other individuals

- Attempting to break into the computer system of another organization or person
- Refusing to cooperate with a security investigation
- Sending or posting chain letters, solicitations, or advertisements not related to business purposes or activities
- Using the Internet for political causes or activities, religious activities, or any sort of gambling
- Jeopardizing the security of the organization's electronic communications systems
- Sending or posting messages that disparage another organization's products or services
- Passing off personal views as representing those of the organization
- Sending anonymous e-mail messages
- Engaging in any other illegal activities

5-22 Workplace Violence Prevention

_____ Company is committed to preventing workplace violence and to maintaining a safe work environment. Given the increasing violence in society in general, _____ Company has adopted the following guidelines to deal with intimidation, harassment, or other threats of (or actual) violence that may occur during business hours or on its premises.

All employees, including supervisors and temporary employees, should be treated with courtesy and respect at all times. Employees are expected to refrain from fighting, "horseplay," or other conduct that may be dangerous to others. Firearms, weapons, and other dangerous or hazardous devices or substances are prohibited from the premises of _____ Company without proper authorization.

Conduct that threatens, intimidates, or coerces another employee, a customer, or a member of the public at any time, including off-duty periods, will not be tolerated. This prohibition includes all acts of harassment, including harassment that is based on an individual's sex, race, age, or any characteristic protected by federal, state, or local law.

All threats of (or actual) violence, both direct and indirect, should be reported as soon as possible to your immediate supervisor or any other member of management. This includes threats by employees, as well as threats by customers, vendors, solicitors, or other members of the public. When reporting a threat of violence, you should be as specific and detailed as possible.

All suspicious individuals or activities should also be reported as soon as possible to a supervisor. Do not place yourself in peril. If you see or hear a commotion or disturbance near your workstation, do not try to intercede or see what is happening. _____ Company will promptly and thoroughly investigate all reports of threats of (or actual) violence and of suspicious individuals or activities. The identity of the individual making a report will be protected as much as is practical.

Anyone determined to be responsible for threats of (or actual) violence or other conduct that is in violation of these guidelines will be subject to prompt disciplinary action, up to and including termination of employment.

_____ Company encourages employees to bring their disputes or differences with other employees to the attention of their supervisors or the Human Resources Department before the situation escalates into potential violence. _____ Company is eager to assist in the resolution of employee disputes and will not discipline employees for raising such concerns.

6-01 Medical Leave

_____ Company provides medical leaves of absence without pay to eligible employees who are temporarily unable to work due to a serious health condition or disability. For purposes of this policy, serious health conditions or disabilities include inpatient care in a hospital, hospice, or residential medical care facility and continuing treatment by a health care provider.

Employees in the following employment classifications are eligible to request medical leave as described in this policy:

Regular full-time employees

Eligible employees should make requests for medical leave to their supervisors at least 30 days in advance of foreseeable events and as soon as possible for unforeseeable events.

A health care provider's statement must be submitted verifying the need for medical leave and its beginning and expected ending dates. Any changes in this information should be promptly reported to _____ Company. Employees returning from medical leave must submit a health care provider's verification of their fitness to return to work.

Eligible employees are normally granted leave for the period of the disability, up to a maximum of 12 weeks within any 12-month period. Any combination of medical leave and family leave may not exceed this maximum limit. If the initial period of approved absence proves insufficient, consideration will be given to a request for an extension.

Employees who sustain work-related injuries are eligible for a medical leave of absence for the period of the disability, in accordance with all applicable laws covering occupational disabilities.

Subject to the terms, conditions, and limitations of the applicable plans, _____ Company will continue to provide health insurance benefits for the full period of the approved medical leave.

Benefit accruals, such as vacation, sick leave, and holiday benefits, will continue during the approved medical leave period.

So that an employee's return to work can be properly scheduled, an employee on medical leave is requested to provide _____ Company with at least two weeks' advance notice of the date the employee intends to return to work. When a medical leave ends, the employee will be reinstated to the same position, if it is available, or to an equivalent position for which the employee is qualified.

If an employee fails to return to work on the agreed-upon return date, _____ Company will assume that the employee has resigned.

6-02 Family Leave

_____ Company provides family leaves of absence without pay to eligible employees who wish to take time off from work duties to fulfill family obligations relating directly to childbirth, adoption, or placement of a foster child or to care for a child, spouse, or parent with a serious health condition. A "serious health condition" means an illness, injury, impairment, or physical or mental condition that involves inpatient care in a hospital, hospice, or residential medical care facility or continuing treatment by a health care provider.

Employees in the following employment classifications are eligible to request family leave as described in this policy:

Regular full-time employees

Eligible employees should make requests for family leave to their supervisors at least 30 days in advance of foreseeable events and as soon as possible for unforeseeable events. Employees requesting family leave related to the serious health condition of a child, spouse, or parent may be required to submit a health care provider's statement verifying the need for family leave to provide care, its beginning and expected ending dates, and the estimated time required.

Eligible employees may request up to a maximum of 12 weeks of family leave within any 12-month period. Any combination of family leave and medical leave may not exceed this maximum. Married employee couples may be restricted to a combined total of 12 weeks leave within any 12-month period for childbirth, adoption, or placement of a foster child or to care for a parent with a serious health condition.

Subject to the terms, conditions, and limitations of the applicable plans, _____ Company will continue to provide health insurance benefits for the full period of the approved family leave. Benefit accruals, such as vacation, sick leave, and holiday benefits, will continue during the approved family leave period.

So that an employee's return to work can be properly scheduled, an employee on family leave is requested to provide _____ Company with at least two weeks' advance notice of the date the employee intends to return to work. When a family leave ends, the employee will be reinstated to the same position, if it is available, or to an equivalent position for which the employee is qualified. If an employee fails to return to work on the agreed-upon return date, _____ Company will assume that the employee has resigned.

6-07 Pregnancy Disability Leave

_____ Company provides pregnancy disability leaves of absence without pay to eligible employees who are temporarily unable to work due to a disability related to pregnancy, childbirth, or related medical conditions. Any employee is eligible to request pregnancy disability leave as described in this policy. Employees should make requests for pregnancy disability leave to their supervisors at least 30 days in advance of foreseeable events and as soon as possible for unforeseeable events. A health care provider's statement must be submitted verifying the need for pregnancy disability leave and its beginning and expected ending dates. Any changes in this information should be promptly reported to _____ Company. Employees returning from pregnancy disability leave must submit a health care provider's verification of their fitness to return to work.

Employees are normally granted unpaid leave for the period of the disability, up to a maximum of four months. Employees may substitute any accrued paid leave time for unpaid leave as part of the pregnancy disability leave period. Subject to the terms, conditions, and limitations of the applicable plans, _____ Company will continue to provide health insurance benefits for the full period of the approved pregnancy disability leave. So that an employee's return to work can be properly scheduled, an employee on pregnancy disability leave is requested to provide _____ Company with at least two weeks' advance notice of the date she intends to return to work.

When a pregnancy disability leave ends, the employee will be reinstated to the same position, unless either the employee would not otherwise have been employed for legitimate business reasons or each means of preserving the job would substantially undermine the ability to operate _____ Company safely and efficiently. If the same position is not available, the employee will be offered a comparable position in terms of such issues as pay, location, job content, and promotional opportunities.

If an employee fails to report to work promptly at the end of the pregnancy disability leave, _____ Company will assume that the employee has resigned.

7-01 Employee Conduct and Work Rules

To ensure orderly operations and provide the best possible work environment, _____ Company expects employees to follow rules of conduct that will protect the interests and safety of all employees and the organization.

It is not possible to list all the forms of behavior that are considered unacceptable in the workplace. The following are examples of infractions of rules of conduct that may result in disciplinary action, up to and including termination of employment:

- Theft or inappropriate removal or possession of property
- Falsification of timekeeping records
- Working under the influence of alcohol or illegal drugs
- Possession, distribution, sale, transfer, or use of alcohol or illegal drugs in the workplace, while on duty or while operating employer-owned vehicles or equipment
- Fighting or threatening violence in the workplace
- Boisterous or disruptive activity in the workplace
- Negligence or improper conduct leading to damage of employer-owned or customer-owned property
- Insubordination or other disrespectful conduct
- Violation of safety or health rules
- Smoking in the workplace

- Sexual or other unlawful or unwelcome harassment
- Possession of dangerous or unauthorized materials, such as explosives or firearms, in the workplace
- Excessive absenteeism or any absence without notice
- Unauthorized disclosure of business "secrets" or confidential information
- Violation of personnel policies
- Unsatisfactory performance or conduct

Nothing is this policy is intended to change the company's at-will employment policy. Employment with _____ Company is at the mutual consent of _____ Company and the employee, and either party may terminate that relationship at any time, with or without cause, and with or without advance notice.

7-02 Drug and Alcohol Use

It is _____ Company's desire to provide a drug-free, healthful, and safe workplace. To promote this goal, employees are required to report to work in appropriate mental and physical condition to perform their jobs in a satisfactory manner.

While on _____ Company premises and while conducting business-related activities off _____ Company premises, no employee may use, possess, distribute, sell, or be under the influence of alcohol or illegal drugs. The legal use of prescribed drugs is permitted on the job only if it does not impair an employee's ability to perform the essential functions of the job effectively and in a safe manner that does not endanger other individuals in the workplace.

Violations of this policy may lead to disciplinary action, up to and including immediate termination of employment, and/or required participation in a substance abuse rehabilitation or treatment program. Such violations may also have legal consequences.

Employees with questions or concerns about substance dependency or abuse are encouraged to discuss these matters with their supervisor or the Human Resources Department to receive assistance or referrals to appropriate resources in the community.

Employees with problems with alcohol and certain drugs that have not resulted in, and are not the immediate subject of, disciplinary action may request approval to take unpaid time off to participate in a rehabilitation or treatment program through _____ Company's health insurance benefit coverage. Leave may be granted if the employee agrees to abstain from use of the problem substance and abides by all _____ Company policies, rules, and prohibitions relating to conduct in the workplace; and if granting the leave will not cause _____ Company any undue hardship.

Employees with questions on this policy or issues related to drug or alcohol use in the workplace should raise their concerns with their supervisor or the Human Resources Department without fear of reprisal.

7-03 Sexual and Other Unlawful Harassment

_____ Company is committed to providing a work environment that is free from all forms of discrimination and conduct that can be considered harassing, coercive, or disruptive, including sexual harassment. Actions, words, jokes, or comments based on an individual's sex, race, color, national origin, age, religion, disability, sexual orientation, or any other legally protected characteristic will not be tolerated.

Sexual harassment is defined as unwanted sexual advances, or visual, verbal, or physical conduct of a sexual nature. This definition includes many forms of offensive behavior and includes gender-based harassment of a person of the same sex as the harasser. The following is a partial list of sexual harassment examples:

- Unwanted sexual advances
- Offering employment benefits in exchange for sexual favors
- Making or threatening reprisals after a negative response to sexual advances

- Visual conduct that includes leering, making sexual gestures, or displaying of sexually suggestive objects or pictures, cartoons, or posters
- Verbal conduct that includes making or using derogatory comments, epithets, slurs, or jokes
- Verbal sexual advances or propositions
- Verbal abuse of a sexual nature, graphic verbal commentaries about an individual's body, sexually degrading words used to describe an individual, or suggestive or obscene letters, notes, or invitations
- Physical conduct that includes touching, assaulting, or impeding or blocking movements

Unwelcome sexual advances (either verbal or physical), requests for sexual favors, and other verbal or physical conduct of a sexual nature constitute sexual harassment when: (1) submission to such conduct is made either explicitly or implicitly a term or condition of employment; (2) submission to or rejection of the conduct is used as a basis for making employment decisions; or (3) the conduct has the purpose or effect of interfering with work performance or creating an intimidating, hostile, or offensive work environment.

If you experience or witness sexual or other unlawful harassment in the workplace, report it immediately to your supervisor. If the supervisor is unavailable or you believe it would be inappropriate to contact that person, you should immediately contact the Human Resources Department or any other member of management. You can raise concerns and make reports without fear of reprisal or retaliation.

All allegations of sexual harassment will be quickly and discreetly investigated. To the extent possible, your confidentiality and that of any witnesses and the alleged harasser will be protected against unnecessary disclosure. When the investigation is completed, you will be informed of the outcome of the investigation.

Any supervisor or manager who becomes aware of possible sexual or other unlawful harassment must immediately advise the Human Resources Department or the President of the company so it can be investigated in a timely and confidential manner. Anyone engaging in sexual or other unlawful behavior will be subject to disciplinary action, up to and including termination of employment.

7-04 Attendance and Punctuality

To maintain a safe and productive work environment, _____ Company expects employees to be reliable and to be punctual in reporting for scheduled work. Absenteeism and tardiness place a burden on other employees and on _____ Company. In the rare instances when employees cannot avoid being late to work or are unable to work as scheduled, they should notify their supervisor or the Human Resources Department as soon as possible in advance of the anticipated tardiness or absence.

Poor attendance and excessive tardiness are disruptive. Either may lead to disciplinary action, up to and including termination of employment.

7-05 Personal Appearance

Dress, grooming, and personal cleanliness standards contribute to the morale of all employees and affect the business image that _____ Company presents to the community.

During business hours or when representing _____ Company, you are expected to present a clean, neat, and tasteful appearance. You should dress and groom yourself according to the requirements of your position and accepted social standards.

Your supervisor or department head is responsible for establishing a reasonable dress code appropriate to the job you perform. If your supervisor feels that your personal appearance is inappropriate, you may be asked to leave the workplace until you are properly dressed or groomed. Under such circumstances, you will not be compensated for the time away from work. Consult your supervisor if you have questions as to what constitutes appropriate appearance. Where necessary, reasonable accommodation may be made to a person with a disability.

7-06 Return of Property

Employees are responsible for all _____ Company property, materials, or written information issued to them or in their possession or control. Employees must return all _____ Company property immediately upon request or upon termination of employment. Where permitted by applicable laws, _____ Company may withhold from the employee's check or final paycheck the cost of any items that are not returned when required. _____ Company may also take all action deemed appropriate to recover or protect its property.

7-08 Resignation

Resignation is a voluntary act initiated by the employee to terminate employment with _____ Company. Although advance notice is not required, _____ Company requests at least two weeks' written notice of resignation from nonexempt employees and two weeks' written notice of resignation from exempt employees.

Prior to an employee's departure, an exit interview will be scheduled to discuss the reasons for resignation and the effect of the resignation on benefits.

7-10 Security Inspections

_____ Company wishes to maintain a work environment that is free of illegal drugs, alcohol, firearms, explosives, or other improper materials. To this end, _____ Company prohibits the possession, transfer, sale, or use of such materials on its premises. _____ Company requires the cooperation of all employees in administering this policy.

Desks, lockers, and other storage devices may be provided for the convenience of employees but remain the sole property of _____ Company. Accordingly, they, as well as any articles found within them, can be inspected by any agent or representative of _____ Company at any time, either with or without prior notice.

7-12 Solicitation

In an effort to ensure a productive and harmonious work environment, persons not employed by _____ Company may not solicit or distribute literature in the workplace at any time for any purpose.

_____ Company recognizes that employees may have interests in events and organizations outside the workplace. However, employees may not solicit or distribute literature concerning these activities during working time. (Working time does not include lunch periods, work breaks, or any other periods in which employees are not on duty.)

Examples of impermissible forms of solicitation include:

- The collection of money, goods, or gifts for community groups
- The collection of money, goods, or gifts for religious groups
- The collection of money, goods, or gifts for political groups
- The collection of money, goods, or gifts for charitable groups
- The sale of goods, services, or subscriptions outside the scope of official organization business
- The circulation of petitions
- The distribution of literature in working areas at any time
- The solicitation of memberships, fees, or dues

In addition, the posting of written solicitations on company bulletin boards and solicitations by e-mail are restricted. Company bulletin boards display important information; employees should consult them frequently for:

- Affirmative Action statement
- Employee announcements
- Workers' compensation insurance information
- State disability insurance/unemployment insurance information

If employees have a message of interest to the workplace, they may submit it to the Human Resources Director for approval. All approved messages will be posted by the Human Resources Director.

7-16 Progressive Discipline

The purpose of this policy is to state _____ Company's position on administering equitable and consistent discipline for unsatisfactory conduct in the workplace. The best disciplinary measure is the one that does not have to be enforced and comes from good leadership and fair supervision at all employment levels.

_____ Company's own best interest lies in ensuring fair treatment of all employees and in making certain that disciplinary actions are prompt, uniform, and impartial. The major purpose of any disciplinary action is to correct the problem, prevent recurrence, and prepare the employee for satisfactory service in the future.

Although employment with _____ Company is based on mutual consent and both the employee and _____ Company have the right to terminate employment at will, with or without cause or advance notice, _____ Company may use progressive discipline at its discretion.

Disciplinary action may call for any of four steps—verbal warning, written warning, suspension with or without pay, or termination of employment—depending on the severity of the problem and the number of occurrences.

Progressive discipline means that, with respect to many disciplinary problems, these four steps will normally be followed. However, there may be circumstances when one or more steps are bypassed.

_____ Company recognizes that there are certain types of employee problems that are serious enough to justify either a suspension or, in extreme situations, termination of employment, without going through the usual progressive discipline steps.

While it is impossible to list every type of behavior that may be deemed a serious offense, the Employee Conduct and Work Rules policy includes examples of problems that may result in immediate suspension or termination of employment. However, the problems listed are not all necessarily serious offenses, but may be examples of unsatisfactory conduct that will trigger progressive discipline.

By using progressive discipline, we hope that most employee problems can be corrected at an early stage, benefiting both the employee and _____ Company.

7-18 Problem Resolution

_____ Company is committed to providing the best possible working conditions for its employees. Part of this commitment is encouraging an open and frank atmosphere in which any problem, complaint, suggestion, or question receives a timely response from _____ Company supervisors and management.

_____ Company strives to ensure fair and honest treatment of all employees. Supervisors, managers, and employees are expected to treat each other with respect. Employees are encouraged to offer positive and constructive criticism.

If employees disagree with established rules of conduct, policies, or practices, they can express their concern through the problem resolution procedure. No employee will be penalized, formally or informally, for voicing a complaint with _____ Company in a reasonable, business-like manner, or for using the problem resolution procedure.

If a situation occurs when employees believe that a condition of employment or a decision affecting them is unjust or inequitable, they are encouraged to make use of the following steps. The employee may discontinue the procedure at any step.

1. The employee presents the problem to his or her immediate supervisor after the incident occurs. If the supervisor is unavailable or the employee believes it would be inappropriate to contact that person, the employee may present the problem to the Human Resources Department or the CEO.

2. The supervisor responds to the problem during discussion or after consulting with appropriate management, when necessary. The supervisor documents this discussion.

3. The employee presents the problem to the Human Resources Department if the problem is unresolved.

4. The Human Resources Department counsels and advises the employee, assists in putting the problem in writing, and visits with the employee's manager(s).

Not every problem can be resolved to everyone's total satisfaction, but only through understanding and discussing mutual problems can employees and management develop confidence in each other. This confidence is important to the operation of an efficient and harmonious work environment.

8-00 Life-Threatening Illnesses in the Workplace

Employees with life-threatening illnesses, such as cancer, heart disease, and AIDS, often wish to continue their normal pursuits, including work, to the extent allowed by their condition. _____ Company supports these endeavors as long as the employees are able to meet acceptable performance standards. As in the case of other disabilities, _____ Company will make reasonable accommodations in accordance with all legal requirements, to allow qualified employees with life-threatening illnesses to perform the essential functions of their jobs.

Medical information on individual employees is treated confidentially. _____ Company will take reasonable precautions to protect such information from inappropriate disclosure. Managers and other employees have a responsibility to respect and maintain the confidentiality of employee medical information. Anyone inappropriately disclosing such information is subject to disciplinary action, up to and including termination of employment.

Employees with questions or concerns about life-threatening illnesses are encouraged to contact the Human Resources Department for information and referral to appropriate services and resources.

8-06 Suggestions

As employees of _____ Company, you have the opportunity to contribute to our future success and growth by submitting suggestions for practical work-improvement or cost-savings ideas.

All regular employees are eligible to participate in the suggestion program.

A suggestion is an idea that will benefit _____ Company by solving a problem, reducing costs, improving operations or procedures, enhancing customer service, eliminating waste or spoilage, or making _____ Company a better or safer place to work. All suggestions should contain a description of the problem or condition to be improved, a detailed explanation of the solution or improvement, and the reasons why it should be implemented. Statements of problems without accompanying solutions or recommendations concerning co-workers and management are not appropriate suggestions. If you have questions or need advice about your idea, contact your supervisor for help.

Submit suggestions to the Human Resources Department and, after review, they will be forwarded to the Suggestion Committee. As soon as possible, you will be notified of the adoption or rejection of your suggestion. Special recognition and, optionally, a cash award will be given to employees who submit a suggestion that is implemented.

14. Acknowledgment of Receipt of Employee Handbook

The Employee Handbook describes important information about _____ Company, and I understand that I should consult the Human Resources Department regarding any questions not answered in the Employee Handbook.

Since the information, policies, and benefits described here are necessarily subject to change, I acknowledge that revisions to the Employee Handbook may occur. All such changes will be communicated through official notices. I understand that revised information may supersede, modify, or eliminate existing policies.

Furthermore, I acknowledge that this Employee Handbook is neither a contract of employment nor a legal document. I have received the Employee Handbook and I understand that it is my responsibility to read and comply with the policies contained in this Employee Handbook and any revisions made to it.

Employee's Name (printed): _____

Employee's Signature: _____

Date: _____

15. Employee Personal Information

You should have your new employee complete this form only after he or she has been hired. This information should be kept with the company's important records and should remain strictly confidential.

Date_____

Last Name_____ First _____ Middle _____

Street Address _____

City_____ State _____ ZIP _____

Home Phone Number _____

Driver's License Number _____

Social Security Number _____

Marital Status: ❑ Single ❑ Married ❑ Divorced

Date of Birth _____

Height _____ft. _____in.

Weight _____lbs.

Sex: ❑ Male ❑ Female

Name of Spouse _____

Phone _____

Spouse's Employer _____

Person to notify in case of emergency other than your spouse:

Name _____ Relation _____

Phone _____ Cell Phone _____

What was your previous address? _____

_____

How long have you been at your present address? _____ Years

Please fill out and return to the Human Resources Department.

16. Employee Vacation Request

Employee Name _____ Date _____

Employee has requested vacation from the following date _____ to the following date _____.

Total Vacation Days Accrued _____

Total Vacation Days Taken _____

Total Vacation Days Available _____

Number of Days Requested _____

Total Vacation Days Remaining _____

(if request approved)

Approval _____

Manager Signature _____ Date _____

17. Payroll Deduction Authorization

I authorize _____

to deduct $ _____

from my gross earnings each payroll period beginning _____

In payment for: Amount:

❏ Credit Union $_____

❏ Employee Savings Plan $_____

❏ 401(k) Plan $_____

❏ Union Dues $_____

❏ _____ $_____

❏ _____ $_____

❏ _____ $_____

❏ _____ $_____

Total $_____

Signature _____ Date _____

Print Name _____

Social Security # _____

Please keep a copy of this for your records.

18. Payroll Deduction Authorization

I authorize _____

to deduct $ _____

from my gross earnings each payroll period beginning _____

in payment for _____

These deductions are to continue until the amount of my obligation is paid in full or until my employment with this company is terminated for any reason. If my employment is terminated before this obligation is paid, I agree to pay the balance owed on or before the termination date.

Signature _____ Date _____

Print Name _____

Social Security # _____

Please keep a copy of this for your records.

19. Direct Deposit Authorization

Name _____

ID # _____

Social Security # _____

Bank Name and Branch _____

Account Number _____

❏ Yes, Direct Deposit:

I hereby request the deposit of my entire net payroll check into the specified bank account each pay period.

I authorize _____ and _____
to withdraw any funds deposited in error into my account.

❏ Yes, Direct Payroll Deduction:

I hereby request and authorize the sum of _____ dollars ($_____)
be deducted from my paycheck each pay period and deposited directly into the bank account named above.

❏ I would like to cancel my deposit authorization:

I hereby cancel the authorization for direct deposit or payroll deduction deposit previously submitted.

Employee Signature _____ Date _____

Please attach a copy of the deposit slip.

20. Pay for Meal Period

To: _____ (employee)

Since the nature of your job prevents us from relieving you of all duty and responsibilities during your regular meal period, we will pay you for an on-the-job meal period at your regular rate of pay.

If you voluntarily agree to this arrangement, please sign below.

Manager _____ Date _____

Agreed:

Employee Signature _____ Date _____

21. Personnel Requisition (Non-Management)

Job Title _____

Department _____

Reports to _____

Pay Grade _____

Date Required _____ ❑ Full Time ❑ Part Time

If part time, what is length needed? _____

Hours/Days _____

New Position? ❑ Yes ❑ No   If yes, approved? _____

Replacement? ❑ Yes ❑ No   Name _____

Position budgeted for? ❑ Yes ❑ No   Amount $ _____

Outside agency used for recruitment? ❑ Yes ❑ No   Name _____

Outside Recruitment Budget Amount $ _____

Major Job Responsibilities _____

_____

_____

Minimum Qualifications _____

_____

_____

Special Knowledge, Skills and Ability Required _____

_____

_____

Requested by _____ Date _____

Approved by _____ Date _____

To be filled out by Human Resources Department.

Date Received_____ Date Job Filled _____

Employee Name _____

22. Personnel Requisition (Management)

Job Title _____

Department _____

Reports to _____ ❑ Exempt ❑ Non-Exempt

Recruitment Start Date _____

Projected Start Date _____

Hiring Salary between _____ and _____ per _____

Bonus Applicable? ❑ Yes ❑ No   Amount $ _____

Other Special Benefits _____

_____

Position budgeted for? ❑ Yes ❑ No   Amount $ _____

Outside agency used for recruitment? ❑ Yes ❑ No   Name _____

Outside Recruitment Budget Amount $ _____

Major Job Responsibilities _____

_____

_____

_____

Minimum Qualifications _____

_____

_____

_____

A successful candidate will possess the following: _____

_____

_____

_____

Number of Subordinates to Supervise _____

Titles of Subordinates _____

Budget Accountability _____

Assets _____

Special Considerations and Requirements (travel, location, hours, etc.) _____

_____

_____

Indicate the level of responsibility and frequency of occurrence for each area of work. Please add areas of work if appropriate. Consider 1 the lowest and 4 the highest. Circle appropriate number.

Area of Work					Comments
Planning/Organizing Others' Work	1	2	3	4	_____
Planning/Organizing Own Work	1	2	3	4	_____
Leadership	1	2	3	4	_____
Training	1	2	3	4	_____
Policy Development	1	2	3	4	_____
Employee Relations	1	2	3	4	_____
Long-Range Planning	1	2	3	4	_____
Problem Solving	1	2	3	4	_____
Personnel Selection	1	2	3	4	_____
Creativity, New Ideas	1	2	3	4	_____
Internal Contacts	1	2	3	4	_____
Outside Contacts	1	2	3	4	_____

Submitted by _____ Date _____

Approved by _____ Date _____

Position Filled Date _____ Salary _____

23. Salary Recommendation Form

Employee Name _____

ID # _____

Location _____

Department _____

	Current	Proposed
Title	_____	_____
Salary Grade	_____	_____
Base Rate	_____	_____
Merit Amount	_____	_____
Promotion Amount	_____	_____
Other Amount	_____	_____
Bonus	_____	_____

Effective Date _____

Type of Proposed Increase: ❏ New Hire ❏ Merit ❏ Promotion ❏ Other _____

Date of Last Increase _____

Type of Last Increase: ❏ New Hire ❏ Merit ❏ Promotion ❏ Other _____

Explanation for Proposed Salary Increase _____

_____

_____

_____

Approvals:

Supervisor _____ Date _____

Manager _____ Date _____

Division Vice President _____ Date _____

Human Resources Department _____ Date _____

24. Job Announcement: Open Position

Job Title _____

Department _____

Pay Grade _____ ❏ Exempt   ❏ Non-Exempt

Reports to _____

Job Summary _____

_____

_____

_____

Job Minimum Qualifications (special skills, education, etc.) _____

_____

_____

_____

_____

_____

_____

_____

Interested candidate should contact the Human Resources Department by _____

Posted Date _____

To be eligible for consideration for the above position you must have been in your current position a minimum of _____ months.

25. Job Posting: Open Position

Job Title _____

Department _____

Pay Grade _____   ❏ Exempt   ❏ Non-Exempt

Reports to _____

Location _____

Job Summary _____

_____

_____

_____

Duties and Responsibilities _____

_____

_____

_____

_____

_____

_____

Minimum Requirements _____

_____

_____

_____

Job Posting Date _____

All bids must be received by the Human Resources Department within 10 days of the job posting.

26. Job Position Description

Job Title _____

Grade _____

Pay Range _____

Reports to _____

Job Class _____

Location _____

Department _____

Job Summary _____

_____

_____

_____

Duties and Responsibilities _____

_____

_____

_____

_____

_____

_____

Supervision:

Received _____

Given _____

Position Minimum Requirements:

Education _____

_____

_____

Experience _____

_____

Responsibility _____

_____

_____

Initiative _____

_____

_____

Skills _____

_____

_____

Physical Requirements _____

_____

_____

Mental Requirements _____

_____

_____

Supervision _____

_____

_____

Equipment Used _____

_____

_____

Other _____

_____

_____

Prepared by _____ Date _____

Approved by _____ Date _____

27. Personnel Data Change Form

Effective Date _____

Employee Name (previous name if changed) _____

For Changes Only:

Name _____

Address _____

_____

Phone Number _____

Marital Status:

❏ Single

❏ Married

❏ Divorced

Note: An employee is not obligated to report marital status to his or her employer, but the employee may wish to report marital status so the employer can adjust the tax withholding amount.

Signature _____ Date _____

Please fill out and return to the Human Resources Department.

28. Employee Status Change

Name _____

Employer ID # _____

Department _____

Effective Date _____

Wage/Salary/Title Change:

	Title	Grade	Pay Rate	Increase %
Present				
Proposed				

Type of Change: (check appropriate type)

❏ New Hire ❏ Voluntary Resignation

❏ Promotion ❏ Leave of Absence

❏ Other ❏ Sick Leave

❏ Transfer ❏ Layoff

❏ Return from Absence ❏ Disability—Not Work-Related

❏ Termination ❏ Disability—Work-Related

If leave of absence, state duration: from _____ to _____

Comments and reasons for change: _____

_____

_____

_____

Submitted by:

Supervisor _____ Title _____ Date _____

Approvals:

Department Manager _____ Date _____

Human Resources Manager _____ Date _____

Original to Department Manager, copy to Human Resources File.

29. Career Development Worksheet for Management Employee Career Interests

Employee _____ Date _____

Job Title _____ Department _____ Job Grade _____

Employees who are satisfied with their present position and do not wish to be considered for other positions should omit Section II when completing this form.

I. Development Goals for the Coming Year:

A. What are your development goals for the coming year? _____

_____

_____

B. Can you meet these goals, or some of them, through your present work assignment?

C. Indicate any specific training programs, developmental experiences, job assignments, or job structure changes that you feel would be beneficial. Please explain.

II. Longer-Range Career Goals:

A. What are your longer-range career aspirations? _____

_____

_____

B. In your judgment, is your present assignment suitable, given your longer-range aspirations? Please explain.

_____

_____

_____

C. Do you want to be considered for assignment in another function or department? If yes, please specify.

_____

_____

_____

D. What are your main strengths that you would like to have considered in future job assignments?

_____

_____

_____

E. Please describe ways you feel the company could help you prepare yourself for future career opportunities.

_____

_____

_____

III. Location Preferences:

A. Are you willing to relocate now to develop your skills? ❏ Yes   ❏ No

B. Will you be willing to relocate within the next five years? If yes, please indicate time frame:

❏ one year   ❏ two years   ❏ three years   ❏ four years   ❏ five years

C. Please describe any location restrictions.

_____

_____

IV. Developmental Progress:

Summarize what you have done this past year to improve work performance and prepare for future responsibilities.

_____

_____

_____

_____

V. Additional Comments:

_____

_____

_____

_____

_____

Employee Signature _____ Date _____

30. Career Development Worksheet for Non-Management Employee Career Interests

Employee _____ Date _____

Job Title _____ Job Grade _____

Department _____

Please answer each question wherever you have a preference or an opinion. However, it is not necessary to state a conclusion in each area. Indicate approximate timing where appropriate. This will help us ensure that your personal goals are considered in the career-planning process.

I. Personal Career Goals

A. What are your short- and long-term career aspirations?

_____

_____

_____

B. Do you feel your present job assignment is suitable, given your longer-range aspirations? If so, for how long? If not, please explain.

_____

_____

_____

C. Do you want to be considered for assignment in another function or department? If yes, please specify.

_____

_____

_____

D. What are your current and future plans for self-improvement? (i.e., education, etc.)

_____

_____

_____

E. Please describe ways you feel the company could help you prepare for future career opportunities. What training programs, developmental experiences, job assignments, or job structure changes do you feel would be beneficial?

_____

_____

_____

II. Location Preferences

A. Are you willing to relocate now to develop your skills? ❑ Yes   ❑ No

B. Will you be willing to relocate within the next five years? _____ If yes, please indicate time frame:

❑ one year   ❑ two years   ❑ three years   ❑ four years   ❑ five years

C. Please describe any location restrictions.

_____

_____

_____

III. Additional Comments

_____

_____

_____

_____

_____

_____

Employee Signature _____ **Date** _____

31. Employee Career Development Worksheet Objectives and Results

Employee _____

Job Title _____

Supervisor _____

Period: from _____ to _____

Date Written _____

Date Results Reviewed _____

Major Objectives

_____

_____

_____

_____

Actions to Achieve Objectives

_____

_____

_____

_____

Performance Measures

_____

_____

_____

_____

Progress or Outside Influences Uncontrollable by Employee

_____

_____

_____

_____

Performance Results

_____

_____

_____

_____

32. Employee Incident and Discipline Documentation Form

Employee Information

Name of Employee _____

Employee's Job Title _____

Incident Information

Date/Time of Incident _____

Location of Incident _____

Description of Incident _____

_____

_____

_____

Witnesses to Incident _____

Was this incident in violation of a company policy? ❑ Yes   ❑ No

If yes, specify which policy and how the incident violated it. _____

_____

_____

Action Taken

What action will be taken against the employee? _____

_____

_____

Has the impropriety of the employee's actions been explained to the employee? ❑ Yes   ❑ No

Did the employee offer any explanation for the conduct? If so, what was it? _____

_____

_____

Signature of person preparing report _____

Date _____

33. Disciplinary Notice

Employee _____

Department _____

❑ Written Warning   ❑ Final Warning

1. Statement of the problem (violation of rules, policies, standards, practices, or unsatisfactory performance):

_____
_____
_____

2. Prior discussion or warnings on this subject (oral, written, dates):

_____
_____
_____
_____

3. Statement of company policy on this subject:

_____
_____
_____

4. Summary of corrective action to be taken (including dates for improvement and plans for follow-up):

_____
_____
_____

5. Consequences of failure to improve performance or correct behavior:

_____
_____
_____

6. Employee comments: _____

_____
_____
_____

(Continue on reverse if necessary.)

Employee Signature _____ Date _____

Management Approval _____ Date _____

Distribution: One copy to Employee, one copy to Supervisor, and original to Personnel File.

34. Employee Performance Review

Name _____

Job Title _____

Department _____

Supervisor _____

Date Hired _____ Last Review Date _____ This Review Date _____

The following definitions apply to each factor rated below

Level 6–Far Exceeds Job Requirements
Performance at this level far exceeds the requirements for this position.
Duties and responsibilities are exceptionally met and consistently exceeded.

Level 5–Consistently Exceeds Job Requirements
Performance at this level is always beyond the requirements for this position.
Duties and responsibilities are not only met excellently, but exceeded consistently.

Level 4–Meets and Usually Exceeds Job Requirements
Performance at this level is above the requirements for this position.
Duties and responsibilities are met well and usually exceeded.

Level 3–Consistently Meets Job Requirements
Performance at this level is up to the requirements for this position.
Duties and responsibilities are met consistently and in a satisfactory and acceptable manner.

Level 2–Inconsistent in Meeting Job Requirements
Performance at this level is at the minimum acceptable requirements for this position.
Duties and responsibilities are met marginally.

Level 1–Does Not Meet Job Requirements
Performance at this level is below the minimum acceptable requirements for the position.
Duties and responsibilities are not met in an acceptable manner.

Circle appropriate number.

Quantity of Work   Level   1 2 3 4 5 6

Volume of work regularly produced, speed and consistency of output.

Comments _____

_____

_____

Quality of Work   Level   1 2 3 4 5 6

Extent to which employee completes assignments.

Comments _____

_____

_____

Job Cooperation   Level   1 2 3 4 5 6

Amount of interest and enthusiasm shown in work.

Comments _____

_____

_____

Ability to Work with Others   Level   1 2 3 4 5 6

Extent to which employee interacts effectively with others in doing his/her job.

Comments _____

_____

_____

Adaptability   Level   1 2 3 4 5 6

Extent to which employee is able to perform various assignments within the scope of his/her job duties.

Comments _____

_____

_____

Communications   Level   1 2 3 4 5 6

Extent to which employee communicates effectively with others in doing his/her job.

Comments _____

_____

_____

Job Knowledge   Level   1 2 3 4 5 6

Extent of job information and understanding possessed by employee.

Comments _____

_____

_____

Initiative   Level   1 2 3 4 5 6

Extent to which employee is a self-starter in attaining objectives of his/her job.

Comments _____

_____

_____

Overall Evaluation of Employee Performance   Level   1 2 3 4 5 6

Comments _____

_____

_____

Attendance ❑ Problem ❑ No Problem

Comments _____

_____

_____

I. Employee's Career Development

A. Strengths _____

_____

_____

B. Development Needs _____

_____

_____

C. Development Plan (including long range) _____

_____

_____

II. Employee Comments (optional)

General comment about the evaluation of your performance:

_____

_____

_____

_____

_____

_____

Read and acknowledged by:

Employee _____ Date _____

III. Approvals

Supervisor _____ Date _____

Department Manager _____ Date _____

Human Resources _____ Date _____

President _____ Date _____

35. Time Sheet–Hourly Employees

Employee Name _____

ID # _____

Social Security # _____

Position _____

Department _____

Number _____

Time Period Covered from _____ to _____

Day	Date	In	Out	Total Regular	Total Overtime	Total Hours	Approval
Sun							
Mon							
Tues							
Wed							
Thur							
Fri							
Sat							
			Totals				

Employee Signature _____ Date _____

Supervisor Approval _____ Date _____

Legend :

A = Absent

H = Holiday

S = Sick

F = Funeral Leave

J = Jury Duty

V = Vacation

O = Occurrence

P = Personal Leave Approved

T = Tardy

U = Unauthorized Absence

I = Job Injury

LO = Leave of Absence

36. Annual Attendance Record

For Calendar Year _____

Employee Name _____ Social Security # _____

Date of Birth _____ Date of Hire _____

Position _____ Department _____

Day	Jan	Feb	Mar	Apr	May	Jun	Jul	Aug	Sep	Oct	Nov	Dec
1												
2												
3												
4												
5												
6												
7												
8												
9												
10												
11												
12												
13												
14												
15												
16												
17												
18												
19												
20												
21												
22												
23												
24												
25												
26												
27												
28												
29												
30												
31												

Legend:

A = Absent	O = Occurrence	H = Holiday	P = Personal Leave Approved
S = Sick	T = Tardy	F = Funeral Leave	U = Unauthorized Absence
J = Jury Duty	I = Job Injury	V = Vacation	LO = Leave of Absence

Comments and Summary of Attendance:

_____

_____

37. Request for Leave of Absence Without Pay

Name _____ Social Security # _____

Address _____

Phone Number _____ Department _____

Position _____ Employment Date _____

Last Day to Work _____

I hereby request a leave of absence without pay, for the purpose indicated:

❑ Disability (including pregnancy)
❑ Family or Childcare Leave
❑ Personal Leave
❑ Military Leave
❑ Educational Leave
❑ Other _____

Start Date _____ Return Date _____

Purpose _____

I understand that the leave, if granted, may be used only for the purpose described above and use of the leave for any other purpose will be grounds for disciplinary action, up to and including termination.

Employee Signature _____ Date _____

Physician's Statement:

If the request for leave is due to medical disability, have your physician complete the following statement:

The above-named is a patient in my care and is expected to be able to resume his/her usual occupation on or about

_____.

Physician's Address _____ Phone Number _____

Physician's Signature _____ Date _____

Approval:

Department Manager: _____

❑ Approved ❑ Denied Reason _____

Manager's Signature _____ Date _____

Human Resources Manager

❑ Approved ❑ Denied Reason _____

Manager's Signature _____ Date _____

To the Employee: The date of expiration of your leave of absence is the date you are expected to return to work. Request for an extension of leave of absence must be made to the Human Resources Department prior to the return date of your leave. You have the responsibility for maintaining contact, by providing an address and a phone number for contacting you.

38. Request to Inspect Personnel File

Employee Name _____

Date of Request _____

Social Security # _____

Department/Location _____

Work Phone _____

I request an appointment with the Human Resources Department to inspect my personnel file.

I last reviewed my file _____

Signature _____ Date _____

Appointment is scheduled for:

Date _____

Time _____

Location _____

File review completed (Date) _____

Employee comments regarding information and accuracy of information in the personnel file:

_____

_____

_____

_____

_____

Human Resources Representative _____ Date _____

Employee Signature _____ Date _____

Employee is to complete top section of request form and forward to the Human Resources Department.

Place one completed copy of this form into personnel file upon completion of review.

39. Employee Grievance Form

Date _____

Name of Employee _____

Department _____

State your grievance in detail, including the date of act(s) or omissions causing grievance.

_____

_____

_____

Identify other employees with personal knowledge of your grievance.

_____

_____

State briefly your efforts to resolve this grievance.

_____

_____

Describe the remedy or solution you would like.

_____

_____

Employee's Signature _____ Date _____

Grievance Team Member–Informal Review

Date Received _____

Actions Taken _____

_____

_____

Disposition _____

❏ Employee Accepted   ❏ Employee Appealed

Assigned Team Member _____ Date Communicated _____

Grievance Team–Formal Review

Date Received _____

Actions Taken _____

_____

_____

Disposition _____

❏ Employee Accepted   ❏ Employee Appealed

Assigned Team Member _____ Date Communicated _____

Grievance Team and Management–Formal Review

Date Received _____

Actions Taken _____

_____

_____

Disposition _____

❏ Employee Accepted   ❏ Employee Appealed

Assigned Team Member_____ Date Communicated _____

Employee and Workplace Safety

The safety and security of you and your employees should be your highest business priority. We have included here several documents that can help you achieve the goal of a 100% safe workplace. Post the *Emergency Instructions* in a conspicuous place to advise your employees of safety procedures. Don't be afraid to add information to this form, such as the location of exits, a safe place to congregate outside the premises following an emergency, and specific instructions about machinery that should be turned off in the event of an emergency. The *Employee Telecommuting Memo* highlights several safety issues related to employees who work at home.

If an accident injures an employee, have the employee's supervisor complete the *Supervisor's Report of Work Injury*. This form should be completed as soon as possible following the incident to ensure that the record keeping is complete and accurate. Finally, we have included several Occupational Safety & Health Administration forms: *OSHA Form 300: Log of Work-Related Injuries and Illnesses*, *OSHA Form 300A: Summary of Work-Related Injuries and Illnesses*, and *OSHA Form 301: Injuries and Illnesses Incident Report*. You may be required to fill out these forms in the event of workplace injury. While a complete description of OSHA record-keeping is beyond the scope of this book, you can find a helpful summary of OSHA compliance on OSHA's Web site at www.osha.gov/dcsp/compliance_ assistance/index.html.

40. Emergency Instructions

These emergency instructions should be posted in a prominent place such as the employee lounge.

Follow these rules in an emergency:

- Stop work and leave the building IMMEDIATELY when the fire alarm sounds or when you are instructed to do so!

- Follow instructions, avoid panic, and cooperate with those responding to the emergency.

- Proceed to the designated or nearest exit.

- Turn off computers, equipment, fans, etc., and close desk drawers.

- Do NOT delay your exit from the building by looking for belongings or other people.

- When leaving the building, go to a clear area well away from the building. Do not obstruct fire hydrants or the responding fire/rescue workers and their equipment.

- Do not re-enter the building until instructed to do so by your supervisor or a fire/rescue worker.

The above rules will be enforced. Periodic fire emergency drills may be conducted. Your life and the lives of others will depend on your cooperation.

If you ever discover a fire:

- Remain calm. Do not shout "Fire!"

- Pull the nearest fire alarm.

- Dial "911" and give the operator the location of the fire—the floor, wing, and room number, if possible.

41. Employee Telecommuting Memo

What follows are some guidelines that we would like our telecommuting employees to follow with respect to their work environment. We want our employees to be safe; these recommendations will ensure the safest home work environment possible. If you have any questions, please contact your manager.

General Lighting

- Use blinds or drapes on windows to eliminate bright light. Blinds should be adjusted during the day to allow light into the room without enabling you to see bright light directly.

- Reorient the workstation so that bright lights aren't in your field of view. Turn off fluorescent light fixtures in your field of view if they're bothersome. (Of course, be considerate of the effect on others who are working nearby.)

- If you use auxiliary desk lighting, it should usually be low wattage and should be directed so that it doesn't directly enter your eyes or directly illuminate the display screen. It's usually inadvisable to put additional lighting on reference documents, because this makes them too bright compared to the screen.

Screen Reflections

- An antireflection screen can be placed over the display. Glass screens perform better than mesh screens. Look for screens that have been approved by the American Optometric Association. (Alternatively, a hood can be purchased and placed over the display to shield it from offending sources; however, hoods often don't perform as well as antireflection screens.)

- Eliminate or cover the sources of the reflections—typically windows and other bright lights behind you.

Flicker Problems

Some people experience a flickering sensation when viewing the screen. If this is bothersome, try turning down the brightness, or use a dark background instead of a light one. If all else fails, using a display with a higher refresh rate might solve the problem. In less than 1% of the population, flickering may trigger epileptic seizures. If this condition applies to you, please immediately notify your supervisor.

Display Characteristics

- Adjust the screen brightness and contrast so that character definition and resolution are maximized. The screen brightness should match the general background brightness of the room. (This is much easier to do with light background screens.)

- Black characters on a white background is probably the best combination. Other combinations can be comfortable as long as the contrast between the characters and the background is high. It's best to avoid dark backgrounds.

- The size of the text should be three times the size of the smallest text you can read. You can test this by viewing the screen from three times your usual working distance; you should still be able to read the text.

- Although 60 Hz is the most common refresh rate, higher refresh rates are preferred. If you need help adjusting your refresh rate, contact your supervisor and we will assist you.

- For color monitors, small dot pitches (less than 0.28 mm) are desirable. If you require a monitor with a higher dot pitch, contact your supervisor and we will assist you.

Workstation Furniture and Arrangement

- Your table should allow for adjusting the keyboard height, have adequate space for both the monitor and reference material, and provide adequate knee space. It's usually best for the keyboard to be 3-5 inches below the standard desktop height of 29 inches; you should not be reaching up to the keyboard.

- Your chair should be easily adjustable in height, provide adjustable lower-back support, and have a flexible, woven seat covering. Five legs provide greater stability than four. Full armrests are not recommended, because they often preclude moving the chair under the table. However, support for the elbow or forearm can relieve strain on the shoulders, arms, and wrists.

- The height of your monitor should be adjustable. The center of the screen should be 10-20 degrees below your straight-ahead gaze (4-9 inches below your eyes, for normal working distances). In most cases, the top of the screen should be just below your eyes. A screen that is higher than these recommendations adversely affects your posture.

- Reference documents should be located close to the screen, with adjustable copy holders. The documents and the screen should be the same distance from your eyes and the brightness of the documents should match that of the screen.

Work Pace

- Take frequent breaks. Get up and walk around at least once an hour. Close your eyes. (People often "forget" to blink when they're concentrating.) Some of the more progressive workplaces even encourage their employees to take naps so that they can be re-energized and be more productive.

- If you feel any physical pain (back pain, headaches, sore wrists, etc.), stop working immediately. Normally these are simply signs of fatigue and can be remedied with sufficient rest or a pain reliever. For 10% of workers, there may be a risk of injury that can easily be prevented or significantly reduced through the use of ergonomic accommodations. If this condition applies to you, please see your human resource specialist to make the necessary accommodations.

Notify

The most important rule of all is to communicate with your superior or manager. If you ever have a question or concern, notify your manager. If you desire an inspection of your workplace, notify your manager.

42. Supervisor's Report of Work Injury

Date of Report _____

Injured Employee _____ Age _____

Job Title _____ Employee Number _____

Location _____

Department _____

Date of Hire _____ Time in this job (months) _____ Time on this shift (months) _____

Date of Injury _____ Time of Injury _____

Exact Location _____

Names of Witnesses _____

_____

Injury to:

❏ Face or Head ❏ Eyes ❏ Body ❏ Arms ❏ Hands or Fingers

❏ Legs ❏ Toes or Foot ❏ Internal ❏ Lungs

Type of Injury:

❏ Lacerations ❏ Strain or Sprain ❏ Hernia ❏ Fracture

❏ Puncture ❏ Abrasion ❏ Amputation ❏ Burns

❏ Foreign Body ❏ Skin ❏ Gas

Treatment:

❏ First Aid ❏ Nurse ❏ Doctor's Care

❏ Serious ❏ Lost Time ❏ Fatality

Remarks: (Be Specific—e.g., L or R arm, etc.)

_____

_____

Describe how employee was injured. (What was employee doing? What duty or task?)

_____

_____

_____

What happened that resulted in this injury? (Examples: slipped, fell, was struck.)

_____

_____

_____

_____

What factors do you believe contributed to this accident? (Consider methods, procedures, tools, machines, equipment arrangements, instructions, rules, inherent hazards, skill, experience, materials, and other factors.)

_____

_____

_____

How could such an accident be prevented or avoided?

_____

_____

_____

Investigating Committee (People to be included in accident investigations are listed below.)

1. Injured Employee _____

2. Immediate Supervisor _____

3. Safety Committeeperson _____

4. Shop Steward _____

5. Department Head (or Representative) _____

6. Witnesses _____

7. Safety Department Representative _____

8. Designated Union Safety Representative _____

9. Manager or Appointed Representative _____

Note: Report to be completed by immediate supervisor and turned in to the Safety Department not later than the end of the day following the injury. All lost-time injuries or fatalities must be promptly reported.

Important: All fatalities or accidents resulting in five or more persons being hospitalized must be reported to the appropriate federal or state agency enforcing OSHA regulations within the time limits applicable.

People to be included in accident investigations:

Near Miss/No Injury
The extent of the investigation will be left to the discretion of the supervisor.

Slight (First Aid)
Immediate Investigation
1. Injured Employee
2. Immediate Supervisor

Nurse Case
Immediate Investigation
1. Injured Employee
2. Immediate Supervisor
3. Safety Committeeperson

Doctor Case
Immediate Investigation
1. Injured Employee
2. Immediate Supervisor
3. Safety Committeeperson
4. Shop Steward
5. Department Head (or Representative)
6. Witnesses

Final Investigation
1. Injured Employee
2. Immediate Supervisor
3. Safety Committeeperson
4. Shop Steward
5. Department Head (or Representative)
6. Witnesses
7. Safety Dept. Representative

Lost Time or Fatality

Immediate Investigation

1. Injured Employee
2. Immediate Supervisor
3. Safety Committeeperson
4. Shop Steward
5. Department Head (or Representative)
6. Witnesses
7. Safety Dept. Representative
8. Designated Union Safety Representative

Final Investigation

1. Injured Employee
2. Immediate Supervisor
3. Safety Committeeperson
4. Shop Steward
5. Department Head (or Representative)
6. Witnesses
7. Safety Dept. Representative
8. Designated Union Safety Representative
9. Manager or Appointed Representative

43. OSHA Form 300: Log of Work-Related Injuries and Illnesses

OSHA's Form 300

Log of Work-Related Injuries and Illnesses

Year

U.S. Department of Labor
Occupational Safety and Health Administration

Form approved OMB no. 1218-0176

Attention: This form contains information relating to employee health and must be used in a manner that protects the confidentiality of employees to the extent possible while the information is being used for occupational safety and health purposes.

You must record information about every work-related injury or illness that involves loss of consciousness, restricted work activity or job transfer, days away from work, or medical treatment beyond first aid. You must also record significant work-related injuries and illnesses that are diagnosed by a physician or licensed health care professional. You must also record work-related injuries and illnesses that meet any of the specific recording criteria listed in 29 CFR 1904.8 through 1904.12. Feel free to use two lines for a single case if you need to.

Establishment name

City   State

Identify the person

(A) Case No.	(B) Employee's Name	(C) Job Title (e.g., Welder)

Describe the case

(D) Date of injury or onset of illness (mo./day)	(E) Where the event occurred (e.g. Loading dock north end)	(F) Describe injury or illness, parts of body affected, and object/substance that directly injured or made person ill

Classify the case

Using these categories, check ONLY the most serious result for each case:

	(G) Death	Days away from work (H)	Remained at work		

CHECK ONLY ONE box for each case based on the most serious outcome for that case:

Remained at work	
(I) Job transfer or restriction	(J) Other recordable cases

Enter the number of days the injured or ill worker was:

(K) On job transfer or restriction (days)	(L) Away from work (days)

(M) Check the "Injury" column or choose one type of illness:

(1) Injury	(2) Skin Disorder	(3) Respiratory Condition	(4) Poisoning	(5) All other illnesses

Page totals

Death	Days away from work	Job transfer or restriction	Other recordable cases	On job transfer or restriction	Away from work	Injury	Skin Disorder	Respiratory Condition	Poisoning	All other illnesses
0	0	0	0	0	0	0	0	0	0	0

Be sure to transfer these totals to the Summary page (Form 300A) before you post it.

Injury	Skin Disorder	Respiratory Condition	Poisoning	All other illnesses
(1)	(2)	(3)	(4)	(5)

Page 1 of 1

Public reporting burden for this collection of information is estimated to average 14 minutes per response, including time to review the instruction, search and gather the data needed, and complete and review the collection of information. Persons are not required to respond to the collection of information unless it displays a currently valid OMB control number. If you have any comments about these estimates or any aspects of this data collection, contact: US Department of Labor, OSHA Office of Statistics, Room N-3644, 200 Constitution Ave, NW, Washington, DC 20210. Do not

44. OSHA Form 300A: Summary of Work-Related Injuries and Illnesses

OSHA's Form 300A
Summary of Work-Related Injuries and Illnesses

All establishments covered by Part 1904 must complete this Summary page, even if no injuries or illnesses occurred during the year. Remember to review the log to verify that the entries are complete and accurate before completing this summary.

Using the Log, count the individual entries you made for each category. Then write the totals below, making sure you've added the entries from every page of the log. If you had no cases write "0."

Employees, former employees, and their representatives have the right to review the OSHA Form 300 in its entirety. They also have limited access to the OSHA Form 301 or its equivalent. See 29 CFR 1904.35, in OSHA's recordkeeping rule, for further details on the access provisions for these forms.

Year _____

U.S. Department of Labor
Occupational Safety and Health Administration

Form approved OMB no. 1218-0176

Number of Cases

Total number of deaths	Total number of cases with days away from work	Total number of cases with job transfer or restriction	Total number of other recordable cases
0	0	0	0
(G)	(H)	(I)	(J)

Number of Days

Total number of days away from work	Total number of days of job transfer or restriction
0	0
(K)	(L)

Injury and Illness Types

Total number of...

(M)	
(1) Injury	0
(2) Skin Disorder	0
(3) Respiratory Condition	0
(4) Poisoning	0
(5) All other illnesses	0

Establishment information

Your establishment name _____

Street _____

City _____ State _____ Zip _____

Industry description (e.g., Manufacture of motor truck trailers)
_____

Standard Industrial Classification (SIC), if known (e.g., SIC 3715)
_____

Employment information

Annual average number of employees _____

Total hours worked by all employees last year _____

Sign here

Knowingly falsifying this document may result in a fine.

I certify that I have examined this document and that to the best of my knowledge the entries are true, accurate, and complete.

_____
Company executive   Title

_____
Phone   Date

Post this Summary page from February 1 to April 30 of the year following the year covered by the form.

Public reporting burden for this collection of information is estimated to average 50 minutes per response, including time to review the instruction, search and gather the data needed, and complete and review the collection of information. Persons are not required to respond to the collection of information unless it displays a currently valid OMB control number. If you have any comments about these estimates or any aspects of this data collection, contact: US Department of Labor, OSHA Office of Statistical Analysis, Room N-3644, 200 Constitution Avenue, NW, Washington, DC 20210. Do not send the completed forms to this office.

45. OSHA Form 301: Injuries and Illnesses Incident Report

OSHA's Form 301
Injuries and Illnesses Incident Report

U.S. Department of Labor

Occupational Safety and Health Administration

Form approved OMB no. 1218-0176

Attention: This form contains information relating to employee health and must be used in a manner that protects the confidentiality of employees to the extent possible while the information is being used for occupational safety and health purposes.

This *Injury and Illness Incident Report* is one of the first forms you must fill out when a recordable work-related injury or illness has occurred. Together with the *Log of Work-Related Injuries and Illnesses* and the accompanying *Summary*, these forms help the employer and OSHA develop a picture of the extent and severity of work-related incidents.

Within 7 calendar days after you receive information that a recordable work-related injury or illness has occurred, you must fill out this form or an equivalent. Some state workers' compensation, insurance, or other reports may be acceptable substitutes. To be considered an equivalent form, any substitute must contain all the information asked for on this form.

According to Public Law 91-596 and 29 CFR 1904, OSHA's recordkeeping rule, you must keep this form on file for 5 years following the year to which it pertains

If you need additional copies of this form, you may photocopy and use as many as you need.

Information about the employee

1) Full Name

2) Street

   City _____ State _____ Zip _____

3) Date of birth

4) Date hired

5) ☐ Male
   ☐ Female

Information about the physician or other health care professional

6) Name of physician or other health care professional

7) If treatment was given away from the worksite, where was it given?

   Facility

   Street

   City _____ State _____ Zip _____

8) Was employee treated in an emergency room?
   ☐ Yes
   ☐ No

9) Was employee hospitalized overnight as an in-patient?
   ☐ Yes
   ☐ No

Information about the case

10) Case number from the Log _____ *(Transfer the case number from the Log after you record the case.)*

11) Date of injury or illness

12) Time employee began work _____ AM/PM

13) Time of event _____ AM/PM ☐ Check if time cannot be determined

14) **What was the employee doing just before the incident occurred?** Describe the activity, as well as the tools, equipment or material the employee was using. Be specific. Examples: "climbing a ladder while carrying roofing materials"; "spraying chlorine from hand sprayer"; "daily computer key-entry."

15) **What happened?** Tell us how the injury occurred. Examples: "When ladder slipped on wet floor, worker fell 20 feet"; "Worker was sprayed with chlorine when gasket broke during replacement"; "Worker developed soreness in wrist over time."

16) **What was the injury or illness?** Tell us the part of the body that was affected and how it was affected; be more specific than "hurt", "pain", or "sore." Examples: "strained back"; "chemical burn, hand"; "carpal tunnel syndrome."

17) **What object or substance directly harmed the employee?** Examples: "concrete floor"; "chlorine"; "radial arm saw." If this question does not apply to the incident, leave it blank.

18) **If the employee died, when did death occur?** Date of death

Completed by _____

Title _____

Phone _____ Date _____

Public reporting burden for this collection of information is estimated to average 22 minutes per response, including time for reviewing instructions, searching existing data sources, gathering and maintaining the data needed, and completing and reviewing the collection of information. Persons are not required to respond to the collection of information unless it displays a current valid OMB control number. If you have any comments about this estimate or any other aspects of this data collection, including suggestions for reducing this burden, contact: US Department of Labor, OSHA Office of Statistics, Room N-3644, 200 Constitution Ave, NW, Washington, DC 20210. Do not send the completed forms to this office.

Employee Termination

All employees come to a company looking for a job and many leave looking for a job. This section is brief, but important. When an employee's employment is terminated with your firm, make sure that all is in order before you part ways. The past few decades have witnessed a significant increase in litigation brought by former employees for wrongful termination. While some of the suits are valid, others are groundless and abusive and exploit poor record keeping by employers. Thus, secure all documentation necessary to memorialize the separation and you can more successfully defend a suit brought for wrongful termination.

If an employee chooses to leave voluntarily, have him or her execute the *Voluntary Resignation*. This form serves as a nearly indisputable record of the employee's willing termination of employment. This form may also go a long way to extinguishing an employee's right to charge your business's unemployment insurance for unemployment benefits. The *Employee's Separation Checklist* advises an employee of outstanding issues that must be resolved before separation. *The Manager's Pre-Dismissal Checklist* ensures that all loose ends are well tied before an employee departs. Finally, the *Employee Exit Interview* helps the company and the employee communicate their final thoughts before terminating the employment relationship.

46. Voluntary Resignation

Employee Name _____

Department _____

I voluntarily resign my employment with _____

Effective: Month _____ Day _____ Year_____

My reasons for leaving are:

_____

_____

_____

_____

_____

_____

_____

_____

_____

_____

Forwarding Address: _____

_____

_____

Employee Signature _____ Date_____

Manager Signature _____ Date_____

47. Employee's Separation Checklist

Employee Name _____

Date of Termination _____

The following items are to have been collected prior to your separation with the company. Please have all these below listed items returned to your manager prior to your separation date. Thank you.

❑ All keys returned.

❑ Company vehicle keys returned.

❑ Company vehicle returned.

❑ Company credit cards returned.

❑ Company phone credit cards returned.

❑ Company equipment (portable phones, beepers, PCs) returned.

❑ COBRA election forms signed and returned.

❑ 401(k) election forms signed and returned.

❑ Profit-sharing election forms signed and returned.

Your files, desk, and work area will be inventoried for all equipment and work utensils given to you by the company.

❑ Desk and working premises inventoried.

48. Manager's Pre-Dismissal Checklist

Employee Name _____

Date of Termination _____

Collect the following items from the employee prior to separation from the company:

❑ All keys returned.

❑ Company vehicle keys returned.

❑ Company vehicle returned.

❑ Company credit cards returned.

❑ Company phone credit cards returned.

❑ Company equipment (e.g., portable phones, beepers, credit cards, laptop computers) returned.

❑ COBRA election forms signed and returned.

❑ 401(k) election forms signed and returned.

❑ Profit-sharing election forms signed and returned.

❑ Company documents and files inventoried.

❑ Desk and working premises inventoried.

❑ Personnel and Payroll Departments notified of departure.

❑ Final expense report received, reviewed, and approved; expense check prepared.

❑ Final check prepared (including all accrued vacation pay, sick pay, accrued wages, bonus, etc.).

❑ Exit interview prepared.

❑ Exit interview given.

❑ Final checks (payroll and expense) given to terminating employee.

All of the above duties have been completed in a satisfactory manner.

Company has no further liability with the terminating employee.

Manager Signature _____ Date _____

49. Employee Exit Interview

Employee Name _____

Title _____

Department _____

Date _____

What did you like best about your current position?
_____
_____
_____

What did you like least about your current position?
_____
_____
_____

What did you like best about the company?
_____
_____
_____

What did you like least about the company?
_____
_____
_____

What are your feelings toward your supervisor?
_____
_____
_____

Why are you leaving the company at this time? What company and position are you going to?
_____
_____
_____

What are your comments about the company's salary and benefits?
_____
_____
_____

What suggestions do you have for improving your current position and other aspects within the company?

_____

_____

_____

Interviewed by _____ **Date** _____

Interviewer's remarks

_____

_____

_____

_____

_____

Miscellaneous Personnel Forms

We have included several miscellaneous personnel forms. Unfortunately, not every résumé you receive will be a perfect match. Thus we have included two versions of a *Job Applicant Dismissal*, which you should send to job seekers who don't fit your needs. Of course, you'll want to invite certain applicants for an interview. You can do so with the *Job Applicant Invitation*. The document is safely worded so as not to convey an offer of employment.

You should strongly consider enacting a formal job applicant referral program. Recommendations from current employees are usually your greatest source of new employees. Also, consider the cost of recruitment firms—often a third of a new hire's first-year salary. You can award your current employees with cash or vacation time. Encourage your employees to submit the *Employee Referral* form to the human resources department to recommend candidates for particular positions. We have included an *Applicant Referral Update* for use when one of your employees refers a potential new hire in the context of a job applicant referral program; this form keeps the referring employee up to date on the status of the referral. Finally, the *Employee Referral Award* notifies the referring employee that his or her referral has been accepted.

The *Notice of Established Workday and Workweek* advises your employees of the establishment of or changes to the standard workday and workweek. Direct your employees to use the *Time Log* to record their job activities. The use of this report can help you pinpoint efficiency problems with certain employees and tasks. Use the *Client Time/Expense Sheet* to track activities and expenses for which a client should be billed. If you have employees who are independent contractors, clarify and document that relationship with the *Independent Contractor's Agreement*.

We have included a helpful and descriptive summary of stock option plans, *The Manager's Guide to Employee Stock Option Plans—A Concise Overview*. If your company grants stock options to its employees, the *Stock Option Memorandum to Employees* can help you communicate to your employees the basic principles of stock option plans. Consult a qualified attorney to implement a stock option plan for your company.

50. Job Applicant Dismissal (Version 1)

From: _____

_____

_____

_____

To: _____

_____

_____

Date: _____

Dear _____

Thank you for your time and the interest you've shown in considering a _____ position here at our firm. We were fortunate to have interviewed a number of applicants with strong backgrounds such as yours, making our selection process difficult.

We regret to say that we are now concentrating our attention on a limited number of other candidates whose backgrounds appear to be the best match for our firm's needs. Be assured that your résumé and interview have received our full attention. Should another opening present itself in the near future for which you appear qualified, we will contact you immediately.

Your regard for our firm is greatly appreciated. Best wishes for your continued career success.

Thank you.

Yours truly,

51. Job Applicant Dismissal (Version 2)

From: _____

_____

_____

_____

To: _____

_____

_____

Date: _____

Dear _____:

Thank you for the interest you've shown in a career opportunity with our firm. We were fortunate to have interviewed a number of applicants with strong backgrounds such as yours, making our selection process difficult.

Be assured that your résumé has received our full attention. While your background is interesting, unfortunately we have no openings that are a match for your skills and experience.

We would like to again thank you for your interest in our firm and wish you continued success in pursuit of your career objectives.

Yours truly,

52. Job Applicant Invitation

From: _____

_____

_____

_____

To: _____

_____

_____

Date: _____

Dear _____:

Thank you for the interest you've shown in considering a _____ position with our firm. Your qualifications have been reviewed by our management team. We feel that your skills could potentially be a good match for the position.

We would like to invite you to visit our firm for an interview to more fully evaluate you as a candidate. This interview is a necessary part of our evaluation process. Please contact _____ at the telephone number that appears above to arrange the interview. Please plan to spend about an hour with us.

Thank you for your interest and we look forward to meeting with you.

Yours truly,

53. Employee Referral

Date _____

Name of Candidate Referred _____

For the Position of _____

Department _____

My relationship and knowledge of this candidate is:

❏ Former Work Peer

❏ Former Supervisor

❏ Former Subordinate

❏ Friend

❏ Other _____

My evaluation of this candidate is: (5 equals highest)

Experience	1	2	3	4	5
Job-Related Skills	1	2	3	4	5
Initiative	1	2	3	4	5
Responsibility	1	2	3	4	5
Related Education	1	2	3	4	5
Interpersonal Skills	1	2	3	4	5

Comments and Other Information:

_____

_____

_____

_____

_____

_____

Submitted by _____ Date _____

Please attach résumé.

54. Applicant Referral Update

To _____

Date _____

From _____

Thank your for recent referral of _____

For the position of _____

The status of this candidate is:

❏ Job offered but declined

❏ Job offer pending

❏ Currently being interviewed

❏ Résumé on file—no current openings

❏ Not qualified

Thank you for your support and participation in the employee referral program. If any further action is taken regarding this candidate, we will notify you.

55. Employee Referral Award

To _____

Date _____

From _____

Congratulations!

We are please to announce that _____, your recent referral, has been hired effective _____.

According to the terms of our employee referral program, your award of _____ will be processed for you on or about _____.

Once the referred employee has completed 90 days of continuous, satisfactory employment, the remainder of your award will be immediately processed for you.

You are to be aware that this award may have tax implications for you. The award ❑ is ❑ is not "grossed up" by 20% to offset part or all of the additional taxes that you can incur.

Thank you again for you support and participation in the employee referral program.

Yours truly,

56. Notice of Established Workday and Workweek

In order to arrange fair and consistent work schedules and to determine when overtime payments are due for hours worked beyond 40 in a week or _____ in a day, the following standard workday and workweek has been established:

Workday:

The 24-hour period beginning at _____ (time) and ending at _____(time).

Workweek:

The seven-day period beginning at _____(time) _____ (day) and ending at _____ (time) _____ (day).

This schedule becomes effective _____(date).

Please contact your supervisor or the Human Resources Department if you have any questions.

57. Time Log

Name _____

Title _____

Department _____

Date _____

Time	Activity and Result	Total Time Spent
_____	_____	_____
_____	_____	_____
_____	_____	_____
_____	_____	_____
_____	_____	_____
_____	_____	_____
_____	_____	_____
_____	_____	_____
_____	_____	_____
_____	_____	_____
_____	_____	_____
_____	_____	_____
_____	_____	_____
_____	_____	_____
_____	_____	_____
_____	_____	_____
_____	_____	_____
_____	_____	_____
_____	_____	_____
_____	_____	_____
_____	_____	_____
_____	_____	_____
_____	_____	_____
_____	_____	_____

58. Client Time/Expense Sheet

Client Name _____

Associate Name _____

Date	Description of Task or Purchase	Time Used	Expense
_____	_____	_____	_____
_____	_____	_____	_____
_____	_____	_____	_____
_____	_____	_____	_____
_____	_____	_____	_____
_____	_____	_____	_____
_____	_____	_____	_____
_____	_____	_____	_____
_____	_____	_____	_____
_____	_____	_____	_____
_____	_____	_____	_____
_____	_____	_____	_____
_____	_____	_____	_____
_____	_____	_____	_____
_____	_____	_____	_____
_____	_____	_____	_____
_____	_____	_____	_____
_____	_____	_____	_____
_____	_____	_____	_____
_____	_____	_____	_____
Totals		_____	_____

59. Independent Contractor's Agreement

Date" _____

Dear _____:

The following will outline our agreement and summarize the terms of the arrangement that we have discussed.

You have been retained by _____ as an independent contractor for the project of _____.

You will be responsible for successfully completing the above-described project according to specifications and within the policy guidelines discussed.

The project is to be completed by _____ (date) at a cost not to exceed $_____.

You will invoice us for your services rendered at the end of each month.

We will not deduct or withhold any taxes, FICA, or other deductions that we are legally required to make from the pay of regular employees. As an independent contractor, you will not be entitled to any fringe benefits, such as unemployment insurance, medical insurance, pension plans, or other such benefits that would be offered to regular employees.

During this project, you may be in contact with or directly working with proprietary information that is important to our company and its competitive position. All information must be treated with strict confidence and may not be used at any time or in any manner in work you may do with others in our industry.

If you agree to the above terms, please sign and return one copy of this letter for our records. You may retain the other copy for your files.

Agreed:

Independent Contractor _____ Date _____

Company Representative _____ Date _____

60. The Manager's Guide to Employee Stock Option Plans–A Concise Overview

Set forth below is an overview of the tax, accounting, and general business considerations applicable to typical equity-based compensation arrangements. Following the overview are general descriptions of how those considerations apply to three basic types of arrangements: incentive stock options, nonqualified stock options, and restricted stock.

Incentive Stock Options (ISOs) Offer Great Tax Benefits, but Are for Employees Only

An incentive stock option ("ISO") provides for the grant to employees only (not to outside directors, consultants, etc.) of options to acquire stock of the employer and, by satisfying a series of statutory requirements, qualifies for a specified set of tax consequences. To satisfy tax requirements, the plan providing for the grant of the ISOs must be approved by the shareholders within 12 months before or after it is adopted, must specify the aggregate number of shares of employer stock that are available for issuance under the plan, and must specify the employees or class of employee eligible for the plan.

The restrictions applicable to terms of the ISO are as follow:

- The option price must at least equal the fair market value of the stock at the time of grant.
- The option cannot be transferable, except at death.
- There is a $100,000 limit on the aggregate fair market value (determined at the time the option is granted) of stock any employee may acquire during any calendar year. (Any amount exceeding the limit is treated as a nonqualified stock option, as described below.)
- All options must be granted within 10 years of either plan adoption or approval of the plan, whichever is earlier.
- The options must be exercised within 10 years of grant.
- The options must be exercised within three months of termination of employment (extended to one year for disability retirement, with no time limit in the case of death).
- Optimum tax treatment to the employee depends on the employee not making a "Disqualifying disposition" (i.e., the employee does not dispose of the shares within one years after the date of grant of the option or within one year of receipt of the shares).

Modification of an existing option is treated as a grant of a new option, which must meet all of the applicable tax requirements as of the date of the modification. Note that, in the case of a 10% or greater shareholder, the option price must be at least 110% of the fair market value of the stock at the time of the grant and the option period must not exceed five years. The number of options granted to each employee at any one time can be discretionary. The exercisability of options typically vests over time. Vesting can be conditioned on performance, in addition to continued employment. The plan may permit the option price to be paid with other stock held by the employee. If stock received on the previous exercise of another ISO is used to exercise an ISO, the disposition of the previously held shares will be nontaxable unless it is a disqualifying disposition.

Tax Consequences of ISOs

For the employer:

No compensation deduction is ever allowed for an ISO, unless the employee makes a disqualifying disposition, in which case the employer receives a deduction equal to the employee's income inclusion for the year in which the disqualifying disposition occurs. Under current rules, the employer is not required to withhold income or employment taxes, even in the case of a disqualifying disposition.

For the employee:

There is no taxable income to the employee at the time of the grant or timely exercise. However, the difference between the value of the stock at exercise and the exercise price is an item of adjustment for purposes of the dreaded alternative minimum tax ("AMT"). In the absence of a disqualifying disposition, gain or loss when the stock is later sold is long-term capital gain or loss. Gain or loss is the difference between the amount realized from the sale and the tax basis (i.e., the amount paid on exercise). In the case of a disqualifying disposition, the employee is treated as having ordinary income subject to tax in an amount equal to the lesser of (i) the difference between the amount realized on the disposition and the exercise price or (ii) the difference between the fair market value of the stock on the date the ISO is exercised and the exercise price. Any gain in excess of the amount taxed as ordinary income will be treated as a long- or short-term capital gain, depending on whether the stock was held for more than 12 months.

Nonqualified Stock Options (NSOs): The Leftovers

In general, nonqualified stock options ("NSOs"), unlike ISOs, are not subject to specific tax eligibility requirements—an NSO is just a plain old option. Thus, any option that is not an ISO is by default an NSO.

The term "nonqualified" means just that—if the option does not qualify as an ISO, it's a stock option that enjoys no special tax treatment. NSOs are typically granted with an exercise price approximating the value of the stock at the time of grant, although they are frequently issued at some discount from such value. Like ISOs, NSOs may become exercisable as they vest over time, conditioned on continued employment or specific performance criteria. Unlike ISOs, NSOs can be issued to anyone, employee or otherwise.

Tax Consequences of NSOs

For the employer:

In general, the employer receives a deduction equal to (and at the same time as) the employee's income inclusion. The employer is required to withhold income and employment taxes on the employee's income amount.

For the employee:

In general, there is no taxable income to the employee at the time of the grant. However, the difference between the value of the stock at exercise and the exercise price is ordinary income to the employee at the time of exercise. The income recognized on exercise is subject to income tax withholding and to employment taxes. When the stock is later sold, the gain or loss is capital gain or loss (calculated as the difference between the sales price and tax basis, which is the sum of the exercise price and the income recognized at exercise).

Accounting Treatment of ISOs and NSOs

Generally, under traditional rules, there is no charge to earnings for accounting purposes, unless the option is granted with an option price of less than the fair market value of the stock, determined at the date of the grant (the measurement date). For companies contemplating an IPO within the foreseeable future, the valuation of stock option grants can be particularly important, as the SEC commonly questions the exercise prices of options granted in the period before the IPO.

Certain conditions, however, may result in an earnings charge if there is a stock value/exercise price disparity at some other measurement date. The exercise of an option with stock already held can result in the earnings charge being calculated at the exercise date if the stock used to exercise the option has been held less than six months. Withholding of stock upon exercise will not result in a new measurement date if the withheld stock is limited to the minimum withholding tax payable by the employee. Withholding of more shares can result in the exercise date becoming a new measurement date for the withheld shares. A cash bonus to pay withholding taxes can result in the exercise date becoming a new measurement date for the option as well as the cash bonus itself.

Under rules adopted by the Financial Accounting Standards Board, companies are "encouraged" to account for equity-based compensation awards based on the fair value of the awards; companies that do not do so nonetheless must disclose such fair value in notes to their financial statements. We believe that most public companies choose the latter approach.

The accounting treatment of option grants to non-employees has recently changed. Grants to non-employees (other than grants to non-employee directors, who for this purpose are treated as employees) will now incur a compensation expense for the company, even if the option price is set at the fair market value of the stock at the time of the grant.

	Incentive Stock Option (ISO)	Nonqualified Stock Option (NSO)
Tax Qualification Requirements?	Many	None
Who Can Receive?	Employees Only	Anyone
How Taxed for Employee?	There is no taxable income to the employee at the time of the grant or timely exercise. However, the difference between the value of the stock at exercise and the exercise price is an item of adjustment for purposes of the alternative minimum tax ("AMT"). When the stock is later sold, the gain or loss is long-term capital gain or loss (calculated as the difference between the amount realized from the sale and the tax basis, which is the amount paid on exercise). Disqualifying disposition destroys favorable tax treatment.	The difference between the value of the stock at exercise and the exercise price is ordinary income. The income recognized on exercise is subject to income tax withholding and to employment taxes. When the stock is later sold, the gain or loss is capital gain or loss (calculated as the difference between the sales price and tax basis, which is the sum of the exercise price and the income recognized at exercise).

61. Stock Option Memorandum to Employees

What follows is an explanation of the current stock option plans offered by _____. Please bear in mind that stock option plans are powerful but complicated devices. Thus, to maximize the benefit to you personally, you should educate yourself about stock options. This memo is meant to be an overview and summary.

What Is a Stock Option? How Do Options Work?

A stock option gives an employee the right to buy a certain number of shares in a company at a fixed price for a certain number of years. The price at which the option is provided is called the "grant" or "strike" price and is usually the market price at the time the options are granted (usually the first day of employment).

Employees who have been granted stock options hope that the share price will go up and that they will be able to make substantial gains by exercising (purchasing) the stock at the grant price and then selling the stock at the (hopefully) higher current market price. The difference between the grant price and the current market price is called the "spread."

A stock option "vests" when the employee earns the right to exercise the option. Typically, an employee's options begin vesting one year after employment begins and continue vesting until three or four years after employment begins. This gradual vesting is called a "vesting schedule." When the vesting schedule is complete, the options are said to be fully vested.

The Two Principal Types of Options

There are two principal kinds of stock option programs, each with unique rules and tax consequences: incentive stock options (ISOs) and nonqualified stock options (NSOs).

Incentive Stock Options (ISOs)

These are also known as "qualified" stock options because they qualify to receive special tax treatment. IMPORTANT: With ISOs, no income tax is due at grant or exercise—rather, the tax is deferred until you sell the stock. This is a valuable benefit to employees. The Company offers ISOs to eligible employees.

Upon sale, the entire option gain (the initial spread at exercise plus any subsequent appreciation) is taxed at long-term capital gains rates, provided you sell at least two years after the option is granted and at least one year after you exercise. The current long-term capital gains rate is 20% (a much lower rate than the 28% to 39% bracket for ordinary income—a huge tax savings). If you don't meet the one- and two-year holding period requirements, the sale is a "disqualifying disposition" and you are taxed as if you had held NSOs (see below).

A warning applies here: the spread at exercise is considered a preference item for purposes of calculating the alternative minimum tax (AMT), increasing taxable income for AMT purposes. The AMT is hopelessly complicated and Congress is actually considering making changes to the law. You need not worry about the AMT until exercise. Also, a disqualifying disposition can help you avoid this tax.

Nonqualified Stock Options (NSOs)

The taxation of NSOs is not as beneficial for employees as ISOs. You are required to pay ordinary income tax on the difference ("spread") between the grant price and the stock's market value when you purchase ("exercise") the shares. Companies get to deduct this spread as a compensation expense.

After that, any subsequent appreciation in the stock is taxed at capital gains rates when you sell. Keep the stock for more than a year and you'll have a long-term capital gain, taxed at a top rate of 20%; hold it for one year or less and your gain is short-term, taxed at higher, ordinary income tax rates. Nonqualified options can be granted at a discount to what is then the stock's market value. They also are "transferable" to children and charity, provided your company permits it.

How to Exercise Stock Options

There are three basic ways to exercise stock options: cash, stock swap, and "cashless exercise."

Cash: This is the most straightforward way. You give your employer money and get stock certificates in return. But what happens, when it's time to exercise the option, if you don't have enough cash to buy the option shares and pay any resulting tax?

Stock swap: Some employers let you exercise stock options by trading company stock you own already. If, for example, your company stock sells for $20 a share and you have an ISO to buy 1,000 additional shares at $10, you can either paying $10,000 in cash or exchange 500 shares you already own for the 1,000 new shares. (This strategy has the extra benefit of limiting your holdings of company stock.) If the stock you're swapping is ISO shares, you must have held them for the required one- and two-year holding periods; otherwise, the exchange is treated as a sale and you incur tax.

Cashless exercise: To exercise a stock option this way, you borrow the money you need from a stockbroker and simultaneously sell at least enough shares to cover your costs, including taxes and commissions. You receive any balance in cash or stock.

There is an important restriction on your ability to sell shares under any of the plans: the shares that you are granted are not registered with the Securities and Exchange Commission and so they're "restricted" from resale. Restricted shares must be held for one year before they can be sold.

When to Exercise Stock Options

Conventional thinking is that you should wait until your options are about to expire before you exercise them, to allow the stock to appreciate and maximize your gain. However, many employees can't wait that long. One study found that the typical employee cashed out of his or her options within six months of becoming eligible to do so—and thus sacrificed an estimated $1 in future value for every $2 realized.

Sales and Revenue Analysis Tools

The forms in this section are all designed to increase your company's sales. The *Sales Call Log* is a log for use by salespersons; it serves as a record of telephone conversations with customers and prospects. The *Client/Prospect Contact Log* is a related form that summarizes the calls and contacts made to a particular prospect. The *Sales Prospect File* is the best log for use by salespersons in industries where the sales are made through incoming calls and during advertising campaigns.

The *Customer Satisfaction Survey* lets you learn from your most valuable critics—your customers. The *Customer Service Request* helps you effectively gather, track, follow, and respond to customer service inquiries.

Use the *Product Information* form to keep a unified and complete description of all of your products and services. The *Order Card* is a handy and simple card that you can include in mailings and facsimile advertisements. It enables your customers to quickly and easily place orders for your products and services. Use the *Work Order/ Request for Quote* form when your customers request custom goods and services. The *Sales Order Form* is a familiar receipt/invoice form.

The *Daily Sales Recap* is an internal sales tracking mechanism; it enables you and your staff to see a day-by-day analysis of your company's sales. The *Month-to-Month Sales Comparison Log* enables your staff to compare sales performance on a month-to-month basis.

The *Cash Receipts Control Log* is an effective tracking mechanism for cash-based businesses; the form may also serve to prevent employee theft and loss. Ensure that the cash on hand at the end of each business day reconciles with the amount on the *Cash Receipts Control Log*.

62. Sales Call Log

Number _____ Date _____

Name of Company _____

Contact _____ Phone _____

Type of Call: ❑ Customer ❑ Prospect

Comments

_____

_____

Purpose of Call

_____

_____

Opening Conversation

_____

_____

Sales Story

_____

_____

_____

Benefits to Customer

_____

_____

_____

Objections or Resistance Response

_____

_____

Closing Conversation

_____

_____

_____

When to Follow Up

_____

_____

63. Client/Prospect Contact Log

Sales Representative _____

Company _____

Contact(s) _____

Address _____

Phone _____

Date	Comments	Next Call/Contact?	Sale?
_____	_____	_____	_____
_____	_____	_____	_____
_____	_____	_____	_____
_____	_____	_____	_____
_____	_____	_____	_____
_____	_____	_____	_____
_____	_____	_____	_____
_____	_____	_____	_____
_____	_____	_____	_____
_____	_____	_____	_____
_____	_____	_____	_____
_____	_____	_____	_____
_____	_____	_____	_____
_____	_____	_____	_____
_____	_____	_____	_____
_____	_____	_____	_____
_____	_____	_____	_____
_____	_____	_____	_____
_____	_____	_____	_____
_____	_____	_____	_____
_____	_____	_____	_____

64. Sales Prospect File

❏ New Prospect   ❏ Current Client   ❏ Follow-up   Date _____

Company Name _____

Contact _____

Title _____

Address _____

_____

Phone _____

Source of Initial Contact

❏ Call-in   ❏ Direct Mail   ❏ Referral—by Whom? _____

Current Supplier _____

Approximate Monthly Sales Volume _____

Action Taken to Follow-up

_____

_____

_____

Sales Calls History

Comments

_____

_____

_____

_____

_____

General Comments

_____

_____

_____

_____

_____

_____

65. Customer Satisfaction Survey

Your input is valuable to us and we are constantly looking for ways to improve the quality of our products and services. Please take a few minutes to fill out the few questions below. Please return this survey by fax at _____ or in the envelope provided.

Please LIST "Outstanding," "Good," "Average," "Needs Improvement," or "Unacceptable" and comment in the area provided:

Products	Outstanding	Good	Average	Needs Improvement	Unacceptable

Services and Support	Outstanding	Good	Average	Needs Improvement	Unacceptable

Delivery	Outstanding	Good	Average	Needs Improvement	Unacceptable

Ordering and Billing	Outstanding	Good	Average	Needs Improvement	Unacceptable

Employees	Outstanding	Good	Average	Needs Improvement	Unacceptable

Comments

_____

_____

_____

_____

_____

Thank you. You are a valued customer!

66. Customer Service Request

Customer Service Request	
Customer	Date
Contact	Originator
	Department
Telephone	Telephone

Customer Complaint:

Person Assigned for Resolution:

Recommended Action/Action Taken:

Customer Follow-up Notes:

Issue Resolved: ❏ Yes

67. Product Information

Product _____

Brand Name _____

ID # _____

Product Description

_____

_____

_____

Features

_____

_____

_____

Applications

_____

_____

_____

Technical Specifications

_____

_____

_____

Materials Required

_____

_____

_____

Distributors

_____

_____

_____

Required Lead Time _____

Prepared by _____ Date _____

Approved by _____ Date _____

68. Order Card

Yes! I'd like to make an order. Please send me:

Quantity	Item Description	Price per Unit	Extended Price
_____	_____	_____	_____
_____	_____	_____	_____
_____	_____	_____	_____
_____	_____	_____	_____

❏ Payment Enclosed ❏ Bill Me   Total _____ $_____

Name _____ Phone _____

Address _____

City _____ State _____ ZIP

✂ ···

Yes! I'd like to make an order. Please send me:

Quantity	Item Description	Price per Unit	Extended Price
_____	_____	_____	_____
_____	_____	_____	_____
_____	_____	_____	_____
_____	_____	_____	_____

❏ Payment Enclosed ❏ Bill Me   Total _____ $_____

Name _____ Phone _____

Address _____

City _____ State _____ ZIP

✂ ···

Yes! I'd like to make an order. Please send me:

Quantity	Item Description	Price per Unit	Extended Price
_____	_____	_____	_____
_____	_____	_____	_____
_____	_____	_____	_____
_____	_____	_____	_____

❏ Payment Enclosed ❏ Bill Me   Total _____ $_____

Name _____ Phone _____

Address _____

City _____ State _____ ZIP

69. Work Order/Request for Quote

Overview

Customer Name _____

Customer Address _____

Contact Person _____

Phone _____

Project Description _____

_____

_____

Specific Instructions

Materials and Quantities to Be Used

_____

_____

_____

_____

Additional Outside Services Required

_____

_____

_____

_____

Comments

_____

_____

_____

_____

Sample of Design or Sketch of Design

Pricing _____

_____

Submitted by _____ Date _____

70. Sales Order Form

Customer Name _____ Date _____

Phone _____

Address _____

City _____ State_____ ZIP _____

Ship to Address _____

City _____ State_____ ZIP _____

Special Instructions

_____

_____

_____

_____

Item Number	Description	Quantity	Unit Price	Extended Price
_____	_____	_____	_____	_____
_____	_____	_____	_____	_____
_____	_____	_____	_____	_____
_____	_____	_____	_____	_____
_____	_____	_____	_____	_____
_____	_____	_____	_____	_____
_____	_____	_____	_____	_____
_____	_____	_____	_____	_____
_____	_____	_____	_____	_____
_____	_____	_____	_____	_____
_____	_____	_____	_____	_____
_____	_____	_____	_____	_____
_____	_____	_____	_____	_____

Gross Total _____

Tax _____

Freight _____

Labor _____

Total Due _____

Order Taken by _____

71. Daily Sales Recap

For the Month of _____ , _____

Date	Taxable Sales	Nontaxable Sales	Total Sales
1			
2			
3			
4			
5			
6			
7			
8			
9			
10			
11			
12			
13			
14			
15			
16			
17			
18			
19			
20			
21			
22			
23			
24			
25			
26			
27			
28			
29			
30			
31			
TOTAL			

72. Month-to-Month Sales Comparison Log

For Year _____

Month	Taxable Sales	Nontaxable Sales	Total Sales
January	_____	_____	_____
February	_____	_____	_____
March	_____	_____	_____
April	_____	_____	_____
May	_____	_____	_____
June	_____	_____	_____
July	_____	_____	_____
August	_____	_____	_____
September	_____	_____	_____
October	_____	_____	_____
November	_____	_____	_____
December	_____	_____	_____

73. Cash Receipts Control Log

Period _____

Date	Check Amount	Customer ID	Reference No.
_____	$_____	_____	_____
_____	$_____	_____	_____
_____	$_____	_____	_____
_____	$_____	_____	_____
_____	$_____	_____	_____
_____	$_____	_____	_____
_____	$_____	_____	_____
_____	$_____	_____	_____
_____	$_____	_____	_____
_____	$_____	_____	_____
_____	$_____	_____	_____
_____	$_____	_____	_____
_____	$_____	_____	_____
_____	$_____	_____	_____
_____	$_____	_____	_____
_____	$_____	_____	_____
_____	$_____	_____	_____
_____	$_____	_____	_____
_____	$_____	_____	_____
_____	$_____	_____	_____
_____	$_____	_____	_____
_____	$_____	_____	_____
_____	$_____	_____	_____
_____	$_____	_____	_____
_____	$_____	_____	_____
_____	$_____	_____	_____
_____	$_____	_____	_____
_____	$_____	_____	_____
_____	$_____	_____	_____

Reconciled to Daily Cash Deposit by _____ Date _____

Authorized by _____ Date _____

D7

Credit, Billing, and Collection Tools

The forms presented in this section are designed to help you and your company receive payment for the goods and services you and your company provide. The forms include credit application forms, credit terms documentation, past due reminder and demand letters, and invoices/statements.

Your company will have an easier time with the challenges of billing and collections if it formalizes its credit application process and consistently applies the credit application process to every customer who comes knocking. When a new customer appears, you should begin by asking the customer to complete *Authorization to Release Credit Information*. This authorization form gives your company the authority to make inquiries with credit reporting bureaus without fear of consequence. Never submit a credit inquiry to a credit reporting bureau without written authorization. You'll also ask your new customer to complete either the *Business Credit Application* or, if the customer is an individual, the *Personal Credit Application*. These credit application forms are invaluable. Not only do they help you evaluate your customer for creditworthiness, but also they serve to obtain information that can make the collection process easier in the event that your customer defaults on the credit arrange-

ments. The *Credit Approval Form* is an internal tracking mechanism that collects certain information gleaned from the credit inquiry process and ensures that all necessary staff authorize the approval of credit for each customer.

Once your organization has agreed to extend credit to a customer, you should document the credit terms by having your customer submit a signed copy of the *Credit Terms Agreement*. This is another powerful protection device that can give you significant leverage if a customer defaults on those credit terms.

Naturally, you can increase the speed at which your customers pay and the reliability with which they pay if you make it fast and easy to pay. The *EasyPay Automatic Payment Agreement* is a notice and agreement signed by your customer that enables you to make automatic withdrawals from either your customer's bank or your customer's credit card. Once this agreement is in place, your customers are far more likely to pay on time and in full.

The *Response to Request for Adjustment of Account* is a letter that your credit or collections department would send to a customer who has formally requested an adjustment to his or her account.

The next four forms in this section address the unfortunate but all too common circumstance of a late-paying or nonpaying customer. The four letters escalate both in tone and consequences. The *Credit Terms Reminder Letter* is a bland and polite reminder for the habitually late-paying customer. We have included two *Past Due Reminder Letter*s, which you should promptly issue when a customer fails to pay after 30 and 45 days, respectively. You should always endeavor to not allow your receivables to age: studies have shown that uncollected customer balances become far less likely to be collected if they are allowed to age beyond 60, 90, and 120 days. The last collection letter is the *Past Due Demand Letter*. This is your last resort when handling a nonpaying customer; the letter terminates the credit privileges of the errant customer and threatens legal and collection action.

It is important to recognize the difference between *invoices* and *statements*. Invoices are individual billing notices; typically, one invoice is delivered to a customer for each order. Statements are billing summaries; typically, a statement is delivered to a customer periodically. The statement will summarize billing and payment activity and will reference each individual invoice. If you invoice your customers, you should issue monthly statements as well. We have included two forms of invoices. Use the *Job Invoice* when you provide both materials and labor to your customers; use the *Customer Invoice* when you provide only goods or only services. Use the *Customer Statement* to advise your customers of billing and payment activity.

The *Request for Payment* form is a simple invoice best used for a one-time customer for whom you do not wish to set up a full-blown account. Use the *Short Pay Inquiry Form* when a customer fails to pay the full amount of an invoice.

74. Authorization to Release Credit Information

From:

_____

_____

_____

_____

To:

_____

_____

_____

_____

Date _____

Dear _____,

Thank you for your recent interest in establishing credit with our company. Please sign the authorization to release information agreement below and complete the enclosed form. Then send them to us with your most recent financial statements. We will contact your credit and bank references. Then we will contact you regarding your credit terms with our company.

Thank you.

[Signature]

Credit Manager

We have recently applied for credit with _____.

We have been requested to provide information for their use in reviewing our creditworthiness. Therefore, I authorize the investigation of me and my firm, _____, and its related credit information.

The release in any manner of all information by you is authorized whether such information is of record or not.

I do hereby release all persons, agencies, firms, companies, etc. from any damages resulting from providing such information.

This authorization is valid for 30 days from the date of my signature below. Please keep a copy of my release request for your files. Thank you for your cooperation.

Signature _____   Date _____

75. Business Credit Application

From:

_____

_____

_____

Thank you for your interest in our company's products and services. We appreciate your business and look forward to a long and prosperous business relationship.

Please complete the credit application and return it to the above address, attention Credit Department. Please note our credit terms. You will be advised shortly of your credit status with our company. Thank you.

Credit Application

Business Legal Name_____

Business Trade Name_____

Web Site Address _____

Business Address Information

Address _____

City/Town _____

State/Province _____ Zip _____

Check one:

Sole Proprietorship _____ Partnership _____ Corporation _____ LLC _____ Other_____

Federal Tax ID Number _____

Contact Person _____ Title _____

Contact Person _____ Title _____

Phone (_____)_____ Ext _____ Fax (_____)_____

E-mail Address _____ Dept _____

Hours of Operation _____

Names of Authorized Account Users _____

Do you require an Invoice? Yes _____ No _____

Invoice Preferred?

Weekly invoice and monthly statement _____ Open item statement _____

Billing Address Information (If different from above)

Address _____

City/Town _____

State/Province _____ ZIP _____

Contact Persons _____ Title _____

Phone (_____)_____ Ext _____ Fax (_____)_____

E-mail Address _____ Dept _____

Other Location Information (i.e., Local Contacts)

Additional Location _____

Address _____

City/Town _____

State/Province _____ ZIP _____

Contact Persons _____ Title _____

Phone (_____)_____ Ext _____ Fax (_____)_____

E-mail Address _____ Dept _____

Hours of Operation _____

Preferred Billing Date _____

Names of Authorized Users _____

Doing Business as (DBA) Names _____

Bank References

Bank Name _____

Account Number _____

City/Town _____

State/Province _____ Phone (_____) _____ Ext _____

Bank Officer _____

Bank Name _____

Account Number _____

City/Town _____

State/ Province _____ Phone (_____) _____ Ext _____

Bank Officer _____

Trade or Supplier Credit References (Must provide at least 3)

Name _____

Address _____

Person to Contact _____

City/Town _____

State/Province _____ ZIP _____

Phone (_____)_____ Ext _____ Fax (_____)_____

Name _____

Address _____

Person to Contact _____

City/Town _____

State/Province _____ ZIP _____

Phone (_____)_____ Ext _____ Fax (_____)_____

Name _____

Address _____

Person to Contact _____

City/Town _____

State/Province _____ ZIP _____

Phone (_____)_____ Ext _____ Fax (_____)_____

Names of Principals: Owners, Officers, Partners

Name _____

Address _____

City/Town _____

State/Province _____ ZIP _____

Phone (_____)_____ Ext _____ Fax (_____)_____

Title _____ Social Security # _____-_____-_____

Name _____

Address _____

City/Town _____

State/Province _____ ZIP _____

Phone (_____)_____ Ext _____ Fax (_____)_____

Title _____ Social Security # _____-_____-_____

Please attach additional pages if you have more than two principals.

I certify that I am authorized to sign and submit this application for and on behalf of the applicant. I also certify that the foregoing information is true and correct to the best of my knowledge.

_____   _____

Name (Please Print or Type)   Title

_____   _____

Signature   Date

76. Personal Credit Application

From:

_____

_____

_____

Thank you for your interest in our company's products and services. We appreciate your business and look forward to a long and prosperous business relationship.

Please complete the credit application and return it to the above address, attention Credit Department. Please note our credit terms. You will be advised shortly of your credit status with our company. Thank you.

Credit Application

Personal Information:

Name_____

Address _____

City/Town _____

State/Province _____ ZIP _____

Social Security Number _____-_____-_____

Phone (_____)_____ Ext _____ Fax (_____)_____

E-mail Address _____ Date of Birth_____

Do you ❑ Own ❑ Rent   Monthly Housing Payment Amount $_____

Prior Addresses for the Last 5 Years:

Address _____ City State ZIP: _____

Address _____ City State ZIP: _____

Employment:

Employer _____

Address _____

Occupation_____

Contact to verify employment _____ Phone # (_____)_____

Length of Employment _____ Monthly Gross Salary _____

Credit References:

Bank Name _____ Account Number _____

City/Town _____

State/Province _____ Phone (_____) _____ Ext _____

Bank Officer _____

Credit Card Type _____ Number _____ Exp. Date _____

Credit Card Type_____ Number _____ Exp. Date _____

I certify that I am authorized to sign and submit this application for and on behalf of the applicant. I also certify that the foregoing information is true and correct to the best of my knowledge.

_____   _____
Name (Please Print or Type)   Date

_____
Signature

77. Credit Approval Form

To be completed by the Credit Department.

Company Name (Applicant)_____

Company Address _____

Contact Name _____

Phone Number _____

Bank References Notes _____

_____

_____

Credit References Notes _____

_____

_____

Approximate Amount of Business Anticipated per Month (as per Sales Manager) $ _____

Credit Terms _____

Credit Limit _____

Any Special Instructions _____

_____

_____

Prepared by _____

Approvals:

Credit Manager _____ Date _____

Sales Manager _____ Date _____

Controller _____ Date _____

General Manager _____ Date _____

78. Credit Terms Agreement

I, the "Applicant," hereby agree to the following credit terms agreement in connection with my application for credit terms from _____ ("Company"). I, Applicant, agree as follows:

1. Applicant represents that the information supplied with the credit application and all associated documentation is in all respects complete, accurate, and truthful. Applicant agrees to notify Company promptly, in writing, of any substantive changes in the information Applicant has provided.

2. Applicant agrees to pay in full for goods and services rendered (without deduction or setoff) on or before the earlier of the 30th day of the month following the date of billing or the due date started on each billing to the order of Company. Any amounts not paid when due shall be assessed a service charge at the rate of _____% per year (_____% per month) or the highest rate allowed by law.

3. If Applicant's account is placed or given to an attorney for collection, Applicant shall pay any and all expenses of collection and attempted collection, court costs, and reasonable attorney's fees in addition to other amounts due. The failure of Company to charge interest on Applicant's account or pursue any other remedy available to it shall not constitute Company's waiver of any rights.

4. The acceptance of this application by Company does not constitute an agreement to extend credit to Applicant or to provide services to Applicant. Company, in its absolute discretion, may set and/or modify credit limits from time to time or terminate credit, with or without notice to Applicant.

5. In the event Applicant or any affiliate of Applicant (i.e., a company or other entity under common control) defaults in the payment of any sums due to Company, all other amounts due from Applicant or any affiliate shall be immediately due and payable, including any amount due for freight in transit. Also, in the event of such default, to the extent allowed under applicable law, Company is hereby authorized by Applicant to take possession of any freight then being shipped by Applicant and hold the same until payment is made, with all the rights of a secured party under the Uniform Commercial Code, as applicable in the State of Company's headquarters.

6. Applicant agrees that Company may set off against monies due it from Applicant or any affiliate any monies owed by Company to Applicant or any affiliate. Applicant agrees that he/she will not set off against any amounts due Company or claimed to be due to Applicant from Company.

7. If any one or more of the above terms becomes invalid or illegal in any respect, such term or terms shall be waived and the validity, legality, and enforceability of the remaining terms shall not be affected.

8. All disputes related to underlying charges must be submitted to Company no later than 30 days following date of billing. Any billing not challenged within 60 days will be deemed accepted and it is agreed will not thereafter be subject to dispute by Applicant. Adjustments must be submitted to Company in writing. All adjustments must reference either an invoice number or an air waybill number, or both numbers, for which the adjustment is being made.

9. I have read, I understand, and I accept the above terms, and I have provided true information to the best of my knowledge. I understand you will rely on the information provided herein in determining whether to extend credit and the limits thereof and that you may wish to periodically update the information given herein. For the purpose of obtaining credit from Company, Applicant hereby authorizes Company or its agents to investigate the Applicant's personal, partnership, or corporate credit and financial responsibility.

_____

Applicant

_____   _____

Name (Please Print or Type)   Title

_____   _____

Signature   Date

79. EasyPay Automatic Payment Agreement

Here's How It Works:

When you enroll in EasyPay, we deduct funds automatically from your local checking account or credit card account to pay your bill. Your bill will be paid for you on time and automatically. You won't have to worry about missing a payment if you are away on a business trip or vacation. You'll continue to receive your monthly statement and you'll have 15 days from the billing date to review it before your bank pays the amount due. If you feel there is a problem with your bill, simply call us at _____. Of course, you can always dispute a bill with us even if the bill was paid automatically—we are always here to listen. You can notify us if you wish to discontinue EasyPay at any time.

It's Easy to Start EasyPay:

Simply complete the attached form and return it with your next payment. Enclose an original check marked "Void" or a photocopy of a check from the checking account you wish to have debited or, if you wish to have your credit card account billed automatically, just fill out the form below. Your next bill will show "No Payment Due" and your financial institution will show the appropriate debit on your monthly statement.

Why wait? Just fill out the form and send it in with your next payment.

EasyPay Authorization Agreement

I hereby authorize _____ ("Company") to deduct funds from my checking account/credit card account listed below to pay my Company bills. I understand that these automatic payments may be cancelled if I notify Company in writing prior to the next billing date.

_____

(Please Print) Name of Your Bank or Credit Card Company

_____   _____

Your Name as Shown on Financial Institution Records   Your Daytime Phone

_____

Address in Our Records

_____   _____

Your Signature as Shown on Financial Institution Records   Today's Date

To Charge a Bank Account: please attach an original check on which you've written "VOID" or a photocopy of a check from your checking account and return it along with this form with your next payment. Deposit slips cannot be accepted.

To Charge a Credit Card: please fill out the following:

_____

Type: VISA/MasterCard/American Express   Card Number   Exp. Date

_____

Credit Card Billing Address

80. Response to Request for Adjustment of Account

From:

_____

_____

_____

_____

To:

_____

_____

_____

_____

Date _____

Dear Customer:

Thank you for writing us regarding an error or adjustment to your account with our firm.

We have received your request and are currently researching your account and its history. We should complete our research shortly and make any necessary adjustment on your next statement. Understand that the accuracy of your account is of vital importance to us and that we will give this matter our highest attention.

Yours truly,

81. Credit Terms Reminder Letter

From:

_____

_____

_____

_____

To:

_____

_____

_____

_____

Date _____

Dear _____:

Thank you for your recent order with our firm. As a reminder to your Purchasing and Accounts Payable Departments, our credit terms are as follows: _____.

If you have any questions about your credit terms or our policies, please feel free to contact us.

Thank you for adhering to our credit policy. We hope our business relationship is a long and prosperous one.

Thank you again.

82. Past Due Reminder Letter

From:

_____

_____

_____

_____

To:

_____

_____

_____

_____

Date _____

Dear Customer:

Please take note that your account is still past due in the amount of $ _____. We sent you a statement a short time ago, which was not acted upon by you. Please submit payment immediately to avoid further charges to your account. We want to continue our relationship with you, but we need your cooperation and your payment to do so.

Thank you for your attention to this matter.

83. Past Due Reminder Letter

From:

_____

_____

_____

_____

To:

_____

_____

_____

_____

Date _____

Dear Customer:

Please take note that your account is still past due in the amount of $ _____. We sent you a statement a short time ago, which was not acted upon by you. Please submit payment immediately.

Your failure to pay the amount due on your account is a violation of the terms of your credit agreement with us. We therefore will suspend your account in seven days from the date of this letter if we do not receive payment. Once we suspend your account, it is unlikely that we will reactivate credit terms on your account.

We sincerely hope that you submit payment in full.

Thank you.

84. Past Due Demand Letter

From:

_____

_____

_____

_____

To:

_____

_____

_____

_____

Date _____

Dear Customer:

This matter requires your immediate attention. Please take note that your account is still past due in the amount of $_____. We sent you a statement a short time ago, and several reminders, upon which you have not acted. This is our final request for payment and we ask that you submit payment immediately.

We had sincerely hoped that we could continue to do business with you, but your failure to pay your outstanding bill has made that impossible. We have suspended your credit privileges with our company.

Furthermore, if we do not receive payment immediately, we will turn this matter over for collection to a collection agency or attorney, or both. Please review your credit agreement. We will be seeking interest and we may also seek court costs and fees and attorney's fees to the extent permitted by law.

We sincerely hope that you submit payment in full to avoid the course of action that we have outlined here.

Thank you.

85. Job Invoice

Seller

Buyer

Date	Your Order #	Our Order #	Sales Rep	FOB	Ship Via	Terms	Tax ID

Materials				Labor			
Quantity	Material	Unit Price	Amount	Date	Hours/Tasks	Rate	Amount
Total Materials					Total Labor		
				Total Materials and Labor			

86. Customer Invoice

Seller

Buyer

Date	Your Order #	Our Order #	Sales Rep	FOB	Ship Via	Terms	Tax ID

Quantity	Item	Units	Description	Discount %	Taxable	Unit Price	Total
					Balance		

87. Customer Statement

Seller

Buyer

Statement Date	Statement #

Reference	Date	Item/Code	Description	Amount	Balance
				Balance	

Codes: C = Credit Memo P = Payment A = Discount Allowed
D = Debit Memo I = Invoice F = Finance Charge

88. Request for Payment

From:

_____

_____

_____

_____

To:

_____

_____

_____

_____

Date _____

Dear Customer:

We have received your order and promptly processed the order according to your instructions. Please send the amount listed below immediately. Payment is expected in the form of a check, money order, VISA, or MasterCard. Please place the reference number on your payment. We appreciate your interest in our product/service and your prompt attention to this matter.

Thank you.

Accounting Department

Amount $ _____   Reference # _____

- -

From:

Check payment $ _____   Check # _____

To Charge a Credit Card: please fill out the following:

_____

Type: VISA/MasterCard/American Express   Card Number   Exp. Date

_____

Credit Card Billing Address

_____

_____

_____

_____

89. Short Pay Inquiry Form

From:

_____

_____

_____

_____

To:

_____

_____

_____

_____

Date _____

Dear Customer:

We recently received payment from you for our invoice # _____. Thank you.

However, the amount that you submitted fell short of the amount of the invoice. We were unable to determine why. Below please tell us the reason for the short pay so that we may review our records and determine if the short pay is acceptable.

Thank you.

Accounting Department

Amount of short-paid $ _____   Reference # _____

From _____

Reason for short payment _____

_____

Contracts and Agreements

The surest way to maintain clear understandings with your customers and vendors is to document your arrangements in written agreements. We have included here several useful and universal contracts and agreements.

Use the *Bill of Sale* to record the terms of a simple sale of goods or property. The *Unsecured Promissory Note* is simply a legal document that documents a promise to pay money at a future date. Use this document to memorialize simple business or personal loans. The *Secured Promissory Note and Security Agreement* is a legal document that memorializes a loan, but it goes a step farther: it grants to the lender the right to repossess property in the event the loan is not repaid. The *Secured Promissory Note and Security Agreement* gives the lender much greater rights and power than the *Unsecured Promissory Note*.

The *Simple Commercial Lease* is a straightforward rental agreement for commercial (non-residential) property. The *Consulting Services Agreement* is a general and universal agreement suitable for nearly all types of consulting services firms. Simply customize the agreement to cover the particular services that you offer. The *Multimedia Development Contract* is a contract suitable for use by Web developers, programmers, and print and graphic designers. Keep in mind, however, that you will need to customize the *Multimedia Development Contract* to cover the particular services that you offer.

The *Mutual Nondisclosure Agreement* is an agreement whereby two parties agree to maintain the confidentiality of information that they share in the context of business discussions or negotiations. The *Mutual Nondisclosure Agreement* is common in many industries where parties will discuss technology, work product, trade secrets, and competitive secrets in the context of negotiations. Finally, the *Mutual Compromise Agreement and Mutual Release* is an agreement to finally and forever settle a dispute between two parties. Use this agreement to finalize the resolution of conflicts and lawsuits between you and third parties.

90. Bill of Sale

BILL OF SALE

This Bill of Sale is made on this _____ day of 20___ between _____ ("Seller") and _____ ("Buyer").

Seller, in exchange for consideration of $_____, the receipt of which funds is acknowledged, hereby do grant, sell, transfer, and deliver to Buyer the following goods:

_____.

Buyer shall have full rights and title to the goods described above.

Seller is the lawful owner of the goods and the goods are free from all encumbrances. Seller has good right to sell the goods and will warrant and defend the right against the lawful claims and demands of all persons.

_____

Signature of Seller

_____

Signature of Buyer

91. Unsecured Promissory Note

UNSECURED PROMISSORY NOTE

Amount: $_____

Date: _____

For value received, _____ ("Borrower") hereby covenants and promises to pay to _____ ("Lender") _____ Dollars ($_____.00) in lawful money of the United States of America, together with interest thereon computed from the date hereof at the rate of ten percent (10%) per annum, on an actual day/365 day basis. All interest, principal, and other costs hereunder shall be due and payable to the holder ("Holder") of this Promissory Note (this "Note") on or before _____ (the "Due Date").

Payments of principal and interest will be made in legal tender of the United States of America. Borrower shall have the right to prepay without penalty all or any part of the unpaid balance of this Note at any time. Borrower shall not be entitled to re-borrow any prepaid amounts of the principal, interest, or other costs or charges. All payments made pursuant to this Note will be first applied to accrued and unpaid interest, if any, then to other proper charges under this Note, and the balance, if any, to principal.

This Note shall be paid as follows: monthly payments of $_____ shall be made upon this Note on the first day of each month, commencing with the date of _____, and shall continue until _____ (the "Repayment Date"), at which time all sums due hereunder shall be paid.

Notwithstanding anything in this Note to the contrary, the entire unpaid principal amount of this Note, together with all accrued but unpaid interest thereon and other unpaid charges hereunder, will become immediately all due and payable without further notice at the option of the Holder if Borrower fails to timely make any payment hereunder when such payment becomes first due and such failure continues for a period of ten days after written notice from Holder to Borrower.

If any amount payable to Holder under this Note is not received by Holder on or before the Due Date, then such amount (the "Delinquent Amount") will bear interest from and after the Due Date until paid at an annual rate of interest equal to the greater of (i) fifteen percent (15%) or (ii) the maximum rate then permitted by law (the "Default Rate"). If the maximum rate then permitted by law is lower than 15%, the maximum legal rate shall be the Default Rate.

All rights, remedies, undertakings, obligations, options, covenants, conditions, and agreements contained in this Note are cumulative and no one of them will be exclusive of any other. Any notice to any party concerning this Note will be delivered as set forth in the Financing Agreement.

Borrower for itself and its legal representatives, successors, and assigns expressly waives presentment, protest, demand, notice of dishonor, notice of nonpayment, notice of maturity, notice of protest, presentment for the purpose of accelerating maturity, and diligence in collection, and consents that Holder may extend the time for payment or otherwise modify the terms of payment or any part or the whole of the debt evidenced hereby.

The prevailing party in any action, litigation, or proceeding, including any appeal or the collection of any judgment concerning this Note, will be awarded, in addition to any damages, injunctions, or other relief, and without regard to whether or not such matter be prosecuted to final judgment, such party's costs and expenses, including reasonable attorneys' fees, and Lender shall be entitled to recover all of its attorneys' fees and costs should Lender place this Note in the hands of an attorney for collection.

_____ ("Borrower")

Signature _____

Date _____

92. Secured Promissory Note and Security Agreement

SECURED PROMISSORY NOTE

Amount: $_____

Date: _____

For value received, _____ ("Borrower") hereby covenants and promises to pay to _____ ("Lender") _____ Dollars ($_____) in lawful money of the United States of America, together with interest thereon computed from the date hereof at the rate of ten percent (10%) per annum, on an actual day/365 day basis. All interest, principal, and other costs hereunder shall be due and payable to the holder ("Holder") of this Promissory Note (this "Note") on or before _____ (the "Due Date").

Payments of principal and interest will be made in legal tender of the United States of America. Borrower shall have the right to prepay without penalty all or any part of the unpaid balance of this Note at any time. Borrower shall not be entitled to re-borrow any prepaid amounts of the principal, interest, or other costs or charges. All payments made pursuant to this Note will be first applied to accrued and unpaid interest, if any, then to other proper charges under this Note, and the balance, if any, to principal.

This Note is secured by a security interest in Borrower's assets, as more particularly described in the Security Agreement attached to this Note.

This Note shall be paid as follows: monthly payments of $_____ shall be made upon this Note on the first day of each month, commencing with the date of _____, and shall continue until _____ (the "Repayment Date"), at which time all sums due hereunder shall be paid.

Notwithstanding anything in this Note to the contrary, the entire unpaid principal amount of this Note, together with all accrued but unpaid interest thereon and other unpaid charges hereunder, will become immediately all due and payable without further notice at the option of the Holder if Borrower fails to timely make any payment hereunder when such payment becomes first due and such failure continues for a period of ten days after written notice from Holder to Borrower.

If any amount payable to Holder under this Note is not received by Holder on or before the Due Date, then such amount (the "Delinquent Amount") will bear interest from and after the Due Date until paid at an annual rate of interest equal to the greater of (i) fifteen percent (15%) or (ii) the maximum rate then permitted by law (the "Default Rate"). If the maximum rate then permitted by law is lower than 15%, the maximum legal rate shall be the Default Rate.

All rights, remedies, undertakings, obligations, options, covenants, conditions, and agreements contained in this Note are cumulative and no one of them will be exclusive of any other. Any notice to any party concerning this Note will be delivered as set forth in the Financing Agreement.

Borrower for itself and its legal representatives, successors, and assigns expressly waives presentment, protest, demand, notice of dishonor, notice of nonpayment, notice of maturity, notice of protest, presentment for the purpose of accelerating maturity, and diligence in collection and consents that Holder may extend the time for payment or otherwise modify the terms of payment or any part or the whole of the debt evidenced hereby.

The prevailing party in any action, litigation, or proceeding, including any appeal or the collection of any judgment concerning this Note, will be awarded, in addition to any damages, injunctions, or other relief, and without regard to whether or not such matter be prosecuted to final judgment, such party's costs and expenses, including reasonable attorneys' fees, and Lender shall be entitled to recover all of its attorneys' fees and costs should Lender place this Note in the hands of an attorney for collection.

_____ ("Borrower")

Signature _____

SECURITY AGREEMENT ACCOMPANYING SECURED PROMISSORY NOTE

Date_____

This Security Agreement is made on this _____ day of _____ between
_____ ("Borrower") and _____ ("Lender").

1. Security Interest. Borrower grants to Lender a "Security Interest" in the following property (the "Collateral"):

_____

_____

_____

_____

_____

The Security Interest shall secure the payment and performance of Borrower's promissory note of given date herewith in the principal amount of _____ Dollars ($_____) and the payment and performance of all other liabilities and obligations of Borrower to Lender of every kind and description, direct or indirect, absolute or contingent, due or to become due, now existing or hereafter arising.

2. Covenants. Borrower hereby warrants and covenants:

   a. The parties intend that the collateral is and will at all times remain personal property despite the fact and irrespective of the manner in which it is attached to realty.

   b. The Borrower will not sell, dispose, or otherwise transfer the collateral or any interest therein without the prior written consent of Lender, and the Borrower shall keep the collateral free from unpaid charges (including rent), taxes, and liens.

   c. The Borrower shall execute alone or with Lender any Financing Statement or other document or procure any document, and pay the cost of filing the same in all public offices wherever filing is deemed by Lender to be necessary.

   d. Borrower shall maintain insurance at all times with respect to all collateral against risks of fire, theft, and other such risks and in such amounts as Lender may require. The policies shall be payable to both the Lender and the Borrower as their interests appear and shall provide for ten (10) days' written notice of cancellation to Lender.

   e. The Borrower shall make all repairs, replacements, additions, and improvements necessary to maintain any equipment in good working order and condition. At its option, Lender may discharge taxes, liens, or other encumbrances at any time levied or placed on the collateral, may pay rent or insurance due on the collateral, and may pay for the maintenance and preservation of the collateral. Borrower agrees to reimburse Lender on demand for any payment made or any expense incurred by Lender pursuant to the foregoing authorization.

3. Default. The Borrower shall be in default under this Agreement if it is in default under the Note. Upon default and at any time thereafter, Lender may declare all obligations secured hereby immediately due and payable and

shall have the remedies of a Lender under the Uniform Commercial Code. Lender may require the Borrower to make it available to Lender at a place that is mutually convenient. No waiver by Lender of any default shall operate as a waiver of any other default or of the same default on a future occasion. This Agreement shall inure to the benefit of and bind the heirs, executors, administrators, successors, and assigns of the parties. This Agreement shall have the effect of an instrument under seal.

_____ ("Borrower")

Signature _____

Date_____

93. Simple Commercial Lease

This Commercial Lease is hereby made between _____, the "Lessor," and _____, the "Lessee," concerning the following property: _____, the "Premises."

Lessee hereby leases from Lessor the Premises.

1. Term and Rent. Lessor will lease the above Premises for an initial term of _____ years and _____ months, beginning on _____, 20_____, and ending on _____, 20_____, as provided herein at the monthly rent of $ _____, payable in equal installments in advance on the first day of each month for that month's rental, during the term of the lease. All rental payments shall be made to Lessor, at the following address: _____
_____.

2. Use. Lessee shall use and occupy the Premises for _____. The Premises shall be used for no other purpose. Lessor represents that the Premises may lawfully be used for such purpose.

3. Care and Maintenance of Premises. Lessee acknowledges that the Premises are in good order and repair, unless otherwise indicated herein. Lessee shall, at his own expense and at all times, maintain the Premises in good and safe condition, including electrical wiring, plumbing and heating installations, and any other system or equipment upon the Premises and shall surrender the same, at termination hereof, in as good a condition as received, normal wear and tear excepted. Lessee shall be responsible for all repairs required, excepting the roof, exterior walls, structural foundations, and the following:
_____, which shall be maintained by Lessor. Lessee shall also maintain in good condition such portions adjacent to the Premises, such as sidewalks, driveways, lawns, and shrubbery, which would otherwise be required to be maintained by Lessor.

4. Alterations. Lessee shall not, without first obtaining the written consent of Lessor, make any alterations, additions, or improvements, in, to, or about the Premises.

5. Ordinances and Statues. Lessee shall comply with all statutes, ordinances, and requirements of all municipal, state, and federal authorities now in force, or which may hereafter be in force, pertaining to the Premises, occasioned by or affecting the use thereof by Lessee.

6. Assignment and Subletting. Lessee shall not assign this lease or sublet any portion of the Premises without prior written consent of the Lessor, which shall not be unreasonably withheld. Any such assignment or subletting without consent shall be void and, at the option of the Lessor, may terminate this lease.

7. Utilities. All applications and connections for necessary utility services on the demised Premises shall be made in the name of Lessee only, and Lessee shall be solely liable for utility charges as they become due, including those for sewer, water, gas, electricity, and telephone services.

8. Entry and Inspection. Lessee shall permit Lessor or Lessor's agents to enter upon the Premises at reasonable times and upon reasonable notice, for the purpose of inspecting the same, and will permit Lessor, at any time within sixty (60) days prior to the expiration of this lease, to place upon the Premises any usual "To Let" or "For Lease" signs and permit persons desiring to lease the same to inspect the Premises thereafter.

9. Possession. If Lessor is unable to deliver possession of the Premises at the commencement hereof, Lessor shall not be liable for any damage caused thereby, nor shall this lease be void or voidable, but Lessee shall not be liable for any rent until possession is delivered. Lessee may terminate this lease if possession is not delivered within ten (10) days of the commencement of the term hereof.

10. Indemnification of Lessor. Lessor shall not be liable for any damage or injury to Lessee, or any other person, or to any property, occurring on the demised Premises or any part thereof, and Lessee agrees to hold Lessor harmless from any claims for damages, no matter how caused.

11. Insurance. Lessee, at his expense, shall maintain public liability insurance including bodily injury and property damage insuring Lessee and Lessor with minimum coverage as follows:_____

_____

Lessee shall provide Lessor with a Certificate of Insurance showing Lessor as additional insured. The Certificate shall provide for a ten-day written notice to Lessor in the event of cancellation or material change of coverage. To the maximum extent permitted by insurance policies that may be owned by Lessor or Lessee, Lessee and Lessor, for the benefit of each other, waive any and all rights of subrogation that might otherwise exist.

12. Eminent Domain. If the Premises or any part thereof or any estate therein, or any other part of the building materially affecting Lessee's use of the Premises, shall be taken by eminent domain, this lease shall terminate on the date when title vests pursuant to such taking. The rent, and any additional rent, shall be apportioned as of the termination date, and any rent paid for any period beyond that date shall be repaid to Lessee. Lessee shall not be entitled to any part of the award for such taking or any payment in lieu thereof, but Lessee may file a claim for any taking of fixtures and improvements owned by Lessee and for moving expenses.

13. Destruction of Premises. In the event of a partial destruction of the Premises during the term hereof, from any cause, Lessor shall forthwith repair the same, provided that such repairs can be made within sixty (60) days under existing governmental laws and regulations, but such partial destruction shall not terminate this lease, except that Lessee shall be entitled to a proportionate reduction of rent while such repairs are being made, based upon the extent to which the making of such repairs shall interfere with the business of Lessee on the Premises. If such repairs cannot be made within said sixty (60) days, Lessor, at his option, may make the same within a reasonable time, this lease continuing in effect with the rent proportionately abated as aforesaid, and in the event that Lessor shall not elect to make such repairs that cannot be made within sixty (60) days, this lease may be terminated at the option of either party. In the event that the building in which the demised Premises may be situated is destroyed to an extent of not less than one-third of the replacement costs thereof, Lessor may elect to terminate this lease whether the demised Premises be injured or not. A total destruction of the building in which the Premises may be situated shall terminate this lease.

14. Lessor's Remedies on Default. If Lessee defaults in the payment of rent, or any additional rent, or defaults in the performance of any of the other covenants or conditions hereof, Lessor may give Lessee notice of such default and if Lessee does not cure any such default within sixty (60) days, after the giving of such notice (or if such other default is of such nature that it cannot be completely cured within such period, if Lessee does not commence such curing within such sixty (60) days and thereafter proceed with reasonable diligence and in good faith to cure such default), then Lessor may terminate this lease on not less than thirty (30) days' notice to Lessee. On the date specified in such notice, the term of this lease shall terminate and Lessee shall then quit and surrender the Premises to Lessor, but Lessee shall remain liable as hereinafter provided. If this lease shall have been so terminated by Lessor, Lessor may at any time thereafter resume possession of the Premises by any lawful means and remove Lessee or other occupants and their effects. No failure to enforce any term shall be deemed a waiver.

15. Common Area Expenses. In the event the Premises are situated in a shopping center or in a commercial building in which there are common areas, Lessee agrees to pay his pro-rata share of maintenance, taxes, and insurance for the common areas.

16. Attorney's Fees. In case suit should be brought for recovery of the Premises, or for any sum due hereunder, or because of any act which may arise out of the possession of the Premises, by either party, the prevailing party shall be entitled to all costs incurred in connection with such action, including a reasonable attorney's fee.

17. Notices. Any notice that either party may or is required to give shall be given by mailing the same, postage prepaid, to Lessee at the Premises, or Lessor at the address shown below [give address], or at such other places as may be designated by the parties from time to time.

18. Heirs, Assigns, Successors. This lease is binding upon and inures to the benefit of the heirs, assigns, and successors in interest to the parties.

19. Subordination. This lease is and shall be subordinated to all existing and future liens and encumbrances against the property.

20. Entire Agreement. The foregoing constitutes the entire agreement between the parties and may be modified only by a writing signed by both parties. The following Exhibits, if any, have been made a part of this lease before the parties' execution hereof:

Signed this _____ day of _____, 20_____.

_____
Signature of Lessor

_____
Signature of Lessee

94. Consulting Services Agreement
CONSULTING SERVICES AGREEMENT

This Consulting Services Agreement (this "Agreement") is hereby made between _____ ("Client") and _____ ("Consultant"). Consultant agrees to provide the "Services," as more fully defined below, to Client and Client agrees to pay to Consultant the Consultant Services Fee, as more fully defined below.

1. Definitions. The following definitions shall apply to this Agreement.

   a. The "Services Fee Payment Schedule" (if applicable) shall include the compensation outlined in Exhibit A, and shall be paid according to the terms outlined in the table attached to this Agreement as Exhibit B.

   b. The "Agreement Term" shall begin with the Commencement Date and shall end with the Termination Date.

   c. The "Commencement Date" shall be the later of (i) the last date upon which a party executes this Agreement or (ii) the first date upon which Services are rendered.

   d. The "Termination Date" shall be any of the following: (i) the one-year anniversary of the Commencement Date or (ii) the date of receipt by either party of a Termination Notice.

2. Services. Consultant shall perform the duties and tasks outlined in the table attached to this Agreement as Exhibit C (the "Services"). The Services may include a development schedule and milestones.

3. Payment. Client shall pay the "Consulting Services Fee" as outlined in the table attached to this Agreement as Exhibit A, and shall pay such Consulting Services Fee according to the "Services Fee Payment Schedule" (if applicable) as outlined in the table attached to this Agreement as Exhibit B.

4. Termination. Either party may without cause terminate this Agreement by delivering to the other party written notice via U.S. Mail, facsimile, or personal delivery (but not by electronic mail transmission) expressing a desire to terminate this Agreement (a "Termination Notice"). Termination shall be effective immediately upon receipt of a Termination Notice.

5. Representations and Warranties. The parties to this Agreement make the following representations and warranties.

   a. Both parties represent and warrant to the other party that they have the full power to enter into this agreement without restriction.

   b. This Agreement shall not establish an employer/employee relationship between the parties. Consultant shall be an independent contractor and shall not enjoy the benefits normally afforded to employees provided either by Client's policy or by law.

   c. Consultant shall not include in the Material (as defined in Paragraph 5, below) any copyrights, trade secrets, trademarks, service marks, patents, or other property that to the Consultant's knowledge would infringe on the rights of third parties.

   d. Consultant shall not be an agent or representative of Client, except as specifically defined in this Agreement. Consultant shall have no authority to, and shall not attempt to, bind Client to contracts with third parties.

6. Confidential Information. Neither party shall, at any time, either directly or indirectly, use for its own benefit, nor shall it divulge, disclose, or communicate any information received from the other party that has been identified as Confidential. Both parties agree to execute standard nondisclosure agreements in connection with this Agreement.

7. Copyrights. Consultant, in the absence of any agreement to the contrary, agrees to irrevocably assign and convey to Client all rights, title, and interest to the copyrights, trade secrets, trademarks, service marks, patents, or

other property created or to be created in connection with the performance of the Services (the "Material"). Client shall be deemed the author of such material and the Material shall be a "work for hire" as defined in 17 U.S.C. § 201 and the cases interpreting it.

8. **Limitation of Damages.** NEITHER PARTY SHALL BE LIABLE TO THE OTHER PARTY FOR ANY INCIDENTAL, CONSE-QUENTIAL, SPECIAL, OR PUNITIVE DAMAGES OF ANY KIND OR NATURE, INCLUDING, WITHOUT LIMITATION, THE BREACH OF THIS AGREEMENT OR ANY TERMINATION OF THIS AGREEMENT, WHETHER SUCH LIABILITY IS ASSERTED ON THE BASIS OF CONTRACT, TORT, OR OTHERWISE, EVEN IF EITHER PARTY HAS BEEN WARNED OR WARNED OF THE POSSIBILITY OF ANY SUCH LOSS OR DAMAGE.

9. **General Provisions.** This Agreement constitutes the entire agreement of the parties and supersedes all prior understandings and agreements of the parties, whether oral or written. If any provision of this Agreement shall be held to be invalid or unenforceable for any reason, (i) the remaining provisions shall continue to be valid and enforceable; or (ii) if by limiting such provision it would become valid and enforceable, then such provision shall be deemed to be written, construed, and enforced as so limited. This Agreement shall be governed by the laws of the State of California. This Agreement is to be performed in (and venue shall lie exclusively in) _____ County, _____. This Agreement shall not be strictly construed against any party to this Agreement. Any controversy or claim arising out of or relating to this Agreement, or the breach thereof, shall be resolved by either (i) adjudication in a small claims court (subject to jurisdictional limitations) or (ii) in binding arbitration administered under the rules of the American Arbitration Association in accordance with its applicable rules.

Date _____   Date _____

_____   _____
Consultant   Client

Exhibit A: The "Consulting Services Fee" shall include the following payments and shall be according to the terms outlined herein:

The "Consulting Services Fee" shall include:

$_____, payable per hour for the time that Consultant devotes to the performance of the Services and for which written itemization for individual tasks is provided to Client (the "Hourly Rate"). The Hourly Rate shall be recorded in increments of time no greater than 1/10 of an hour (6 minutes). Payment shall be made within 15 days of the receipt of a written invoice by Client.

The "Consulting Services Fee" shall include:

$_____, payable in cash, by negotiable draft(s), or by transfer(s) to Client's bank account, according to the Services Fee Payment Schedule, which appears as Exhibit B.

Exhibit B: The "Services Fee Payment Schedule" shall include the following payments and according to the terms outlined herein:

The "Consulting Services Fee" shall be paid as follows:

$_____ shall accrue to the consultant upon the completion of each calendar month of service. Partial months shall be prorated on a daily basis. Payment shall be made within 15 days following the later of (a) the end of any applicable calendar month or (b) the submission of a written invoice to Client.

Exhibit C: The "Services" to be performed under the Agreement shall include the following:

Describe services to be performed.

95. Multimedia Development Contract

MULTIMEDIA DEVELOPMENT CONTRACT

This agreement is entered into by and between _____("Client") and _____ ("Developer") (together, the "Parties").

The effective date of this agreement is _____ ("Effective Date").

Recitals

WHEREAS, Developer offers the following services and related services: digital media design and development, corporate identity design and development, print design, Web site design and development, interactive kiosk design and development, CD-ROM design and development, logo design and development, computer graphics design and development.

WHEREAS, Client wishes to have Developer provide services for compensation.

NOW, THEREFORE, in consideration of the promises and mutual covenants and agreements set forth herein, Client and Developer agree as follows:

Definitions

"Existing Client Content" means the material provided by Client to be incorporated into the Product.

"Developer Tools" means the software tools of general application, whether owned or licensed to Developer, which are used to develop the Product.

"Development Schedule" shall be, only when applicable, as set forth in Schedule B to this Agreement, which lists the deliverable items contracted for ("Deliverables") and the deadlines for their delivery.

"Error" means, only when applicable, any failure of a Deliverable or Product to (i) meet the Specifications, if any, or (ii) to properly operate.

"Payment Schedule" shall be set forth in Schedule C to this Agreement and is the schedule by which payments under this agreement shall be made.

"Product" means the material that is the subject of this agreement, as further described in paragraph 1.1, below.

"Specifications" for the product, only when applicable, shall be set forth in Schedule A.

DEVELOPMENT AND DELIVERY OF DELIVERABLES, PAYMENT

1.1. Developer agrees to develop, on behalf of Client, the following (the "Product"): (describe what you are making, e.g., interactive Kiosk, educational CD-ROM, Web site, etc.).

1.2. Developer shall use his best efforts to develop each Deliverable and/or Product in accordance with the Specifications, if any.

1.3. All development work will be performed by Developer or his employees or by approved independent contractors who have executed confidentiality agreements, where appropriate.

1.4. Developer shall deliver all Deliverables and/or Product within the times specified in the Development Schedule and in accordance with the Specifications, if any.

1.5. Developer agrees to comply with all reasonable requests of Client as to the manner of delivery of all Deliverables, which may include delivery by electronic means.

1.6. Client agrees to pay according to the Payment Schedule.

1.7. If the Client, following the execution of this Agreement, alters the Specifications, or alters the nature and/or scope of the project as described in paragraph 1.1, or requests additional work, Developer reserves the right, upon notification to the Client, to (i) modify the Payment Schedule or (ii) charge Client on an hourly basis for the additional time at the rate of $_____ per hour.

1.8. Except as expressly provided in this Agreement or in a later writing signed by the Client, Developer shall bear all expenses arising from the performance of its obligations under this Agreement.

1.9. Except as expressly provided in this Agreement, this Agreement does not include any maintenance work on the Product or later enhancements to the product.

TESTING AND ACCEPTANCE

2.1. All Deliverables shall be thoroughly tested by Developer (if applicable) and all necessary corrections as a result of such testing shall be made, prior to delivery to Client.

2.2. When applicable, in the event that a Deliverable or Product delivered to Client has an Error, Client shall notify Developer within 7 days of delivery or shall waive its objections. Upon notification to Developer, Developer shall have 7 days to make a correction to the Deliverable or Product and present the repaired Deliverable or Product to Client. If the Payment Schedule calls for work under this Agreement to be paid by piece rate, time spent correcting Errors is to be included in the amounts in the Payment Schedule. If the Payment Schedule calls for work under this Agreement to be paid by hourly rate, time spent correcting Errors shall be billed to Client according to the hourly rate in the Payment Schedule.

COPYRIGHTS

3.1. Client will retain copyright ownership of Existing Client Content.

3.2. Developer will retain copyright ownership of the following material ("Developer's Components") to be created in the development of the Product and to include any and all of the following:

   a. Developer's existing tools, such as (source code, pre-existing code, scripts, stock images—basically your tools that you bring to the project: these should be non-negotiable items and should appear here in every contract.)

   b. Content created in connection with development of the Product, including: (simply insert the components that you are creating to which you wish to retain the rights—HTML code, source code, Java code, computer code in any language, images, animations, scripts, script code, text, logos).

3.3. Client will retain copyright ownership of, and Developer agrees to irrevocably assign and convey to Client all rights, title, and interest in the same, the following material ("Client's Components") to be created in the development of the Product and to include any and all of the following: (HTML code, source code, Java code, computer code in any language, images, animations, scripts, script code, text, logos—simply insert the components that you are creating to which you wish to give the rights).

3.4. Developer will retain copyright ownership of any copyrights not specifically granted to either party by this Agreement ("Non-specified Components").

3.5. Developer, however, grants to Client a royalty-free, worldwide, perpetual, irrevocable, non-exclusive license, with the right to sublicense through multiple tiers of sub-licensees, to use, reproduce, distribute, modify, publicly perform, and publicly display the Developer's Components and Non-specified Components in any medium and in any manner, unless such rights are specifically limited by this Agreement. This license includes the right to modify such copyrighted material.

3.6. Client, however, grants to Developer a royalty-free, worldwide, perpetual, irrevocable, non-exclusive license, to use, reproduce, distribute, modify, publicly perform, and publicly display its Existing Client Content and Client's Components (if any) for the sole and limited purpose of use in Developer's portfolio as self-promotion and not for direct commercial sale.

3.7. For the purposes of this agreement, "copyright" shall be deemed to include copyrights, trade secrets, patents, trademarks, and other intellectual property rights.

3.8. If any third party content or Developer Tools are used in the development of the Product, Developer shall be responsible for obtaining and/or paying for any necessary licenses to use third party content.

CONFIDENTIALITY

4.1. The terms of this Agreement, Existing Client Content, and other sensitive business information are confidential ("Confidential Information"). Developer and Client agree, except as authorized in writing, not to disclose to any third party Confidential Information. Developer agrees to return to Client promptly, upon completion of the Product, all Existing Client Content.

WARRANTIES, COVENANTS, AND INDEMNIFICATION

5.1. Developer represents and warrants to Client the following: (i) Developer has the full power to enter into this agreement without restriction, (ii) except with respect to Existing Client Content, and properly licensed materials, the performance, distribution, or use of the Product will not violate the rights of any third parties, and (iii) Developer agrees to defend, hold harmless, and indemnify Client and its representatives from and against all claims, defense costs, judgments, and other expenses arising out of the breach of the foregoing warranties.

5.2. Client represents and warrants to Developer the following: (i) Client has the full power to enter into this agreement without restriction, (ii) the performance of this Agreement will not violate the rights of any third parties, and (iii) Client agrees to defend, hold harmless, and indemnify Developer and its representatives from and against all claims, defense costs, judgments, and other expenses arising out of the breach of the foregoing warranties.

TERMINATION

6.1. If Developer fails to correct an Error according to paragraph 2.2 after 3 attempts, Client may terminate this agreement without making any further payments according to the Payment Schedule.

6.2. No termination of this Agreement by any party shall affect Developer's rights to receive his hourly rate for all time spent producing Deliverables and/or Product.

MISCELLANEOUS PROVISIONS

7.1. This Agreement contains the entire understanding and agreement of the parties, supersedes all prior written or oral understandings or agreements, and may not be altered, modified, or waived except in a signed writing.

7.2. EXCEPT AS PROVIDED ABOVE WITH RESPECT TO THIRD PARTY INDEMNIFICATION, NEITHER PARTY SHALL BE LIABLE TO THE OTHER PARTY FOR ANY INCIDENTAL, CONSEQUENTIAL, SPECIAL, OR PUNITIVE DAMAGES OF ANY KIND OR NATURE, INCLUDING, WITHOUT LIMITATION, THE BREACH OF THIS AGREEMENT OR ANY TERMINATION OF THIS AGREEMENT, WHETHER SUCH LIABILITY IS ASSERTED ON THE BASIS OF CONTRACT, TORT, OR OTHERWISE, EVEN IF EITHER PARTY HAS BEEN WARNED OR WARNED OF THE POSSIBILITY OF ANY SUCH LOSS OR DAMAGE.

_____

Developer

_____

Client

Schedule A

Specifications

(This will depend on the job, obviously, and may not apply to all jobs.)

Schedule B

Development Schedule

(This will depend on the job, obviously, and may not apply to all jobs.)

Schedule C

Payment Schedule

(For hourly rate:)

Developer shall be paid on an hourly basis, and his rates and billing procedures are as follows: Charges are $_____ per hour. The minimum billing increment is six minutes or 1/10 of an hour. Time spent on individual tasks is rounded up to the next 10th of an hour.

(For piece rate:)

Deliverables	Due Date	Payment Due
Down payment (1/3)	_____	$_____
Milestone 1	_____	$_____
Milestone 2	_____	$_____
Final Completion	_____	$_____
Total Payment	_____	$_____

96. Mutual Nondisclosure Agreement

This agreement is made effective on _____ (date) by and between _____ (first party) and _____ (second party) (collectively, the "Parties"), to ensure the protection and preservation of the confidential and/or proprietary nature of information disclosed or made available or to be disclosed or made available to each other. For the purposes of this agreement, each Party shall be deemed to include any subsidiaries, internal divisions, agents, and employees. Any signing party shall refer to and bind the individual and the entity that he or she represents.

Whereas the Parties desire to ensure the confidential status of the information that may be disclosed to each other.

Now, therefore, in reliance upon and in consideration of the following undertakings, the Parties agree as follows:

1. Subject to limitations set forth in paragraph 2, all information disclosed to the other party shall be deemed to be "Proprietary Information." In particular, Proprietary Information shall be deemed to include any information, marketing technique, publicity technique, public relations technique, process, technique, algorithm, program, design, drawing, mask work, formula, test data research project, work in progress, future development, engineering, manufacturing, marketing, servicing, financing, or personal matter relating to the disclosing party, its present or future products, sales, suppliers, clients, customers, employees, investors, or business, whether in oral, written, graphic, or electronic form.

2. The term "Proprietary Information" shall not be deemed to include information that (i) is now, or hereafter becomes, through no act or failure to act on the part of the receiving party, generally known or available information, (ii) is known by the receiving party at the time of receiving such information as evidenced by its records, (iii) is hereafter furnished to the receiving party by a third party, as a matter of right and without restriction on disclosure, (iv) is independently developed by the receiving party without reference to the information disclosed hereunder, or (v) is the subject of a written permission to disclose provided by the disclosing party.

   Not withstanding any other provision of this Agreement, disclosure of Proprietary Information shall not be precluded if such disclosure:

   (a) is in response to a valid order of a court or other governmental body of the United States or any political subdivision thereof,

   (b) is otherwise required by law, or,

   (c) is otherwise necessary to establish rights or enforce obligations under this agreement, but only to the extent that any such disclosure is necessary.

   In the event that the receiving party is requested in any proceedings before a court or any other governmental body to disclose Proprietary Information, it shall give the disclosing party prompt notice of such request so that the disclosing party may seek an appropriate protective order. If, in the absence of a protective order, the receiving party is nonetheless compelled to disclose Proprietary Information, the receiving party may disclose such information without liability hereunder, provided, however, that such party gives the disclosing party advance written notice of the information to be disclosed and, upon the request and at the expense of the disclosing party, uses its best efforts to obtain assurances that confidential treatment will be accorded to such information.

3. Each party shall maintain in trust and confidence and not disclose to any third party or use for any unauthorized purpose any Proprietary Information received from the other party. Each party may use such Proprietary Information in the extent required to accomplish the purpose of the discussions with respect to the subject. Proprietary Information shall not be used for any purpose or in any manner that would constitute a violation on law regulations, including without limitation the export control laws of the United States of America. No other rights or licenses to trademarks, inventions, copyrights, or patents are implied or granted under this Agreement.

4. Proprietary Information supplied shall not be reproduced in any form except as required to accomplish the intent of this Agreement.

5. The responsibilities of the Parties are limited to using their efforts to protect the Proprietary Information received with the same degree of care used to protect their own Proprietary Information from unauthorized use or disclosure. Both Parties shall advise their employees or agents who might have access to such Proprietary Information of the confidential nature thereof and that by receiving such information they are agreeing to be bound by this Agreement. No Proprietary Information shall be disclosed to any officer, employee, or agent of either party who does not have a need for such information for the purpose of the discussions with respect to the subject.

6. All Proprietary Information (including all copies thereof) shall remain the property of the disclosing party and shall be returned to the disclosing party after the receiving party's need for it has expired, or upon request of the disclosing party, and in any event, upon completion or termination of this Agreement. The receiving party further agrees to destroy all notes and copies thereof made by its officers and employees containing or based on any Proprietary Information and to cause all agents and representatives to whom or to which Proprietary Information has been disclosed to destroy all notes and copies in their possession that contain Proprietary Information.

7. This Agreement shall survive any termination of the discussion with respect to the subject and shall continue in full force and effect until such time as Parties mutually agree to terminate it.

8. This Agreement shall be governed by the laws of the United States of America and as those laws that are applied to contracts entered into and to be performed in all states. Should any revision of this Agreement be determined to be void, invalid, or otherwise unenforceable by any court or tribunal of competent jurisdiction, such determination shall not affect the remaining provisions of this Agreement, which shall remain in full force and effect.

9. This Agreement contains final, complete, and exclusive agreement of the Parties relative to the subject matter hereof and supersedes any prior agreement of the Parties, whether oral or written. This Agreement may not be changed, modified, amended, or supplemented except by a written instrument signed by both Parties.

10. Each party hereby acknowledges and agrees that, in the event of any breach of this Agreement by the other party, including, without limitations, the actual or threatened disclosure of a disclosing party's Proprietary Information without the prior express written consent of the disclosing party, the disclosing party will suffer an irreparable injury such that no remedy at law will afford it adequate protection against or appropriate compensation for such injury. Accordingly, each party hereby agrees that the other party shall be entitled to specific performance of a receiving party's obligations under this Agreement as well as further injunctive relief as may be granted by a court of competent jurisdiction.

11. The term of this agreement is for two (2) years, commencing on the "Effective Date."

AGREED TO:

Signature _____

Printed Name _____

Date _____

AGREED TO:

Signature _____

Printed Name _____

Date _____

97. Mutual Compromise Agreement and Mutual Release

THIS MUTUAL COMPROMISE AGREEMENT AND MUTUAL RELEASE ("Agreement") is entered into as of
_____, by and between _____ ("Debtor") and
_____ ("Creditor") (collectively "Parties or Party"). For the purposes of the Agreement,
"Party" includes subsidiaries and parents of a Party and includes individuals serving as directors, officers, employees, agents, consultants, and advisors to or of a Party.

A. BACKGROUND

1. Debtor and Creditor entered into an agreement or series of agreements (the "Contract") whereby Debtor provided a series of services to Creditor for an agreed-upon fee.

2. Since the time of entering into the Contract, the Parties have determined that a settlement of the mutual obligations between them is appropriate and would best serve the interests of all of the Parties. This Agreement is intended to express the Parties' intent to equitably settle the obligations arising from or related to the Contract.

B. AGREEMENT

NOW, THEREFORE, IN CONSIDERATION OF THE FOLLOWING, THE FOREGOING, THE MUTUAL COVENANTS,
PROMISES, AGREEMENTS, REPRESENTATIONS, AND RELEASES CONTAINED HEREIN, AND IN EXCHANGE FOR
OTHER GOOD AND VALUABLE CONSIDERATION, THE RECEIPT, SUFFICIENCY, AND ADEQUACY OF WHICH IS
HEREBY ACKNOWLEDGED, THE PARTIES HEREBY AGREE AS FOLLOWS:

1. Settlement.

    a. Debtor shall pay the following amounts to Creditor: _____, such payment to be made no later than _____ date.

    b. Debtor shall owe no further liability or obligation to Creditor in connection with any services.

2. Confidentiality. Debtor and Creditor shall keep the terms of the Agreement confidential and shall not disclose such terms to any other Party except as is necessary for the proper conduct of the disclosing Party's business.

3. No Other Payments. No additional funds shall be required to be paid or transferred by Creditor to Debtor or by Debtor to Creditor.

4. Nature and Effect of Agreement and Conditions Thereon. This Agreement consists of a compromise and settlement by the Parties of claims arising from the Contract described in Section A, Paragraph 2, above, and a release given by the Parties relinquishing their claims against the other. By executing this Agreement, the Parties intend to and do hereby extinguish the obligations heretofore existing between them and arising from that dispute.

    The nature and effect of this agreement, and the enforcement of any of the provisions found herein, is strictly conditioned upon the actions described in Paragraph 1. The shares must bear the medallion guaranteed signature of an authorized officer of the entity whose name appears on the face of the certificate and the shares must be accompanied by a resolution of the board authorizing transfer of the shares.

5. Admissions. This Agreement is not, and shall not be treated as, an admission of liability by either Party for any purpose, and shall not be admissible as evidence before any tribunal or court.

6. Compromise Agreement. The Parties hereby compromise and settle any and all past, present, or future claims, demands, obligations, or causes of action for compensatory or punitive damages, costs, losses, expenses, and compensation, whether based on tort, contract, or other theories of recovery, which the Parties have or which may later accrue to or be acquired by one Party against the other, the other's predecessors and successors in interest, heirs, and assigns, past, present, and future officers, directors, shareholders, agents, employees, parent and subsidiary organizations, affiliates, and partners, arising from the subject matter of the claim described in

Section A, Paragraph 2, above, and agree that this compromise and settlement shall constitute a bar to all such claims. The Parties agree that this compromise and settlement shall constitute a bar to all past, present, and future claims arising out of the subject matter of the action described in Section A, Paragraph 2, above.

7. **Release and Discharge.** The Parties hereby release and discharge the other, the other's predecessors and successors in interest, heirs, and assigns, past, present, and future officers, directors, shareholders, agents, employees, parent and subsidiary organizations, affiliates, and partners from, and relinquish, any and all past, present, or future claims, demands, obligations, or causes of action for compensatory or punitive damages, costs, losses, expenses, and compensation, whether based on tort, contract, or other theories of recovery, which the Parties have or which may later accrue to or be acquired by one Party against the other arising from the subject of the claim described in Section A, Paragraph 2, above.

8. **Unknown Claims.** The Parties acknowledge and agree that, upon execution of the release, this Agreement applies to all claims for damages or losses that either Party may have against the other, whether those damages or losses are known or unknown, foreseen or unforeseen, and in the event that this Agreement is deemed executed in California, the Parties thereby waive application of California Civil Code Section 1542.

The Parties certify that each has read the following provisions of California Civil Code Section 1542: "A general release does not extend to claims which the creditor does not know or suspect to exist in his favor at the time of executing the release, which if known by him must have materially affected his settlement with the debtor."

The Parties understand and acknowledge that the significance and consequence of this waiver of California Civil Code Section 1542 is that even if one Party should eventually suffer additional damages arising out of the facts referred to in Section A, Paragraph 2, above, that Party will not be able to make any claim for these damages. Furthermore, the Parties acknowledge that they intend these consequences even as to claims for damages that may exist as of the date of this release but that the damaged or harmed Party does not know exist and that, if known, would materially affect that Party's decision to execute this release, regardless of whether the damaged Party's lack of knowledge is the result of ignorance, oversight, error, negligence, or any other cause.

9. **Conditions of Execution.** Each Party acknowledges and warrants that its execution of this compromise agreement and release is free and voluntary.

10. **Representation of Understanding.** All Parties and signatories to this Agreement acknowledge and agree that the terms of this Agreement are contractual and not mere recital, and all Parties and signatories represent and warrant that they have carefully read this Agreement, have fully reviewed its provisions with their attorneys, know and understand its contents, and sign the same as their own free acts and deeds. It is understood and agreed by all Parties and signatories to this Agreement that execution of this Agreement may affect rights and liabilities of substantial extent and degree and, with the full understanding of that fact, they represent that the covenants and releases provided for in this Agreement are in their respective best interests.

11. **Construction.** The provisions of this Agreement shall not be construed against either Party.

12. **Entire Agreement.** This Agreement constitutes the entire agreement between the Parties and signatories and all prior and contemporaneous conversation, negotiations, possible and alleged agreements, and representations, covenants, and warranties, express or implied, or written, with respect to the subject matter hereof, are waived, merged herein, and superseded hereby. There are no other agreements, representations, covenants, or warranties not set forth herein. The terms of this Agreement may not be contradicted by evidence of any prior or contemporaneous agreement. The Parties further intend and agree that this Agreement constitutes the complete and exclusive statement of its terms and that no extrinsic evidence whatsoever may be introduced in any judicial or arbitration proceeding, if any, involving this Agreement. No part of this Agreement may be amended or modified in any way unless such amendment or modification is expressed in writing signed by all Parties to this Agreement.

13. **Counterparts.** This Agreement may be executed in multiple counterparts, each of which shall be deemed an

original but all of which together shall constitute one and the same instrument. When all of the Parties and signatories have executed any copy hereof, such execution shall constitute the execution of this Agreement, whereupon it shall become effective.

14. Governing Law. THIS AGREEMENT WILL BE GOVERNED AND CONSTRUED IN ACCORDANCE WITH THE LAW OF THE STATE OF _____ AND THE UNITED STATES OF AMERICA, WITHOUT REGARD TO CONFLICT OF LAW PRINCIPLES. This Agreement shall not be strictly construed against any Party to this Agreement. Any controversy or claim arising out of or relating to this Agreement, or the breach thereof, shall be resolved by arbitration administered under the rules of the American Arbitration Association in accordance with its applicable rules. Such arbitration shall take place within San Mateo County, California, and shall be binding upon all Parties, and any judgment upon or any an award rendered by the arbitrator may be entered in any court having jurisdiction thereof.

15. Binding Effect. The provisions of this Agreement shall be binding upon and inure to the benefit of each of the Parties and their respective successors and assigns. Nothing expressed or implied in this Agreement is intended, or shall be construed, to confer upon or give any person, partnership, or corporation, other than the Parties, their successors and assigns, any benefits, rights, or remedies under or by reason of this Agreement, except to the extent of any contrary provision herein contained.

16. Authority. The Parties hereto represent and warrant that they possess the full and complete authority to covenant and agree as provided in this Agreement and, if applicable, to release other Parties and signatories as provided herein. If any Party hereto is a corporation or limited liability company, the signatory for any such corporation or limited liability company represents and warrants that such signatory possesses the authority and has been authorized by the corporation or limited liability company to enter into this Agreement, whether by resolution of the board of, upon the instruction by an authorized officer of, as authorized in the bylaws of the corporation on whose behalf the signatory is executing this Agreement, or otherwise.

17. Severability. If any provision of this Agreement is held by a court to be unenforceable or invalid for any reason, the remaining provisions of this Agreement shall be unaffected by such holding.

18. Exchanges by Fax. The exchange of a fully executed Agreement in counterparts or otherwise by fax shall be sufficient to bind the Parties to the terms and conditions of this Agreement.

IN WITNESS WHEREOF, the Parties and signatories execute this Agreement on the dates indicated.

_____, "Debtor"

Date _____

Signature _____

_____, "Creditor"

Date _____

Signature _____

Business Operation Tools

Controlling business operations is essential to generating a profit and meeting your business expectations. This section provides you with a range of worksheets to develop and control key operation issues, production schedules, and costing.

The *Vendor Information Sheet* helps you compile and maintain complete information on current and potential vendors. Use this form initially to confirm approval of new vendors. When deciding among the goods or services of several vendors, use the *Vendor Price and Comparison Analysis* to compare the offerings of each.

If your business conducts manufacturing operations, use the *Daily Production Planning/ Schedule* to formalize your production goals. Use the *Production Completion Notice* to internally notify departments (sales and billing, especially) of the completion of an order.

The *Marketing Department Budget Recap* helps you analyze the sales, margins, and marketing expenses for your products or services. The *Sales Price Estimate* helps you budget and calculate the expenses you'll incur in the production of goods; this calculation helps you determine a sales price for your production with an adequate profit margin. The *Job Costing Report* helps you budget and calculate the expenses you'll incur in the completion of a job or project; this calculation helps you determine your profit. The *Job Costing Comparison Report* is an analytical tool that compares your estimated and actual revenues, material costs, and labor costs.

The *Ratio Analysis Worksheet* is a powerful analytical and budgeting tool. It helps you analyze key financial ratios by comparing your current year ratios with prior year ratios. The *Ratio Analysis Worksheet* can pinpoint trouble areas in your business and reveal areas where your business operations are improving.

The *Commission Report Worksheet* helps you compile sales and commission information for your sales staff, but it can also serve an analytical function by comparing the performances of sales staff members.

The *Production Efficiency Worksheet* analyzes the hour-by-hour performance of production facilities or production lines.

98. Vendor Information Sheet

Name of Firm _____ Phone _____

Address _____

_____

Headquarters Office _____

❏ Corporation ❏ Partnership ❏ Individual ❏ Other _____

Date Business Started _____

President/Principal Owner _____

Other Officers _____

_____

Has this company provided products or services to our company before? ❏ Yes ❏ No

If so, when and what type? _____

_____

List current customers and their approximate purchase value _____

_____

List trade references (name, phone) _____

_____

List bank references (name, branch, phone) _____

_____

Completed by _____ Date _____

Approved by _____ Date _____

99. Vendor Price and Comparison Analysis

Item Description _____ Item # _____

Enter quantity here and price per item below.

Vendor Name					Lead Time	Other Factors
_____	$_____	$_____	$_____	$_____	_____	_____
_____	$_____	$_____	$_____	$_____	_____	_____
_____	$_____	$_____	$_____	$_____	_____	_____
_____	$_____	$_____	$_____	$_____	_____	_____
_____	$_____	$_____	$_____	$_____	_____	_____
_____	$_____	$_____	$_____	$_____	_____	_____
_____	$_____	$_____	$_____	$_____	_____	_____
_____	$_____	$_____	$_____	$_____	_____	_____
_____	$_____	$_____	$_____	$_____	_____	_____
_____	$_____	$_____	$_____	$_____	_____	_____
_____	$_____	$_____	$_____	$_____	_____	_____
_____	$_____	$_____	$_____	$_____	_____	_____
_____	$_____	$_____	$_____	$_____	_____	_____
_____	$_____	$_____	$_____	$_____	_____	_____
_____	$_____	$_____	$_____	$_____	_____	_____
_____	$_____	$_____	$_____	$_____	_____	_____
_____	$_____	$_____	$_____	$_____	_____	_____

Comments

_____
_____
_____
_____
_____
_____
_____
_____
_____
_____

100. Daily Production Planning/Schedule

Date _____ Shift _____ Plant _____

Product Description	Product I.D.#	Quantity
1. _____	_____	_____
2. _____	_____	_____
3. _____	_____	_____
4. _____	_____	_____
5. _____	_____	_____
6. _____	_____	_____
7. _____	_____	_____
8. _____	_____	_____
9. _____	_____	_____
10. _____	_____	_____

101. Production Completion Notice

Customer I.D.# _____ Sales Order # _____ Production Order # _____

Scheduled Completion Date _____ Actual Date _____

Scheduled Shipping Date _____ Actual Date _____

Signed by _____ Date _____

Description of changes made to original sales order:

_____

_____

_____

_____

_____

_____

_____

_____

_____

_____

_____

_____

_____

_____

_____

_____

_____

102. Marketing Department Budget Recap

For the Reporting Period of _____

Product A _____

Product B _____

Product C _____

Product D _____

		Product A	Product B	Product C	Product D	Total
Gross Sales		$_____	$_____	$_____	$_____	$_____
Discounts & Returns	–	$_____	$_____	$_____	$_____	$_____
Net Sales	=	$_____	$_____	$_____	$_____	$_____
Cost of Goods Sold	–	$_____	$_____	$_____	$_____	$_____
Gross Margin	=	$_____	$_____	$_____	$_____	$_____
Marketing Expenses:						
Sales Department Expense		$_____	$_____	$_____	$_____	$_____
Delivery	+	$_____	$_____	$_____	$_____	$_____
Warehousing	+	$_____	$_____	$_____	$_____	$_____
Advertising	+	$_____	$_____	$_____	$_____	$_____
Sales Promotion	+	$_____	$_____	$_____	$_____	$_____
Marketing Research	+	$_____	$_____	$_____	$_____	$_____
Development Cost	+	$_____	$_____	$_____	$_____	$_____
Total Marketing Expense	=	$_____	$_____	$_____	$_____	$_____
Gross Margin		$_____	$_____	$_____	$_____	$_____
Total Marketing Expense	–	$_____	$_____	$_____	$_____	$_____
Profit	=	$_____	$_____	$_____	$_____	$_____

103. Sales Price Estimate

For Job #/Name _____

Materials:	Quantity	x Unit Cost	= Extended
Raw Materials - A _____	_____	$_____	$_____
Raw Materials - B _____	_____	$_____	$_____
Raw Materials - C _____	_____	$_____	$_____
Raw Materials - D _____	_____	$_____	$_____
Total Raw Materials			$_____

Labor:	Time	x Rate	= Extended
Set Up Labor	_____	$_____	$_____
Direct Labor	_____	$_____	$_____
Post Labor	_____	$_____	$_____
Benefit Factoring (Add benefit/hour for the hours of employees included in Labor)	_____	$_____	$_____
Total Labor			$_____

Other Costs: Costs

Outside Services $_____

Delivery + $_____

Burden Rate (Overhead expense directly related to each unit produced) + $_____

Other _____ + $_____

Other _____ + $_____

Total Other Costs = $_____

Total Raw Materials + Total Labor + Total Other Costs = Total Job Cost = $_____

Total Job Cost x Your Desired Profit Margin _____% = Total Price of Job = $_____

104. Job Costing Report

Description _____

Job Number _____

Start Date _____

Completion Date _____

Invoice #	Transaction Description	Amount	Revenues:
_____	_____	_____	$_____
_____	_____	_____	+ $_____
_____	_____	_____	+ $_____
_____	_____	_____	+ $_____
_____	_____	_____	+ $_____
_____	_____	_____	+ $_____

Total Revenues   = $_____

Material and Outside Services Costs:

          _____ $_____

          _____   + $_____

          _____   + $_____

          _____   + $_____

          _____   + $_____

Total Materials & Services   = $_____

Labor Cost:

_____   _____ $_____

_____   _____   + $_____

_____   _____   + $_____

_____   _____   + $_____

_____   _____   + $_____

_____   _____   + $_____

Total Labor   = $_____

Total Materials and Services + Total Labor = Total Costs   = $_____

Total Revenues – Total Costs = Profit   = $_____

105. Job Costing Comparison Report

Description _____

Job Number _____

Start Date _____

Completion Date _____

Revenues:

Invoice #	Transaction Description	Amount	– Estimated	= Difference
_____	_____	$_____	$_____	$_____
_____	_____	$_____	$_____	$_____
_____	_____	$_____	$_____	$_____
_____	_____	$_____	$_____	$_____
_____	_____	$_____	$_____	$_____
_____	_____	$_____	$_____	$_____
Total Revenues		$_____	$_____	$_____

Material and Outside Services:

	Amount	– Estimated	= Difference
_____	$_____	$_____	$_____
_____	$_____	$_____	$_____
_____	$_____	$_____	$_____
_____	$_____	$_____	$_____
_____	$_____	$_____	$_____
_____	$_____	$_____	$_____
Total Materials and Services	$_____	$_____	$_____

Labor Cost:

	Amount	– Estimated	= Difference
_____	$_____	$_____	$_____
_____	$_____	$_____	$_____
_____	$_____	$_____	$_____
_____	$_____	$_____	$_____
_____	$_____	$_____	$_____
_____	$_____	$_____	$_____
Total Labor	$_____	$_____	$_____

	Amount	– Estimated	= Difference
Total Materials and Services + Total Labor = Total Costs	$_____	$_____	$_____
Total Revenues – Total Costs = Profit	$_____	$_____	$_____

106. Ratio Analysis Worksheet

For the Month Ending _____

Current Ratio = Current Assets ÷ Current Liabilities

Current Ratio = _____ ÷ _____ = This Year

Current Ratio = _____ ÷ _____ = Last Year

Inventory Turnover = Cost of Goods Sold ÷ Inventory

Inventory Turnover = _____ ÷ _____ = This Year

Inventory Turnover = _____ ÷ _____ = Last Year

Total Asset Turnover = Net Sales ÷ Total Assets

Total Asset Turnover = _____ ÷ _____ = This Year

Total Asset Turnover = _____ ÷ _____ = Last Year

Average Collection Period = Accounts Receivable ÷ Average Credit Sales/Day

Average Collection Period = _____ ÷ _____ = This Year

Average Collection Period = _____ ÷ _____ = Last Year

Long-Term Debt to Equity = Long-Term Debt ÷ Stockholders' Equity

Long-Term Debt to Equity = _____ ÷ _____ = This Year

Long-Term Debt to Equity = _____ ÷ _____ = Last Year

Total Debt to Total Assets = Total Liabilities ÷ Total Assets

Total Debt to Total Assets = _____ ÷ _____ = This Year

Total Debt to Total Assets = _____ ÷ _____ = Last Year

Earnings per Share = Earnings after Tax less Dividends ÷ Number of Common Shares Outstanding

Earnings per Share = _____ ÷ _____ = This Year

Earnings per Share = _____ ÷ _____ = Last Year

107. Commission Report Worksheet

Name of Sales Rep:

#1 _____

#2 _____

#3 _____

#4 _____

#5 _____

#6 _____

#7 _____

#8 _____

		Sales Rep #1	Sales Rep #2	Sales Rep #3	Sales Rep #4
Monthly Net Sales		$_____	$_____	$_____	$_____
Less Adjustments		$_____	$_____	$_____	$_____
Net Sales Applicable	=	$_____	$_____	$_____	$_____
Commission Rate	x	_____	_____	_____	_____
Commission Due	=	$_____	$_____	$_____	$_____

		Sales Rep #5	Sales Rep #6	Sales Rep #7	Sales Rep #8
Monthly Net Sales		$_____	$_____	$_____	$_____
Less Adjustments		$_____	$_____	$_____	$_____
Net Sales Applicable	=	$_____	$_____	$_____	$_____
Commission Rate	x	_____	_____	_____	_____
Commission Due	=	$_____	$_____	$_____	$_____

108. Production Efficiency Worksheet

Date _____ Shift _____ Supervisor _____

Comments _____

Standard Output is 100% capacity of output for production line. Actual Output ÷ Standard Output = % Efficient

	Hour									
	1	2	3	4	5	6	7	8	9	10
Line 1 Product										
Actual Output/Hour										
Cumulative Output										
Standard Output/Hour										
Standard Cumulative										
% Efficient/Hour										
Comments										

	Hour									
	1	2	3	4	5	6	7	8	9	10
Line 2 Product										
Actual Output/Hour										
Cumulative Output										
Standard Output/Hour										
Standard Cumulative										
% Efficient/Hour										
Comments										

	Hour									
	1	2	3	4	5	6	7	8	9	10
Line 3 Product										
Actual Output/Hour										
Cumulative Output										
Standard Output/Hour										
Standard Cumulative										
% Efficient/Hour										
Comments										

	Hour									
	1	2	3	4	5	6	7	8	9	10
Line 4 Product										
Actual Output/Hour										
Cumulative Output										
Standard Output/Hour										
Standard Cumulative										
% Efficient/Hour										
Comments										

Cash Disbursements and Purchasing

This section offers tools that streamline and control your purchasing procedures. The *Purchase Order* is likely familiar; use it to place orders with vendors. You and your employees can use the *Expense Report* both internally and in connection with expenses billable directly to clients. The *Petty Cash Voucher* helps you keep track of funds spent from the petty cash account. The *Check Requisition* is an internal control and record-keeping tool; instruct your staff members to use this form to request checks for purchases.

109. Purchase Order

From:

_____

_____

_____

_____

To:

_____

_____

_____

_____

Purchase Order Number _____

Please supply and deliver the goods or services specified below to the address above. The stated goods or services shall be delivered no later than _____.

This order is subject to the following conditions: _____

_____

Item #	Quantity	Description	Net Unit Price	Total
		Net Total Price	$

Invoices, quoting the order number, should be submitted for payment to:

Signed _____

Name _____

Title _____

This order is not valid unless it is signed.

Please acknowledge receipt of this order.

110. Expense Report

Period covered: From _____ To _____

Name		Dept/Sales Office	Report Date	Date of Trip	From / /	To / /

Business Purpose			Account No.			

Day	Date	Transportation (Air, Rail, Taxi, Limousine, Bus, Car Rental, etc.)	Automobile Expense (Gas Mileage, Tolls, Parking)	Lodging	Meals (Itemize Business: Breakfast/ Lunch/Dinner)	Entertain-ment	Misc.	Totals
Sunday								
Monday								
Tuesday								
Wednesday								
Thursday								
Friday								
Saturday								
Totals								

Automobile Expenses				Entertainment and Business Meals Only				
Date	Location	Mileage, Gas, Parking, Repairs, Service	Amount	Date	Entertained (name, company, title)	Place	Business Purpose	Amount

Miscellaneous Expenses			Expense Summary		Instructions
Date	Detail	Amount	Total Expenses Reported	Amount	Deduct from my advance
					Mail to:

Employee Signature	Date
Approved By	Date

111. Petty Cash Voucher

Account	Description	Amount
	Total Cash Amount	$
Received by	Authorized by	

Account	Description	Amount
	Total Cash Amount	$
Received by	Authorized by	

Account	Description	Amount
	Total Cash Amount	$
Received by	Authorized by	

Account	Description	Amount
	Total Cash Amount	$
Received by	Authorized by	

112. Check Requisition

Requestor		Date of Request		Date Check Needed by	
Make Payable to	Description of Item Needed				Amount
				Total Cash Amount	$
Authorized by			Date		

Requestor		Date of Request		Date Check Needed by	
Make Payable to	Description of Item Needed				Amount
				Total Cash Amount	$
Authorized by			Date		

Requestor		Date of Request		Date Check Needed by	
Make Payable to	Description of Item Needed				Amount
				Total Cash Amount	$
Authorized by			Date		

Requestor		Date of Request		Date Check Needed by	
Make Payable to	Description of Item Needed				Amount
				Total Cash Amount	$
Authorized by			Date		

Inventory Movement and Valuation Tools

This section will guide you in managing and evaluating your inventory. Maintaining the accuracy and integrity of your inventory system is important, but so are identifying and correcting all causes of variances.

Use the *In-House Stock Requisition* form to request inventory internally. This form will serve as a written record of both the request and the delivery from inventory. When you ship goods to a customer, you should accompany the goods with a *Shipping Verification*. Request that a signed copy of the *Shipping Verification* be returned to you and instruct your carrier to secure a signed copy on your behalf. This document serves as your proof of delivery of the shipment.

Use the *Physical Inventory Count Sheet* when performing a physical count of your inventory. The *Physical Inventory Gain or Loss* form enables you to track inaccuracies and shrinkage to your inventory by comparing your *book count*—the amount of inventory shown in your records—and your *physical count*—the amount of inventory shown by an inspection.

Substantial differences between book count and physical count can mean poor record keeping, entry errors, and, in some cases, employee theft. The *Raw Material Shrinkage Report* helps calculate and track losses due to shrinkage of inventory. This tool can help you pinpoint problem areas.

The *Physical Inventory Valuation Report* will determine your total physical inventory value. Simply enter the quantity of each item based on a physical inventory count and multiply the quantity by the cost per unit to determine the value. The *Book Inventory Valuation Report* works the same way as the *Physical Inventory Valuation Report,* except that you use the book count of inventory. The advantage of the *Book Inventory Valuation Report* is that it does not require a full physical inventory count. The obvious disadvantage, however, is that book inventory counts are typically less accurate than physical inventory counts. The *Physical vs. Book Inventory Cost Variance Report* reveals the differences between the book value and the physical value of your inventory.

The *Inventory Status Sheet* helps you maintain an accurate physical count of individual items. Use the *Authorization to Destroy Inventory* to secure approval before disposing of inventory and to notify appropriate personnel of the inventory change. Use the *Property Loss Report* whenever your business suffers loss to its inventory or property. Be sure to fill the form out completely and as soon as possible after the loss. A promptly completed *Property Loss Report* will carry more evidentiary weight with insurance adjusters.

113. In-House Stock Requisition

Requisition # _____

From _____

Job Reference Number _____ Date Needed _____

Department _____

Location _____

Description of items requested from in-house stock:

Quantity	Item Number	Description	Quantity Issued	Date Issued	Initials

Requested by			Date		
Approved by			Date		

114. Shipping Verification

From:

_____

_____

_____

_____

Shipper _____ Date _____

Ship to:

_____

_____

_____

_____

Carrier

_____

_____

_____

_____

Quantity Shipped	Item Number	Description

Proof of shipment received:

Signature of Receiving Clerk   Date

115. Physical Inventory Count Sheet

Sheet #		Location	
Item Number	Description	Quantity	Location
Counted by		Date	

116. Physical Inventory Gain or Loss

For the Period Ending:

Item Number	Description	Book Count	Physical Count	Difference

Prepared by		Date
Reviewed by		Date

117. Raw Material Shrinkage Report

For the Period Ending:

Item Number	Description	Cost per Unit	Quantity Lost	Total Value Lost

All shrinkage losses greater than $_____ per item are to be explained below.

_____

_____

_____

_____

Prepared by _____ Date _____

Reviewed by _____ Date _____

118. Physical Inventory Valuation Report

For the Period Ending:

Item Number	Description	Quantity	Cost per Unit	Total Value
			Total Value	$

Prepared by	Date
Reviewed by	Date

119. Book Inventory Valuation Report

For the Period Ending:

Item Number	Description	Quantity	Cost per Unit	Total Value
			Total Value	$

Prepared by		Date	
Reviewed by		Date	

120. Physical vs. Book Inventory Cost Variance Report

For the Period Ending:				
Item Number	Description	Book Value	Physical Value	Difference
			Total Value	$

Prepared by	Date
Reviewed by	Date

121. Inventory Status Sheet

Item Description				Item Number		
Quantity on Hand	Quantity Ordered	Date Ordered	Unit Cost	Quantity Received	Date Received	Usage

Quantity on Hand: The present quantity of inventory per book inventory report
Quantity Ordered: The quantity of item ordered from vendor
Date Ordered: The date item was ordered from vendor
Unit Cost: The unit cost of item per vendor
Quantity Received: The quantity of item received from vendor
Date Received: The date item was received from vendor
Usage: The actual usage of item in production or sales

Add Quantity on Hand to Quantity Received and subtract Usage to get next Quantity on Hand.

122. Authorization to Destroy Inventory

Date _____

Reason for Request to Destroy Inventory:

_____

_____

_____

_____

Item Number	Description	Quantity to Be Destroyed

Prepared by		Date
Reviewed by		Date

Copy to: Inventory Control, Accounting, Warehouse Manager, and Files.

123. Property Loss Report

Department	Date
Completed by	Date

Cause of Loss
❑ Theft
❑ Vandalism
❑ Burglary
❑ Tools and Equipment
❑ Fire/Arson
❑ Accident/Damage
❑ Unexplained
❑ Other:
_____
_____
_____

Type of Loss
❑ Property Damage
❑ Inventory
❑ Money/Cash
❑ Tools and Equipment
❑ Employee Time
❑ Business Interruption
❑ Other:
_____
_____
_____

Type of Loss	Description	Value Lost

Date and Time Loss Occurred _____

Date and Time Loss Reported _____

❑ Police Report Made   Report ID # _____

List Police Department Contacts and Notes _____

Besides the property loss, were there any other consequences of the loss? _____

_____

_____

_____

Could this loss have been avoided? ❑ Yes   ❑ No

If Yes, how? _____

_____

Other Comments, Notes: _____

_____

_____

Financial Reports

This section offers a full range of financial reports and supporting schedules that will help you quickly produce accurate financial reports for your business. Many of the forms are interactive spreadsheet files that will calculate most of the figures for you.

The *Period-End Closing and Analysis* is a control tool that will greatly increase the accuracy and integrity of your financial statements. You can use this form to close out the month, the quarter, and the year. The *Actual vs. Budget Income Statement* is an interactive computer spreadsheet file that calculates the variance between budgeted income statement items and actual income statement items. You'll find a copy of the file on the disk included with this volume. Enter the actual and budgeted items and the worksheet calculates the dollar variance for each item.

The seven *Balance Sheet Support Schedules* help you accumulate information for individual balance sheet items. These can be real money-savers; they make it unnecessary for your accountant or auditor to accumulate the information on his or her own. The *Balance Sheet Support Schedule—Cash Balance* accumulates information on cash accounts. The *Balance Sheet Support Schedule—Marketable Securities* accumulates information on stocks, bonds, and other marketable instruments. The *Balance Sheet Support Schedule—Accounts Receivable* aggregates accounts receivable information. The *Balance Sheet Support Schedule—Inventory* accumulates information on inventory. The *Balance Sheet Support Schedule—Prepaid Expenses* amortizes prepaid expenses and aggregates period-end totals. The *Balance Sheet Support Schedule—Accounts Payable* summarizes and accumulates accounts payable information. The *Balance Sheet Support Schedule—Notes Payable* accumulates information on notes and loan obligations.

The *Cash Flow Forecast—12-Month* is an interactive spreadsheet that forecasts sales, expenses, and available cash for a 12-month period. The *Cash Flow Forecast—Five Year* does the same for a five-year period. The files are on the disk included with this volume. Simply enter your anticipated sales and expenses and the worksheet calculates the surplus or deficit and the running cash balance.

The *Income Statement—12-Month* is an interactive spreadsheet that accumulates and totals income statement items for a 12-month period. The *Income Statement—Quarterly* calculates the same data for four quarters. The files are on the disk included with this volume. Enter your sales and expenses and the worksheet records the information and calculates the total annual balance for all items.

The *Quarterly Balance Sheet* is an interactive spreadsheet that accumulates and totals balance sheet items for four quarters. The *Year-End Balance Sheet* calculates the same data at the end of your year. The files are on the disk included with this volume. Enter your assets and liabilities and the worksheet records the information and calculates the total balance for all items.

124. Period-End Closing and Analysis

Using this form will increase the level of accuracy and integrity of the financial statements and general ledger. Use to ensure that all month-end tasks have been completed and reviewed.

1. Cash in Banks	Done by	Date	Reviewed by	Date
All bank accounts reconciled from month-end balance per the bank statement to the general ledger balance, with all unusual reconciling items investigated and resolved. (Ensure that, prior to reconciliation, the general ledger balance has been updated to reflect all quarterly entries.)				
Bank reconciliations prepared by an employee who is independent from the cash receipts and disbursements functions.				
Bank reconciliations initialed and dated by the preparer.				
Bank reconciliation reviewed by manager, as evidenced by his/her initials and date.				
2. Accounts Receivable—Trade				
General ledger balance reconciled to balance per detailed accounts receivable aging. All reconciling items investigated and resolved, with journal entries prepared as required.				
All customer account receivable balances have been reviewed for collectibility, giving proper consideration to: • All significant past due accounts • All disputed invoices and erroneous billings • All unissued credits				
The allowance for doubtful accounts has been determined as the sum of the specific and general reserves and has been treated as an offset of current trade receivables. The journal entry to record the specific reserve for disputed invoices, erroneous credits, and doubtful accounts and the general reserve has been made against bad debt expense: • Debit bad debt expense • Credit allowance for doubtful accounts				
All specific invoices determined to be uncollectible have been written off against the allowance for doubtful accounts by the following entry: • Debit allowance for doubtful accounts • Credit accounts receivables–trade				
The approval for the write-offs of uncollectible accounts has been made by individuals who do not have direct access to incoming cash receipts or to the accounts receivable ledgers.				
3. Other Receivables (Including notes)				
All other receivables are supported by account analyses and have been evaluated as to collectibility. Adjustments have been made as required.				

4. Inventory	Done by	Date	Reviewed by	Date
Physical inventory of supplies and materials taken and compared with stock status. Any discrepancies are to be identified, researched, and corrected for the following inventory items: • Raw Materials • Finished Goods • Other				
The physical inventory reconciliation worksheets between physical and stock status report are to be reviewed and approved by manager, as evidenced by his/her initials and date.				
Determine that the stock status report properly reflects month-end quantities on hand and current unit costs.				
Update the inventory cost summary spreadsheet with the following information: • Beginning year inventory value by item and category • Current month-end inventory value by item and category • Determine inventory value difference between beginning inventory values and current month-end values • Journal entry prepared to record inventory • Reverse the prior period's inventory entry				
Record inventory using the net inventory amount obtained in earlier mentioned step, as follows: • Debit/credit inventory account • Credit/debit cost of costs sold (If difference between beginning and current month valuations is positive, debit inventory and credit COGS; if difference is negative, debit COGS and credit inventory.)				
Attach supporting schedules to the journal entry sheet.				
5. Prepaid Expenses				
Changes in account balances have been analyzed and composition of account balances listed on support schedules, which agree with general ledger for each account: • Prepaid state income taxes • Prepaid IRS • Prepaid insurance				
6. Property, Plant, and Equipment				

Journal entry prepared to record depreciation expense for the current month from prepared detail property records, as follows:
• Debit depreciation expense
• Credit accumulated depreciation for each account:
  ❑ Equipment
  ❑ Automobiles
  ❑ Leasehold improvements				

6. Property, Plant, and Equipment (continued)	Done by	Date	Reviewed by	Date
Review and ensure that cost and general ledger agree with detailed records of fixed assets for each account: • Equipment • Automobiles • Leasehold improvements				
Changes in asset costs (additions and disposals) are substantiated by vendor invoices or cash receipts. Gain or loss computed and recorded after taking into account related accumulated depreciation.				
7. Deposits and Other Assets				
Changes in account balances have been analyzed and composition of account balances listed on support schedules, which agree with general ledger for each account.				
8. Accounts Payable				
Accounting department completed matching of invoices received by month-end to open receivers (merchandise received by month-end and included in inventory, for which invoices have not been received), prepared accounts payables vouchers, and processed through A/P system. (Cut-off procedures for accounts payables must coincide with those for inventory.)				
Prepare schedules listing open receivers and other open payables.				
Merchandise recap schedule prepared from accounts payable schedules, listing accruals, returns for credits, merchandise returns, merchandise returns deducted from payments, holding for credit, overage, and freight applicable for the month.				
Journal entry prepared to record above prepared schedules: • Debit applicable cost of sales or expense account • Credit accounts payables				
Journal entry prepared reversing prior month accrual for open receivers and other accounts payables adjustments.				
Check registers issued by accounts payables covering the period between month-end and date of the accounts payable expense. Distribution report reviewed to determine what checks were issued subsequent to month-end.				
Journal entry prepared to record above: • Debit cash • Credit accounts payable				
Accounts payable per detailed listing, reconciled to the general ledger balance. All discrepancies are to be identified, researched, and corrected.				

9. Accrued Expenses	Done by	Date	Reviewed by	Date
All accounts analyzed and composition of account balance schedules in agreement with the general ledger balances: • Federal tax payable • State income tax payable • Payroll tax payable • Workers comp payable • Sales tax payable • Other taxes payable • City tax payable • Accrued wages payable				
Inquiries made regarding services received for which invoices not received (e.g. legal, accounting, consulting, etc). Proper journal entries prepared to record such expenses in the month that the services were received, as follows: • Debit various expense accounts • Credit various accrued expense accounts				
Amount of accrued payroll expense determined by obtaining the payroll recap for the first payroll subsequent to month-end and prorating the total to the month prior to and subsequent to month-end. Journal entry prepared as follows: • Debit payroll expense by department • Credit accrued wages payable				
10. Other Liabilities				
General ledger balances in agreement with the detailed support schedules and amortization schedules. Any discrepancies should be identified, researched, and corrected.				
Evaluate propriety of short-term versus long-term general ledger balances and classify accordingly.				
11. Sales				
Total monthly sales—including gross, sales tax, discounts, and net—have been accumulated from the accounts receivable subsystem into a monthly sales journal, cash receipts, and discounts taken journal.				
12. Other Income				
Interest-bearing investments reviewed and interest earned through month-end but not received is accrued as follows: • Debit interest income receivable • Credit interest income				
13. Work in Progress				
Review open orders file. Prepare list of open orders reflecting all related costs incurred with open orders (jobs).				

13. Work in Progress (continued)	Done by	Date	Reviewed by	Date
Prepare appropriate journal entry to match costs with revenues from above mentioned schedule, as follows: • Debit work in progress • Credit various cost of sales, wages, and other related expense accounts				
Prepare reversing entry of prior month's work in progress entry, as follows: • Debit various cost of sales, wages, and other related expense accounts • Credit work in progress				
14. Commissions				
Review open job orders, ensuring that all closed jobs are recorded closed.				
Review job costing detail reports, ensuring that total revenues and related costs tie out to revenues and costs reflected in preliminary trial balance. If any discrepancies, identify, research, and correct as appropriate.				
Summarize the month's closed job cost detail reports by number of closed jobs, revenues, and related costs from above reconciliation.				
Generate and review commission recap schedule by salesperson, to ensure that closed jobs, revenues less sales tax, and related costs tie out to the summarized job costing detail reports.				
Extend net sales less related expenses at commission rate _____% for each salesperson by closed job. Total and cross-foot commission recap schedule.				
Accrue commissions expense by the following journal entry: • Debit commission expense • Credit accrued commissions				
15. Income Taxes				
Quarterly tax provisions and tax liability calculated based upon pro rata share of annualized net income, giving consideration to tax payments made, net operating loss carry forwards, etc.				

125. Actual vs. Budget Income Statement

For the Period:	Actual	Budget	Variance-$
Sales			
Sales			$0.00
Other			$0.00
Total Sales	**$0.00**	**$0.00**	**$0.00**
Less Cost of Goods Sold			
Materials			$0.00
Labor			$0.00
Overhead			$0.00
Other			$0.00
Total Cost of Goods Sold	**$0.00**	**$0.00**	**$0.00**
Gross Profit	**$0.00**	**$0.00**	**$0.00**
Operating Expenses			
Salaries and wages			$0.00
Employee benefits			$0.00
Payroll taxes			$0.00
Rent			$0.00
Utilities			$0.00
Repairs and maintenance			$0.00
Insurance			$0.00
Travel			$0.00
Telephone			$0.00
Postage			$0.00
Office supplies			$0.00
Advertising/Marketing			$0.00
Professional fees			$0.00
Training and development			$0.00
Bank charges			$0.00
Depreciation			$0.00
Miscellaneous			$0.00
Other			$0.00
Total Operating Expenses	**$0.00**	**$0.00**	**$0.00**
Operating Income	**$0.00**	**$0.00**	**$0.00**
Interest Income (expense)			$0.00
Other Income (expense)			$0.00
Total Nonoperating Income (expense)	**$0.00**	**$0.00**	**$0.00**
Income (Loss) Before Taxes	**$0.00**	**$0.00**	**$0.00**
Income Taxes			**$0.00**
Net Income (Loss)	**$0.00**	**$0.00**	**$0.00**

126. Balance Sheet Support Schedule–Cash Balance

For the Period:			
Bank Account Detail Description		Balance, This Month, This Year	Balance, This Month, Prior Year
Bank Name	Account		
Total Cash Balances		$	$

Detail totals must agree with Cash on Balance Sheet.

This table reflects bank balances that comprise the cash balance on a company's balance sheet. This is a detailed report often used in CPA review. If management prepares this report before CPA review, CPA fees can be dramatically reduced.

Prepared by _____ Date _____

Reviewed by _____ Date _____

127. Balance Sheet Support Schedule—Marketable Securities

For the Period:		Balance, This Month, This Year	Balance, This Month, Prior Year
Marketable Securities Detail Description			
Investment Type	Description		
Total Marketable Securities Balances		$	$

Detail totals must agree with Marketable Securities on Balance Sheet.

This table reflects bank balances that comprise the marketable securities balance on a company's balance sheet. This is a detailed report often used in CPA review. If management prepares this report before CPA review, CPA fees can be dramatically reduced.

Prepared by _____ Date _____

Reviewed by _____ Date _____

128. Balance Sheet Support Schedule—Accounts Receivable

For the Period:		
Accounts Receivable	Balance, This Month, This Year	Balance, This Month, Prior Year
Balance per Accounts Receivable Detail:		
Current		
Over 30 days		
Over 60 days		
Over 90 days		
Total Accounts Receivable Balances	$	$

Detail totals must agree with Accounts Receivables on Balance Sheet.

Prepared by _____ Date _____

Reviewed by _____ Date _____

129. Balance Sheet Support Schedule—Inventory

For the Period:		
Inventory	Balance, This Month, This Year	Balance, This Month, Prior Year
Balance per Inventory Detail:		
Raw Materials		
Work in Progress		
Finished Goods		
Other		
Total Inventory Balances	$	$

Detail totals must agree with Inventory on Balance Sheet.

Prepared by _____ Date _____

Reviewed by _____ Date _____

130. Balance Sheet Support Schedule—Prepaid Expenses

For the Period:		
Prepaid Expenses	Balance, This Month, This Year	Balance, This Month, Prior Year
Balance per Prepaid Expenses Amortization Schedules:		
Prepaid Insurance		
For the Period _____ / _____ to _____ / _____ Total of Payments Months in Period Monthly Amortized Amount Remaining Periods	÷ = X	
Total Prepaid Insurance Balance	$	$
Prepaid Worker's Compensation		
For the Period _____ / _____ to _____ / _____ Total of Payments Months in Period Monthly Amortized Amount Remaining Periods	÷ = X	
Total Prepaid Worker's Compensation Balance	$	$
Prepaid Other		
Description: For the Period _____ / _____ to _____ / _____ Total of Payments Months in Period Monthly Amortized Amount Remaining Periods	÷ = X	
Total Prepaid Other Balance	$	$
Grand Total All Prepaid Expense Balances	$	$

Detail totals must agree with Prepaid Expenses on Balance Sheet.

Prepared by _____ Date _____

Reviewed by _____ Date _____

131. Balance Sheet Support Schedule—Accounts Payable

For the Period:		
Accounts Payable	Balance, This Month, This Year	Balance, This Month, Prior Year
Beginning Balance		
Purchases		
Disbursements		
Adjustments		
Ending Balance		
Total Accounts Payable Balances	$	$

Detail totals must agree with Accounts Payable on Balance Sheet.

Prepared by _____ Date _____

Reviewed by _____ Date _____

132. Balance Sheet Support Schedule—Notes Payable

For the Period:		
Notes Payable	Balance, This Month, This Year	Balance, This Month, Prior Year
Note 1 Description:		
Beginning Balance		
Principal Payments		
Adjustments		
Note 1 Balances	$	$
Note 2 Description:		
Beginning Balance		
Principal Payments		
Adjustments		
Note 2 Balances	$	$
Note 3 Description:		
Beginning Balance		
Principal Payments		
Adjustments		
Note 3 Balances	$	$
Note 4 Description:		
Beginning Balance		
Principal Payments		
Adjustments		
Note 4 Balances	$	$
Total Notes Payable Balances	$	$

Detail totals must agree with Notes Payable on Balance Sheet.

Prepared by _____ Date _____

Reviewed by _____ Date _____

133. Cash Flow Forecast—12-Month

Period/Month:	1	2	3	4	5	6	7	8	9	10	11	12	Total
Receipts													0
Cash sales													0
Collections from credit sales													0
Other													0
Total Receipts	0	0	0	0	0	0	0	0	0	0	0	0	0
Payments													0
Cash purchases													0
Payments to creditors													0
Salaries and wages													0
Employee benefits													0
Payroll taxes													0
Rent													0
Utilities													0
Repairs and maintenance													0
Insurance													0
Travel													0
Telephone													0
Postage													0
Office supplies													0
Advertising													0
Marketing/promotion													0
Professional fees													0
Training and development													0
Bank charges													0
Miscellaneous													0
Owner's drawings													0
Loan repayments													0
Tax payments													0
Capital purchases													0
Other													0
Total Payments	0	0	0	0	0	0	0	0	0	0	0	0	0
Cash Flow Surplus (+) or Deficit (–)	0	0	0	0	0	0	0	0	0	0	0	0	0
Start Cash (Owner's Equity + Loans – Start-Up)	0	0	0	0	0	0	0	0	0	0	0	0	0
Closing Cash Balance	0	0	0	0	0	0	0	0	0	0	0	0	0

Note: This form is available on the accompanying CD as an Excel template.

134. Cash Flow Forecast—Five-Year

Period/Month:	1	2	3	4	5	Total
Receipts						
Cash sales						0
Collections from credit sales						0
Other						0
Total Receipts	**0**	**0**	**0**	**0**	**0**	**0**
Payments						
Cash purchases						0
Payments to creditors						0
Salaries and wages						0
Employee benefits						0
Payroll taxes						0
Rent						0
Utilities						0
Repairs and maintenance						0
Insurance						0
Travel						0
Telephone						0
Postage						0
Office supplies						0
Advertising						0
Marketing/promotion						0
Professional fees						0
Training and development						0
Bank charges						0
Miscellaneous						0
Owner's drawings						0
Loan repayments						0
Tax payments						0
Capital purchases						0
Other						0
Total Payments	**0**	**0**	**0**	**0**	**0**	**0**
Cashflow Surplus (+) or Deficit (–)	**0**	**0**	**0**	**0**	**0**	**0**
Start Cash (Owner's Equity + Loans – Start-Up)	**0**	**0**	**0**	**0**	**0**	
Closing Cash Balance	**0**	**0**	**0**	**0**	**0**	

Note: This form is available on the accompanying CD as an Excel template.

135. Income Statement–12-Month

Period/Month:	1	2	3	4	5	6	7	8	9	10	11	12	Total
Sales													
Sales													0
Other													0
Total Sales	0	0	0	0	0	0	0	0	0	0	0	0	**0**
Less Cost of Goods Sold													
Materials													0
Labor													0
Overhead													0
Other													0
Total Cost of Goods Sold	0	0	0	0	0	0	0	0	0	0	0	0	**0**
Gross Profit	0	0	0	0	0	0	0	0	0	0	0	0	**0**
Operating Expenses													
Salaries and wages													0
Employee benefits													0
Payroll taxes													0
Rent													0
Utilities													0
Repairs and maintenance													0
Insurance													0
Travel													0
Telephone													0
Postage													0
Office supplies													0
Advertising/Marketing													0
Professional fees													0
Training and development													0
Bank charges													0
Depreciation													0
Miscellaneous													0
Other													0
Total Operating Expenses	0	0	0	0	0	0	0	0	0	0	0	0	**0**
Operating Income	0	0	0	0	0	0	0	0	0	0	0	0	**0**
Interest income (expense)													0
Other income (expense)													0
Total Nonoperating Income (Expense)	0	0	0	0	0	0	0	0	0	0	0	0	**0**
Income (Loss) Before Taxes	0	0	0	0	0	0	0	0	0	0	0	0	**0**
Income Taxes	0	0	0	0	0	0	0	0	0	0	0	0	**0**
Net Income (Loss)	0	0	0	0	0	0	0	0	0	0	0	0	**0**
Cumulative Net Income (Loss)	0	0	0	0	0	0	0	0	0	0	0	0	**0**

Note: This form is available on the accompanying CD as an Excel template.

136. Income Statement—Quarterly

Period/Quarter:	Quarter 1	Quarter 2	Quarter 3	Quarter 4	Total
Sales					
Sales					0
Other					0
Total Sales	0	0	0	0	0
Less Cost of Goods Sold					
Materials					0
Labor					0
Overhead					0
Other					0
Total Cost of Goods Sold	0	0	0	0	0
Gross Profit	0	0	0	0	0
Operating Expenses					
Salaries and wages					0
Employee benefits					0
Payroll taxes					0
Rent					0
Utilities					0
Repairs and maintenance					0
Insurance					0
Travel					0
Telephone					0
Postage					0
Office supplies					0
Advertising/Marketing					0
Professional fees					0
Training and development					0
Bank charges					0
Depreciation					0
Miscellaneous					0
Other					0
Total Operating Expenses	0	0	0	0	0
Opeating Income	0	0	0	0	0
Interest income (expense)					0
Other income (expense)					0
Total Nonoperating Income (Expense)	0	0	0	0	0
Income (Loss) Before Taxes	0	0	0	0	0
Income Taxes					0
Net Income (Loss)	0	0	0	0	0
Cumulative Net Income (Loss)	0	0	0	0	0

Note: This form is available on the accompanying CD as an Excel template.

137. Quarterly Balance Sheet

	Quarter 1	Quarter 2	Quarter 3	Quarter 4
ASSETS				
Current Assets				
Cash				
Marketable securities				
Accounts receivable, net				
Inventory				
Prepaid expenses				
Other				
Total Current Assets	0	0	0	0
Long-Term Assets				
Property, plant, and equipment				
Less accumulated depreciation				
Net property, plant, and equipment	0	0	0	0
Goodwill				
Other long-term assets				
Total Long-Term Assets	0	0	0	0
Total Assets	0	0	0	0
LIABILITIES AND SHAREHOLDERS' EQUITY				
Current Liabilities				
Short-term debt				
Current maturities of long-term debt				
Accounts payable				
Income taxes payable				
Accrued liabilities				
Other				
Total Current Liabilities	0	0	0	0
Long-Term Liabilities				
Long-term debt less current maturities				
Deferred income taxes				
Other long-term liabilities				
Total Long-Term Liabilities	0	0	0	0
Shareholders' Equity				
Common stock				
Additional paid-in capital				
Retained earnings				
Other				
Total Shareholders' Equity	0	0	0	0
Total Liabilities and Shareholders' Equity	0	0	0	0

Note: This form is available on the accompanying CD as an Excel template.

138. Year-End Balance Sheet

	Year Ending 20___
ASSETS	
Current Assets	
Cash	
Marketable securities	
Accounts receivable, net	
Inventory	
Prepaid expenses	
Other	
Total Current Assets	0
Long-Term Assets	
Property, plant, and equipment	
Less accumulated depreciation	
Net property, plant, and equipment	0
Goodwill	
Other long-term assets	
Total Long-Term Assets	0
Total Assets	0
LIABILITIES AND SHAREHOLDERS' EQUITY	
Current Liabilities	
Short-term debt	
Current maturities of long-term debt	
Accounts payable	
Income taxes payable	
Accrued liabilities	
Other	
Total Current Liabilities	0
Long-Term Liabilities	
Long-term debt less current maturities	
Deferred income taxes	
Other long-term liabilities	
Total Long-Term Liabilities	0
Shareholders' Equity	
Common stock	
Additional paid-in capital	
Retained earnings	
Other	
Total Shareholders' Equity	0
Total Liabilities and Shareholders' Equity	0

Note: This form is available on the accompanying CD as an Excel template.

Miscellaneous Forms

This section offers a mix of useful forms that do not fit any of the preceding 12 sections. Use the *Trademark Infringement Cease and Desist Letter* when you feel that a party is using a trademark or service mark for which you have priority rights.

We have included a familiar *Fax Cover Sheet*, but we have added a confidentiality warning to protect your correspondence in the event of wrongful delivery. The *Message Notes* will also be familiar.

The *Web Site Terms of Service* is a strongly worded legal disclaimer for any business that operates a Web site.

Finally, we have included two sample letters to use in regard to the Digital Millennium Copyright Act of 1998, which updates U.S. copyright law for the Internet. The Act protects online service providers from civil and criminal liability for copyright infringement under some circumstances. If a copyright holder discovers that his or her content appears on the Internet without proper authorization, the holder may take advantage of the Act's "notification and takedown" provisions to have the content removed from the Web site where it appears. Those provisions govern the process of notification by copyright holders and the rights and responsibilities of online service providers once they receive notice of infringing material. The copyright owner would deliver to the online service provider the *Notification of Infringement Letter Under the Digital Millennium Copyright Act*. A subscriber who feels his or her material is not infringing then may deliver a *Counter-Notification Letter Under the Digital Millennium Copyright Act* to respond to the notice.

139. Trademark Infringement Cease and Desist Letter

From:

_____

_____

_____

_____

To:

_____

_____

_____

_____

Re: Evolution Trademark

To whom it may concern,

This matter requires your immediate attention.

We are the owners of a U.S. trademark registration for the trademark _____ for the following services: _____.

We have used our trademark consistently for _____ years.

Your company is currently using a similar mark, specifically, _____. A comparison of your mark to our trademark reveals that you are in violation of state unfair competition laws and several provisions of the Federal Trademark Act (15 U.S.C. § 1125 et seq.).

We ask that you immediately cease the manufacture and distribution of any products and/or undertaking any services bearing the trademark _____. Your failure to notify me by _____, 20_____, that you have taken these steps will result in the prompt initiation of legal proceedings against your company. I eagerly await your response, and as a courtesy to you, I will temporarily abstain from contacting any retail establishments in which the offending mark is offered.

Be advised that this matter is of the gravest concern to us and that the protection of our trademark is one of our highest priorities. However, if you agree to cease the manufacture and distribution of products and undertaking any services bearing the infringing mark, we will consider the matter resolved. We sincerely hope that you will take this opportunity to avoid a legal dispute.

Please contact my office if you require any further information.

Yours truly,

140. Fax Cover Sheet

To:	From:
Fax:	Date:
Phone:	Pages:
Re:	CC:

❑ Urgent   ❑ For Review   ❑ Please Comment   ❑ Please Reply   ❑ Please Recycle

THIS MESSAGE IS INTENDED ONLY FOR THE USE OF THE INDIVIDUAL OR ENTITY TO WHOM OR WHICH IT IS ADDRESSED AND MAY CONTAIN INFORMATION THAT IS PRIVILEGED, CONFIDENTIAL, AND EXEMPT FROM DISCLOSURE. If the reader of this message is not the intended recipient or an employee or agent responsible for delivering the message to the intended recipient, you are hereby notified that any dissemination, distribution, or copying of this communication is strictly prohibited. If you have received this communication in error, please notify us immediately by telephone and return the original message to us by mail. Thank you.

141. Message Notes

IMPORTANT MESSAGE

For:

Date: Time: ❑ AM
                                        ❑ PM

Mr./Ms.

of

Phone:

Fax:

Mobile:

❑ Telephoned   ❑ Please call
❑ Came to see you   ❑ Will call you again
❑ Wants to see you   ❑ Rush
❑ Returned your call   ❑ Will fax you

Message: _____

_____

_____

_____

_____

Taken by:

IMPORTANT MESSAGE

For:

Date: Time: ❑ AM
                                        ❑ PM

Mr./Ms.

of

Phone:

Fax:

Mobile:

❑ Telephoned   ❑ Please call
❑ Came to see you   ❑ Will call you again
❑ Wants to see you   ❑ Rush
❑ Returned your call   ❑ Will fax you

Message: _____

_____

_____

_____

_____

Taken by:

IMPORTANT MESSAGE

For:

Date: Time: ❑ AM
                                        ❑ PM

Mr./Ms.

of

Phone:

Fax:

Mobile:

❑ Telephoned   ❑ Please call
❑ Came to see you   ❑ Will call you again
❑ Wants to see you   ❑ Rush
❑ Returned your call   ❑ Will fax you

Message: _____

_____

_____

_____

_____

Taken by:

IMPORTANT MESSAGE

For:

Date: Time: ❑ AM
                                        ❑ PM

Mr./Ms.

of

Phone:

Fax:

Mobile:

❑ Telephoned   ❑ Please call
❑ Came to see you   ❑ Will call you again
❑ Wants to see you   ❑ Rush
❑ Returned your call   ❑ Will fax you

Message: _____

_____

_____

_____

_____

Taken by:

142. Web Site Terms of Service

Terms of Service

Some or all of the information on this Web site(s) is provided by _____ ("Company") on one or more Company Web sites. The Company Web sites include the following Web sites: _____. Company provides this service to you, subject to the following Terms of Service ("TOS"), which may be updated by us anytime without notice to you. When using particular Company services, you shall be subject to any posted guidelines or rules applicable to such services that may be posted from time to time. All such guidelines or rules are hereby incorporated by reference into the TOS. For specific services, Company also may put forth specific Terms of Service that differ from this TOS. It is your responsibility to periodically review the TOS. If you do not agree with or understand the TOS, do not use a Company site.

The TOS apply to both "Affiliates" (persons or entities that receive the Service, as defined below, for redistribution and/or republication on a non-Company Web site) and "Users" (all persons, including Affiliates, that make any use whatsoever of any Service, as defined below). Company currently provides Affiliates and Users with several resources, including news feeds, message boards, financial calculators, articles, and stock quotes (the "Service"). Unless expressly stated otherwise, new resources added to the current Service shall be subject to the TOS. You understand and agree that the Service is provided "as is" and that Company assumes no responsibility for the timeliness, deletion, misdelivery, or failure to store any user communications or personalization settings.

In consideration of your use of the Service, you agree to (a) provide true, accurate, current, and complete information about yourself as prompted by the Service's registration form (such information being the "Registration Data") and (b) maintain and promptly update the Registration Data to keep it truthful, accurate, current, and complete. If you provide any information that is untrue, inaccurate, not current, or incomplete, or Company has reasonable grounds to suspect that such information is untrue, inaccurate, not current, or incomplete, Company has the right to suspend or terminate your account and refuse any and all current or future use of the Service (or any portion thereof). You will receive a password and account designation upon completing the registration process for the use of some Services. You are responsible for maintaining the confidentiality of the password and account and are fully responsible for all activities that occur under your password or account. You agree to (a) immediately notify Company of any unauthorized use of your password or account or any other breach of security and (b) ensure that you exit from your account at the end of each session. Company cannot and will not be liable for any loss or damage arising from your failure to comply with this Paragraph.

You understand that all information, data, text, software, music, sound, photographs, graphics, video, messages, or other materials ("Content"), whether publicly posted or privately transmitted, are the sole responsibility of the person from which such Content originated. This means that you, and not Company, are entirely responsible for all Content that you upload, post, e-mail, or otherwise transmit via the Service. Company does not control the Content posted via the Service and thus does not guarantee its accuracy, integrity, or quality. By using the Service, you may be exposed to Content that is offensive, indecent, or objectionable. Under no circumstances will Company be liable in any way for any Content, including, but not limited to, for any errors or omissions in any Content, or any loss or damage of any kind incurred as a result of the use of any Content posted, e-mailed, or otherwise transmitted via the Service.

You agree to not use the Service to:

i. upload, post, e-mail, or otherwise transmit any Content that is unlawful, harmful, threatening, abusive, harassing, defamatory, vulgar, obscene, libelous, invasive of another's privacy, hateful, or racially, ethnically, or otherwise objectionable;

ii. impersonate any person or entity or falsely state or otherwise misrepresent your affiliation with a person or entity;

iii. forge headers or otherwise manipulate identifiers in order to disguise the origin of any Content transmitted through the Service;

iv. upload, post, e-mail, or otherwise transmit any Content that you do not have a right to transmit under any law or under contractual or fiduciary relationships;

v. upload, post, e-mail, or otherwise transmit any Content that infringes on any patent, trademark, trade secret, copyright, or other proprietary rights ("Rights") of any party;

vi. upload, post, e-mail, or otherwise transmit any unsolicited or unauthorized advertising, promotional materials, "junk mail," "spam," "chain letters," "pyramid schemes," or any other form of solicitation, except in areas designated for such purpose;

vii. upload, post, e-mail, or otherwise transmit any material that contains software viruses or any other computer code, files, or programs designed to interrupt, destroy, or limit the functionality of any computer software or hardware or telecommunications equipment;

viii. interfere with or disrupt the Service or servers or networks connected to the Service, or disobey any requirements, procedures, policies, or regulations of networks connected to the Service;

ix. intentionally or unintentionally violate any applicable local, state, national, or international law, including, but not limited to, regulations promulgated by the U.S. Securities and Exchange Commission, any rules of any national or other securities exchange, including, without limitation, the New York Stock Exchange, the American Stock Exchange, or the NASDAQ, and any regulations having the force of law; or

x. "stalk" or otherwise harass another or collect or store personal data about other Users.

You acknowledge that Company does not pre-screen Content, but that Company and its designees shall have the right (but not the obligation) in their sole discretion to refuse or move any Content that is available via the Service. Without limiting the foregoing, Company and its designees shall have the right to remove any Content that violates the TOS or is otherwise objectionable. You agree that you must evaluate, and bear all risks associated with, the use of any Content, including any reliance on the accuracy, completeness, or usefulness of such Content. In this regard, you acknowledge that you may not rely on any Content created by Company or submitted to Company, including without limitation information in Company Message Boards and in all other parts of the Service.

You acknowledge and agree that Company may preserve Content and may also disclose Content if required to do so by law or in the good faith belief that such preservation or disclosure is reasonably necessary to (a) comply with legal process; (b) enforce the TOS; (c) respond to claims that any Content violates the rights of third parties; or (d) protect the rights, property, or personal safety of Company, its Users, and the public.

You understand that the technical processing and transmission of the Service, including your Content, may involve (a) transmissions over various networks and (b) changes to conform and adapt to technical requirements of connecting networks or devices.

Recognizing the global nature of the Internet, you agree to comply with all local rules regarding online conduct and acceptable Content. Specifically, you agree to comply with all applicable laws regarding the transmission of technical data exported from the United States or the country in which you reside.

With respect to all Content you elect to post to other publicly accessible areas of the Service, you grant Company the royalty-free, perpetual, irrevocable, non-exclusive, and fully sublicensable right and license to use, reproduce, modify, adapt, publish, translate, create derivative works from, distribute, perform, and display such Content (in whole or part) worldwide and/or to incorporate it in other works in any form, media, or technology now known or later developed.

You agree to indemnify and hold Company and its subsidiaries, Affiliates, officers, agents, co-branders or other partners, and employees harmless from any claim or demand, including reasonable attorneys' fees, made by any third party due to or arising out of Content you submit, post to, or transmit through the Service, your use of the Service, your connection to the Service, your violation of the TOS, or your violation of any rights of another.

You agree not to reproduce, duplicate, copy, sell, resell, or exploit for any commercial purposes any portion of the Service, use of the Service, or access to the Service, except in accordance with the TOS.

You acknowledge that Company may establish general practices and limits concerning use of the Service, including without limitation the maximum number of days Content will be retained by the Service, the maximum number of messages that may be sent from or received by an account on the Service, the maximum size of any message that may be sent from or received by an account on the Service, the maximum disk space that will be allotted on Company's servers on your behalf, and the maximum number of times and the maximum duration for which you may access the Service in a given period of time. You agree that Company has no responsibility or liability for the deletion or failure to store any messages and other communications or other Content maintained or transmitted by the Service. You acknowledge that Company reserves the right to log off accounts that are inactive for an extended period of time. You further acknowledge that Company reserves the right to change these general practices and limits at any time, in its sole discretion, with or without notice.

Company reserves the right at any time and from time to time to modify or discontinue, temporarily or permanently, the Service (or any part thereof), with or without notice. You agree that Company shall not be liable to you or to any third party for any modification, suspension, or discontinuance of the Service.

You agree that Company, in its sole discretion, may terminate your password, account (or any part thereof), or use of the Service and remove and discard any Content within the Service for any reason. Company may also, in its sole discretion and at any time, discontinue providing the Service, or any part thereof, or may change the price for the Service, all with or without notice. You agree that any termination of your access to the Service under any provision of this TOS may be affected without prior notice, and acknowledge and agree that Company may immediately deactivate or delete your account and all related information and files in your account and/or bar any further access to such files or the Service. Further, you agree that Company shall not be liable to you or any third party for any termination of your access to the Service.

Your correspondence or business dealings with, or participation in promotions of, advertisers found on or through the Service, including payment and delivery of related goods or services, and any other terms, conditions, warranties, or representations associated with such dealings, are solely between you and such advertiser. You agree that Company shall not be responsible or liable for any loss or damage of any sort incurred as the result of any such dealings or as the result of the presence of such advertisers on the Service.

The Service or third parties may provide links to other World Wide Web sites or resources. Because Company has no control over such sites and resources, you acknowledge and agree that Company is not responsible for the availability of such external sites or resources and does not endorse and is not responsible or liable for any Content, advertising, products, or other materials on or available from such sites or resources. You further acknowledge and agree that Company shall not be responsible or liable, directly or indirectly, for any damage or loss caused or alleged to be caused by or in connection with use of or reliance on any such Content, goods, or services available on or through any such site or resource.

You acknowledge and agree that the Service and any necessary software used in connection with the Service (the "Software") contain proprietary and confidential information that is protected by applicable intellectual property and other laws. You further acknowledge and agree that Content contained in sponsor advertisements or information presented to you through the Service or advertisers is protected by copyrights, trademarks, service marks, patents, or other proprietary rights and laws. Except as expressly authorized by Company or advertisers, you agree not to modify, rent, lease, loan, sell, distribute, or create derivative works based on the Service or the Software, in whole or in part.

Company grants you a personal, non-transferable, and non-exclusive right and license to use the object code of its Software on a single computer, provided that you do not (and do not allow any third party to) copy, modify, create a derivative work of, reverse engineer, reverse assemble, or otherwise attempt to discover any source code, sell, assign, sublicense, grant a security interest in, or otherwise transfer any right in the Software. You agree not to modify the Software in any manner or form or to use modified versions of the Software, including (without limitation) for the purpose of obtaining unauthorized access to the Service. You agree not to access the Service by any means other than through the interface that is provided by Company for use in accessing the Service.

YOU EXPRESSLY UNDERSTAND AND AGREE THAT:

a. YOUR USE OF THE SERVICE IS AT YOUR SOLE RISK. THE SERVICE IS PROVIDED ON AN "AS IS" AND "AS AVAILABLE" BASIS. COMPANY EXPRESSLY DISCLAIMS ALL WARRANTIES OF ANY KIND, WHETHER EXPRESSED OR IMPLIED, INCLUDING, BUT NOT LIMITED TO, THE IMPLIED WARRANTIES OF MERCHANTABILITY, FITNESS FOR A PARTICULAR PURPOSE, AND NON-INFRINGEMENT.

b. COMPANY MAKES NO WARRANTY THAT (i) THE SERVICE WILL MEET YOUR REQUIREMENTS, (ii) THE SERVICE WILL BE UNINTERRUPTED, TIMELY, SECURE, OR ERROR-FREE, (iii) THE RESULTS THAT MAY BE OBTAINED FROM THE USE OF THE SERVICE WILL BE ACCURATE OR RELIABLE, (iv) THE QUALITY OF ANY PRODUCTS, SERVICES, INFORMATION, OR OTHER MATERIAL PURCHASED OR OBTAINED BY YOU THROUGH THE SERVICE WILL MEET YOUR EXPECTATIONS, AND (v) ANY ERRORS IN THE SOFTWARE WILL BE CORRECTED.

c. ANY MATERIAL DOWNLOADED OR OTHERWISE OBTAINED THROUGH THE USE OF THE SERVICE IS DONE AT YOUR OWN DISCRETION AND RISK AND THAT YOU WILL BE SOLELY RESPONSIBLE FOR ANY DAMAGE TO YOUR COMPUTER SYSTEM OR LOSS OF DATA THAT RESULTS FROM THE DOWNLOAD OF ANY SUCH MATERIAL.

d. NO ADVICE OR INFORMATION, WHETHER ORAL OR WRITTEN, OBTAINED BY YOU FROM COMPANY OR THROUGH OR FROM THE SERVICE, SHALL CREATE ANY WARRANTY NOT EXPRESSLY STATED IN THE TOS.

YOU EXPRESSLY UNDERSTAND AND AGREE THAT COMPANY SHALL NOT BE LIABLE FOR ANY DIRECT, INDIRECT, INCIDENTAL, SPECIAL, CONSEQUENTIAL, OR EXEMPLARY DAMAGES, INCLUDING BUT NOT LIMITED TO DAMAGES FOR LOSS OF PROFITS, GOODWILL, USE, DATA, OR OTHER INTANGIBLE LOSSES (EVEN IF COMPANY HAS BEEN ADVISED OF THE POSSIBILITY OF SUCH DAMAGES) RESULTING FROM (i) THE USE OR THE INABILITY TO USE THE SERVICE; (ii) THE COST OF PROCUREMENT OF SUBSTITUTE GOODS AND SERVICES RESULTING FROM ANY GOODS, DATA, INFORMATION, OR SERVICES PURCHASED OR OBTAINED OR MESSAGES RECEIVED OR TRANSACTIONS ENTERED INTO THROUGH OR FROM THE SERVICE; (iii) UNAUTHORIZED ACCESS TO OR ALTERATION OF YOUR TRANSMISSIONS OR DATA; (iv) STATEMENTS OR CONDUCT OF ANY THIRD PARTY ON THE SERVICE; OR (v) ANY OTHER MATTER RELATING TO THE SERVICE.

SOME JURISDICTIONS DO NOT ALLOW THE EXCLUSION OF CERTAIN WARRANTIES OR THE LIMITATION OR EXCLUSION OF LIABILITY FOR INCIDENTAL OR CONSEQUENTIAL DAMAGES. ACCORDINGLY, SOME OF THE ABOVE LIMITATIONS OF LIABILITY MAY NOT APPLY TO YOU.

THE SERVICE IS PROVIDED FOR INFORMATIONAL PURPOSES ONLY AND NO CONTENT INCLUDED IN THE SERVICE IS INTENDED FOR TRADING OR INVESTING PURPOSES. COMPANY SHALL NOT BE RESPONSIBLE OR LIABLE FOR THE ACCURACY, USEFULNESS, OR AVAILABILITY OF ANY INFORMATION TRANSMITTED VIA THE SERVICE AND SHALL NOT BE RESPONSIBLE OR LIABLE FOR ANY TRADING OR INVESTMENT DECISIONS MADE BASED ON SUCH INFORMATION.

Company respects the intellectual property of others and we ask our Users to do the same. If you believe that your work has been copied in a way that constitutes copyright infringement, please contact Company:

_____

_____

_____

The TOS constitute the entire agreement between you and Company and govern your use of the Service, superseding any prior agreements between you and Company. You also may be subject to additional terms and conditions that may apply when you use affiliate services, third-party content, or third-party software. The TOS and the relationship between you and Company shall be governed by the laws of the State of California without regard to its conflict of law provisions. You and Company agree to submit to the personal and exclusive jurisdiction of the courts located within the county of _____, _____. The failure of Company to exercise or enforce any right or provision of the TOS shall not constitute a waiver of such right or provision. If any provision of the TOS is found by a court of competent jurisdiction to be invalid, the parties nevertheless agree that the court should endeavor to give effect to the parties' intentions as reflected in the provision and that the other provisions of the TOS remain in full force and effect. You agree that, regardless of any statute or law to the contrary, any claim or cause of action arising out of or related to use of the Service or the TOS must be filed within one (1) year after such claim or cause of action arose or be forever barred.

143. Notification of Infringement Letter Under the Digital Millennium Copyright Act

Date _____

To:

_____

_____

_____

_____

To Whom It May Concern:

I am writing to you to avail myself of my rights under the Digital Millennium Copyright Act (DMCA). This letter is a Notice of Infringement as authorized in § 512(c) of the U.S. Copyright Law. I wish to report an instance or what I feel in good faith is an instance of copyright infringement. The infringing material appears on a service for which you are the designated agent.

You are registered with the U.S. Copyright Office as the Designated Service Provider Agent to receive notifications of alleged Copyright infringement with respect to users of the Service for which you are the Designated Agent.

1. The material that I contend belongs to me and that appears illegally on the service is the following:
   (describe the infringing material: e.g., "a song entitled "Legal Battle Blues" and a song entitled "A Little Litigation," both performed by Lawyers in Love).

2. The material appears at the Web site address:
   (provide the full Web site address and a link to the page on which the material appears).

3. My contact information is as follows:
   (provide your name, address, telephone number, and e-mail address).

4. I have a good-faith belief that the use of the material that appears on the service is not authorized by the copyright owner, by its agent, or by operation of law.

5. The information in this notice is accurate and I am either the copyright owner or authorized to act on behalf of the copyright owner.

I declare under the perjury laws of the United States of America that this notification is true and correct.

_____
Signature

_____
Printed Name

144. Counter-Notification Letter Under the Digital Millennium Copyright Act

Date _____

To:

_____

_____

_____

_____

To Whom It May Concern:

I am writing to you to avail myself of my rights under the Digital Millennium Copyright Act (DMCA). You recently provided me with a copy of Notice of Infringement from (Name the party who submitted the Notice of Infringement). This letter is a Counter-Notification as authorized in § 512(g) of the U.S. Copyright Law. I have a good-faith belief that the material that was removed or disabled as a result of the Notice of Infringement was removed or disabled as a result of mistake or misidentification of the material. I therefore request that the material be replaced and/or no longer disabled.

You are registered with the U.S. Copyright Office as the Designated Service Provider Agent to receive notifications of alleged copyright infringement with respect to users of the Service for which you are the Designated Agent.

1. The material in question formerly appeared at the Web site address:
   (provide the full Web site address and a link to the page on which the material appears).

2. My contact information is as follows:
   (provide your name, address, telephone number, and e-mail address).

3. I consent to the jurisdiction of the Federal District Court for the judicial district in which my address is located (solely for the purposes of the resolution of this dispute) and I agree to accept service of process from the person who provided the Notice of Infringement.

4. I have a good-faith belief that the material removed or disabled following the Notice of Infringement was removed or disabled because of mistake or misidentification of the material. I therefore request that the material be replaced and/or no longer disabled.

I declare under the perjury laws of the United States of America that this notification is true and correct.

_____
Signature

_____
Printed Name

Index